"Fantastic!

. . . Any author who wants to sell books *must* have this incredible book by the Rosses. *Jump Start Your Book Sales* will be the bible for book selling. Own it, and don't loan it out. This book belongs in your professional and personal library. My only regret is that it wasn't available when I published my first book in 1981."

Dr. Judith Briles
Author of *Woman to Woman 2000*

"You'll understand my excitement about the Rosses' new book when I tell you that their classic, *The Complete Guide to Self-Publishing*, has helped me greatly to sell millions of books. Guess what—they've done it again!"

Dave Chilton
Author of Canada's #1 best-selling book, *The Wealthy Barber*

"Call it a jump start cable, crutch, helping hand, or how-to—whatever you call it, get yourself a copy today. This sensible, comprehensive step-by-step guide is an invaluable tool for anyone who understands that publishing is neither an art nor a science but a lot of sheer, hellish hard work."

Letty Cottin Pogrebin, President
The Author's Guild of America

"Any serious author or publisher should be able to make hundreds of times what this book costs from following its treasure-trove of promotional ideas and suggestions. My copy is riddled with highlighting and notes of things to follow up on."

Marcia Yudkin
Author of *Six Steps to Free Publicity* and eight other books

"*Jump Start Your Book Sales* is absolutely terrific. Every page overflows with sound, practical advice and actual usable information and sources. We will carry this excellent book in our *Sharing Ideas* Magazine catalog."

Dottie Walters, President of Walters International Speakers
Bureau and Author of *Speak & Grow Rich*

"No doubt about it, *Jump Start Your Book Sales* will help you sell more books—a lot more books. Whether you're self-publishing your first book or you've been a publisher for twenty years, you're sure to profit by putting a few of these proven strategies into action. If you really want people to buy your book, you need to buy this one!"
Stephen Hall Harrison
Publisher of *Radio-TV Interview Report*

"This book's a gem! It sparkles brilliantly with unlimited points of light. Don't enter the book biz without it!"
Irwin Zucker, President of Promotion in Motion
Past President/Founder of Book Publicists of So. Calif.

"*Jump Start* is a great book. Even after twenty years in publishing, I am finding new ideas and leads on almost every page."
Bernard B. "Bear" Kamoroff
Author of *Small Time Operator: How to Start Your Own Business*

"Along come the Rosses with a reference information entrepreneurs will use, sparkling full of samples, examples, loads of detailed information needed by authors and small publishers to generate publicity, market their books and special reports, and make money in publishing. Bravo!"
Paul and Sarah Edwards
Co-authors of *Getting Business to Come to You*

"Marilyn and Tom Ross's newest book is an indispensable guide for authors and publishers. Creating books (publishing) is easy; it's selling books that's difficult; and making money in this industry is really difficult! *Jump Start Your Book Sales* is a practical guide and inspirational idea book for beginners and experts alike."
Gregory J.P. Godek
Author of *1001 Ways To Be Romantic*

"Whoa. If ever a book packs in the information, this is *the one.* We recommend *Jump Start Your Books Sales* to all our clients and it is required reading for our Account Management Team."
Tami DePalma, MarketAbility

"Wow! This is the book you've been waiting for. Everything you need to promote and market your book for maximum profitability. A winner!"
Nido R. Qubein, Chairman, Creative Services, Inc.

"Once again Tom and Marilyn have provided the small press publisher with information that is necessary to succeed. Congratulations for a job well done."
Carolyn Olson, Manager of Publisher Relations
Quality Books Inc.

"It's harder these days to generate interest in—and sales for—a new book, especially for the backlist. *Jump Start Your Book Sales* gives you a fighting chance."
Bob Bly
Author of *Getting Your Book Published*

"The Rosses have done it again! *Jump Start Your Book Sales* is a wonderful grab bag of ideas that authors and publishers can use before, during, and after publication of their books. No matter how many marketing guides you may have read, I can guarantee that you'll find something new and innovative here. Buy it."
Connie Shelton, President of Intrigue Press and
Author of *Publish Your Own Novel*

"Whoever must sell your book, must also *read* this book! I've learned from the Rosses for years. Now they have compiled their best sales tips into one excellent volume. Get it, read it, keep it, review it!"
Jim Cathcart
Author of *The Acorn Principle* and *Relationship Selling*

"Wow! I'm amazed at the amount of information and inside secrets in this great book! Anyone with a book to sell better get this resource to help them do it. It's worth gold!"
Joe "Mr. Fire!" Vitale, Marketing specialist and
Author of *There's A Customer Born Every Minute*

"*Every* author need this book. You'll find more ways to generate publicity, market books, and make money in publishing that you ever imagined. It's the ideal guide for those who want to take charge of their publishing destiny and *really* sell books. I recommend it without reservation."
Dianna Booher, Author of 37 books including
Communicate with Confidence!, Get a Life Without Sacrificing
Your Career, and The Worth of a Woman's Words

"Bravo! Your new *Jump Start Your Book Sales* is jam-packed with even more industry secrets and proven bookselling strategies. Every author and every person employed in the publishing field should have a copy of this 'bible' on his or her desk."

Tony Alessandra, PhD
Author of *Charisma* and *The Platinum Rule*

"If you have ever longed to have all the wisdom you ever needed to become a best-selling author in one place—this is it! A 'book sales' bible!"

Glenna Salsbury,
Professional speaker, Author of *The Art of the Fresh Start* and 1997-98 President of the National Speakers Association

"Rosses' new book has 25 chapters, each loaded with ideas. Ideas are a dime a dozen. The person who puts them into practice is priceless. Buy this book, put the ideas into action, and *you* too will become priceless."

Joe Sabah, Speaker, Author, Publisher

"Sure to become a Must-Have book for the publishing industry, *Jump Start Your Book Sales* is comprehensive, detailed and full of action-oriented ideas. A glance at the Table of Contents alone will send you scrambling for your to-do list."

Kim Dushinski, MarketAbility

"If you have written a book, or someday dream of writing a book, then you need to pick up a copy of *Jump Start Your Book Sales*. It is easy to read and packed with quick short ideas that can be read in about a minute. And it only takes one good idea to make you wealthy. Take a Minute and read this book…It Might Just Change Your Life!"

Willie Jolley
Author of *It Only Takes A Minute To Change Your Life!*

"Tom and Marilyn more than deliver what their book promises. It's a cornucopia of great ideas that captures their warmth and their can-do approach to making books successful. Authors and publishers who use these proven techniques will guarantee their books' success."

Michael Larsen, AAR
Author of *Literary Agents: What They Do, How They Do It, and How to Find and Work with the Right One for You*

"Attention all authors, independents, and self-publishers: You, too, can bask in the glory of bestsellers—if you'll use the dynamic strategies found in this book."
   Bud Gardner, America's most inspirational writing coach and Co-author of *Chicken Soup for the Writer's Soul*

"Been there, done that, needed this. Easily worth five, even fifteen, times its modest price—*Jump Start Your Book Sales* pierces the deadly "I'm not a marketer" barrier that often condemns authors to oblivion. A must-have, must-use marketing tool for every publisher, author, and book industry employee."
   Fred Holden, Author of *TOTAL Power of ONE in America: Discover What You Need to Know, Why and How to be a More Powerful Person and Citizen*

"*Jump Start Your Book Sales* is a combination of industry knowledge and disciplined directions for small press publishers."
   Harold Sterling, Senior Vice President
   Quality Books Inc.

"Thousands of great ideas—any one of which is worth the price of admission to authors and independent presses."
   Peter McWilliams
   Author/publisher of *How to Survive the Loss of a Love* **and** *Do It!*

"*Jump Start Your Book Sales* is chock-full of advice that authors and publishers can—and must—follow if they want to turn their books into money-makers. It's terrific! Nobody has a better understanding of today's competitive publishing market than Tom and Marilyn Ross."
   Margaret Coel, Author of *The Story Teller* **and other novels in the Wind River Mystery Series**

"*Jump Start Your Book Sales* is an excellent source of traditional and creative strategies for people at any stage of book marketing. The sidebars alone are worth the price."
   Brian Jud, Author of *You're On The Air*

"If your book is the least bit promotable, you are crazy not to pick up a copy of the Rosses' book. The names and numbers in the appendix alone will get you up and running on book promotion."
   Pat McNees, Editor of *Dying: A Book of Comfort*

"The best of the best—*indispensable* advice for every serious publisher. This book can increase your sales tenfold."
Elaine Floyd, Author of *Marketing with Newsletters*

"*Jump Start Your Book Sales* directs your actions to the highest return on investment for your time. It describes an industry in transition and helps you focus your energies on the best place to sell books. With this gem you could randomly open to any page and sell twice as many books."
Terri A. Boekhoff, Publisher of Rudi Publishing
Co-author of *The Insiders' Guide to Book Publishing*

"*Jump Start Your Book Sales* is a lively and engaging marketing primer for publishers and would-be publishers. If more publishing entrepreneurs followed the advise outlined in this book—they wouldn't need to call me because they run out of money."
Stephen J. Kerr, President, Business Marketing Consultants

"The most comprehensive, reader-friendly resource you're ever going to find on the topic of taking entrepreneurial responsibility for your book's success."
Sam Horn, Author of *Tongue Fu!* **and** *ConZentrate!*
M.C. of Maui Writers Conference

"Since the Rosses' *Self-Publishing Encyclopedia* was invaluable when I became a self-publisher, I wasn't surprised to find *Jump Start Your Book Sales* an equally valuable treasure-trove. In fact, there are a number of ideas which will go straight into the marketing plans for my upcoming books. Kudos to Tom and Marilyn for giving us 'indies' a leg—no, a whole football field—up on the competition."
Shel Horowitz, Author of *Marketing Without Megabucks:*
How to Sell Anything on a Shoestring **and** *The Penny-Pinching*
Hedonist: How to Live Like Royalty with a Peasant's Pocketbook

"*Jump Start Your Book Sales* is a herd-of-elephants-sized collection of resources, contacts and ideas no author, publisher or marketer of books should be without."
Dan Kennedy
Author of *No Rules: 21 Giant Lies About Success*

JUMP START YOUR BOOK SALES

A Money-Making Guide for
Authors, Independent Publishers
and Small Presses

Marilyn and Tom Ross

COMMUNICATION
CREATIVITY
Buena Vista, Colorado

This book contains information gathered from many sources. It is published for general reference and not as a substitute for independent verification by users when circumstances warrant. It is sold with the understanding that neither the authors nor publisher is engaged in rendering any legal, psychological, or accounting advice. The publisher and authors disclaim any personal liability, either directly or indirectly, for advice or information presented within. Although the authors and publisher have used care and diligence in the preparation, and made every effort to ensure the accuracy and completeness of information contained in this book, we assume no responsibility for errors, inaccuracies, omissions, or any inconsistency herein. Any slights of people, places, publishers, books, or organizations are unintentional. Some of this material previously appeared in the *SPAN Connection* newsletter.

First printing 1999
Second printing 2005
Third printing 2006

Ross, Marilyn Heimberg
    Jump start your book sales: a money-making guide for authors, independent publishers, and small presses / Marilyn and Tom Ross.
       p.   cm.
    Includes bibliographical references and index.
    ISBN 0-918880-41-6 (trade paper)
    1. Books—United States—Marketing.   I. Ross, Tom, 1933-
II. Title.
Z471.R67   1999
381'.45002'0973—dc21
                                       99-11466
                                        CIP

ATTENTION: WRITING & PUBLISHING ORGANIZATIONS, EDUCATIONAL INSTITUTIONS, AND INDUSTRY PUBLICATIONS: Quantity discounts are available on bulk purchases of this book for reselling, educational purposes, subscription incentives, gifts, or fund raising. Special books or book excerpts can also be created to fit specific needs. For information, please contact our Special Sales Department at POB 909, Buena Vista, CO 81211-0909, 800-331-8355.

OTHER BOOKS BY THE AUTHORS

The Complete Guide to Self-Publishing

Shameless Marketing for Brazen Hussies

Country Bound!

Big Ideas for Small Service Businesses

How to Make Big Profits Publishing City & Regional Books

National Directory of Newspaper Op-Ed Pages

Marketing Your Books

Discover Your Roots

The Encyclopedia of Self-Publishing

Be Tough or Be Gone

Creative Loafing

ACKNOWLEDGMENTS

This book couldn't have been birthed without our wonderful staff. Our appreciation goes to Cathy Bowman, who designed and typeset a book that is both reader-friendly and fun. To Sue Collier and Helen Stastny for their editing expertise. To Katrina Borg-Becker for her fact checking skills, and to Lurina Thieman and Orpha Paape for their help. Thanks to Gloria Brown for her patience and creativity in developing a dynamite cover. Bravo!

Many people contributed their knowledge, advice, and experiences to enrich this manuscript. We thank each of you. We're especially grateful to Clarissa Pinkola Estes, Ph.D., who lovingly went over every page and made suggestions for changes and nuances we would never have realized. Also to Shel Horowitz, who voluntarily donned his editing hat and thus made it a better book. And we applaud Mary Westheimer for caring enough to add her superior wisdom of the Web throughout.

We were astounded by the vast number of people who agreed to provide advance blurbs for this book. That they graciously agreed to take time to look at the manuscript during the busy holiday season only intensifies our gratitude. Thank you so much Judith Appelbaum, Dan Poynter, Letty Cottin Pogrebin, Dave Chilton, Marcia Yudkin, Dottie Walters, Irwin Zuker, Stephen Hall Harrison, Bear Kamoroff, Paul and Sarah Edwards, Greg Godek, Tami DePalma, Nido Qubein, Carolyn Olson, Bob Bly, Connie Shelton, Jim Cathcart, Tony Alessandra, Ph.D., Joe Vitale, Dr. Judith Briles, Dianna Booher, Glenna Salsbury, Joe Sabah, Kim Dushinski, Willie Jolley, Bud Gardner, Michael Larsen, Fred Holden, Harold Sterling, Peter McWilliams, Margaret Coel, Brian Jud, Pat McNees, Elaine Floyd, Terri Boekhoff, Clarissa Pinkola Estes, Ph.D., Mary Westheimer, Shel Horowitz, Sam Horn, Dan Kennedy, Jay Levinson, and Stephen Kerr.

HOW TO CONTACT THE AUTHORS

Professional speaker Marilyn Ross has been delighting and informing audiences in writing and publishing organizations across North America for more than two decades. She speaks about publishing business startup secrets, unabashed creative marketing, and awesome PR for books and authors. To discuss hiring her for your next conference, fundraiser, or special event, contact:

Marilyn Ross / Self Publishing Resources
Marilyn@SelfPublishingResources.com / phone: 719-395-8659
P. O. Box 909-JS, Buena Vista, CO 81211-0909
www.SelfPublishingResources.com

NEED PERSONALIZED MARKETING HELP?

Marilyn accepts a few select clients for phone consultations, ongoing coaching, and book packaging. You may find her helpful in a variety of ways: Need a brainstorming partner for titles, subtitles, or chapter heads? Want your book cover critiqued? Require professional copywriting for your brochure, sales letters, ads, bookmark, media kit, etc.? Seeking website guidance or evaluation? Want a strategic book marketing campaign that will get you tons of publicity and sell books? Hoping to tap into the Internet in a BIG way? Marilyn can help make your dreams come true! Contact her today.

CONSIDERING SELF-PUBLISHING?

The Rosses' *Complete Guide to Self-Publishing* is often called the "bible" of the industry. It has sold over 100,000 copies and launched thousands of authors on an exciting trajectory to take control of their destiny and get on bestseller lists. The whopping 4th edition (521 pages) provides everything you need to know about the publishing business (yes, it *is* a business!). Discover writing tips and shortcuts, creative design and typesetting ideas, money-saving printing strategies, plus much more. Only $19.95 at http://www.CommunicationCreativity.com/g.

NOW AVAILABLE: *The Complete Guide to Self-Publishing Companion.* This new eBook provides current contacts and bonus resources to make your job easier, faster, and more profitable. Access the wonderful sources in the print book with a keystroke or two because we've hot-linked things for you. And it's all cross referenced. Don't miss the latest way to let the Internet work for you. Go to http://www.CommunicationCreativity.com/gc.

TABLE OF CONTENTS

Part I: Jump Start Your Marketing Engine

1. Step on the Gas for Revved-Up Profits 3
2. Energized Editorial + Electrified Titles =
   Marketing Magic. 11
3. Endorsements Equal Souped-Up Success 27

Part II: Illuminating Publicity Techniques

4. Reviews and Galleys Accelerate Your Sales. 39
5. Publicity Horsepower: Shameless Print Promotion
   for Brazen Hustlers 55
6. Putting Your Self-Propelled Author Tour and
   Book Signings in Overdrive. 75
7. Op-Ed Pieces for High Gear Results 91
8. Radio Interviews: How to Be Hip and
   Shoot from the Lip 95
9. Opening the Throttle: Touting Titles on TV 109

Part III: Muscling Your Way into Traditional Channels

10. Outdistancing Distribution Doldrums: How to
    Capture Booksellers, Wholesalers, and Distributors . . . 119
11. High-Voltage Ideas for Getting on
    the Library Speedway 135
12. Educational Sales: Steering Toward
    Impressing Academics 145
13. Amplify Your Presence with Book Clubs 155

Part IV: Flip the Switch
with Nontraditional Retail Markets

14. Nonbookstore Merchandising Channels to
Make Sales Sizzle 167

15. Turn Up the Current with Catalog Sales 179

16. Enterprising Internet Strategies: Tech It to the Max . . . 189

17. Premiums and Incentives
Super-Charge Your Bottom Line 207

18. LinkThink: Strategic Alliances to
Ignite Your Book Sales 221

19. QVC and Home Shopping Network:
Adding Mileage to Your Campaign 233

Part V: Powerhouse Direct Marketing Techniques

20. Your Consumer Brochure: Tips to Fuel
a Fabulous Sales Piece 243

21. Lightning-Charged Possibilities in Direct Mail 253

22. Speaking and Teaching to Speed Up Profits 271

Part VI: More Methods to Fire Up Your Sales

23. Alternative Master Moves to Outrun the Herd 283

24. Sidelines, Spinoffs, Special Reports, and Stuff:
Getting a Power Boost 299

25. Moving Up to Indy: Selling Your Self-Published
Book to New York 311

Afterword 321

About the Authors 323

Appendixes 325

Ideas to Accelerate Your Progress

Publisher's and Author's Bill of Rights—and Obligations

Mastering Your Marketing Plan

Resource Roundup of Contacts to Help You Roar Ahead

Key Review Galley Recipients (chapter 4)

Selected Newswire Services (chapter 5)
Op-Ed Newspaper Contacts (chapter 7)
Master (Exclusive) Distributors (chapter 10)
Bookstore Contacts (chapter 10)
Selected Major Catalogs (chapter 15)
Premium/Incentive Trade Associations (chapter 17)
Home Shopping Networks (chapter 19)
Specialty Booklet Printers (chapter 24)

Bibliography 339

Index 341

LIST OF SIDEBARS AND VISUALS

Rosses' Rules of Order: 13 Tips for Awesome Results 6

Genre-Specific Web Sites 8

The 7 Habits of Highly Successful Publishers 44

Galley Cover Example 49

Flyer Giveaway: Top 10 Free Vacations 57

Follow-Up Piece: "You're Missing a Lot" 66

The Ross Marketing Idea Generator: 26 Winning Strategies . . . 68

Sample Autographed Copy Stickers 80

Media Reminder Card 100

Potent Radio Maneuvers 102

Sales Rep Monthly Contact Newsgram 122

Catalog/Retail Information Sheet 185

Examples of Premium Book Sales 212

Special Dates to Piggyback On 224

Features Versus Benefits 246

Direct Marketing Sales Letter Checklist 256

Direct Marketing "Freebies" 262

17 Ways to Outdistance the Herd 288

Ancillary Product Possibilities 305

12 Self-Publishing Success Strategies 312

PART I

Jump Start
Your Marketing
Engine

CHAPTER 1

Step on the Gas for Revved-Up Profits

Marketing does *not* mean going to the grocery store.

It means getting behind your books with publicity, promotion, and creative sales activity. It means you start before the manuscript is even written (if you're an author) and as soon as you receive a viable proposal (if you're a publisher). And though it starts early, it never ends. Older books, called "backlist" titles, actually are your most profitable because the costs of developing the book are long past. With ongoing publicity, these products can continue to garner exposure and sales year after year.

"But I hate marketing," you lament. You are not alone. Of all the hats an author wears, the marketing fedora itches the worst. Authors like to write. Stoop to crass commercialism? Never! Okay then, forget about your book being a success. Scratch the idea of making your living as a writer.

Does that make you feel as nervous as an acrobat on a high wire during a hurricane? Never fear. You *can* develop the mind set and skills to make your book a winner. And you can do it without forfeiting your good taste or embarrassing your mother. You can actually become as excited and eager about the marketing process as a hunting dog on a hot scent. As we stand on the edge of the millennium, this is an incredible time in the publishing industry.

Each book has enormous competition. The copyright office estimates there are 63,000 new titles released each year. The August 1997

3

edition of *Books in Print* listed 1,350,000 titles currently in print and available.

As long ago as March 1, 1988, *The Wall Street Journal* reported, "Best-selling books are made, not born. Authors are starting to grasp this simple fact. Now, as publishers increasingly invest most of their promotion budgets in a few big books, many authors are paying large sums to hire personal publicists."

Must you do this? No. Must you do something? Yes. What you lack in money, you can make up for in moxie.

Letty Cotton Pogrebin, president of the Authors Guild and author of eight books herself, was interviewed on NPR's "Talk of the Nation" recently. When asked her opinion of the new trend to place more marketing responsibility on the author, she observed, "It isn't just the case for new authors. It's also the case for established authors."

She told of a conversation with Gore Vidal who had spent his own money to buy advertising and haul himself around to do speaking dates because his publisher had not delivered for him. "Publishers simply take the book, take the manuscript, don't necessarily edit it, don't necessarily copy edit it, and certainly don't promote it in all too many cases," Letty said.

An industry in transition

The way books are born, promoted, bought, and sold is changing. This trend is transforming the face of publishing. With Bertelsmann's purchase of Random House and other companies being bought and sold like baseball cards, power is now concentrated in the hands of four behemoth publishers: Random House/Bantam Doubleday Dell (30%), Simon & Schuster (14%), Penguin Putnam (10%), and HarperCollins (7%).

Today the attitude of New York publishers is, they only want household names and sure-fire books. So-called "midlist authors," an industry label for writers whose books sell modestly and whose names lack marquee value, are getting short shrift from Publishers Row. Small to mid-sized publishers, however, are much more likely to nurture these authors and their books.

In the wake of mammoth mergers, small publishing is also growing. The R. R. Bowker Company, which assigns ISBN publisher prefixes, told us that more than 7,000 new publishers start up every year. Though there is naturally some attrition, estimates place the number of total publishers at more than 50,000.

In 1994 Barnes & Noble reported that books from the 10 largest publishers accounted for three-quarters of their purchases. By 1997, these 10 leaders accounted for less than half of the books bought. Thus independent publishers, self-publishers, and university presses are now generating more than their share of bookstore revenue.

Independent bookstores that were thriving a decade ago now feel the effect of chains that offer huge discounts on bestsellers. And the Internet will continue to have an ever-growing impact on how books are sold as it gobbles up more market share.

We can either think of all these changes in the book industry as a death knell—or as a rally cry for erasing old boundaries and rejuvenating how things are done. We can—as authors—groan that our publishers are ignoring our books. Or we can be proactive and create a positive stir on our own behalf. We can—as publishers—bemoan heavy returns and too many books being published. Or we can find fresh ways to sell books and publicize our titles more innovatively to put our promotional and sales campaigns into overdrive. We can all stop breathing our own exhaust.

What you get in these pages

If you create a quality product and approach the chains and independents wisely, you can penetrate the bookstore market. Getting books on the shelves, however, is only the beginning. It's your job to drive buyers into the bookstore, to create demand so consumers will come in and buy your book. Throughout these pages we show you how to do just that, how to pluck the very marrow out of the bones of book marketing.

But be aware that the majority of books—53%—are *not* sold in bookstores. (The sad fact is 37% of all Americans have never been in a bookstore.) Fortunately, there are many other venues for merchandising books. For smaller publishers these often make more sense than forcing the issue with booksellers. We'll reveal what these venues are and coach you on strategies for succeeding with them.

You really can turn yourself into a marketing master and make tens of thousands of extra dollars with the concepts in this one-of-a-kind resource. This is a book about ideas and substance rather than flash. You'll discover how to get your book into catalogs, rack up lucrative bulk premium sales, and do radio interviews and author signings that get outrageous results. And you'll find the secret to generating lots of free publicity, then master how to *capitalize* on it.

Rosses' Rules of Order: 13 Tips for Awesome Results

Marketing begins the minute you get the book idea or decide to purchase a manuscript.

Forge strategic alliances with others who are already reaching your customer base.

Write all promotional materials from a *benefit* standpoint.

Use direct mail only for a book over $25, or for a collection of titles.

Avoid advertising, except to tightly focused target markets or in trade publications.

Work with distributors and wholesalers rather than individual bookstores.

Use reputable book manufacturers or savvy print brokers rather than generic printers.

Price the book a *minimum* of five times first-run production costs.

Authors are your best salespeople; involve them and give them good buy-back discounts.

Position your books so they have a unique selling proposition (USP); separate them from the herd.

Be aggressive about pre-publication marketing to generate working capital.

Strive for publicity *off* the book review pages: aim at lifestyle, business, sports sections, etc.

Include an order form in the back of every book.

Add to this the insider information on how to make the Internet a fabulous sales generator, how to penetrate libraries, sell to book clubs, get your titles onto QVC and Home Shopping Network—and you can see why this guide has been called a wealth-building bonanza!

Another unique feature only found here is a section after each chapter called Web Sites, Wisdom, and Whimsey. Here you'll find relevant URLs, miscellaneous tidbits of advice, and quips to tickle your funny bone.

Who should read this book?

Authors: Unless your name is Stephen King, Danielle Steel, or Tom Peters, your passion and involvement will mean life or death to your book. This resource takes you by the hand and shows you how to effectively breathe new sales life into your masterpiece.

Expectant authors: Are you about to have a book? Then read fast and furiously. *Now* is the time to begin making your book a success. Good prenatal care ensures the birth of a healthy baby. You wouldn't have a baby, then ignore it. Don't do that to your book either.

Self-publishers: You've elected to take control of your destiny. But if you're so preoccupied with the writing and production of your book that you ignore *pre-publication publicity* (not to mention all the ongoing possibilities), you're flushing money down a toilet. You'll likely have 3,000 books sitting in your garage for a very long time. We'll explain how to avoid that dilemma.

Small presses: Those with a few books in print stand on the edge of exciting growth. If this describes you, allow us to challenge you to leap to the next level by following the guidance here and doing an extraordinary job with your present titles.

Independent presses and university presses: As a medium-sized publisher, are you using all the ammunition at your disposal to position your books ahead of the herd? The strategies here will accelerate your publicity plans, open new doors for special sales, and boost your bottom line.

Publicists, sales directors, and marketing coaches: Sure you know your stuff. But those who stop learning, stop growing. We defy you to not find several nuggets of wisdom here that will make your job better, easier, and give greater results.

Be passionate about marketing! Stomp on the gas pedal. Nobody cares as much about your book as you do. Don't turn on the cruise control. Dream BIG dreams. Educate yourself. Then get out there and make it happen.

Jump Start Your Book Sales transcends the typical how-to book. It inspires and entertains as it informs. But it is not for the faint-hearted. It separates the wannabes from those who are serious about making money with books. If the latter describes you, read on.

Publishers Weekly survey reveals encouraging statistics. *PW* polled 1,000 adults about their reading habits and preferences and came up with some startling revelations.

1. "Bestseller lists" don't count for much. Only 8% of the responders said they were "very important" or "extremely important." Our

Genre-Specific Web Sites

Great site for children's books. "Books for Children and More: an Editor's Site" doesn't pretend to be all things to all people. It is a highly selective, not an all-inclusive starting point, but attractively designed and full of good tidbits. Under the *Articles* section there is basic information for writers and illustrators, followed by additional sophisticated advice. Under *Children's* you'll find links to "Children's Literature Web Guide," not to mention other intriguing places. Come browse at http://www.users.interport.net/~hdu/ even if you don't do children's books; we guarantee you'll find something useful.

Web resources for those doing children's books. The Society of Children's Book Writers and Illustrators has an informative site at http://www.scbwi.org. Here you can locate individuals to illustrate or write a children's book, plus access articles from their *SCBWI Bulletin*. We found many useful tips in their articles. The "Events" section lists meetings and conferences of interest. Anyone connected with children's publishing should pay them a visit. Also check out another site called The Children's Literature Web Guide at http://www.ucalgary.@ca/~dkbrown/. They have Internet resources related to books for kids and young adults. Here you'll find links to book awards, recommended books, bestsellers, and children's literature Internet discussion groups—not to mention resources for parents and for teachers (a great place to get your books listed).

(continued on next page)

chances of capturing a spot on these coveted lists is iffy at best. And the general public couldn't give a tinker's damn. So there!

2. Readers really care about cover copy. The information about a book, which is printed on the back cover and inside flaps of hardcovers, was rated as either "extremely important" or "very important" by two-thirds of potential readers. Cover *design* on the other hand, was only important to 23% of the people. Think about that! Much emphasis is put on the graphics, yet readers say good copywriting is what compels them to buy a book.

3. In other findings, we learned that fiction is ahead of nonfiction 53% to 43%, with mystery and suspense being the favorite fiction categories.

4. Happily, the survey also revealed that younger book buyers are more likely to buy a larger number of books. It was previously believed that older people were the biggest book purchasers.

Consumer spending on books to explode. That's the good news from the Book Industry Study Group, which projects domestic consumer spending on books will reach $31.2 billion by the year 2000. This is up from an estimated $19 billion in 1990. Another prognosis from the 10th Annual Communications Industry Forecast, projects more slimmed down numbers. They predict total consumer spending on books will increase from $15.7 in 1955 to $20.7 billion in 2000.

In either case, those who feared that the Internet and CD-ROMs would signal the end of books as we know them can take heart. Books sales will continue to be healthy despite the advent of the digital age. This is fueled by the fact that those most likely to buy books—baby boomers aged 35 to 54—are at an all-time high. Technology, competition, and consumer lifestyles are redefining book retailing and distribution. Consumers seek value pricing, convenient purchasing, and broad selection. Our challenge is to help them achieve these desires.

Did you hear that researchers have learned how to transplant brains into the feet of dogs? I don't know about you, but it certainly gives me paws for thought.

Statistics that can shape your business life. We're happy to report that more Americans enjoy reading than any other activity according to the fourth annual Harris Poll of U.S. leisure activities. When asked, "What are your two or three most favorite leisure-time activities?" 30% said reading. It was followed by watching TV (21%) and gardening (14%). The American Booksellers Association commissioned a consumer

---

Genre-Specific Web Sites (continued)

Additionally, they have a forum called "Talk About Books." It features a message board for posting your comments, recommendations, questions/answers about children's books, and other useful related material.

Are you into romance? Then take yourself to http://www.romantictimes. com/ where *Romantic Times* resides. Dubbed "the bible of romantic fiction," it is dedicated to news of romance books and the behind-the-scenes world of romance publishing. You can view the current issue, back issues, and 150 new book reviews each month. (*You* are represented there, right?) We found intriguing industry pieces on foreign rights, contracts, agent news, even a story on promotion titled, "Selling Yourself for Fun and Profit."

Attention mystery and romance buffs. You may want to visit *The Rock*. (No, we don't mean Alcatraz.) This is a free online magazine with content likely to tickle your fancy. In the October 1997 issue there is an article, "Make Mine Hard-boiled," about cooking up great detective mysteries. "Romance that Goes Bump in the Night" was about exploring paranormal romance. Regular features include Up Close & Personal (a Harlequin Intrigue editor was interviewed), news releases about romance and mystery genres, plus reviews of all genres. There is also a section titled "Authors on the Road" that covers book signings, workshops, events, and kudos. This is a site to educate yourself and use as a promotional vehicle, so check it out at http:/

(continued on next page)

Genre-Specific Web Sites (continued)

/www.paintedrock.com/memvis/ rockmag/oct97/oct97htm.htm.

Treasure trove for fiction authors. Surf on over to http://www.eclectics. com/writing/writing.html and you'll discover The Eclectic Writer. They indeed have a menu of tantalizing offerings: "Spot Newsletter" is about promotion and publicity for authors; the "Writers' Message Board" is a Web-based discussion board for writers. Then there are collections of articles on writing in general, plus crime, romance, horror, children's, technical, sci-fi, poetry, mystery, even screen writing! You'll also be able to locate Usenet newsgroups for writers here as well as links to many reference works. And the articles are worth their weight in gold. Here's a sampling: "What Makes a Hot Book Hot?" addresses sensuality, "Setting" talks about how to create an ideal place for your novel, while the "Fiction Writers Character Chart" provides a detailed guideline for getting to really know your characters.

Calling all word-aholics. Want a fun site where you can tease your brain cells? Then go to http://www. wordmuseum.com. It features reviews, contests, classes, and how-to articles in many genres. It's also a very imaginatively designed site; for instance, the Horror page has blood dripping from the top. But you'll find more than horror and blood. There are also sections for mystery, westerns, science fiction, children, teens, even the paranormal. Surfers can enter writing contests, the readers club, or pursue fun trivia.

research study conducted by the NPD Group, Inc. It found that Popular Fiction, though always the most prevailing category, slipped two percentage points in 1997. While this doesn't seem like much, it represents a decline of over 21 million books purchased in that category! Popular Fiction represented 50%. Cooking/ Crafts came in second at 10%, while General Nonfiction and Religion each captured 9%.

Noel Coward once said that "having to read a footnote resembles having to go downstairs to answer the door while in the midst of making love."

Looking for a powerful online publishing community? Then surf on over to http://www.bookzone.com. The premier Web developer and host for publishing professionals, this huge site has something to help every publisher—and book lover! From their retail Super Catalog to Literary Leaps (the Web's largest searchable collection of book-related links) to their BookFlash promotion service to BookZone Pro (a section chock-full of articles, links and tools for publishers), you'll find something for you.

CHAPTER 2

Energized Editorial + Electrified Titles = Marketing Magic

In today's competitive world of publishing, smart authors and publishers start thinking "marketing" when they first begin a book project. Sound like a strange statement? Not really. There are things you can include as you create and shape the manuscript that will furnish additional clout when it comes time to sell that book. There are also things you may want to omit; more on that later.

Determining your "USP"

Every product—from soap to refrigerators to cars—has a Unique Selling Proposition, or USP. Books need this differentiating element too. Some people call it "positioning." It takes something common and makes it uncommon. So how do you make your books better, more unusual than the competition's?

You need to *know* the competition. Authors tell us almost daily, "There's no other book like this." Not so. They just don't know about the other books because they haven't done their homework. Stopping by a big chain store and checking the shelves for similar works is *not* the way you determine what else is available. That store, no matter how huge, only carries a fraction of all the books available.

11

Here's how to really check out the competition: First, go online to www.amazon.com and bring up your subject area. Then study the information on the books that come up and note which ones you want to investigate further. Second, go to an independent bookstore. Chat with the owner or buyer about your project and ask their opinion for recommendations on the topic and why those books are good. Buy them. Devour them.

Third, go to a large library and look in the Subject Guide of current copies of *Books in Print* and *Forthcoming Books in Print*. (These are often housed in the Acquisitions Department.) Photocopy the relevant pages. Study them. This research can also be done on CD-ROM, which has updates monthly, and can be downloaded to a printer. Then check out the 10 top books you want to peruse. You can ask for an interlibrary loan to obtain those not readily available.

Once you know the good books out there, you're ready to determine how to tempt people to review, purchase, and read yours. After you've identified their strengths and weaknesses, you can position your book to outshine their weaknesses. Will you make yours shorter? Funnier? More complete? Will you add illustrations? Quizzes and checklists? Take a different approach?

That's what the authors of *What to Expect When You're Expecting* did. There were scores of guides on preparing for baby when they were writing their book. They added a new twist: taking readers through the process month by month. Did it work? That book has sold over 4,500,000 copies, continues to sell at the rate of 75,000 copies a month, and has led to three companion volumes that are also racking up huge sales numbers.

Whatever you do, give your all. If you make the quality and research of your book a prime concern, then you'll have a superior product to promote. Love your readers and make a passionate commitment to them. Tell your readers *everything* you know on the subject. And stretch yourself to learn more. By making content king you turn up the juice and blast out of the gate at a run instead of at a trot.

Adding chapters for greater diversity

The more promotional angles you provide for a book, the more sales will sizzle instead of fizzle. You widen the book's appeal by thinking through your topic and slanting parts of it to different target audiences. One reason this is a shrewd approach is that magazines and newspapers often buy what are called serial or excerpt rights. That means they purchase a small portion of your book to run in their publication. And even though the overall thrust of your message might not be applicable, they may be encouraged to find a section, chapter, quiz, or list of tips that appeals to their particular readers. Such exposure can be crucial in bringing your title to the attention of hundreds of thousands of extra people and stimulating word-of-mouth sales.

Let's suppose you have a book on alcoholism. Have you included a chapter on teenage alcoholics? This will open a whole new niche for marketing the book to schools, professional counselors, even progressive churches. What about a chapter for the mate of an alcoholic? Adding such information could turn a book that has no appeal to women's magazines into one they would consider reviewing or excerpting.

Maybe your title is *The Second Time Around*. Besides the usual focus on how to meet someone and develop a good relationship, probe deeper. How about a chapter on dealing harmoniously with ex-spouses? How about adding advice on visiting arrangements for grandparents when normal family ties no longer exist? Such information may be just the hook you need to interest *Modern Maturity* or one of the host of other publications slanted to the grandparenting crowd. Wouldn't a section on handling hostile stepchildren be useful to many?

Look for ways to give your book more universal appeal. Until recently, there was no book on how to produce, package, and market cassette tapes. Let's pretend we're doing one. When developing the Table of Contents, think about the kinds of people who might use such a book. Publishers to be sure. But what about a separate chapter for aspiring musicians? And how about specific sections for ministers—speakers—trainers—authors—sales managers—politicians—even meeting planners who are often responsible for making arrangements to tape conventions? Thus a book that might appeal only to one major market is expanded to many potential outlets.

Planting strategic editorial "zingers"

Just as one has to water, fertilize, weed, and otherwise nurture a garden before it produces, there are more things you can do at the writing stage to boost sales later. Sometimes it makes a lot of sense to mention key places or people.

When Marilyn wrote her first book, *Discover Your Roots*, back in 1978, she tried to sell it to the bookstore at Cabrillo National Monument in San Diego, which is the most visited of all such sites in the U.S. Their answer was "no." The book had no relationship to the monument, they said. She filed this away for future reference. When writing *Creative Loafing* a year later, guess which national monument was prominently featured in this guide of leisure pursuits? Sure enough, they were happy to carry the book.

In our *How to Make Big Profits Publishing City & Regional Books*, we shared hundreds of specific anecdotes and referenced book titles within the body of the text to show how broad this specialty publishing field actually is. When making the index, we listed each book that was mentioned.

Then we used the index to help prepare a special mini-mailing to the publishers covered. It cited the page on which each was mentioned and suggested purchasing a copy of the book. The orders rolled in. One marketing director even sent along this note: "Enclosed is our order for a copy of your new book. We received your flier and I do want to congratulate you on a clever and effective marketing technique." You can use this tip to increase your sales as well.

Adding quotes from key people can also boost interest in your book. Let's suppose you hope to make a bulk premium sale to XYZ corporation. If you include a relevant statement or two from the CEO it's only natural they will look more fondly on your project. You might also want to mention key companies or products in the text. Imaginative use of a tie-in can lead to corporate sponsorship of your project.

Corporate America is always looking for creative ways to draw attention to itself. And these companies have gigantic advertising budgets. Let's say you're an author or publisher doing a cookbook on southwestern foods. Many of the recipes will contain salsa as an ingredient. If you mention a particular brand of salsa, your book could launch a whole national publicity campaign for the company that manufacturers that salsa. They might buy books in the tens of thousands of copies. The author could even sign a deal to be a company spokesperson. Yes, premium sales can equate to enormous profits. Yet the groundwork must often be laid early.

You may *not* want to mention a specific company or product, however. Why? Because staying generic is far safer if you anticipate making bulk sales of this title to *several* different companies in the same industry. If you plug XYZ company, sure you'll make points with them. But should you *also* hope to sell this book to ABC firm, and DEF, Inc., and GHI corporation, it is wiser to stay neutral and not mention any company or product by name.

Today speakers, doctors, attorneys, and a wide variety of entrepreneurs contact our publishing consulting firm, About Books, Inc., to help them put their specialized knowledge between book covers. Most of them do it not only to create a new revenue center, but also to use as a marketing tool. People read their books, perceive them as "the expert," and want their services or products.

In such cases, it's prudent to sprinkle a few self-serving plugs in the manuscript. (See About Books, Inc. in the above paragraph.) This can be done tactfully by citing examples of what you've done, including case studies, mentioning "my patient, my client, my customer," etc. Be sure to make it obvious how to contact you both at the front and back of the book. Include not only the usual information, but also an email address and a URL if you have an Internet site. (No, a URL is not a European nobleman. It's the abbreviation for your Web address and stands for Uniform Resource Locator.)

Another ingenious approach is to build your book *around* your target audience. Who is your customer? Truly know this person. What are their problems and frustrations? Their bliss? Their buzz words? Their educational and income level? What do they read? What groups do they join? How can you reach them? If you create a manuscript with the end user constantly in mind, you'll build a better book.

Thinking "foreign rights" from the outset

Not all power tools are in the Black & Decker catalog. Foreign rights sales are often an underappreciated power tool with great potential. Few people realize that what keeps many smart mid-sized to small publishers thriving is the revenue generated from these sales. *Publishers Weekly* revealed that a title from Jossey-Bass, *Emotional Intelligence at Work*, has been bought by no less than 14 foreign publishers to be translated into such languages as Chinese, Japanese, Korean, and Indonesian. Advances from these deals total a whopping $212,750! The Brazilian edition alone brought in $100,000. Will this work for your books? Here's how to assess the potential.

First, your topic must be in demand. Business is very popular. New age and metaphysical subjects are popular as well, especially holistic medicine and natural healing. Titles on aging that deal with second careers, care giving, travel, disease, and dating after middle age have appeal. Relationship and parenting topics do well also. And because the PC is just emerging as a popular trend in foreign countries, computer books sell like hot cakes. Happily, many backlist titles are just as viable as brand new books.

Second, your books must "travel." That means they must be as appropriate in other countries as here. If you include a lot of U.S. addresses and phone numbers in the text, you'll hurt your chances of foreign sales. (Consider whether you can group such material in an Appendix—which they can elect to delete.) Other countries depend on the metric system of measurement, so cookbooks with ingredients specified in the American standard will meet with resistance. Books referencing dollars and prices are doomed. But perhaps you can condense your U.S.-oriented material into one chapter, which can be omitted from the foreign language version. Naturally, having "America/American" or "U.S." in the title or subtitle is frowned upon.

Knowing how lucrative foreign rights can be is a real impetus for evaluating how you write, edit, and slant a book in the early stages.

Front matter as sales stimulators

Most people wouldn't think the front and back matter—those things that come before and after the main text in a book—would have much bearing on how it sells. Not so. This material can have a dramatic impact on your book's success! Let us first consider front matter.

Face it: you want to stand out. Right? One of the more positive things you can do to accomplish that is to get a person widely recognized in the field to write a Foreword. (Notice it's spelled "Foreword" not "Forward"!) Physicians, attorneys, and certain other professionals can be tapped for Forewords. They are often thrilled to get their names on book covers. And there may be an additional benefit for you; a doctor, for instance, will read your manuscript for accuracy as well because he or she would be embarrassed by errors.

Acknowledgments are another place to mention key names—not only those you genuinely wish to thank for their help, but also people you want to favor and impress. Sometimes they will be so flattered to be singled out they will buy your book and help with promotion by recommending it to others.

Have you ever gone to a bookstore and watched browsers? (That's called "shelf-awareness.") At first they look at the front cover. If the book still holds their attention, they turn it over and examine the back cover. The next thing they'll usually do is flip through the pages, then turn to the Table of Contents and either decide to buy—or move on to another book.

Therein lies a profound revelation: The Table of Contents is one of your most valuable sales tools! Make it meaty. Exciting. Benefit-oriented. Include the subheads as well as the chapter titles. Tell potential buyers specifically what the book delivers, what problem it solves for them. Use punchy phraseology and active verbs.

If the book will be rolling off the press at the end of the year, use the *next year* in your copyright notice. It will seem fresh for a much longer time and have a better crack at ongoing reviews. It's an industry standard to do this for any book coming out from September on.

Back matter that rings cash registers

Now let's examine some of the ingredients that come after the main part of the book and can mean extra dollars in your pocket.

Fat Appendixes pay big dividends. In fact, some people buy a book solely because of the unique reference information presented in the Appendix. If your book contains enough such data, it may qualify for a listing in the *Directory of Directories.*

We had a client several years back who had written an autobiographical expose decrying slipshod medical practices. Her topic lent itself to listings of various associations dealing with specific diseases, consumer medical advocacy groups, state medical policing agencies, etc. We counseled her to add these additional sources of information in the Appendix to increase the book's worth. That way her autobiography became a "reference work" because it included a compendium of valuable resources not previously collected in one place.

Adding a Glossary can also be a smart move, especially if you use a lot of unfamiliar terms. When our best-selling *Complete Guide to Self-Publishing* was reviewed by John Kremer in *Small Press* magazine (now *Independent Publisher*), one of the things he said was, "The Rosses have defined over 400 publishing terms in a separate glossary, an indispensable reference resource for neophytes." Sometimes people who need to know the terminology of a certain industry will buy your book strictly for the Glossary.

A nonfiction book without an Index is like bread without butter. Readers want—and deserve—to be able to locate specific pieces of information quickly. The only way they can do that is through an Index. Librarians expect them; educational sales will be dampened for a book lacking one. (And as we pointed out earlier, Indexes can also serve as a marketing tool to pinpoint individuals or groups who might be interested in purchasing your book.)

Last, but certainly not least, should be an Order Form. It amazes us how seldom books include this obvious sales opportunity. How often do you use a library book, and subsequently want to purchase a personal copy? Or borrow a book from a friend, then want one yourself? Our philosophy is to make it easy to buy. At our sister company, Communication Creativity, we get orders every week on the order forms we provide in the back of the books we publish.

We've heard some decry, "But the bookstores and wholesalers won't carry my book if I include an Order Form." Nonsense. Our books are carried by Ingram, Baker & Taylor, Barnes & Noble, Borders, Tattered Cover—shall we go on? To avoid alienating bookstores unnecessarily, however, your Order Form should always say: "Check your leading bookstore or order here."

Design it as an actual Order Form—complete with a benefit-oriented headline and places for name, address, city, state, zip, phone number, and email address. If you offer credit card purchasing, include logos for the various cards, a place for the card number, expiration date, and a signature line. Compute the state sales tax and express it in exact dollars and cents rather than a percentage. Add a postage and shipping fee; $3 or $4 per book works well. Remember to indicate you offer a discount on quantity orders. (You do, don't you?) This form should appear on the last recto (right-hand) page of the book where it is easily seen. Few people will tear it out, most simply photocopy it.

The ideas we've been sharing are guaranteed to hike your book sales and keep you from looking like a turtle in a horse race. But they are things that must be done early in the writing or editing process. Good marketing planning begins when you first start thinking about the shape of a manuscript. By employing the strategies we've discussed at that early stage, you're assured of stronger sales throughout the life of the work.

Christening your masterpiece with a sensational title

You think you have a tough time coming up with a fantastic title? Just be grateful you don't have to name thoroughbred racehorses. In that situation the colt's name must reflect the names of both equine parents. For example, if mom was named *Southern Dancer* and dad was *Hot Sounds*, you might name the colt *Jazzy Two-Step* or *Waltzing Blare*—or you might not.

Some book titles, like horse names, simply "work." Take for instance, *Men are from Mars, Women Are from Venus; Don't Sweat the Small Stuff . . . and It's All Small Stuff;* and *Gone with the Wind.* A new book out by Andre Bernard (*Now All We Need Is a Title),* tells us that some very famous books were almost doomed to obscurity by their original titles. *Pride and Prejudice* was initially *First Impressions. The Blackboard Jungle* was first titled *To Climb a Wall. The Red Badge of Courage* was originally dubbed *Private Fleming, His Various Battles.*

If our friend, Sam Horn, had called her first book *Handling Difficult People,* she would have lost an exceptional opportunity to be unique and command attention. Instead, she titled it *Tongue Fu!* In the subtitle, she erases any doubts what the book is about: *How to Deflect, Disarm, and Defuse any Verbal Conflict.*

Notice how well the title and subtitle function together. One is short and catchy; the other embellishes it. We were pleased when *Publishers Weekly* commented about our *Country Bound! Trade Your Business Suit Blues for Blue Jean Dreams* that it was "enticingly titled." Again there is a short title with a longer, catchy explanatory line. All who work in nonfiction need to be considering not just titles but also subtitles. One must reinforce the other.

Of course, what really makes the two above books work is that each promises a *benefit*. In just a few words, they take a problem and explain how the book will solve it. Magazines do this as well. They use article titles to grab potential readers. Study *Readers Digest* and *The National Enquirer,* for instance, to get a better feel for how their headlines tease, titillate, and sell.

A benefit addresses the pain a person feels or the gain they want. Pain is stronger than gain. That's why books on losing weight or becoming sexier are infinitely popular. Here are two titles that appear on Quality Books Small Press Top 40 List: *Find Anyone Fast* and *Stop Memory Loss!* If you can't locate a loved one (or an ex-husband behind in his child-support), or you're beginning to forget names, these titles hold much appeal to you. They state the benefit clearly and succinctly.

So how do you come up with a title that promises a robust meal rather than thin gruel? Collect ideas. Mix and match concepts. Brainstorm. Start a journal, manilla folder, or computer file where you dump every possible thought. Maybe it's just one word, or a phrase or slogan. Begin gathering tidbits from which you can weave a compelling title tapestry. Don't be judgmental. Include everything that intrigues you. Then begin mixing and matching. In the end, part of something you were considering for a subtitle may emerge as your title, or vice versa.

And go online to www.amazon.com. There you'll find some 4 million book titles. By searching on key words you plan to have in your title, you can see what is already taken, as well as prospect for new notions.

Get others involved. This expands your pool of possibilities. Ask the opinion of colleagues on an Internet listserv, talk about your potential titles at the next meeting of your writers' or publishers' group, ask clients or customers about their viewpoint. Not only will you get feedback on what you already have but probably a slew of new ideas to consider. So then you get to brainstorm all over again. This doesn't end until the fat lady (of title magic) sings.

People may also reveal a problem you had never thought of, such as a word that's offensive to some segments of the population, or perhaps an embarrassing double entendre. Do be aware of another danger: If you discuss a book with a group of people who are *not* its potential market, you'll usually get jaded feedback. A group of engineers will not likely give good input about the title of a cookbook any more than a gathering of Mensa members can be relied on to help title a volume for blue-collar workers.

Though you don't want cutsie simply for cutsie's sake, look at how you can add a twist to make it more interesting or fun. Patricia Schroeder, former congresswoman and current president/CEO of the Association of American Publishers, recently wrote *24 Years of Housework . . . and the Place Is Still a Mess: My Life in Politics.*

Fire "Captain Bob" Smith tells of titling his book *Transform Stress and Fear* and not getting much play for it. One day at breakfast his wife said, "Why don't we change it to 'Eat Stress for Breakfast'?" When he approached radio producers with this headline, they gobbled it up (pun intended). So the book will carry the new title on the second printing. Virtually everyone chuckles and is curious when they hear it.

Such was not the case when Sterling, which has a 2,300-title backlist catalog, first put out a book on optical illusions and called it *Eye Spy*. It didn't sell. Nobody knew what it meant. Next they tried titling it *Eye Teasers*, which also bombed. But when it was republished as *The Great Book of Optical Illusions*, they went on to sell 200,000 copies. They had finally hit on a high-octane title.

Now let's look at how your title will be treated by the industry. Databases typically enter the first 30 characters. Only. If you have a long title they will cut off part of it. Some publishers intentionally use the main word of their subject as the first word in the title, feeling this helps them in searches and databases. Thus, *A Handbook for Veterinary Medicine* would become *Veterinary Medicine: A Handbook*.

Joe Sabah, who speaks on "How to Create Book Titles that Sizzle and Sell," swears by a "how-to" beginning. And it certainly works for him. He has sold over $357,000 worth of his *How to Get the Job You Really Want and Get Employers to Call You*. You'll also notice that Joe's title is loaded with benefits, another strategy he preaches: "Benefits. Benefits. Benefits. This is the secret to a *great* book title," counsels Joe.

Think about how a clerk in a bookstore will interpret your title when a potential customer comes asking for it. If your book is about *no smoking*, and she looks under *know smoking*, you're sunk. Hyphenation can also present a problem. That's why we intentionally titled this *Jump Start Your Book Sales* instead of the correct *Jump-Start Your Book Sales*. Most clerks wouldn't think to put in the hyphen; then the database would say there is no such book. (Thank you, Bear Kamoroff, for that great tip at the 1997 SPAN Conference.)

Attention bibliophiles. For those of you collectors and admirers of books, surf over to http://www.bibliomag.com for a real online treat. Here you'll find both the latest and previous issues of *Biblio* magazine. One of their lead stories the month we visited was on Oprah and how she has single-handedly spearheaded a reading revival. They also have a Genre of the Month and extensive lists of book-related links. This is a great jumping-off place for other intriguing sites for book lovers.

Quick quotation resource. Go to http://www.quotations.com for quotes on over 150 different subjects. You can order a group—such as fame (82 entries), humility (62), learning (114), marriage (101), pain (59), action (108), etc.—for $2 each set via disk or email. You can even commission custom quotation research for a book or speech. Quotes can support an idea, open a news release, begin a chapter, or serve other useful purposes.

"A memoir is when you put down the good things you ought to have done and leave out the bad ones you did do."

Will Rogers

Need information on patents and trademarks? Newcomers to publishing often think they can copyright their book title. Not so. But there are ways around this. You can establish a trademark, for instance. For basic facts, specific questions and answers, plus more information than you ever wanted to know, we recommend three Web sites: http://www.uspto.gov/web/offices/tac/doc/basic, http://www.uspto.gov/web/offices/pac/doc/basic, and http://www.uspto.gov/web/offices/pac/doc/general.

Dictionary, dictionary, where art thou? At http://www.bucknell. edu/~rbeard/diction.html that's where. Not just dry pedantic stuff here, however. This is a treasure trove of specialized tomes (about such fun things as beer, rap, and college slang) and serious subjects (such as dictionaries of legal, medical, computer, and real estate terms). There is also a Shakespeare glossary and dictionaries of terminology on such subjects as music, theology, the textile industry—even epidemiology, cell biology, and orthodontics. And for those who enjoy penning poetry, you'll also find a simple rhyming dictionary. This site has links to dictionaries for languages from Afrikaans to Zulu: 85 in all.

Have a grammar question? Short queries about writing, correct usage, and syntax can be directed to various universities and community colleges. Simply go to www.tc.cc.va.us/vabeach/writcent/wchome.html. (Well, that isn't so simple after all, is it?) They are listed alphabetically by state and also include days and hours of operation. If you would like a copy, send a #10 SASE to Grammar Hotline Directory, Tidewater Community College Writing Center, 1700 College Crescent, Virginia Beach, VA 23456.

One definition of a beginning publisher: An international literary conglomerate in the formative stages.

Need a fresh way to write your book? Try storyboarding! Walt Disney used storyboards to plan all his movies. Ad agencies also employ this technique to plan commercials. Get a 4- by 8-foot piece of foam board from an art store and several sizes of Post-it Notes in various colors. Across the top of the board, use the largest notes for chapter level ideas or major parts of your marketing plan. Below each, use smaller and smaller Post-its for each progressively lower-level idea, story, thought, quote, contact, or whatever. Use just a few key words to capture the idea. Because Post-it Notes are easy to move around, you have complete flexibility and your whole project is available at a glance.

Publishers: Looking for alternative sources for good manuscripts? There are options all around you. What about buying rights to out-of-print and underexploited books the original publisher ignored? Have you thought of recombining components from some of your other titles? What about an anthology? Conference proceedings and symposia sometimes contain the foundation for developing an outstanding text. If you're a small press, you could pull a switch—and buy translation rights for a strong foreign title that travels well to the United States. How about bringing out something in the public domain but adding a foreword or other information or illustrations to make your version unique? You could record interviews with notables on a specific theme, then hire a ghostwriter to clean up the transcript. And if you have a stunning idea in-house, don't forget the "work for hire" option. Ideas for winning books proliferate in unusual places once you start looking for them.

New way to play the name game. Having trouble titling your next book? How about getting your potential customers engaged in the process? They love feeling involved and appreciated. And they may come up with some angles *you* never thought of. I (Marilyn) once stood outside a market, clipboard in hand, with a dozen or so possible titles and subtitles and polled shoppers as they walked out. Not only did they graciously make choices, but several offered new ideas or told me why a concept bothered them. It's cheap market research!

Want to know the copyright status of a work? The Library of Congress publishes an eight-page circular that explains how to use its research staff to find out whether a particular book is copyrighted and, if so, who currently holds ownership. This is a real bonanza for any publisher who wants to reprint an existing work it thinks is out of copyright or adapt one for republication. Check your nearest government document depository, often housed at a large university or library, for circular number 22 titled, "How to Investigate the Copyright Status of a Work." If you can't find a depository, call the Library of Congress reference and bibliography section at 202-707-6850 or visit their Web site at http://lcweb.loc.gov/copyright. (And if copyright issues interest you, be sure and read the article "How Much of Someone Else's Work May I Use Without Asking Permission?" on page 9 of that brochure.)

Book topics that won't fade with the next fad. Sometimes being on the "cutting edge" can take a big slice out of your momentum. If you want to publish a "safe" book, consider *evergreen* topics like diet and weight-loss techniques, nutrition, sex, parenting, finding a good job, etc. These perennial topics have long-term potential; they never go out of fashion.

He writes poems from bad to verse.

Want to know more about the *process* of publishing? *The Insiders' Guide to Book Publishing* tells you how to develop and sell books by understanding the whole process. Hot off the press, this new title by Terri A. Boekhoff and Joshua Bagby offers practical advice so publishing professionals can make smart, timely decisions to reduce costs and increase sales. Order it by calling 800-331-8355.

Romance writer uses Internet to research book. Nora Roberts, author of *Montana Sky*, has never been to the state. "I just didn't have time to go there," she admits. But her hundreth novel needed to be set in an isolated locale a little claustrophobic, yet open. The plot revolves around a ranch that's in the middle of nowhere with acres and acres of land. She put out the word, "I'm starting to research a book," and stuff just started coming in. Someone told her of friends who ran a Montana cattle ranch. She called and asked what they did from dawn to dusk. "It gave me a real feel for what they had to do. What kind of equipment there is, what you do in the spring and what you do in the fall," Roberts reports. With the Internet, the *world* is a fiction writer's oyster.

Looking to pinpoint trends before they're common knowledge? *American Demographics* may well become your best online buddy. The magazine covers consumer trends and presents tons of useful statistics. While it's targeted to advertising types, writers and publishers wanting to be on the cutting edge will find the offerings here tantalizing. Reach them at http://www.marketingtools.com.

Comment from writer:
I made no attempt to be inaccurate, but I want to be clear
I was not attempting to be precise.

Meet Scoop Cybersleuth—your Internet guide. Scoop Cybersleuth is the Internet's ace reporter. He'll help you find some great sites such as those for the U.S. government and politics, state and local governments, reference and demographics, journalism tools, academic experts, and on and on. Tune in to him at http://www.evansville.net/courier/scoop/.

Need answers to English questions? It's all waiting for you at the Purdue University's On-Line Writing Lab at http://owl.english.purdue.edu. They can deal with your grammar quandaries and troubleshoot other writing problems. And you'll find *Elements* of *Style* online here. (Did you know this classic was originally self-published in 1918 by William Strunk, Jr. to use in his English classes at Cornell University?) They can also link you to other writing labs on the Internet and additional resources of interest.

CHAPTER 3

Endorsements Equal Souped-Up Success

"Buzz" is influential talk—a big-time, no-nonsense force. Buzz might be called the Tornado Alley of communication. But it needs an igniter. Several igniters actually. That's where advance comments, also known as "blurbs," come in. If you can get several celebrities or really well-known people in your industry to say nice things about your book, people will start talking about it. So in this chapter we'll be searching for one of the most elusive forces in marketing: the buzz of testimonials.

Prepare *now* for getting blurbs later

Ideally, you have developed a personal relationship with key individuals. This is one reason to continually network within your industry. Attend national conventions and regional seminars where you can reach opinion makers. Get to know these people. Follow up the meetings with personal notes. Keep in touch every six months or so.

Join associations in your field and volunteer to serve on committees. It's only human nature to be more willing to help out a friend or acquaintance than a stranger. When you come a callin' with a prepublication endorsement request, your chances of going away a winner are much greater if you are approaching someone you know—and who knows you.

Use your contacts. If, for instance, you happen to be a member of the American Society of Journalists and Authors (ASJA) and you're trying to reach a celebrity, check the membership directory for those who specialize in writing about "Entertainment/Performing Arts." One of your colleagues just might have recently interviewed the luminary you're trying to reach for an article, or written a book about him or her.

This can work for other topic areas as well. Want to reach a fitness guru? Maybe one who writes about "Fitness & Exercise" can help. Those who specialize in such subjects as Music, Personal Finance, Women's Issues, Lifestyles, or Historical Subjects might also provide wonderful liaisons to important people in their fields. We've found our ASJA colleagues to be very generous of spirit.

If you're working really far out, here's another idea, once you've identified your potential endorsers: Determine their birthdays and interests by looking them up in a Who's Who directory. Purchase a book you know they would enjoy, autograph it appropriately, and send it to them on their birthday. It's guaranteed they will remember you when the time comes!

Researching for appropriate endorsers

But suppose you're not on a first-name basis with appropriate people? Don't fret. Get ye to the Internet! You don't have to kiss a million frogs to find a prince on the Net. Just for grins go to amazon.com as a starting point. (Also see the many specific appropriate sites for locating experts and celebrities under Web Sites, Wisdom, and Whimsey.) Often finding someone who matches your needs is as easy as typing a few keywords in an online search engine.

Or you might consider prospecting on a listserv that covers your topic. We know of one celebrity author who waxed eloquently via email after he replied to a request for advance reviews on a listserv—and found he loved the book.

Many people you can't access any other way are on the Information Superhighway. Check various Web sites for their email addresses. (This is a great way to go around gatekeepers, as many important people respond personally to their email.)

If the Web doesn't solve your problem, try a large library. Look under your subject in *Readers' Guide to Periodical Literature, Magazine Index,* and any of the specialized indexes such as *Business Periodicals Index, Applied Science and Technology Index,* or *Index Medicus.* Often article writers are the experts in the field.

And don't overlook book authors, especially if you have a novel. Those who write in your genre are the ideal people to blurb your book.

Other authors published by your same house or clients of your agent will be easier to reach since the publisher or agent can intervene in your behalf.

You can also find appropriate authors in *Subject Guide to Books in Print* (which is usually housed in the library's order department rather than in the open stacks in the patron section.) For best-selling authors who are deluged with requests, you usually have to write them in care of their most recent publisher. Find those addresses in *Literary Market Place (LMP).* (Or for a more sneaky approach, read the acknowledgments in their most recent book; they'll usually name their agent. Then look up that person in *LMP.*)

One resourceful author, who obtained a quote from none less than John Bradshaw, discovered how to reach him while preparing a reading list for her own book. When going through one of Bradshaw's books she noticed a phone number telling where to buy his tapes. It rang into his office and resulted in a rich and laudatory testimonial. Always keep your antenna out; sometimes a hot trail waits in disguise.

More strategies for locating the object of your affection

There are many useful directories that can serve as lightning rods for your search. Try the following: *The Yearbook of Experts, Authorities & Spokespersons; Celebrity Directory; VIP Address Book.* Always use the most current volume. In these three directories you'll find thousands of film and television stars, authors, politicians, recording stars, athletes, and other famous people.

Bury yourself in various Who's Who references or specialized directories to get contact information and background data. Ask the reference librarian for help. While recently researching for a client who had a sports title he wanted us to promote, we discovered *The Sports Address Book.* It proved to be a treasure trove of information for our purposes. There are many such industry-specific resources.

If you're after Hollywood types, try locating their agents or personal publicists through the Screen Actors Guild in Los Angeles at 323-549-6797. The New York Guild can be reached at 212-944-6797. As you might guess, the Guilds are deluged with requests and will only give out information on three actors at a time. Once you get an agent's name, call him or her and ask if the performer has a publicist. If not, the agent is your contact, so come on with your big guns.

Even if the agent or publicist offers to verbally pass along your request, it's wise to send it in writing. It's hard for another person to convey your passion for the project.

Need to corner a political type? Find out who their press secretary is by contacting the White House, Capital, or Supreme Court, whichever applies. Party headquarters can also be helpful in reaching certain elephants or donkeys.

Making it actually happen

Now that you know who you want to contact and how to reach them, the challenge is how to *motivate them* to agree. It's not that they object to giving a quote, it's the time needed to read the book. The celebrity or expert is often too busy to accommodate your request. Is all lost? Not necessarily.

Offer to draft appropriate comments yourself. You might say, "I know how busy you are. Why don't I put together a few lines for you—subject to your approval or revision, of course?" They often agree. Yes, *you* will write the blurb. It's done all the time. This saves the other person valuable time and gives you more control over both the content and the turnaround period.

Tailor the quote to the person by using language the individual would be comfortable with. Craft a quote that is specific rather than general. Saying something is "a good read" really says nothing. Instead, qualify and quantify to develop a strong testimonial. An evocative and credible quote might say something like, "With the ideas in XYZ book, I discovered how to accomplish the same amount of work in half the time."

It's the wise author or publisher who understands the agenda and hot buttons of the person from whom they are requesting a quote. Then you can explain that your book furthers his or her aims. Make it clear you understand the other person's causes and concerns by referring specifically to his or her work.

To expedite things, you might fax the quote, along with a Table of Contents, cover or catalog copy, and author bio for nonfiction. For fiction, it's harder to get a commitment without the other person reading the manuscript. If you wish to try, offer an author bio, synopsis, and a few sample pages so the potential endorser can see your actual writing style.

You may need to work through a personal assistant, agent, publicist, or secretary. If so, woo this person as diligently as you would the endorser. The gatekeeper can either get you in or slam the door shut permanently.

For really important blurbs, call and get the name of the gatekeeper and let him or her know to be on the lookout for a priority or overnight package. Send not only the manuscript, but also write the secretary a personal note of thanks for passing the manuscript along. Call four days later to be sure it got there. Send the gatekeeper a registered letter again thanking him or her for facilitating your contact. Nobody treats these assistants this way. You will be remembered and valued.

How do you proceed once you've garnered these precious testimonial gems? Promote the heck out of them! The advance comments you collect from expert or famous people can be put on the back cover of the book, added to the inside at the very front before the title page, and interwoven in promotional materials. If you manage to get a dynamite testimonial from a heavyweight, you may want to incorporate it on the *front* cover.

How does all this work in "real life?" We decided to be very aggressive about seeking blurbs for *Jump Start Your Book Sales,* so we sent out 67 bound manuscripts to notable authors and key players in the industry. Marilyn's goal was to get 25 advance quotes. When the dust settled we had a whopping 42! This was amazing because we gave people less than a month to reply and it was over the holiday season.

Many read the whole book; others skimmed it and penned a testimonial; four used quotes we developed for them. We sent the bound manuscripts priority mail with a cover letter asking that they let us know if they could provide something. That way we knew the solid contributors early on. When the deadline loomed and we had nothing, we faxed a gentle reminder. Several genuinely appreciated this "heads up" notification.

To our knowledge, no other book in the manuscript stage has garnered so many early rave reviews. This feat seemed worthy of—you guessed it—a news release. It was sent to 26 industry reporters, plus our master distributor, to help fuel the early buzz.

Accolades win sales. Blurbs also lend credibility to your ads and flyers. Try using one as the headline to grab readers' attention. Instead of an abstract claim from you, how much more powerful is a brag from Mr. or Mrs. Big! A headline carries enormous clout if it comes from someone important. Testimonies are also great to add to bookmarks, postcards, or perhaps for a photo caption.

Don't be backward about getting a Foreword

In today's competitive publishing world, each new book must be carefully nurtured to be successful. One of the ways you can help your new baby grow into robust adulthood is by christening it not only with advance quotes, but also with a Foreword.

To be effective, the Foreword should be by someone who is known to, and respected by, your potential reading audience. You want a "name" so you can use it to help promote the book. One of our clients' books, a basketball novel titled *Are You Watching, Adolph Rupp?,* went into a second printing in less than two months. The Foreword by Bob Cousy, Hall of Fame basketball star, was a big boost to sales.

When you're ready to launch your campaign, put together a powerful one-page letter to people telling why your book is important and different from others, and why it will be of special interest to them. Customize each letter with information or comments relevant to that individual to give it personal appeal. Invite the person to read your book and give you *comments*. You're not asking for a Foreword at this point. Ask only for their feedback.

Include the Table of Contents, Introduction, and promotional material to titillate their interest—and offer to send a copy of the book upon request. (If your book is short, include a photocopy of the entire manuscript.)

When you get a glowing response, *then* approach that person about writing a Foreword. This shouldn't be a saga: one to three double-spaced typewritten pages is normal. People who attend our seminars ask, "Should I pay for a Foreword?" No! This is not accepted industry practice.

As in all aspects of any business, persistence pays off. Meredith Rutter of VanderWyk & Burnham tells of her authors sending a copy of their manuscript, *How to Enjoy Your Retirement: Activities from A to Z,* to noted humorist Steve Allen. His personal assistant replied that he would look at it.

But there was no further word. So Rutter sent the assistant a copy of the bound typeset pages with art to "give Mr. Allen a better idea about the final book," plus she mentioned the publication date and their hope that he might want to provide a quotation. Suddenly out of the blue came a faxed Foreword from the man himself . . . just in time to make changes on the bluelines.

But what happens if more than one person is willing to do a Foreword? Take a lesson from Don Dible, who wrote *Up Your Own Organization*. He did so well prospecting for a Foreword he ended up with three notables willing to write about his business book. Dible solved this happy dilemma by having Robert Townsend, of Avis Rent-a-Car fame, do the Introduction; William P. Lear, chairman of the board of Lear Motors Corporation, wrote the Foreword; and John L. Komives, director of the Center for Venture Management, put his name on a Preface. Then Dible splashed *their names* on the cover of his book to give his project added credibility.

Career Press's *Breaking the Rules* takes a slightly different approach. This book carries a Foreword by John Cleese, a "Backward" by Eric Idle, and a "Sideways" by Terry Jones.

So when you're looking for ways to help your book stand out from the crowd, don't be backward about getting a Foreword. It can give you added visibility, credibility, and profitability—not to mention starting a "buzz."

ProfNet is perhaps the best known and most prominent of the spokesperson suppliers. While it used to be the domain of strictly Academe and research institutions, they have now expanded the scope to include corporations, government contacts, think tanks, medical centers, etc. Although they exist primarily as a resource point for journalists and other media personnel, you can make good use of their 5,100 entries as well. Find them on the Internet at http://www.profnet.com/. Send your specific query via email to profnet@profnet.com, or phone 800-776-3638. They usually serve as expert interviewees, but some of the more prominent could also serve as blurb creators.

SCExperts is a service offered by New York University's School of Continuing Education. Their faculty of 1,300 members consists of professionals who practice what they teach on a daily basis. For more details visit their Web site at www.sce.nyu.edu and click on "press kit." Or call 212-998-7070 and ask for SCExperts.

Think about the various markets for your book. Who do these people respect? Get testimonials from different segments of each population so prospective buyers will recognize at least one of them. When we wrote and published the predecessor to this guide, *Marketing Your Books*, the blurbs we acquired represented many segments of the writing and publishing industry. There was one from Dan Poynter, author of *The Self-Publishing Manual;* from Richard Morris, then executive director of the trade association called COSMEP; from James Lee Young then executive director of the National Writers Club.

We also got a glowing comment from Cavett Robert, CPAE and founder of the National Speakers Association. (Speakers were beginning to realize they needed books and they needed to sell them in other ways besides just back-of-the-room when they spoke.) And Tom Drewes, who was then president of Quality Books, Inc., an important distributor of small press titles to libraries, gave us a great quote. See the broad breadth represented?

If a word in the dictionary was misspelled, how would you ever find it?

Seeking an expert for research purposes, advance quotes, etc.? Members of the National Speakers Association can be reached on the Web at http://www.nsaspeaker.org. These folks are typically up-to-the-minute on facts and trends within their subject areas. And they love publicity! If you're publishing books about customer service, gender issues, diversity, change, negotiation, humor, health, networking, relationships, technology, team building—and a variety of other subjects—you can find experts (even celebrities) here. Simply hit "topic" and browse to your heart's content.

Looking for a phone number? Search no further than http://www.switchboard.com. It's a nationwide residential and business directory. Over 10 million businesses are listed, whether or not they're on the Web. And while you're there, be sure *you* are listed so your prospective customers can find you easily.

Experts Searchable Database can be found at http://www.experts.com/. It's a global online directory of experts with a search engine to make your job easier.

BznetUSA is another possibility. It is designed to connect the nation's business press to academic, government, and think tank information sources nationwide. Find them at http://top.monad.net/~gehrung/.

Find an Expert is the Web site of Matthew Lesko. It deals solely with government resources but covers a wide range: sewing machines to eggs, fishnets to hemorrhoids. To tap into this free expert service go to http://www.lesko.com/expert_search.html.

Directory of news sources is the online site of the National Press Club. Access it at http://npc.press.org/sources/. You can search it three different ways.

Genius is the ability to focus on the objective ... too often we focus on the obstacles.

Yearbook of Experts, Authorities & Spokespersons is also available online at http://www.yearbook.com/search.html. You can search for a specific individual or organization, or do a topic list search to click your way to a group that meets your criteria. Unlike many of the above sites, this one contains more diversity of entities, so you may be more likely to find the expert you want.

PART II

Illuminating Publicity Techniques

CHAPTER 4

Reviews and Galleys Accelerate Your Sales

When critics sing, registers ring. Reviews—and their close cousins, editorial mentions—are often responsible for igniting hugely successful book campaigns. The beauty of this publicity is that it's free (paid advertising rarely comes close in generating results); it works whether a book is brand new or a backlist title; and it can be acquired by individual authors, freelance publicists, or publishing companies.

There is no question about whether reviews work. We had more than 500 full-price orders for one of our books when a review by a syndicated columnist broke. Bookstore sales leaped as well. Others have enjoyed even greater success when their books were plugged in major print media.

What are the criteria for getting reviews?

Let us differentiate between general reviews that can occur anytime and those that must be prepublication. Prepublication reviews have to appear before the book's official publication date, which is usually about four months after it rolls off the press. They are triggered by sending a "galley" (an early bound copy that resembles the final book) to a handful of key review sources. We'll talk more about them later.

So how do you attract the attention of the thousands of other possible review sources without offering extravagant bribes, throwing temper tantrums, or disgracing the national anthem? Step number one is to produce a quality product. If you're the author, hopefully you've researched the competition and written a book that is somehow better, more complete, funnier, easier to use, or in some way superior to what is already available. A mediocre book won't outshine the rivals any more than a splash of lipstick will change the bride of Frankenstein into a trophy wife. If you're the publisher, you've dressed this masterpiece in an eye-catching cover and designed an interior that is appealing and user-friendly.

Where do you garner reviews?

Armed with a polished product, you're ready to move on to step number two and contemplate the question, "Who cares?" Precisely, who is your customer? And how do you reach him or her? Of the thousands of consumer magazines and trade journals published in North America, you'll be amazed to find literally hundreds are probable places to obtain reviews. Your job is to match your books with these niched publications.

Then there are editors and reporters at newspapers, both dailies and weeklies, who must fill endless column inches with material interesting to their readers. What about syndicated columnists who write in your subject area . . . and have their material picked up by publications all over the country?

Additionally, there are associations that cater to your potential buyer. Seven out of 10 Americans belong to an association. And there are nearly 23,000 such organizations in the United States. Guess what? They develop bibliographies in which certain titles are recommended, sell books related to their members' interests, and produce publications for their members. Bingo! Another wonderful place for exposure. (Check them out in the *Encyclopedia of Associations*.)

Step number three is to research, either online or in a major public or university library, to amass an electrifying media mailing list. Possible directories include *Bacon's, Ulrich's, Standard Periodical Directory*, and *Gebbie's*. But we prefer a set of reference tools you may never have heard of. Our favorite is *Standard Rate and Data Services (SRDS)*. It comes in several volumes; the two most promising are *Business Publications* and *Consumer Magazines*.

Business Publications gives you access to critical information on more than 7,500 U.S. trade journal publications arranged into 185 market classifications. They range from architecture and banking to legal and woodworking. Listings include the publisher's editorial profile, personnel, circulation numbers, and a lot of other particulars.

Consumer Magazines has descriptions of over 2,700 domestic magazines. It is subdivided into 75 market classifications ranging from affluence to youth. If you haven't heard of the *SRDS* volumes before, don't feel like you've been operating in the dark ages. They are primarily used by advertising agencies, but we've found them of particular value in putting together marketing programs.

The especially appealing aspect of this resource is its timeliness. It is updated every month. Rather than getting a reference work that was obsolete before it was printed, you have extremely current information at your fingertips.

And for newsletters, you can't beat *Oxbridge Directory of Newsletters*. It's fun to work with newsletter editors as they are entrepreneurial souls and often willing to go the extra mile. You might get them to excerpt your book (reprint a small section with full ordering information) as well as run a review.

To find out who's who in more than 7,000 daily, weekly, and specialized newspapers, check out *Working Press of the Nation*. They also list Sunday supplements—plus ethnic, religious, college, and alumni papers.

Editor & Publisher does an issue in August of each year that lists syndicated columnists. It has a handy page that classifies syndicate features by subject matter, helping you precisely target your most likely possibilities. Here you'll find those who write about religion, travel, the outdoors, child rearing, consumerism, business and economics, entertainment, women's issues, and dozens of other topics. You can order it by calling 800-562-2706.

Don't overlook the plethora of other specialized directories and reference works available. For instance, there is a wonderful *Senior Media Directory* (702-786-7419) that lists newspapers, magazines, syndicates, columns, and special newspaper sections devoted exclusively to the mature market. If your titles are slanted to metaphysical/New Age readers, invest in Sophia Tarila's all-encompassing *New Marketing Opportunities* (520-282-9574). The *Sports Market Place Directory* (800-776-7877) contains sport-by-sport listings, sports professional and trade associations, even promotion, event, and athlete management services.

What's the process?

Once you've developed a database of prospective reviewers, the next step is to create a promotional package that will make them sit up and take action. How do you make this unbelievable feat achievable? You *don't* accomplish it with gifts, graft, or gimmicks. In fact, in today's frenetic society, less seems more. Rather than sending an expensive full-blown media kit, we simply mail a carefully crafted news release and a mock review.

"So what's a mock review?", you're probably wondering. Reviewers are busy, so we make it easy for them. We write and typeset our own review! You'd be surprised how often the reviews we get sound surprisingly familiar. When we compare them to the book's cover copy, the news release, and the mock review, a strange phenomena emerges: About 75% of the time, the review is from one of these three promotional pieces—verbatim!

Naturally, there are other options besides regular mail for contacting print media. Broadcast fax is extremely popular today. Email lets you offer a brief message to pique journalists' interest, then follow up with a media kit and book when they request more. Bill Gates believes email will replace phone numbers.

Seeking email addresses for general business magazines and newspapers? Mosey over to http://www.editpros.com/magsgen.html and editpros.com/npapers2.html. At the first one you'll find trade journals and general magazine editors, special columnists, and places to submit email news releases and story ideas. (And there are names of alternate staff, so if you've struck out with one person, this may be a way to locate another possible contact at the same publication.) Going to the latter URL, you'll discover how to reach newspaper business editors and reporters electronically.

When you send out a book for review, *never* send it "naked." That means sending only the book. We're on the review mailing list for several New York publishers. The majority of them send a book and a packing slip—no news release, no mock review, no author bio, no nothing! Help reviewers help you by including promotional materials they can work from. And once you've amassed other reviews from strategic places, include them as well. People like to climb on a moving bandwagon.

To make doubly sure your review copies *and galleys* have all the vital information intact, Jim Cox of the *Midwest Book Review* suggests taping a small sheet to the inside of the front cover containing the following information:

Title	■ Publisher's email address
Author	■ Publisher's URL, if available
Publisher	■ ISBN
Publisher's address	■ Price
Publisher's phone	■ Publishing date
Publisher's fax	

Capturing the attention of reviewers

Short of having a professional sales staff capable of selling sand to a sheik, reviews are your foremost sales generators. People put a lot of stock in reviews because they are perceived as impartial third-party commentaries. But before you can garner appropriate reviews, you must identify your prime review sources. Earlier we discussed getting complimentary copies to area VIP's. That, however, only scratches the surface.

If you're a self-publisher or independent press, even before you have printed books, you need to send out bound galleys. They automatically go to *Publishers Weekly, Booklist, Library Journal, Kirkus Reviews, Independent Publisher,* and *ForeWord* magazine—plus other appropriate places. Finished books should be sent to the "Source Department" editor at *American Libraries* and the editor of *Choice.* These are the kingpin reviewers for general trade books. Garnering a review in one or more of these publications will go a long way toward selling out your first print run.

When we put together a nationwide marketing plan for a client, we usually begin by scouring our corporate library copy of *Standard Rate and Data.* This is actually a tool of advertising agencies but proves especially effective for discovering all sorts of magazines you've probably never heard of. Since it costs several hundred dollars a year to subscribe, use the one at the library. You'll want the editions for "business" and "consumers." By playing detective in these volumes for a few hours you can uncover many solid review possibilities. Other volumes from our reference library that get a lot of use are *The Standard Periodical Directory, National Directory of Magazines,* the *All-in-One Directory, Ulrich's International Periodical Directory, Hudson's Newsletter Directory,* and the *Editor & Publisher Syndicate Directory.*

Now determine what other national newspapers might review your book. You can find major ones listed in *LMP.* Another favorite resource

The 7 Habits of Highly Successful Publishers

1. **Own your niche.** Decide what major subject area you'll publish in and concentrate on it exclusively. Know all about it. Join relevant associations, subscribe to all the trade journals and newsletters, get to know the movers and shakers in the subject area. Become *the* authority, the place where others turn for trustworthy information.

2. **Select highly promotable authors and treat them as your partners.** No one cares as much as they do, probably not even you. Make sure they can function articulately with the media. Use their contacts, their expertise, their enthusiasm. Give them a deep discount on purchasing their own book so they can resell it at a profit. Keep them in the loop. Tell them promptly about great reviews and important book club or special sales. Encourage them not only at the manuscript stage but throughout the life of the book. Their passion and energy make them the book's best salesperson.

3. **Cultivate word-of-mouth.** Getting a buzz started—people talking about the book—is the result you desire. Do it by soliciting advance blurbs, getting reviews *everywhere*, tenaciously pursuing feature stories *off* the book pages, giving away tons of free review and reading copies. A complimentary book is your cheapest and most effective advertising.

4. **Make it easy.** To get people to do what *you* want, make it easy for them to cooperate. Write and typeset a mock review. You'll be amazed how often it comes back as "the" review. Get a toll-

(continued on next page)

of ours is *Working Press of the Nation*, volume 1, titled "Newspaper Directory." Not only does it list daily and weekly papers for every place in the U.S. with editorial department names, it also catalogs special interest publications. These include college papers, black newspapers, those with a religious bent, and others with a business emphasis. While we're talking about newspapers, don't overlook the alternative press. Most larger U.S. cities sport a weekly alternative or "underground" paper. It could be one of your most ardent supporters if you have a controversial or offbeat subject that appeals to the younger crowd.

Of course, to the most important of reviewers you'll automatically send a complimentary book (or maybe a bound galley), accompanied by promotional literature. At a minimum, include a news release with all the pertinent information about your book. For less important reviewers, promo materials along with an offer of the book will probably suffice. While giving away books is cheap promotion, there's no point in throwing them at people who have no intention of giving you any mention.

If you don't crack a vital review source at first, keep in front of it by sending copies of other reviews or comments from respected authorities in your field. Be alert to possible hooks into timely news events or issues. Follow-up is especially important in all areas of promotion. After all, you're competing with many other products for free exposure. So remember that persistence often opens strange and exciting doors.

Talk about excitement: Vic Spandaccini about turned flips when he learned *Parade* magazine planned on reviewing his *The Home Owner's Journal* in their "Bright Ideas" column. He had no sense of what to expect. How many of *Parade's* 30,000,000 readers would take the bait? Well, the last time we heard, Vic had received 5,400 orders and they were still coming in at the rate of 30 per week four months later!

This is certainly proof that reviews are one of your chief sales tools. Successful authors and independent publishers aren't just lucky, they're plucky. They are adept at using media promotion and reviews to leverage themselves into positions of power and profit. And they are wise enough to recognize the original review is just the beginning. An even greater advantage awaits those who skillfully reprint, quote, and use that review for future clout.

Reviews spark sales

Now it's time to address how to know when you've been reviewed, what to do with these gems, and the important role galleys play in the review procedure.

In a perfect world, a journalist would send you a tearsheet of the

The 7 Habits of Highly Successful Publishers (continued)

free number and merchant status so you can accept credit cards. Put order forms in the back of your books and on your flyers.

5. Ask for what you want. A national magazine contacted us about excerpting our *Big Ideas for Small Service Businesses*. After we negotiated how many words they could use and a generous ordering blurb, we asked how much they were offering. The reply? A dollar per word. For years afterwards we sold them marketing articles based on the book for the same dollar per word.

6. Apply the 80/20 rule. You'll get 80% of your PR results (or orders) from 20% of your efforts (or customers). Determine who these biggies are and concentrate your efforts on them. In 1980, we were helping a client with a raw food cookbook. We determined the book needed to be in health food stores. Yet the distributor's buyer turned it down flat. So we romanced this guy with tearsheets of reviews and copies of large purchase orders stamped "This order could be coming to *you!*" He finally bought a case out of self-defense. That book become their bestseller and launched a publishing empire for our client.

7. Follow up, *follow up*, **FOLLOW UP.** It has been proven to us repeatedly that the squeaky wheel gets the grease. When we were trying to sell *Country Bound!* to *Mother Earth News* magazine for their back-of-the-book catalog, nothing seemed to move them off dead center. Finally—on the fifth phone call—the buyer grabbed the book off a stack, examined it, and gave us a hefty purchase order over the phone. It sold into that market for years afterwards.

review or mention of your book that appears in their magazine or newspaper. But we don't live in a perfect world. While *Publishers Weekly, Library Journal,* and *Booklist* will send you an advance copy of a review (hoping to get you to advertise), other sources seldom do.

So how do you even know if something appeared? You track every individual consumer order you get! People will often clip a copy of the item that mentions your book to their order or make reference to it in their letter. On phone orders, we always ask how they heard about the book. Then you contact the publication and request a copy.

Maximizing the reviews you get

Not only will good reviews generate orders immediately, they have long-range selling power if used properly. The industry standard is you can usually excerpt a statement from the review for future promotion. Find the most glowing quotable bit to capitalize on.

You may want to add it to the back cover or the first interior pages for the next printing of the book. After we've amassed several reviews, we typically put together a sheet called "Here's what reviewers are saying . . . " to include with future complimentary copies of the book and to use for direct mail promotions.

Use this praise in every way possible. It is much more impressive when a national magazine or major newspaper says how good your book is than when *you* plug it. If you have an exclusive arrangement with a master distributor, fax them copies of major reviews immediately (or better yet, advance notice if you have it). Then the sales reps can use this as ammunition when contacting booksellers. If you're working with several distributors, let each of them know of major publicity.

Periodically send a copy of all reviews to your authors. They will be pleased to see the good exposure, will realize you're aggressively backing their project, and may find some creative ways to expand on it.

Suppose you get a bad review. Then what? First, realize the world is not going to stop turning on its axis. This is just one person's opinion. Second, look to see if there is something said that's salvageable. Such "review pruning" needs to be ethical, however. If the reviewer said, "While there is many a wonderful book on the subject, this is not one of them," it would not be honorable to excerpt " . . . a wonderful book on the subject."

More insider secrets

A book needn't be new to generate reviews. While those magazines listed in the Appendix under Key Review Galley Recipients are persnickety about only doing brand new books—there are thousand and thousands of consumer magazines, trade journals, newsletters, and syndicated columnists who couldn't care less that the book is a few years old as long as the content is still relevant. In fact, a backlist book may suddenly become very hot because it addresses a topic that's just become newsworthy. Then is the time to roll out an extensive media campaign.

Never refuse to give a review copy to a valid source. We've called more than one New York publisher to request a review copy for plugging in a book we're writing or adding to a bibliography, only to be told, "We've already given out our allotted review copies," or something similar. Hogwash! Review copies are the cheapest advertising there is. If you question the legitimacy of the person requesting the book, ask that the individual send you a copy of the publication or in some way justify themselves. But it's smart to err on the side of generosity.

Our seminar attendees often ask us the best way to sell to librarians. In a word: Reviews! Librarians are very review-driven. They don't like hyperbole. They especially adore a favorable review in *Library Journal, Booklist,* or *Publishers Weekly.* For more specialized titles, *School Library Journal, Kirkus Reviews, The Horn Book Magazine,* and *Choice* also make their pulses beat faster. (See *LMP* for contact information.) When preparing sales flyers for this market, always stress reviews.

In today's high-tech world, another major source for reviews is amazon.com. This behemoth Web site, dubbed the "Earth's Biggest Bookstore," has a staff of reviewers who will consider your book. A positive nod here often translates into many additional book sales.

Moustafa Gadalla of Bastet Publishing tells of sending four of their titles to individual amazon.com reviewers. The last we heard, two reviewers placed their *Historical Deception: The Untold Story of Ancient Egypt* as number 30 on their list of 50 for history/ancient Egypt, while *Pyramid Illusions: A Journey to the Truth* came in as number 31 of 50 for travel/Africa/Egypt. These placements triggered Ingram to order 623 books after the reviews broke.

To toss your literary hat in this Internet ring, go online at http://www.amazon.com and look on their home page under "Browse Subjects." Then click on "View all subject areas." Here you will find 25 categories ranging from Arts & Music to Young Adult. Determine which one fits your books best, then send information and review copies to: Editorial Coverage for (subject), amazon.com; 1516 Second Avenue, 4th Floor; Seattle, WA 98101-1544.

Another relatively new twist on the book scene is Oprah Winfrey's talk show book club. Because she is convinced that reading changes lives, she aims to "help people create the highest vision for themselves." The show is broadcast in more than 130 countries and chosen novels immediately leap to bestseller lists.

Oprah is determined to keep the book club "pure," however, and refuses to even consider submissions from anyone in the publishing or writing business. So how does she learn of possible candidates? From *book reviews* and friends' recommendations. What a compelling reason to get your fiction widely reviewed!

Like the rest of us, reviewers appreciate being appreciated. Smart publishers send thank-you notes, cards, letters, even email posts saying what they liked about the review or expressing appreciation for being chosen from the thousands of possible candidates.

Jim Cox of the *Midwest Book Review* reminds us that reviewers love to know when a quote from their review is featured on a book cover or jacket. (And what a wonderful way to cement a relationship for possible future reviews.)

The importance of galleys

A galley is an early copy of the typeset book. It may still contain typos. Sometimes small publishers send F&G's (folded and gathered pages), but *bound* galleys are preferable. They should be trimmed to the actual size of the finished book.

You can get them several places: Many Kinko's stores have a Docutech and a perfect binder; other quick print shops have duplicating and binding capabilities as well. Printing-on-demand companies are sprouting like dandelions. Or your book manufacturer may be able to provide them. You'll want from 5 to 20 copies, depending on how assertive your plans are.

With some 63,000 books published each year, the competition for review space is fierce. *Library Journal*, for instance, receives about 40,000 books annually. Yet they run only 5,500 evaluations.

Each galley should be accompanied by a sheet of paper including all the book's "vital statistics": title and subtitle, author, price, publication date (month and year), ISBN, LCCN, page count, binding, trim size, illustration details and samples, plus full publisher contact information. A brief description and author bio should be included too. For nonfiction, be sure it establishes his or her credentials for writing this book. Much of this information can appear on the cover of your galley.

UNCORRECTED PROOF
FOR LIMITED DISTRIBUTION

Jump Start Your Book Sales

A Money-Making Guide for Authors, Independent Publishers and Small Presses

by Marilyn & Tom Ross

Category: Writing/Publishing
ISBN: 0-918880-41-6
CIP: 99-11466
Pub Date: July 1999
Price: 19.95
Pages: 352
Trim Size: 6 x 9
Binding: Softcover
Illustrated: 71 illustrations
Backmatter: Appendixes, bibliography, index
Rights: Ann Markham
Editor: Tammy "Sue" Collier
Distributed by: Writer's Digest Books/ F&W Publishing
Publisher: Communication Creativity
POB 909
Buena Vista, CO 81211
719-395-8659

Also tell where it's available: from Ingram, Baker & Taylor, a master distributor, other distributors, local wholesaler, or only the publisher. Be aware that availability is often the determinant for review consideration with these key review sources. They don't want to devote space to a title that isn't easily accessible. The size of your print run will also influence them. If you're only printing 1,000 or 2,000 copies they won't take you seriously, so don't mention it.

Note any advance subsidiary rights sales, such as a book club or foreign rights deal. Indicate the number of cities if you plan an author tour. If the print run or marketing budget is exceptional for a small press (over 10,000 copies or $20,000) this should also be noted so potential reviewers know this book is a lead title for the publisher. (By the way, it's a safe bet to double your proposed advertising/PR budget. Everything always costs more than you anticipate.) A good way to assure this important sheet of paper and the book aren't separated is to paste it inside the front cover. *Publishers Weekly* also now requests the name of any foreign rights agent and the editor.

If you have the cover or dust jacket printed early, or have it on disk, by all means send this along too. At least include an artist's proof. Occasionally colored photos of book covers adorn the pages of review publications. They stand out like a hockey player on a football field and immediately command readers' attention.

Does the book deal with an especially timely topic? Include a news release explaining that angle as well. And if you've garnered impressive advance comments, lay them on!

Have you had late-breaking news, such as a sale of first serial rights to a major magazine or a change in the retail price? Fax the information to everyone immediately.

We've included full contact information for each of the key review publications in the Appendix, but let's discuss them briefly here. Be aware they work with long lead times. They want your galleys three to four months before the official publication date. (The "publication date" is actually three to four months *after* the books come off the press. But never fear, some publishers sell out their whole press run before the official pub date.) Don't ignore this important detail, however; once the pub date is past they will not review your book.

Publishers Weekly is the dominant trade journal in our industry. They reach more than 40,000 paid subscribers and boast a total audience of nearly 100,000 people. They include bookstores, wholesalers and distributors, libraries, media, literary agents, movie and studio executives, and publishers. *PW* runs more than 7,500 book and spoken-word audio reviews annually. Sybil Steinberg tries to review all first novels.

Library Journal is an adult book selection tool. About 43% of *LJ's* readers are in public libraries; 20% are in academic libraries; 19% are in special or school libraries. (We know, that doesn't add up to 100%.) Books chosen for review range from the most popular to the scholarly and encompass all subject areas except textbooks, children's books, or very technical or specialized works. (Their "Classic Returns" column covers reissues of out-of-print titles or special editions.) Librarians use their reviews to make purchasing decisions.

Booklist is another publication relied on heavily by librarians. They receive more than 30,000 volumes a year for review covering adult books, children's and Young Adult titles, reference books, plus audiovisual media. In addition to the galley, send them two copies of the *finished* book. It may be used throughout the year in compilation of bibliographies and Editors' Choice lists.

Independent Publisher, previously *Small Press* magazine, is published six times a year. They run approximately 100 book, periodical, and audio reviews in each issue and concentrate solely on products from independent, university, and small press publishers. Each review runs about 200 words and includes publisher contact information. Of further interest, they have an arrangement whereby amazon.com puts all their reviews on its site.

ForeWord is the new kid on the block. A monthly, they review 40 to 50 prepub galleys each month and accept galleys three months in advance of publication date. Their primary readership is booksellers and librarians, although publishers also subscribe.

Kirkus Reviews, unlike the previous magazines, carries only reviews and no advertising. They review all new major hardcover or trade paperback fiction. Beyond that, they make individual judgments based on many separate factors having to do with merit or potential interest. Although they say they do not review self-published works, we've had several clients' books appear within their pages. They come out twice a month, publish approximately 5,000 pre-publication reviews a year, and have a well-deserved reputation for cheeky, tough evaluations.

Choice is the primary collection development resource for academic libraries and does nearly 7,000 reviews a year spanning all disciplines. Their primary emphasis is on books and computer-readable materials for libraries that serve students at the undergraduate level. *Choice* reviews are divided among four main categories: Social and Behavioral Sciences (40%), Humanities (30%), Science and Technology (15%), and Reference and General (10%). (Another case where their figures don't equal 100%.) One word of caution: They do *not* want galleys; finished books are the order of the day here.

Quill & Quire is Canada's magazine of book news and reviews. Send only galleys with a Canadian connection such as those by a Canadian author or photographer, books originating in Canada, or those about a Canadian subject. They are trade-oriented rather than strictly scholarly and work from galleys.

For complete and up-to-date submission guidelines, call each of the publications listed in the Appendix when you're ready to submit. Produce a good book. Follow their protocols. And we'll see you on the review pages!

Free gifts from cyberspace. Everyone enjoys getting flowers and receiving greeting cards. Did you know you could give them to anyone on the WWW at no cost to you? Directions for sending a "virtual bouquet" await you at http://www.virtualflowers.com. (Of course, you can order the real thing there too.) And if you wander over to http://www.bluemountain.com you'll find lovely greeting cards to send to loved ones, customers, and prospects. What a clever way to express your appreciation for a nice review or media interview. Perhaps put a business twist to a Valentine about how you'd "love" to have their business. The one drawback? Both these sites have been discovered; but your patience will prevail.

Sending thank-you notes opens media doors wider. "I can't remember ever being thanked for a story or receiving a thank-you note from a publicist," states Don Douglas, managing editor of *Health World* magazine. If Don is typical, what an opportunity this affords us! It's not only good manners but good business to send a thank-you note to every reporter, editor, or producer who does a review or story about your books or authors. To stand out even more, use an attractive note card rather than letterhead, handwrite your message, and slip in your business card. The next time you make a pitch, chances are you'll be favorably remembered.

Tap into online magazines and newsletters. "Zines" is the term for online periodicals. While most of us cultivate traditional magazines, newsletters, and newspapers with a zeal—how many of us have exploited the promotional opportunities available through this medium online? To begin, go to http://www.dominis.com/Zines. There is a flourishing cadre of publications listed here. They cover everything from art to cooking, literature to humor, sports to travel . . . and oodles in between. A search will quickly locate likely candidates, then links allow you to jump right to appropriate zines.

Three sure-fire ways to annoy your colleagues:
. . . Staple papers in the middle of the page.
. . . Leave their printer in compressed-italic-cyrillic landscape mode.
. . . TYPE LONG MEMOS IN ALL UPPERCASE.

Penetrating the legislature. Do you have a regional title, or a book that addresses an issue that might be interesting to legislators? Visit your state capital. Each government official has a press box. There is little to stop you from putting your promotional literature, or a review copy of the book, in each pigeonhole. What a direct way to reach people of influence!

CHAPTER 5

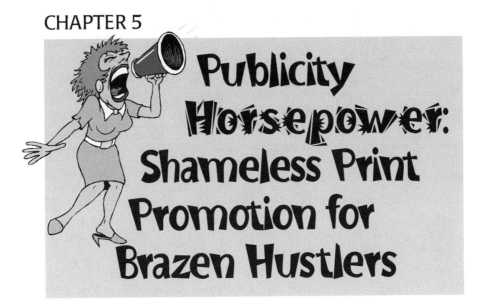

Publicity Horsepower: Shameless Print Promotion for Brazen Hustlers

Today it's "Publicize or Perish." Unlike the author of *Primary Colors*, YOU cannot afford to be anonymous. (As it turned out, neither could he; political columnist Joe Klein eventually 'fessed up to writing the book.) Savvy PR people at independent publishers and small presses should pay particular attention to this chapter.

So should *every author*. Those who expect to have a successful book must develop a passion for promotion, even if they are trade published. One author told us, "I make twice the money promoting and selling my own book as I do on royalties."

Some self-publishers are made to feel second-rate. But if they produce a quality product, this is ridiculous. Publicity is the great equalizer. The book buying public is indifferent to who publishes what. They don't choose a book because it is published by Simon & Schuster, Rodale, or St. Martins. They buy a book because if contains the information they need or because they recognize the author's name. Though we are certain to know the maker of a car we buy, we're unlikely to know the publisher of any book we own.

Why print is so powerful

Print publicity is the most valuable of all. It has staying power. While a radio or TV interview has immediate appeal, articles and reviews sell for you not only at the time of publication but months, sometimes years, later. We recently received a Christmas card from a lady who had clipped an article about us from *The Washington Post* in 1988! She was now ready to do her book and had just purchased a copy of our *The Complete Guide to Self-Publishing*. She wrote to say how much she loved it. You don't get that kind of residual play from anything but print. (Should you want a copy, simply call 800-331-8355.)

Success in publicity is a numbers game. The more media contacts you make, the more publicity you'll garner—and the more juice you'll have. You want to build momentum. Remember Newton's law of inertia? An object at rest tends to stay at rest; one in motion tends to stay in motion . . . maybe even accelerate. So let's get going and never stop!

PR is the ideal marketing tool. It gives an enormous boost for virtually no cost, a very appealing fact for those without ad budgets approaching the size of General Motors.

Promotion starts a chain reaction. People begin to hear about your book, read about it, see it, buy it, tell others about it. Like a pebble tossed in a pool, this promotes word-of-mouth gossip—the ripple effect. It doesn't start all at once but develops gradually over time. A few key "opinion leaders" spread information within their own circles. In turn, these people spread it to other circles and so on. The key to creating positive word-of-mouth is to locate the opinion leaders and find a way to get them talking about your book.

How important is it really? A Gallup poll, which investigated why people bought fiction, revealed that a whopping 26% purchased the book because a friend or relative recommended it.

In an interview in *The New York Times*, the former president of B. Dalton said, "I would probably rate the most effective techniques for selling books as being the individual telling a friend, reviews, and the author's ability to appear on talk shows."

It's like yeast; sales expand rapidly when the book world begins to talk about your title. Beautiful *free* publicity, more than anything else, is what stimulates this fermentation process. Here's how to get it started.

Develop an arsenal of promotional materials

Having the right materials at your fingertips puts you in a more powerful position to generate meaningful publicity. Below is an exhaustive list of the things you could use. If necessary, you can get by with just the first five.

News release: One or two pages maximum. Include a coupon at the end for requesting a free review copy of the book.

Mock review: This is a review *you* write and typeset so it looks as though it is clipped from a newspaper. Lesser-known review sources sometimes use it as their review!

Author bio: We have a full-page biography (see page 323 for a sample) and an abbreviated version.

Pitch letter: Customize this one-pager to the media and the occasion. Make it a great letter!

Customer order flyer: A benefit-oriented flyer or brochure to use for soliciting consumer orders.

Photographs: Of both the author and the book. It's a good idea to have both black and white and color.

List of questions for the media: "10 things people often ask about this topic."

Postcards of the cover: Use these to stay in touch, say thank you, distribute at bookstores, etc.

Quiz: It is based on the book and offered as a freebie on radio, TV, and in articles.

Top 10 List: Again based on the book. Use it everywhere. (See the adjacent sample.)

Here's what people are saying: Excerpted quotes from reviews when you get plenty.

Q&A piece: Interview yourself (or the author) and come up with an interesting question and answer article.

Trend article: Use the author's expertise to write a commentary on what is projected for the future.

Round-up article: Work with three or four others in the field to create an overview of the subject.

- ■ Newsletter: Put a one-pager (front and back) out quarterly to keep in touch.
- ■ Clips: Copies of the publicity you or your author have received, or articles written.
- ■ Radio interviews: Sample cassette tapes of strong radio shows.
- ■ Video: Three minutes of video clips from appearances on TV.

Judith Appelbaum, author of *How to Get Happily Published*, describes selective marketing as a braid, with all promotional efforts interweaving, supporting, and complementing each other. With the ammunition above you are sure to have just the marketing piece needed for any campaign. Be aware, however, that the trend is away from ponderous media kits. Use just a few pieces initially. Come back a second or third time with something different. Most editors, reporters, and producers prefer receiving full media kits only after they have shown some interest.

Midget moves for mighty results

Create a sell statement. Define your book in 25 words of less. Mention who the audience is and quantify what benefit they will receive. There's no business that isn't show business, so don't be modest. You'll use this statement over and over in a myriad of different situations. It's a wonderful introduction when you do follow-up calls to the media and must be brief. It gives your sales reps a succinct way to present the book. You can use it when explaining your book to others.

Here's what we came up with for *Jump Start Your Book Sales*: "It's a thorough and irreverent guide for selling 10 times more books. The imaginative, results-oriented strategies work for authors, independent publishers, and small presses."

Develop a list of key contacts. It is vital to identify your most important customers. These will usually be middlemen of some sort: important book review editors, feature writers, talk show producers, catalog buyers, pivotal people at wholesalers and chains, sales reps, rights buyers, etc. The list will probably run over 100 names. These people hold your future in the palm of their hands. You want to favorably impress them—over and over and over again. By honing in on the most important, you can establish *personal* contact with them. Use any excuse to get in front of them . . . not "in their face" but tactfully. Of course, as your publishing program develops, this list will evolve.

Use postcards. We are great believers in the often undervalued post-card. They can help you build your sales because people *read* them in this cluttered mail world. They are also fast, easy, and cheap. No envelop to print, stuff, and seal—and they're only 20¢ to mail if you stay under the 4½- by 6-inch size. Put the cover of your book on one side, a brief sales plug and PR/ordering information on the other. (Be sure to leave room to write a message.) Or do them blank on the back, write custom-ized messages on your computer, and run them through your printer or copier if it has the appropriate feeder.

Once upon a time we sent out a very expensive media kit promot-ing our *Country Bound!* It got dismal results. So we sent out a follow-up postcard mailing asking, "Did you receive the media kit we sent?" The phones went berserk. So we got an idea. Now we send postcards *first.* They say, "Did you get our media kit?" (Of course they didn't because we haven't sent it!) They call and say "No, and we want it." Bingo—you have qualified your leads and can now afford to send the expensive, full-blown media kit. Plus you've made a person-to-person contact, so working with them is more congenial in the future.

Get off the book pages. (No offense to book review section editors intended.) There's a knack to deciding whom to approach on a newspa-per staff. While the book review editor seems a logical choice, this may not be the ideal place for optimum exposure. Individuals who could use a consumer guide, for instance, aren't typically avid book readers. They would rarely turn to the Book Review section. You'd be better off approaching the Lifestyle Editor or whatever they call what used to be the "Women's Pages." Likewise, a management title would be more appropriately promoted to the Business Editor, a book about horticul-ture to the Gardening Editor, a tome about theology to the Religion Editor.

Understand and use wire services. Speaking of newspapers, one of the best-kept secrets is the enormous power of the national newswire services. Capturing publicity here gives you coast-to-coast coverage that often appears in literally hundreds of papers. Every daily and most week-lies subscribe to at least one wire service. Of perhaps even more significance, these wires are monitored by TV and national magazines, so your story could be catapulted to even greater acclaim. The Associ-ated Press reaches more than 1,550 newspapers. Book review editor Ron Berthel looks for general interest books with a broad audience ap-peal for middle America.

Interestingly, many wire service stories actually originate with a feature in a daily newspaper. Give you any ideas? If you get a good story in a daily complete with contact information, you could approach it one of two ways: 1) While thanking the writer, suggest she or he submit it to a wire service. This gets their byline broadcast across the country and nets you more orders, or 2) *You* contact the bureau in the city where the article appeared with something like "Today's XYZ paper carries a story of great interest about us on page X. I thought you might want to pick it up."

Area newswire reporters can be found several ways. Either look up the newswire service in the phone book, contact the headquarters number listed in the Appendix, and ask for the local representative, or call the editor of your local paper and ask where the regional reporter for XYZ newswire is stationed. Then contact information for the number.

Subscribe to appropriate newsletters. There are five national newsletters that can help you peddle more books and keep you on the cutting edge. They are not cheap. Yet you must spend money to make money. We use all of the following:

- *Book Marketing & Publicity* is published 24 times a year and covers successful book techniques and media placement opportunities for independent publishers, book marketers, and publicists. It is $249 a year. Call 510-596-9300.

- *Book Marketing Update* comes out twice monthly, is published by Bradley Communications, and edited by John Kremer. It follows a similar format as the above and sells for $247 a year. Call 800-989-1400, ext 432.

- *PartyLine* is a two-sided 8½- by 11-inch weekly jammed with media requests, breaking news, and PR opportunities. It sells for $180 a year. Call 212-755-3487.

- *SPAN Connection* is the official newsletter of the Small Publishers Association of North America. It's a monthly, 24 pages, contains oodles of marketing tips, and is edited by yours truly, Marilyn Ross. It comes as a part of association membership, which is $95 a year. Call 719-395-4790.

- *The Publicity Hound* is a bimonthly that features tips, tricks, and tools for free (or really cheap) publicity. Subscriptions are $49.95. Call 414-284-7451.

Capitalize on timing. It can be everything. Exploiting a breaking news story can propel a backlist book into bestseller status. But you must act immediately. Waiting even a day can signal a death peal. Call. Fax. Email. Communicate straightaway how your book (and *the expert* who wrote it) relates to, explains, embellishes—or discredits—the current scoop.

When you approach the media is also a consideration. Newspapers usually hold an editorial meeting early in the morning and make decisions before noon about what will appear in the next day's edition. So you'd better fax them early if you have a time-sensitive topic. Televison and radio producers are always on the lookout for expert commentary on a breaking news story. Be sure they also know of your availability.

Customize to win ink in national magazines. Study publications for the right editorial spin. Knowing the editorial focus of a magazine gives you a distinct advantage when pitching a story. Once you've determined a half dozen major magazines you want to penetrate, call the *advertising* department and request a media kit, including the three most recent issues. When you get the kit you'll be sitting on a profusion of fascinating facts. You'll know the demographics of their subscribers: age, income, education, interests, etc. This helps you pinpoint who their readers are. Included will also be an editorial statement and other literature telling how they view themselves. Tune in!

Now read those three magazines cover to cover. Delve into the Editorial Director's statement that appears early. *Family Circle's* Managing Editor Susan Ungaro typically praises her editors in her column. In other instances, the editorial director or editor-in-chief will show a passion for a specific subject or leaning.

Next study the masthead, which also appears early. It tells who is who. Often job titles are listed or columnists are specifically named. You can also determine the pecking order by examining the hierarchy of name listings.

The most practical inroad is to approach a columnist. Find a column that fits your book, then dissect it. What is the length and flavor of the headline? Is the style breezy? Serious? Intellectual? How long does the column run? Now write a short "exclusive" for that magazine. (That doesn't mean you won't submit similar pieces to noncompeting publications; simultaneous submissions are a proven way to establish momentum.) Naturally, you'll slip in the title of your book and an order number, but the piece must focus on your expertise, not the book. Also include a book and news release to help solidify your credentials.

Once you've graduated from columns to full-fledged articles, be prepared to present a full and holistic package. Make it easy for the editor to say "yes." Besides a headline, you'll include a blurb they can use in a call-out box. Additionally, you'll suggest lines to appear on the cover announcing the article inside. (You've really studied those three magazine issues. Right?) Is there a sidebar of related information? What about photos? Now be sure you send it to the right editor, and your chances of success are greatly improved.

Don't eliminate potential magazines too quickly. *U.S. News & World Report*, not a publication we'd normally target for a book on parenting, did a third page recently on *The War Against Parents* in the "Outlook" section. Besides a color photo of the authors, the story included four points from the book's proposed entitlements called the "Parents' Bill of Rights."

A more likely candidate to print your news is *Publishers Weekly*. Don't just think of it as a review source though. Nineteen columns or departments appear either every week or occasionally. There are many opportunities for creative publicists to get attention focused on their house or books. Once again, *read* the magazine.

Judy Byers, author/publisher of *Words on Tape: How to Create Profitable Spoken Word Audio on Cassettes and CD's* (800-331-8355), snared a terrific two-column article under Audio Bits. *PW* said more quotable stuff in the article than they often do in reviews: "This extensively researched, intelligently written book covers virtually every aspect of audio production: choosing content, writing a script, selecting a narrator . . ." Way to go, Judy!

Every month you can research more and more publications via cyberspace. Are you taking advantage of the Web in this way? Hundreds of magazines, newsletters, and broadcast agencies are now online. By using Yahoo or one of the other search engines you can find their address, visit their site, and study their material. What a perfect way to get the pulse of their editorial direction—and learn how best you can fit in.

Have photos ready. We live in a visually stimulating world. Pictures in print publications increase the readership of an article by 35 to 40% according to content analysis studies. Newspapers and magazines have to compete with TV and the Internet. They can do that more effectively with photographs. And you can compete for space more effectively by offering them a selection of quality professional photographs. Hire a professional photographer. Examine his or her portfolio ahead of time and look for imaginative settings, good composition, and sharp contrast.

Shoot in both black and white and color. To be graphically appealing, don't rely on just head shots. Get creative with the setting and props. Have your pictures tell a story. Papers often put color shots on the covers of sections. You might want to send 5- by 7-inch black and whites initially, but tell them color slides are available.

Finally, be sure you include a caption. It should contain both the author's name and the book title. Many people only read photo captions, so make it easy for them to determine how to get your book.

Don't overlook little media. Sometimes it pays to be a big fish in a little pond . . . and ripple out from there. Early in his career, bestselling author Wayne Dyer was interviewed by a little obscure radio station. A producer from the old Johnny Carson Show happened to hear him. It led to Dyer being on Carson's show some 20 times! The biggies like Letterman, The Tonight Show, The Today Show, *National Enquirer,* and *USA Today* have staff members who constantly scour small town newspapers, radio and TV, specialty magazines, etc., for interesting story leads. If you are lucky enough to be selected by major media, rejoice! There is no way you could afford to buy 10 minutes with Jay Leno.

One independent publisher tells of the *National Enquirer* running excerpts from their book. The very next day after it hit the newsstands, they sold 200 books. But the fascinating twist is that two national newspapers and three smaller ones heard of them as a result and did stories.

In another case, a simple short release in the author's hometown newspaper was picked up by a freelancer working on an article for *Aspire* on the same topic. When she finished that article, she did one for a slightly better-known publication: *Woman's Day!* It talked about spending quality time with the family, mentioned the book title, and included their 800 number. The orders poured in.

We had an interesting experience as a result of a four-line listing in *Publishers Weekly.* Shortly after the Spring Announcement issue came out, we got a call from the person who lines up instructors for the Learning Annex. She had read about *Jump Start Your Book Sales* and wanted to book us for seminars in Los Angeles, San Diego, San Francisco, and New York!

Get publicity for getting publicity. The old axiom, "Success breeds success" is so true. The media like to climb on the bandwagon. Consequently, the more exposure you get, the more exposure you'll get. And you can see to it that this happens by recycling your publicity. Recycling should be done with more than bottles, papers, and aluminum cans. It should be done with any print coverage that appears. While an amateur will be satisfied with what they get, a pro will milk it for all it's worth. But how?

"Do a mailing right away," advise home-based business gurus Paul and Sarah Edwards. "Use a copy of the article as the lead for your mailing. Accompany it with a letter or announcement that proclaims 'Look what we're up to.'" They remind us that publicity is as much about opening doors to future possibilities as it is about obtaining immediate sales.

Augmenting that thought, are there catalogs or nontraditional outlets you're trying to sell? Send them a copy. Fire one off to radio and TV producers you want to influence. Scan and place it on your Web site as well. Add it to your media kit.

Joan Stewart, publisher of *The Publicity Hound* newsletter, recommends, "If a national publication prints a story by or about you or your book, write a short news release about it for your daily and weekly newspapers, trade publications, chamber of commerce newsletter, and alumni magazine." Conversely, work it in the other direction. Should a weekly do a story, send reprints to editors at dailies; forward reprints from dailies to national magazines. Of course, if you're dealing with a big copyrighted publication and you want to send the article itself, you need to get permission or purchase reprints from them.

We have a specific strategy for recycling our publicity. Because we belong to many associations that publish newsletters which include "Member News," we have the newsletter editors all on a database. When something happens, we write a short generic news release—then customize the beginning to match their format for name—and mail, fax, or email it immediately. (That is, we did this before getting consumed writing *Jump Start Your Book Sales!*) Publicity is sort of like a boomerang: You have to throw it before it can come back.

Recycling your media contacts can also net enormous results. Do you maintain a database or have some method of keeping track of editors, reporters, and freelancers who have written about you or your authors before? Have you a list of producers and hosts from past radio appearances? If not, start one today! Send them news releases about new developments, copies of your newsletter, new product information, etc.

When sales get sluggish, one of the smartest and most economical things you can do is put out a mailing or launch a calling campaign to these contacts. Assuming you did well initially, they're already sold on you.

And these folks have a challenging job: They're constantly trying to come up with new ideas, fascinating concepts, interesting experts. It's wise to stay in touch with a postcard or note about every three months. Keep feeding them. When they have a page to fill or a guest drops out at the last minute, you'll be there to save the day. One publisher who took this approach had 400 calls from a story that appeared as a result of her tenacity.

Remember that persistence pays off. Those who expect to send a news release, a review copy, or a media kit, and be overwhelmed with interest, have lost touch with reality. If you are not diligent, your book will sink like a stone. It takes ongoing contact to get results.

Jim Cox, of the *Midwest Book Review,* offers a solid way to follow up via phone. Say, "I'm calling to verify that you received (book title) okay and to inquire into its status with you and if there is anything further you need from us?" With today's voice mail, you'll probably need to leave several voice messages before you connect with a live human being. Be perpetually upbeat; letting your frustration show in your voice is the sign of an amateur.

Follow up needn't be confined to phone calls, however. Mail a postcard. Use email. Fax. That's what moved the producer of C-SPAN2's "Business of Books" TV show to ultimately cover the SPAN 1998 annual conference. We called about a month before the conference to suggest it would provide engrossing viewing for their audience. The producer sounded interested and requested information. We instantly fired off a package. A week later we called and left a message. No reply. In a few days we called again and left another message. Nada.

So we decided to fax over a one-pager with a huge, titillating headline of "You're missing a lot . . .". It seemed to be what moved him off dead center. Soon they were on the phone with us arranging to have a camera crew there to shoot part of the first day's activities.

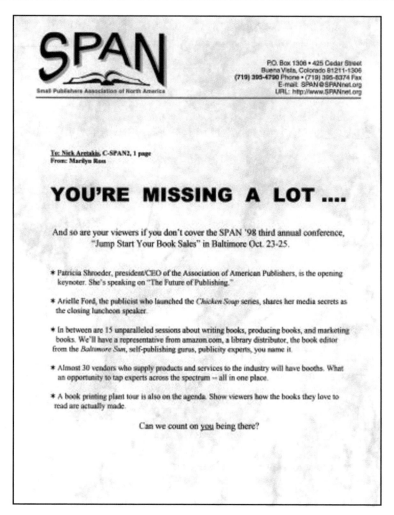

Tenacity is an incredible quality. If it weren't for sticktoitiveness, the bestseller *Midnight in the Garden of Good and Evil* would never have even been published. The first agent didn't think it would sell (so of course it didn't...funny how we can set ourselves up for failure). The second agent author John Berendt engaged took *seven years* to sell it. When Random House brought it out, it only shipped 22,000 copies the first three years—and more than 2 million recently!

The same thing happened with *Chicken Soup for the Soul*. Authors Jack Canfield and Mark Victor Hansen relate that their agent took it to eight major New York publishers who all said, "Sorry, we don't think it will sell." Then 22 smaller New York publishers rejected it before tiny Health Communications had the wisdom to gobble it up. But Jack

Canfield tells of being discouraged initially as they expected word-of-mouth to quickly shoot it onto bestseller lists. It didn't happen. After six months only 135,000 copies had been sold. (Certainly a respectable figure most of us would be grateful for, but these guys think BIG.) What occurred after that has made publishing history.

So don't give up too early. A backlist title that may have languished can be given a fresh start by luck, by tenacity, and by just plain time. Something so boring it could give you dry mouth one day can be so dynamic it could light road flares the next.

Capitalizing on free regional opportunities

By beginning on a local level, you can generate a ripple effect that will carry you regionally, then nationally. You can accomplish real saturation with a regional campaign. Greater New York, for instance, has

some 600 newspapers. You'll generate much more thorough coverage by going after more than just the four large dailies. Additionally, people are impressed when your products are written up in *their* hometown paper. You can often start developing a mailing list by inquiring at the chamber of commerce or visitor and convention bureau for their local media resources list.

A little thinking will quickly reveal several influential locals who should receive a complimentary copy of your book. Start your list with the book review editor of the largest daily and deliver his or her copy personally. Don't overlook regionally oriented magazines. And contact the main branch librarian responsible for acquisitions in your subject area. Once you've convinced this individual you have a good book, branch libraries will probably order.

Would adding the honcho at the visitor and convention bureau or your chamber of commerce be of any value? What about area politicians? A publisher of a tourist guide told us one of her best channels of distribution is legislators who use her book as a giveaway to visiting dignitaries. She lobbied them extensively when her book first came out. Consider hand delivering an autographed copy to the mayor.

Depending on the nature of your publication, think about others with special interests who would appreciate having a copy. They will be

The Ross Marketing Idea Generator: 26 Winning Strategies

Find an angle that makes you controversial.

Do radio phone interviews originating from your home or office.

Go after *all* TV (few can crack Oprah).

Pursue newspaper features about your topic.

Write op-ed pieces addressing the subject.

Submit letters to the editor commenting on related articles.

Plant news items with local newspaper/magazine columnists.

Provide gratis articles to national magazines.

Solicit plugs in newsletters.

Go after mentions in nationally syndicated columns.

Develop alliances with complementary associations.

Request testimonials from leaders in the industry.

Create a sales flyer and customer order form.

Prepare a "Here's What People Are Saying" flyer.

Generate a mailing list of interested buyers.

Create an "event" centered around your topic.

(continued on next page)

excellent goodwill ambassadors. These people can often be persuaded to provide written testimonials you can use to catapult the book to wider acclaim and further impact sales by recommending it to colleagues.

Books that cover timely issues, are highly controversial, or have a strong local hook may warrant a press conference. If you plan to call an official press conference, here are a few tips: Choose a time and place convenient for the media. Mornings are best. There will be less competition Tuesday through Thursday. Double-check on the possibility of any other important conflicting function such as a sports playoff game or the kick-off of a big charity affair that would cut your attendance to a trickle. Arrange for news releases to arrive about a week before the event. Try to create something visually exciting so TV camera crews will have a reason for showing up.

It's a good idea to place follow-up calls a couple of days before the press conference to be sure appropriate people know about it (and as a subtle reminder). At the event itself, have media kits and refreshments available, give out books lavishly, deliver a short well-prepared talk, answer any questions, and be your most charming self.

New place to get ink: the internal press

Want an innovative, untapped publicity outlet? Corporations all across America produce internal newsletters for their employees. This is a completely underutilized source for exposure! The newsletter editors at major corporations rarely hear from outside PR people, yet these company publications represent a terrific source for stories about books that appeal to a cross section of consumers—or relate to what the company or association does.

Many of these newsletters have circulations in the thousands. Lock into a half dozen such company periodicals and you've reached as many potential customers as most trade or consumer magazines. And because this is such a well-kept secret (until now!), you have little competition

for space. Harried editors welcome items of value.

No less than Hallmark uses this approach to get ink. They fax frequent season-specific "Tip Sheets" to keep visible and encourage purchase of their greeting cards. The blurbs on the Tip Sheets are usually filler material of 50 to 100 words containing an interesting statistic or humorous story. They also include a reply fax sheet that allows editors to ask for more information, a product sample, and/or a publicity photo. By doing everything via fax, the whole frustrating issue of missed phone calls and voice mail becomes a moot point. This courting of the internal press is a new and important component in their overall marketing plan.

Certainly we as authors and publishers can come up with interesting or fun details about the subjects of our books. Right? (There is probably a wealth of material lurking in the books themselves, just waiting to be rescued—a paragraph here, a section there.)

The Ross Marketing Idea Generator: 26 Winning Strategies (continued)

■ Establish an award that correlates with your subject.

■ Tie in with a special national day/week/month activity.

■ Develop "P.I." (per inquiry) advertising arrangements.

■ Speak about your topic.

■ Do co-op mailings with others who have complementary books.

■ Be alert to news events and hot issues you can use as a segue.

■ Enter any contests for which you qualify.

■ Take out inexpensive classified ads in targeted magazines.

■ Always make it *easy* for people to do what you want.

■ Follow up always and often.

Hallmark goes to the corporate communications director of Fortune 500 companies. Most of us don't have the budget to research the fax numbers for these people. Plus our marketing efforts must typically be more sharply targeted. So here's another solution for figuring out how to reach this bonanza.

To research where to locate these internal employee newsletters, check the library for volume number 2 (*Magazines and International Publications Directory*) of *Working Press of the Nation*. Be sure to work from a current edition.

Locate appropriate company publications by industry. They range from advertising and agriculture to banks and drug companies, from hospitals and insurance firms, to office equipment and utility companies. There is also a meaty section that covers newsletters from associations in the health field and those that serve various trade and fraternal organizations.

And you'll really salivate when you get to section 10 as it lists specific newsletters that do book reviews. Additionally, it categorizes company publications by subject area (baby care, beauty hints, business, ecology, education, entertainment, food . . . get the idea?)

In section 11 you'll find full contact information. Besides the usual data, listings include the editor's name, how many pages the newsletter is (typically 8, 16, or 24), how often they publish, and the lead time required. Have a business book? Why not contact the Amarillo Chamber of Commerce and the Kansas City, Kansas, Chamber of Commerce to name just two? A humorous gift book about flying? Go after Beech Aircraft Corporation's *Beechcrafter*.

Have a religious guide for teaching youth? Certainly the Baptist Sunday School Board would be interested. A book about wise investing? *New Horizons*, published by the Florida Horizons Federal Credit Union, may well be a match. If you've just published a title on classic cars, it could get exposure in *Olds Line*, which goes to the Oldsmobile employees at General Motors. The possibilities run on like a stream rushing downhill.

This goldmine can also be worked if you have a regional title. For instance, let's say you have a guidebook to Michigan. You might contact Michigan Mutual Insurance Company, Michigan State University, Michigan Bell Telephone Company, etc.

Why not spend a few hours in a good library and prepare a marketing list of internal company publications? You have virtually no competition for their space. Chances are they will welcome your contributions. And the cumulative impact can sell a lot of books!

Borders may give you free ink. *Inside Borders* is a 35-page tabloid available in all Borders chain stores. Before you can be considered for inclusion, however, they must carry your book, either regionally or nationally. There are several possible ways to get press here. Author essays, especially tagged to a seasonal or holiday theme, are very popular. They also run book excerpts of 250 to 350 words. Or you might be fortunate enough to snag an author interview with an editorial staff member. The editor is Beth Fhaner, Borders Group, Inc., 100 Phoenix Drive, Ann Arbor, MI 48108; 734-477-1100.

Need a reminder for important follow-up dates, birthdays, or prioritized "to-do" lists? Then you'll be delighted to learn about eOrganizer, your free personal online electronic organizer. Simply customize it for your needs and this nifty site will nudge you via email on the morning of any must-dos. In addition to providing space for tasks, appointments, and special days, eOrganizer lets you enter names and addresses of key contacts. So if you need access to these people when away from home or office, just bring it up on your laptop and presto!—everything is at your fingertips. Find it at http://www.eorganizer.com.

A bus station is where a bus stops. A train station is where a train stops. On my desk I have a work station.

***Sell* articles to national publications.** When our ASJA colleague Sharon Lloyd Spence finished writing the manuscript for her guidebook, *101 Great Choices: Chicago*, she immediately sent out 40 query letters to national magazines. In them she explained that she had just spent three months driving the city and finding out what was "new and wonderful" and wouldn't they like an article? It turned out five of those she contacted did. She got assignments from *American Air Lines Admiral, The Robb*

Report, Physicians Travel & Meeting Guide, Convention & Meeting Guide, and *Windy City Woman.* (Notice the interesting breadth of the places she connected with. Many would think this topic only had local appeal.) Every article was customized to each magazine and they all ran an author bio with the book's title. Not only did she earn substantial income from the articles but also generated superb plugs for the book.

Look at everything long-term. Best-selling author Greg Godek offers this piece of wisdom: "If you want to be a successful author, you have to look at what you're doing long-term. It's not just about selling books—it's about having a career that you'll live for the next 20 to 30 years. That means getting known, developing lasting relationships, having a plan, and putting everything you've got into marketing and promoting your books."

There's no such thing as "bad publicity"! Got a lousy review? Dust off your ego, put on your rhinoceros skin, and forge ahead. Chances are the public will remember the title of your book before they remember the nasty comments.

Or you might spin the negative into a positive by turning it around. Put out a news release headlined: "Find out why the American Medical Association doesn't want you to read this book!" or "Bankers Banned This Book: Here's Why." Gotcha!

Strategies for penetrating newspapers. Did you know there are 1,500 daily newspapers with a total circulation of 58 million? Not to mention 8,500 weeklies with 70 million readers, most of whom live in the wealthy suburbs? Have any interest in infiltrating this institution? Your best ammunition lies in the following strategies: 1) Don't just go to departmental editors, who are already swamped. Seek out feature and Sunday editors who are often hungry for material. 2) Send what they want: releases on diskettes. New information reveals that most top 500 dailies and nearly 9,500 other dailies and weeklies are using more diskette releases and fewer paper manuscript releases. 3) Go with color. Nearly all newspapers now print in full color. They give color huge space: often full pages and half pages in weekend sections—sometimes even page one of special sections or inside front positioning. To get what *you* want, give them what *they* want!

New angle for getting into *USA Today*. Although you might feel like Cinderella before the ball trying to interest reporters in doing a feature article about your topic or book for this widely circulated national newspaper, there's another way in the door that is seldom explored. Ever noticed the "Voices" column on the editorial page? They seek people to offer opinions on major news items. To toss your hat in the ring, simply send your name, address, occupation, and age—plus a day and evening phone number and your photo—to *USA Today*, Voices Submissions, 1000 Wilson Boulevard, Arlington, VA 22229.

Have you seen the new coffee-table book? It's over 1,000 pages. A great book—if you have a very strong coffee table. You've heard of books you can't put down? This one you can hardly lift up! Don't let your kids get at it. Who needs an eight-year-old with eyestrain and a hernia?

Great links await you at Media Central. This is a site overflowing with useful and unusual places for media and marketing folks. Within Media Links you'll find electronic paths not only to newspapers and magazines but also television and radio. Under Critical Links there are URLs you can't live without . . . well, maybe that's a *slight* exaggeration. Seriously, a conglomeration of intriguing resources live here. Doing a mystery or thriller? Check out *Court TV*. Here you'll find synopses of the cases shaping contemporary law. The *Internet Advertising Resource Guide* will lead you to sites containing advertising, should you be so inclined. Looking for software freebies? www.Shareware.com overflows with stuff you probably want to download. Under their Agency Links you can find ad agencies on the Web and perhaps connect with one who has a client that would like to purchase quantities of your book. There is also a Zine & Noted E-Zine Resource Guide for finding your way around cyberspace publications. A whole new way of publicizing awaits you here! All this resides at http://www.mediacentral.com/Site.

Always carry your book. Your book needs to become as much a part of your persona as your underwear. Seriously! Carry a copy in your briefcase, handbag, and vehicle. We've sold books to people while waiting in line to ship a UPS package, while renewing a drivers license, and at a filling station. The attendant saw a copy laying in the back seat and asked about it. (He was a goner from then on.)

PR coach extraordinaire awaits you online. We're very impressed with the content at http://www.netrageous.com/pr/. Surfers are welcome at "The NETrageous publicity resource center" and it's just that. The free publicity advice here is based on successful, proven experience—not theory. By the time you finish exploring their Web site, you'll know exactly why their experts have received over $6 million of free publicity—and how you can do the same thing! Be sure to check out the following: Paul's "Brooklyn Bridge" story, how you can write a killer press release, sample press release, and how to distribute your press release. Then just keep clicking for information and links to other interesting publicity sites.

Personalized Post-it Notes give you individuality. Want to appear as though you personally handwrote a note on your press kit? Write out your brief message, order a self-inking rubber stamp, then stamp your message on a Post-it Note. Bingo . . . you've given it the individual touch.

Faulkner took 15 years to finish a story.
Hemingway rewrote a manuscript 39 times.
Updike never completed half of his work.
It's a wonder we ever get out a publicity mailing!

Need to influence industry insiders quickly? For a small fee, you can post your news release, exactly as you want it to appear, by going to www.bookflash.com. Your release is submitted to major search engines, then their over 3,000 subscribers hear about it through an email BookFlash Bulletin. This lets you take advantage of the Net's immediacy. For more details visit their site, call 800-536-6162, or email newsnow@bookflash.com.

Take it from the pros. Judith Appelbaum, author of *How to Get Happily Published*, has packed her Web site full of tips and links. You can feast your eyes at http://www.happilypublished.com.

CHAPTER 6

Putting Your Self-Propelled Author Tour and Book Signings in Overdrive

Does it make sense to do in-store book signings? Are they author ego food—or savvy sales moves? And is it viable to put yourself on tour for two, three, or six months to promote your books all over the U.S.? The answers to these questions are "yes" and "no."

Exploring the pros and cons of book signings

There are many variables and divergent opinions. We'll explore them here. Marcella Smith of Barnes & Noble commented at a Small Press Center function that there seems to be a prevailing notion among small or start-up publishers that author appearances and author autographings are the best way to get a foot in the door. Regrettably, nine times out of ten they are not. Usually 10 or 15 books are sold and the time and energy taken to do this would be better devoted to obtaining review or media attention that hits the largest possible audience for the book, in her opinion. Curt Matthews of Independent Publishers Group (IPG) feels signings are a completely inadequate substitute for the broad-based publicity and promotion efforts necessary to sell books in really meaningful quantities.

Yet some booksellers disagree. Two independent stores feel author appearances pay off for them. Dutton's Brentwood in southern California has authors speak or read about 20 minutes almost every weeknight. They host all sort of gatherings from local-author receptions with a handful attending, to visits from household names like Anne Rice or Rosalynn Carter—who need special security and crowd control.

The Elliott Bay Book Company in Seattle hosts more than 600 authors a year. They have a special place adjacent to their store cafe where writers read, speak, and take questions for 60 to 90 minutes. "It fills in the information behind a book, the story of how it came to be," explains owner Walter Carr. And it does sell books, he says.

All concur that for a regional title, a book-signing blitz covering the major stores in the area serves to prime the pump. Signings as an adjunct to a media tour also work if the stores are given enough lead time to order in books.

Besides the obvious benefit of selling books, there are also hidden values in book signings. You increase distribution because a signing forces the store to order a much larger quantity of books than they would usually carry. And because you will sign them all before you leave, these sales are likely to "stick." Stores don't normally return autographed books. Key people begin to know you; your reputation starts to blossom. Free advertising and promotion are yours—features in store newsletters, newspaper ads, prominent positioning of the book. They may even display it on a table in the front for a week or so after you leave.

Residual sales are also a big plus. After store personnel have met you and learned about your book, you become more personal in their minds. Your title stands out from the other nondescript ones on the shelf and they are much more likely to recommend it.

Remember one cardinal rule when setting up signings, events, or tours: You are not selling, you are *giving*. You are a person willing to share his or her time and expertise. With this mind set, you will come across professional, unstressed, and benevolent.

Escaping from the humdrum of ordinary book signings

The reason book signings often fail is simple: They are just signings. Nothing is happening. There is no energy. No draw. No way to attract people. Sitting placidly waiting for folks to come up to you to buy a book is the kiss of death. This approach—like owning a goose—can get you down.

Plan instead to create an "event." If your book is nonfiction, give a mini-seminar on the topic. If the subject lends itself—such as quilting, flower arranging, or calligraphy—provide a demonstration. You might set up a question and answer format, where the store manager, events coordinator, or an articulate friend you bring along, interviews you.

For novelists and poets the ideal is a reading. A writer may actually reach a larger audience through a series of readings than from the published work itself. Readings are a way to introduce your work to people who might otherwise never read it.

Several guidelines will help you be more successful: Think of a reading as a performance. While few of us want to be considered "actors," you must dramatize what you say and how you say it to hold the audiences' attention. Fiction writers sometimes use a range of voices to differentiate dialogue between characters. Another trick is to snap your fingers to indicate a quotation (having explained why you are doing this first, of course, so you don't appear to have an odd affliction).

Choose your material carefully. Passages that work well on the printed page may not play well aloud. Be sure to practice and listen for the rhythm of what you are reading. Twenty minutes is preferred; a half hour is maximum. Leave them hungry for more. And consider your physical appearance as you will be the center of attention. Dress appropriately. Conservative wins over flamboyant. And lose any jangly jewelry that would be picked up by the microphone. (Yes, in many cases you'll have one.)

Is there any way you can combine your reading with something else? Jesse May, for instance, is a fiction writer and professional poker player. He wrote a novel titled *Shut Up and Deal.* Interest in gambling has increased enormously over the last decade as many states legalized some form of wagering. Jesse recently did a national tour during which he combined readings with poker instructions.

More creative spins

If you're going to be a guerilla publisher or author—one who competes with imagination and energy rather than money—you need to think "out of the box." Karen Dowell, the author of *Cooking with Dogs,* did a Saturday afternoon event at Borders in Bangor, Maine. She wasn't alone, however. Her two labrador retrievers participated as well. When the store events coordinator saw Karen's dogs, the decision was made to set the event up next to the information desk on the first floor. Consequently, the first thing you saw when you walked in were two friendly labs. The area was never empty, reports Karen. People were always petting the pooches or asking questions about the book, which sold 30 copies.

Nicole Rubel, illustrator of the children's book *Rotten Ralph*, had a smashingly successful event at The Bookstore in Longview, Washington. The store charged $3 for tickets for each child to attend her drawing lesson (parents could attend free). It was promoted via direct mail, school libraries, radio spot ads and giveaway tickets, word-of-mouth, and in-store signage. Bookmarks attached to suckers were also a sweet inducement for parents and children alike. The ticket revenue was used to buy each child a drawing tablet, pencil, helium balloon, and cookie. After the lesson, Nicole autographed books for an hour.

The author of *Robin-Robin*, Mary Balcomb is also a firm believer in audience participation. When she and her husband do signings and readings, they also frequently discuss the art of etching. She deep-etched three small zine plates: a bird's nest with four eggs, a baby bird, and "Mad Baby," all from the book. As a finale to the event, children and adults can print from one of these on her small press. They end up with a blind-embossed bookmark (no ink, no mess) and they love it, she reports. Along with exposure to the book and the antics of Robin-Robin, people get a taste of etching as well.

Captain Bruce Warren Ollstein applies military strategy to the game of golf to make his book, *Combat Golf*, entertaining and practical. He regales audiences during his signings by demonstrating the book's tactical moves on a six-foot portable green.

Of course, bookstores don't have to be the exclusive domain of events. (Mary Balcomb does events for community groups and Audubon Societies as well.) Alice Low is the author of more than two dozen books for children and teenagers. The end of one October found her in the lobby of the Emelin Theater in New York signing copies of *The Witch Who Was Afraid of Witches* during a special Halloween production of a musical version of her book.

Looking for a location with lots of foot traffic? How about the local grocery store? This works especially well for regional or local books. Rod Colvin signed and sold 300 copies of his book in four hours. And the regional appeal of a book titled *Fountain of Highlandtown* led to the sale of 200 copies at a Moose Lodge (no less) in the heart of the featured neighborhood. Music stores are perfect for books about music; nurseries and garden centers for titles dealing with horticulture. The possibilities of place are limited only by your imagination.

If it isn't practical to do an official event, consider a drive-by signing. (That's *signing*!) This is just what it implies: You stop by a bookstore for a brief visit and sign their stock. It's a good idea to comb the Yellow Pages and call ahead to be sure they have some. All you need is a vehicle, a map, and a little daring. Ask to meet the manager, schmooze a bit, and add your John Henry to the books. Be sure they affix "autographed copy" stickers and suggest they display the book face-out.

You're probably going to find the best results at specialized independents, such as Christian bookstores, feminist bookstores, gay bookstores, mystery bookstores, etc. Once you've met the staff, they will recommend your book and purchase more when it sells out.

Ways to turn signings into extravaganzas

So what do you do when you show up—and nobody else does? Plain vanilla signings can be the loneliest experience in the world. Be proactive. Be as much on your toes as a ballerina. Be willing to put yourself out there.

Lorilyn Bailey, author of *The Little Book of Online Romance*, brings a pretty glass bowl of Hershey kisses. Then she brazenly asks everyone who comes through the door, "Excuse me (sir/ma'am), would you like a kiss?" It usually gets a laugh and she snares them. Offering a Hershey kiss with one hand, she gives them a book to look at with the other.

Other authors walk the aisles carrying a copy of their book and engage those in the store in general conversation, leading up to the fact that they're the author of such and such a book. Then they put the book in the prospect's hands and point out certain sections.

Mark Victor Hansen tells of a mall signing in Canada where the store manager dropped the ball and hadn't advertised the event. So Mark put two tables out in front of the store. Then he got a bunch of balloons and had a clerk pop one every few minutes to get the attention of passersby. He grabbed people and asked them to read page 24 from *Chicken Soup for the Soul* aloud. In an hour and a half he sold 400 books to people who had no idea he was there and no intention of buying books.

He is also famous for inspiring multiple sales. "People who buy books, buy books," says Mark. He and coauthor Jack Canfield encourage and excite people to invest in more than one book as a signed gift for a loved one or friend. At special holidays like Christmas they cajole buyers to do all of their shopping on the spot and get *Chicken Soup* books for everyone on their list.

Larry James suggests bringing along a Polaroid camera and when someone buys your book offering to have your picture taken together. After you've signed and dated the bottom, give it to the customer and suggest they use it for a bookmark. "This increases the odds that your book and the picture will become more of a conversation piece," says Larry. He further recommends having your picture taken with the manager and other key people in the store. Send it with your thank-you note to keep you and your book fresh in their minds.

People love autographed books. They are perceived as having more value and make wonderful gifts. Decide ahead of time on a couple of brief original statements that are general enough to fit anyone, yet have a personal feeling. Inscribe the book to the purchaser, or whomever they designate (double-check the spelling so you don't ruin a book), add your statement, sign and date it, and you're done.

When you are through, sign all the remaining stock so the store won't return the books. Ask them to affix "autographed" stickers. (We carry our own as some stores can't seem to find theirs. SPAN members can order stickers at the rate of $10 for 200.) Before you leave the store, suggest that they shelve the remaining books face-out.

If you want to reach out to Barnes & Noble stores beyond your local area for events, call Thomasina Rose at 212-633-4082. She will mail you a 30-page list of contacts for all their stores, plus a list of the six regional community relations managers. When you contact the individual stores, be very enthusiastic on the phone. They want to feel the author they're considering bringing in will be entertaining for their customers.

This can work on a regional level even if the chain hasn't yet placed a national buy. "We are able to buy directly from small presses for special events," reports Amy Tharp, the Walnut Creek, California, community relations coordinator (CRC). It's preferable, however, to work through the community relations managers as they can help you target the most appropriate stores and have the clout to place books in several locations in their area. Payment is also simplified.

B&N does a nice monthly "Events" flyer to promote upcoming author appearances. Keep in mind they also sponsor a Singles Series and a Senior Citizen Series where your books might fit in.

The Borders chain has made the financial commitment to have a publicist, or CRC, in every store. "We strive to establish each of our bookstores as a neighborhood store and community cultural center," commented one CRC. They stage about 30 events a month per store and can get books ordered when managers don't want to mess with it.

Working in tandem with the media

Signings serve as bait. They provide the "news" angle local media needs to warrant interviewing you. Ask the store for ideas about media contacts; they usually have a very complete and up-to-date list. Target community newspapers as well as the big daily; the former will give you more space, and have a cadre of loyal readers who support things the newspaper promotes. Also submit a brief news release to the calendar editor of every paper within a 50 mile radius.

Doing radio interviews a day or two before a signing and mentioning on the air when and where the event will take place boosts attendance. If you can't snag an actual interview, consider offering six or eight free books to the morning drive-time disk jockeys of the most popular area show to use as contest prizes. As they give them out, they mention the author will be appearing at . . .

And don't overlook public service radio or TV programs. Although they usually air at ridiculous times like 6:00 A.M. on Sunday morning, some people do listen or watch. Additionally, their community affairs director may include your event in the station's daily listing of community activities.

Bobbie Christensen, who is a real pro at doing successful signings, suggests if you're doing one on Saturday or Sunday you call the local TV network affiliates on Friday. Ask for the news director. Say something like, "Hi, I wanted to let you know that Waldenbooks at the (whatever mall in town) is having the author Bobbie Christensen doing a book signing on *Getting Your Dream Life: Career, Sex & Leisure* on Saturday at 1:00. If you need a filler for your nightly news, she can give you a great 60-second spot." Bobby reports having had camera men show up simultaneously from two networks!

The event itself is also news. Leverage it by sending out a news release afterwards. It should be a short piece that summarizes the high points of the event and provides book ordering information.

What to do *before* your event

The meek may inherit the earth—but they won't sell many books. There are countless things you can do prior to your event to ensure that it will be more successful. Here they are:

■ If you're working on a local event, take a copy of the book, key reviews, press clippings, your biography, and a one-page list of suggested workshops/seminar topics to help the event planner determine how best to fit you into their plans.

■ Consider timing. Discuss with the event planner what days and times are best for your genre. Signings and events are usually held weekday nights, plus Saturdays and Sundays. For stores in downtown locations, however, weekday lunch time is often preferable if you have a business book. Work three to four months out, if possible. They need plenty of time to write, produce, and mail their newsletter. By the way, scheduling yourself for the end of the month has an advantage: Your information will be visible in the newsletter longer. When considering timing also look at what periods during the year are best. July and August, for instance, are typically slow months. Major publishing houses don't tour their authors as much then, so you have a better chance of getting premier exposure.

■ Explore the possibilities of putting together a fuller program with perhaps three other authors with books complementary to yours. Each panelist could present a 15-minute segment, then you open it up for Q&A. Of course, everybody's book is available for sale. This might even warrant inexpensive ticket sales of perhaps $5 with the proceeds going to a worthy cause.

Take or send an 8- by 10-inch color photo of yourself, extra book covers, and a sign with impressive advance quotes in large bold lettering. These will give the person ammunition for making a compelling "Meet the Author" poster or display announcing your upcoming event.

Provide postcards they can slip in the package of each book bought ahead of time. And design a customized flyer that shows the book, your photo, has a brief bio, and includes key bullets about the content and details on when the event occurs.

Send out announcements. Don't depend on the bookstore to generate all the attendance; promote the event yourself, too. Search your database by zip code and send postcards to those in the area. Also include appropriate candidates from your Rolodex and your holiday greeting card list. Do you belong to a national association that has a local group? Perhaps you can gain access to their mailing list as well.

Cultivate local media as we explained above.

Have your book front cover enlarged so it becomes a color poster approximately 11- by 17-inch and mount it on posterboard with a stand-up easel on the back. Take this with you to every signing (and retrieve it afterwards).

Have a button made of your book cover that you can wear, or create a name badge that says "Author," your name, and book title.

Write your own announcements to be delivered over the store's intercom. Make them brief and intriguing. It's a good idea to create several as this encourages them to announce you multiple times. If there is no PA system, suggest a clerk be stationed at the front door as a greeter and to alert customers that an author is in the store.

Call and confirm the event a week ahead to be sure they have stock on hand, are prepared for you, etc. And if you're coming in from out of town, it's courteous to let them know you have arrived.

Try to arrange a window display featuring not only multiple copies of the book you're signing, but your other titles as well if you're a frequently published author. If the window is off limits, suggest an end-aisle display near the checkout desk or front door.

Come bearing gifts. Make up a gift box of goodies for the staff—especially if you have a cookbook. Treat the person who booked you as king or queen for a day. Bring a small box of chocolates, a red rose, or some other small present. This will set you apart in their mind.

If you are a cookbook author, always take samples made from a recipe in the book. Customers flock to tasty treats.

Devise a way to capture attendees' names, addresses, emails, etc. You can then do a follow-up mailing for those who didn't purchase and add them all to your database for promoting future titles. Some people have a guest book. Others have a fish bowl and invite people to put in their business cards. If you do this, also have little forms handy for those who don't have business cards. Have a drawing for a tee shirt, button, or some other related item.

Ask the store not to put out too many chairs unless you anticipate a big crowd. It's always better to have 20 occupied chairs than 40 that are half empty.

If you end up with the typical signing, don't let them stick you in some obscure place. For some strange reason some event planners put autographing tables in back corners, in the music section, up-stairs, etc. You want to be front and center . . . even outside in the mall or on the sidewalk, if that's possible.

Request a short meeting with the staff before the signing so they have an understanding of the book and can funnel people to you for the event or intelligently discuss the book afterwards.

Pre-sign several books with a generic statement, your name, and the date if you expect a big crowd. Then you can simply customize them to the individual when the crush hits. (Be sure to use the same color pen!) Speaking of which, some authors swear by the Sharpie extra-fine permanent marker.

Things to do *during* your event

Captivate the audience by incorporating interesting anecdotes and stories about your own experiences. But always go back to the book.

Find ways to add humor to your presentation. Even if your book isn't humorous, keep your remarks on the light side. People love to laugh.

Try to achieve visual variety. Show and tell is a big hit with audiences. When we speak on *Jump Start Your Book Sales* we begin with a set of automobile jumper cables. One end is attached to a book, the other to million dollar bills. Sharyn McCrumb, who wrote *The Hangman's Beautiful Daughter,* brings a quilt for her signings as it demonstrates an Appalachian folk art that plays a large part in the book. Jane Langton, who illustrates her own mysteries, shows a story board for one of them in which thumbnail sketches of the major scenes are arranged and rearranged until she is satisfied with the sequence. The author of a book for children could dress up like a clown; one on applying make up or dressing for success could do half of her face/body the wrong way and half the right way. Get the idea?

■ Jeeni Criscenzo tells of bringing props to decorate her signing table. She went to a fabric store and got material in a Mayan pattern to make a table cloth. Then she added Mayan artifacts to attract the curious.

■ At the beginning, or early in your talk, personally hand a copy of your book to each member of the audience. Walk them through certain sections to get them involved and feeling a sense of owner-ship. In the end they are really buying the author, not the book. They'll want to take it home with them almost as a souvenir of the experience. Retail merchants know that getting their merchandise into the hands of prospective customers is one secret of success.

■ Don't be afraid to point our why your book is better than or differ-ent from the rest. Although no one wants a half-hour commercial, your audience deserves to know why yours is superior. Point to something unique in your book and say matter-of-factly, "Don't go looking for this in other books. No one has done this before."

■ Leave time for questions and answers. Inquiring readers can lead you on a merry chase. Often the most interesting information is revealed during this time. You have a chance to become human to them.

Action plans for book tours

Author tours put on by major publishers for their best-selling au-thors may cost upwards of $50,000 and send the celebrity on a trek of up to 26 cities. Publicists readily admit that such tours almost never recoup the expense in resulting book sales. They are to salve the ego of the author as much as anything.

Your author tour will look very different. It will probably be a com-bination of bookstore events, media coverage, and talks or seminars to various groups. Happily, you can do it for a fraction of the above cost. Rather than hiring an expensive publicist for several months, it will be a do-it-yourself campaign. Instead of paying for tickets to fly hither and yon you'll either cash in frequent flyer miles, drive your own vehicle, or rent a van or RV for the tour. Instead of staying in posh hotels you may crash on the sofa of relatives or renew distant friendships that had gone stale.

One thing is universal, however: Book tours are grueling. You're going to get tired. Very tired. So get plenty of rest before you start and plan to take one day a week off for R&R. Another tip is to reread your book. It will energize you, get your creative juices flowing, and avoid embarrassing questions about a section you've forgotten.

Here's the formula for using an author tour to create sales: First, determine the route you want to take and contact bookstores to secure signings during the targeted time frame. Next, line up speaking or teaching engagements. (See more about this in chapter 22.) Contact civic organizations, such as Rotary, Kiwanis, and Lions, that are always looking for weekly programs. Check with libraries. Offer to speak free as long as you can sell your book. See if there is a Learning Annex or other adult education facility that might provide you a platform.

If your book relates to children, hone in on schools. This is what Dale Smith, author of *The Rabbit* and *The Promise Sign* does. The schools are thrilled to have an author speak. He hands out flyers telling the parents where his book is available and the dates of his local signings.

Last, contact the media. Once book signings and speeches are lined up, you have a reason to be local news. During interviews mention the dates and places of your signings. See how everything feeds the other? The tour is a success because everything you do relates to selling books.

By the way, sometimes small publishers and authors shun the big cities in favor of medium-sized towns that can't command the attention of best-selling authors. Smaller places are more receptive, media-wise, than big metropolitan areas.

Examples of successful author tours

Bobbie Christensen, whom you met earlier in this chapter, is the queen of low-budget, high-results author tours. With each new book, she tools around the country in a 24-foot Winnebago. That allows her to stay for less than $20 a night in KOA campgrounds and cook her own meals. Does it work? Here is a recent note we received from her: "My 5-week Midwest (26 Waldens) trip was great. Totally sold out the new book in every store *and* took orders." That means she peddled from 15 to 30 copies of *Building Your Financial Portfolio on $25 a Month or Less* per stop.

Since then, Bobbie has refined her approach even more. She now stays overnight in rest areas or in store parking lots, thus saving the $20 per day campground fees. She also does radio shows while on the road. One week that resulted in 300 orders from one show and 350 from another. Back home, her husband and son frantically fill book orders that come in on their 800 number.

She has been spending a total of about five months out of the year on the road for several years now. She plans the trips to avoid heavy winter snow when possible, yet heads out April and May to take advantage of bad spring weather when people are in the shopping malls. October and November often find her in the south; January and the summer months she heads for Oregon and Washington. Her home state of California she works all year.

Each trip, as she develops more contacts, yields her additional seminar business, which means full-price sales. People she meets at the signings sometimes book her for speeches. Since Bobbie now has four books and a newsletter, seminar attendees have a nice array to choose from. She typically sells an average of one to two books to everyone in the audience.

Bobbie works strictly with Waldenbooks. Except for Oregon, Washington, and New England, which have district managers, she deals directly with store managers. If the chain hasn't stocked your title, this still works. You simply fax (313-913-1643) their main office in Ann Arbor, Michigan, and tell them such and such a store has booked you for a signing and they need to place a special order.

In an article she wrote for the *SPAN Connection* newsletter, she tells of just finishing a book signing at a large Waldenbooks in Buffalo, New York: "Last Saturday a nationally known best-selling romance writer sat in this same store and did not sell a single book. I, an unknown self-published author, sold 16 books on a Tuesday and made another 10 after-signing sales. Why do store managers ask me back over and over?" And she goes on to make five points:

1. *Don't feel confined to just two hours.* Stay as long as you can and there is interest.

2. *Have lots of signs.* A big sign announcing "Book Signing Today" draws attention. Posters of the book cover are easy and inexpensive to produce.

3. *Plan on handing out 100 to 200 flyers.* Produce a professional 8½- by 11-inch one on your computer. What you say on that flyer decides whether customers who walk away reading it will come back to buy or never be seen again.

4. *Cultivate the media.* Newspaper articles and radio and TV interviews will sell books before you get to the store, while you are there, and after you leave.

5. *Do* not *sit down.* (The best-selling author mentioned earlier sat at a table waiting for people to come to her.) Bobbie takes her display table as far out into the mall as the store allows and stands a couple of feet to the side asking passersby if they "would like information on changing careers or starting your own business" as she hands them a flyer.

Richard J. Maturi, an author from Cheyenne, Wyoming, had two new investment books out and decided to promote them via a "Wyoming to Wall Street Tour." He followed the Lincoln Highway Route, the nation's first transcontinental highway, to New York City while driving his 1936 Oldsmobile. In the process he garnered lots of newspaper, radio, and television coverage as the Lincoln Highway was 80 years old that year and his mode of transportation was unique. In addition, he held numerous book signings and gave a number of investment seminars as he traveled across the country. Richard reports the trip is still paying off as he became a speaker for the Wyoming Speakers Bureau, which led to increased book sales.

Hal Higdon took a different approach to his tour for *Boston: A Century of Running.* He concentrated on his very specific target market. Over a period of six months he visited 46 cities selling books at running clubs and marathons. He and his wife traveled by van so they could carry books with them rather than shipping them. They would set up at races where there were expos or make appearances at the monthly meetings of running clubs. Their best haul was one night when they sold $1,200 worth of product.

So don't believe that signing and tours are a waste of time. Handled creatively, they can provide viable bookselling opportunities.

Web Sites, Wisdom, and Whimsey

A place to sell and sign damaged books. Book fairs, those street events where consumers are often drawn by the thousands, is a perfect place to sell hurt and slightly marred books. Publishers report that consumers who would be horrified by a bent cover in a bookstore love the idea they can pickup a slightly damaged book for a 75% discount at a book fair . . . especially when it is autographed by the author.

When is a signing not a signing? Many feel that using automatic signature pens, which have been around in government offices for years, to autograph books is cheating. Hillary Rodham Clinton gave this approach new meaning when she toured to promote her *It Takes a Village*. The print run was auto-signed and sent to sites hosting the author. Stacks of Clinton's books, advertised as "signed copies," revealed several different computerized versions of her signature. Normally an authentically signed copy indicates the author has actually touched the book.

Touring an author? Get publicity online. BookWire and *PW* have formed an alliance to create an author tour database for Internet browsers. "Authors on the Highway" lets both the general public and industry professionals know about authors touring in their area. For more information call 212-982-7008. You can check BookWire for yourself at http://www.bookwire.com.

A different twist to autographed copies. If you have a good mail database you might consider a ploy Hal Higdon used when promoting his *Boston: A Century of Running*. He sent out a direct-mail solicitation to runners all over the country and presold 500 copies at $35 apiece. They were each stamped "Collector's Edition," then signed and numbered by the author. (This is book number X of 500 special copies.)

Virtual book signing breaks new ground. Leave it to David and Tom Gardner, authors of *The Motley Fool Investment Guide*, to make book-hustling history by holding a live, America Online, interactive, online meet-the-authors event—with autographed books yet! Here's how it worked: Participants could not only click onto a separate screen and order the book, they could also dictate a brief personalized inscription. The next morning the brothers, who worked in tandem with Borders in Fairfax, Virginia, promptly signed the books. The authors came up with the concept as a way to autograph books for fans who didn't live near any of the cities they were touring. Give you any ideas?

God put me on this earth to do a certain number of things. Now I'm so far behind I will never die.

Escorts (the book kind!) are available to take you on the town. When major publishers send an author on tour, they provide a knowledge-able local person to take the author around. These people are called "escorts" (they're really guardian angels) and they schlep you from inter-view to interview, bookstore to bookstore. We've had exceptional ones and impossible ones.

A good escort knows not only the city, but all the book and media people in it. In the hands of an exceptional escort, when you walk into a store to autograph their stock, you are greeted with open arms. When you arrive at a TV studio, you're fawned over. He or she will take you to a wonderful restaurant for lunch, find you a doctor if you become ill, even run a quick errand if necessary. But they don't come cheap. Costs usually run around $150 to $200 per day. It can be a terrific investment.

We've piloted ourselves around strange towns—and gone the es-cort route. And we're here to tell you it's a wonderful relief not to be crouching over unfamiliar maps, fighting rush-hour traffic, and gener-ally getting as stressed as a mouse in a snake's cage. Going into an important interview relaxed and calm is a big plus. There is no national association that we know of, so you have to be resourceful to find local escorts. Check with the chamber of commerce, look in the Yellow Pages, or call a larger publisher or publicist in the area for names.

CHAPTER 7

Op-Ed Pieces for High Gear Results

The newspaper "op-ed" (short for opposite editorial) page refers to a physical location rather than an analytical or political position. It doesn't mean that pieces necessarily oppose the editorial point of view of the paper, rather it literally denotes where these pieces are found: opposite the editorial page.

Newspaper op-ed essays build visibility

This is a forum for opinion and observation that has come into its own over the last couple of decades as a wonderful vehicle for bringing attention to issues, authors, and books. These brief essays have been deemed by publicists as an effective and overlooked means of gaining visibility. It's a place where grassroots go-getters mingle with political pundits, where many people have their "public say." It's not just a place to rebut, settle accounts, serve notice, or exact revenge.

Pat Eisemann, vice president and director of publicity at Scribner, definitely believes in them. The broadcast media, such as *The Today Show*, see the op-eds—and not just those in *The New York Times*. Eisemann said *USA Today* creates a big stir for Scribner.

Op-ed page editors need fresh voices with new thoughts, classy writing, mind-bending revelation. "I like to think of the op-ed page as the people's page," says Diane Clark of *The San Diego Union Tribune*. It's where an informed outsider is granted a forum.

"We consider our Commentary page as a marketplace of ideas," reports Phil Joyce from the *Philadelphia Inquirer*. The op-ed page is a vehicle for an intellectual transaction between writer and reader, believes Richard Liefer of the *Chicago Tribune*. He calls it "a meeting place of the minds."

Book authors will find here a venue ideal for addressing their passions. And since op-ed pieces carry a bio line, your book and publisher are plugged as you sound off about topics close to your heart. With newspaper review space at a premium, and competition for off-the-book pages extremely competitive, a citation in the editorial pages can yield dramatic results.

Because of the immediacy of newspapers, writers no longer have to submit a query or an article—then wait months to learn if an editor is interested. Newspapers make decisions in days not months. And in many cases you can self-syndicate your material, offering exclusive rights in several circulation areas simultaneously as long as they don't compete.

The hows and whys of op-ed pages

Timeliness often dictates what essays will appear. Monitor what's going on in the news carefully and seize the moment. Respond immediately if you have an idea that ties in with a current event. A week later the subject will probably be dead. Faxing, emailing or calling is wise when you're suggesting an especially timely piece. Make the importance of the piece obvious in the title or lead paragraph.

Extraordinary things can result from an op-ed. A few years ago the op-ed page of *The New York Times* printed a piece extolling the desirable simplicity of earlier times and how modern inventions are not so terrific after all. A literary agent who read the essay was struck by the literary skill with which it was written. He was determined to locate the author. The result was a contract with Harper for a book of previously published and new essays, which was published on Mother's Day when the author was a mere 96 years old. Editors and other agents have been known to contact a writer when the germ of an idea presented in an op-ed essay piqued their interest.

A *Newsweek* "My Turn" essay attacking the college loan pay-back system not only helped its author pay off those loans, it helped him get a job at the *Washington Monthly* and led to his becoming a contributing editor to the magazine.

Be sure to learn the submission requirements of papers you are targeting: How long are their pieces? Do they want it double-spaced? Do you fax or email?

To help you, we've supplied a partial list of editors in the Appendix. A good reference source for more is *Bacon's Newspaper Directory.*

Under Daily Newspapers it notes "Editorial/Opinion Page" in bold and gives the name and contact information for the op-ed Page Editor.

Crafting compelling essays

Syndicated columnist James J. Kilpatrick observed that perhaps half of all columns "are pontifical, portentous, pointless; their writers boil not, neither do they grin. They merely plod."

Be a flame thrower not one who timidly lights a pilot. Earn the right to see your byline on the op-ed page by the strength of your argument, the appeal of your subject, and the quality of your writing.

Forget the middle road. It's boooooorrring. Your challenge is to make people view things from a different angle. The best compliment an op-ed page editor can receive is "you made me think." They want a good mix: a balance between the weighty and the whimsical, the expected and the surprising. They're seeking more than warmed-over work from news services. They need views to satisfy a broad range of reader tastes. This is a place where controversy can bloom, where blandness is forbidden, and readers' blood pressure rises.

Because the competition goes up as the circulation numbers increase, it behooves contributors to write the most forceful piece possible. Said an editor at *Newsday,* "We look for clarity of language and logic as well as freshness of approach." Find a creative slant. Offer facts the paper hasn't used before. Take a strong position. Use vibrant language. Consider analogy or metaphor to give your piece an offbeat flavor. If applicable, insert a couple of potent statistics to add validity to your case.

One of the best ways to score is by developing a local hook to a major national event or anniversary date. A broad-brush approach will only work with the national dailies. Otherwise, if you tie in a local person, institution, or event to a topic of general relevance, you'll hit a home run more often. Most papers rely on wire services for national or international events. They look for something they can't get there. "It must have a Colorado angle or it won't make the cut," explains *Denver Post* op-ed editor Bob Ewegen. Many papers are reluctant to accept submissions from people living outside of their immediate area. In this situation it's vital to find a local angle if you want serious consideration.

Be sure you present your credentials in a strong cover letter. Most op-ed pieces are the purview of guest experts with proven knowledge on important issues of the day. If you've got the background to write about a topic, flaunt it! And include both a day and evening phone number so you're easily reached.

Be proactive rather than reactive. A forward-thinking freelancer or PR practitioner anticipates. For instance, is Congress voting on a bill relevant to your titles? Then have a "reaction" piece already in the hands of a key op-ed editor *before* the vote.

One freelancer writer who has fine success with this medium advises putting your argument right up front. It's got to grab interest immediately. And if you're writing a piece of national scope, be aware that the guy in Denver—who's bouncing his baby son while downing his morning Cheerios—needs to be able to relate.

Be careful about self-aggrandizing. If you become blatant about mentioning the title of your book or company, it will be edited out totally. Instead, sign the cover letter with your name, book title, and the publisher. Include it in a brief bio blurb at the end of your piece as well

Publishers can also submit a half-page overview of their authors' credentials on certain subjects. Then when an op-ed piece is needed, the editor can turn to a stable of qualified writers.

Try a Letter to the Editor. If doing an op-ed essay seems unwieldily to you, perhaps a letter to the editor is more your style. Often articles lend themselves to responses. One publisher, who read a piece in a trade journal that lent itself to her book, replied to the piece also citing her book and how it could be ordered. Her letter was printed and she felt she got the equivalent of a nice big ad for the cost of a postage stamp.

Did you hear about the combination word processor/food processor? It's for authors who have to eat their own words.

Peg your op-ed essay to the calendar. Lynne Lamberg is the author of *Bodyrhythms*, which explores recent advances in understanding our biological clock. She published an op-ed story in *The Oregonian* for Labor Day ("24-Hour Schedule Hurts Workers, Society"). And for daylight-savings time changes, *The Indianapolis Star* ran her piece "Disoriented by Daylight-Savings Time."

CHAPTER 8

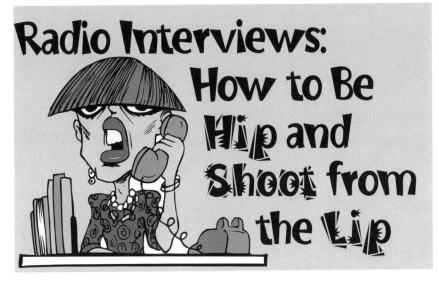

Radio Interviews: How to Be Hip and Shoot from the Lip

Talk is *hot*, whether it's on the radio, TV, or Internet. In 1983 there were only 53 radio stations with news/talk formats. The February 1998 issue of *American Demographics* reports there are more than 1,000 today! And while the number of stations has remained constant, syndicated, network, and cable shows—some with millions of listeners—have ballooned from only a handful when Oprah first went into syndication in 1986 to several dozen now.

This emergence of talk radio seems to serve the need for connection with others. Today we often don't know our neighbors; we don't visit over the backyard fence like we used to. Instead we have a virtual, electronic, sometimes global, media community . . . people with like minds and interests. Show topics often revolve around what you would talk about with your best friend over lunch: such things as relationships, saving money, dealing with an illness or a difficult boss—real-life subjects.

Since commutes to and from work are growing longer each year, Americans on the road are a captive audience for talk radio. Forty-two percent of radio listeners are in their cars, 37% listen at home, and 21% at work, often while engaged in other activities. According to *Talkers* magazine, the industry trade journal, the typical talk fan is between 35 and 64, 66% are white, 47% are female, 32% have at least a college degree, and 58% of them make $50,000 or more a year. Impressive demographics.

Advertising agencies have realized that talk radio listeners tend to participate more directly in the actual listening process than music radio listeners. Talk show devotees use the medium as primary foreground entertainment. Not only are they educated, attentive, and affluent, they're also activists. These characteristics make them ideal targets for book publishers.

The author as radio guest

You (or your authors) can talk to literally millions of people over a short time—without ever leaving your home or office! And you can do it in your robe and slippers by going on the air via your telephone. Radio stations across the land will interview you long distance. These are called "phoners." If you work them right and have a general-interest title that retails for under $20, you can sell thousands of books this way. Author Joe Sabah has been on 630 shows and has sold $357,000 worth of books! (Tips from him later.)

Another advantage to this way of promoting is you don't have to get in front of the camera or a live mike in a radio station if that makes you uncomfortable. It's kind of like chatting over the phone with a friend. So if you're a shy author who can really identify with why the *Book of Lists* ranks fear of public speaking ahead of death, flying, and loneliness—here's your answer!

Statistics have shown results from radio promotion are often even more imposing than those from TV. First, you have more time to expand upon your subject. On television, the guest spots usually last less than five minutes whereas with radio, many talk shows give you an hour. Besides discussing your particular book, you also interact with the audience, answering questions posed by listeners, and getting into an extended conversation about the topic.

Publishers find putting authors on the air, without either party having to worry about travel expenses, an extremely viable way to sell books. With today's lower long distance charges, radio talk shows are now able to team up with a variety of experts in subject areas from aardvarks to zoology. Chances are you can be one of these experts.

Prospecting for appropriate shows

There are radio stations all across the country that would welcome you telling your tale. You could do this virtually all day for months and still not have reached all of them. However, this isn't what we suggest. It doesn't make sense to repeatedly spend hours of your time talking to people in tiny places like Podunk, Idaho. We suggest going for the numbers. And there's a practical way to do it. This is just one of the secrets we will reveal to you.

There are several different directories that list radio shows. Go to your library, or online, and research. If you want the greatest reach, look for "syndicated" or "network" shows. Just be sure you're using the most current information available. Media people seem to change jobs like most of us change underwear. Always call and verify who is the producer or guest booker (and the correct name spelling), plus the current address. With time and tenacity, you can find the big time *yourself* instead of paying thousands of dollars each month to a publicist.

Some of the newsletters currently hawking authors to the media generate a dismal return for your investment. You can probably get on the air, but you're not likely to capture plums like NPR or Oprah. The producers that depend on these newsletters are often with shows that have meager coverage in out-of-the-way places. Unless you need experience (and this is a viable reason to use them) or have loads of time on your hands, it may be too small an audience. That said, we do know of some big media plums that have resulted from producers or editors initially hearing authors on small stations.

Those who pin their hopes on these newsletters should realize they are one of scores being advertised to the radio producers. The big names and scandalous subjects win the most attention. Another drawback is that some of these newsletter publishers work both sides of the street. Not only do they charge authors for listings, they also charge a subscription fee from the radio station. Naturally, the paid subscription ones don't have the circulation base of a newsletter sent free to the stations.

One such publication that has gotten good results for some authors (it's a magazine that typically runs to 80 pages) is Bradley Communications' *Radio-TV Interview Report* (800-553-8002, ext. 312), which is mailed free to some 4,000 producers nationwide.

Another possibility for showing the media you're available is www.RadioTour.com. For a reasonable package price you get a Web listing including an audio message, fax service to the top 1,000 shows, plus email to 10,000 shows and journalists. For details go to their Web site or call 202-333-4904.

There's nothing wrong with doing some smaller stations in out-of-the-way places for practice, to really get your act together and refine it. Start small and craft a thing of beauty: an interview that is really powerful. Then graduate to the larger shows.

As we mentioned, when creating your own mailing, you ideally want to find syndicated or network shows. Some of these go to as many as 1,000 different radio stations around the country! That really makes your time count. Sure the competition is tough. But after you get some experience doing the little shows, it's time to graduate to the big time. New York and Los Angeles are where most syndicated and network shows originate.

Many excellent directories will lead you on a profitable journey to major radio shows. A good librarian, or an inventive search of the Internet, can yield impressive results. Always check whether or not the producers schedule telephone interviews and if they are interested in your topic. Then create a mailing list.

What's your approach? You're not promoting a book; you're providing *a solution to people's problems.* Always keep that uppermost in your mind. Remember it when you're creating your news release, pitch letter, making follow-up phone calls, and appearing on the show.

Send them a personalized pitch letter or a news release with a copy of the book. Full-blown media kits are typically a thing of the past. Everybody is too busy. Follow up with a phone call. Be prepared to follow up with *many* phone calls for popular shows. Have ready a brief, provocative reason why their listeners would want to hear from you.

You are being considered because you're an "expert." (You might even pitch radio and newspapers by saying you've just completed research on XYZ [your particular topic], and if they need an expert in that area, you're available.) The book becomes secondary. You are filling a need, responding to a problem listeners have. It may be how to entertain themselves, how to be sexier, how to be skinnier, how to be healthier, how to be wealthier.

"Be prepared" is the motto of the successful

One of the biggest secrets is to be fully ready. Mark Twain once said it takes three weeks to prepare a good ad-lib speech. Perhaps the easiest way to prepare is to role-play with another individual, or use a cassette recorder to tape what you say. The point is you need to get used to talking about your subject in short, colorful phrases. These are called "sound bites." The idea is to train yourself to present your message in an abbreviated, punchy way. Use Velcro words, vivid statements and phrases that stick in listeners' minds.

Have two or three major points you want to make. What is the core message of your book? You need to refine it, hone it, sharpen it until you've got 20 to 25 words. It's a good idea to write out this "mission statement." Choose forceful words. Use the active voice. Then literally memorize it—not so it becomes a rote announcement, but rather a lively and precise declaration.

Practice aloud. We see things differently with our eyes than we hear with our ears. As you're role-playing, also get in the habit of presenting your main point right at the very beginning. Don't wander into an interview. Dive in! Say something stimulating. The same rules that apply to good writing apply to good interviewing. You must capture the imagination and the interest of the audience at the onset.

Get in the habit of making a short statement or giving a brief answer, then elaborating on it. That way if you are put in a position where time is limited, you've already said the most important thing. When you're on a more leisurely show you can then expound by telling a story (listeners *love* stories!), sharing a startling statistic, giving a case history, or in some way embellishing your initial statement.

Don't try to become too perfect. You don't want to sound like a suave politician. Be human. Strive to come across as someone who's deeply credible and involved in the subject. Be excited. Enthusiastic. Forthright. It's much more important on a longer radio show to be captivatingly conversational than perfectly polished.

If your subject lends itself, try to think of something that would be  easy for the average listener to understand and relate to. For instance, a computer company explained, "Today we can put all the intelligence of a room-sized computer from the 1950s into a silicon chip the size of a corn flake." Not everyone relates to silicon chips, but everybody understands corn flakes. Look at your own subject. See what you can find that makes it easy for the average person to grasp.

Don't be afraid to let people get to know the real you. If you love sports, why not use an analogy about football or baseball? Or if you're a music buff, perhaps you want to use a comparison to an orchestra or a jazz band. Allow listeners to learn a little about you as a person. After all, authors are perceived as glamorous, exciting people. Don't you want to reinforce that image?

Setting the stage

Now that we've talked about the preparation you're going to do for your actual verbal presentation, let's discuss another kind of preparation. There are two items you should create before you ever go on the radio. First is a set of 3- by 5-inch cards, three for each interview. They should contain the name of the book, the author, the publisher, the price, and the toll-free order number. (See the adjacent sample.)

You're going to send these to prime people *before* you go on the air so they have them in their hot little hands when your interview occurs. These cards go to the following: the producer of the show, the host or hostess who will be interviewing you, and the station switchboard operator or the phone receptionist. For the switchboard operator, put a little flag on the card noting when you're going to be interviewed. Also write a notation that this is for her convenience so if calls come in about the book, the information is readily at hand. By doing this you've helped these folks help you. Make it easy for them to direct people to you for orders.

The other item we're going to create is some sort of a giveaway, a "freebie" you can announce and make available while you're being interviewed. It doesn't have to be elaborate, just a one-pager will do. Americans love trivia. Why not create a trivia quiz from information in your book? Or perhaps a list of tips would be helpful to people. Maybe it's a four-page booklet that gives an overview of the subject. Your giveaway should be a fun, intriguing gift or something of value.

Media Reminder Card

Guests Marilyn and Tom Ross

authors of

Country Bound!
Trade Your Business Suit Blues
for Blue Jean Dreams

Publisher: Dearborn/Upstart Publishing

Call orders to 1-800-331-8355
($19.95 plus $3 shipping)

Day/Date _____ Time _____

Paula Ryan, of Prosperity Books and Seminars, offers 10 Tips to Break the Debt Cycle, an excerpt from her new book. Of course, she also includes a flyer (coded to show radio responses) for both that book and her other title, *Bounce Back from Bankruptcy*. Paula gets a 45% response rate, meaning 45% of the people who request her free tip sheet order a book. And she also has the names and addresses to add to her database; these people have already "qualified" themselves for future mailings on related books.

"Look over the tip sheet you're considering using," Paula counsels. "Ask yourself: If I was the person listening, is this something that would encourage me to buy the end product? Is it something that is useful by itself?" If you can answer these questions with a "yes," you probably have a winning free gift.

Andrea Reynolds took a different approach to tip sheets. She *sells* them. After a foray into a TV show where she offered a free tip sheet, spent $60 of her own money on postage, and only sold $40 worth of books, she decided there had to be a better way. Her solution was to create some 20 tip sheets, which she sells for $2 each. Her most successful is the Writer's Fortune Cookie Predictions. Of course, her brochure/order form is included and she gets many multiple orders.

Certainly some people will look for your title in bookstores. If you or your publisher are aggressive about getting books placed in the area, that's wonderful. But very often it isn't practical. If you live in Miami, for instance, how do you personally see that books are stocked in bookstores in the Northwest if that's where the show is airing?

By offering a tip sheet or quiz, you encourage people to get in touch with you directly. You provide a way for listeners to get your book without having to go to bookstores or being frustrated because they can't find it.

The curtain rises

When you're on the air, it's important to be lively and animated. Put yourself in the audience's position: If a guest starts in a monotone, disinterested voice, you fail to become excited as well. Be dynamic in that first minute when you're welcomed by the host or hostess. Show passion for your message! Begin with something important. Remember, you are the authority on your book's subject; that's why you're being interviewed. It's essential you show that expertise in your explanations.

One of the biggest flaws in most interviews is the author typically talks about "my book." It's "my book" this and "my book" that. Unfor-

More Potent Radio Maneuvers

■ As soon as you pick up the phone, assume you're on the air. This won't usually be true as the producer typically comes on first, but you never know when your comments will be broadcast live.

■ Try to listen to the station and show ahead of time. If it's out of your area, one idea is to call the station and ask to be placed on hold: You'll hear the show airing!

■ When you have a guest spot solidified in a specific area, check with a couple of local independent bookstores and tell them if they order 12 copies, you'll plug them on the air. (Of course, if it's an area show, you should be alerting *all* bookstores in the vicinity they will have demand for the book.)

■ Target your pitches for the season. Grace Housholder does Top 10 Funny Kid Christmas Stories, then Top 10 List of Funny Kid Stories Involving Love for Valentine's Day. Of course there's Mother's Day, Halloween, Easter, you name it. Can you give your message a seasonal twist and get on the air again and again?

■ If you're offering a demo tape, don't send it to a station in the same market. Nobody likes to be a runner-up. Producers prefer exclusives in big markets.

■ Stand and deliver. When you do an interview from a chair, you're

(continued on next page)

tunately, this doesn't help listeners interested in buying that specific book. Name your book! You don't have to reiterate the tit le every other sentence, but several times throughout your interview you will have opportunities to gracefully introduce the title of your book. You can do this by saying, "In chapter fourteen of *The Complete Guide to Self-Publishing,* I cover . . . ," or you might say "What people tell us they like most about *The Complete Guide to Self-Publishing* is . . . ." There are all kinds of ways to weave in the title of your book. Think about it and have some ready.

Get the name of the person who will be interviewing you ahead of time; use his or her name as you talk. It gives the interview a more personal touch. Remember, however, that you're not talking to only that individual. You're addressing the entire audience. Frame your comments for all listeners, not just the host.

Don't overlook the opportunity to capitalize on controversy. If you can link your subject to a timely, current issue—or use it as a springboard to discuss something controversial in the news—by all means do so. Controversy presents an opportunity for wonderful interaction with your listeners. A talk show really hums when you get a lot of audience involvement. Of course, when you're dealing with controversy, there will be times you are asked difficult questions. Keep your cool. Some interviewers will deliberately attempt to provoke you.

Even in noncontroversial situations, the host may try to blindside you with an offbeat or hostile question. You simply "bridge" to solid ground. A bridging technique is "I'm not an expert on XYZ, but I *can* tell you . . . ." And you're back on track. As long as you know your subject well and stay calm, you're not likely to get into trouble.

A good tactic when you're asked a question you don't quite know how to deal with is to use a stalling phrase to give yourself time to think. One technique is to simply repeat the question. Another good ploy is to say to the host or hostess, "You know, John, that's a very good question." As you're saying this, your mind has a chance to regroup and decide on an appropriate reply.

What do you do when the host or hostess starts rambling and gets totally off the subject, focusing the show in a direction of no value to you? Take a lesson from Jacqueline Susann. She was a master at handling the media. If an interviewer tried to get her onto a topic she

> **More Potent Radio Maneuvers (continued)**
>
> slouched and your diaphragm is scrunched. Stand. Walk. Pace. You'll sound more dynamic. You may want a longer phone cord—maybe even a headset—to allow this flexibility.
>
> ■ Relate your book to newspaper headlines. Maybe you have an alternative viewpoint. Attack the commonly held notion. Explode a myth.
>
> ■ You may want to "plant" friends or loved ones to get the call-in ball rolling. Coach them with a leading question.
>
> ■ Remember that radio producers and hosts talk . . . to each other. There are sites on the Internet, such as Bit Board and Morning Mouth (closed to the general public), where they gab about outstanding guests. They also have conventions where they network. Be outstanding and they will seek you out like butterflies quest after nectar.
>
> ■ Always be on your best vocal behavior. You are "auditioning" from the moment you open your mouth. Think a producer is calling just to check that detail? Nope. He or she wants to hear your voice inflection, how enthusiastic you sound, if you're quick on the mental uptake, etc. Same thing when you call them. Turn on the charm.

didn't like, she'd say something like, "You know, that's a fascinating subject. It reminds me of a chapter in my novel . . . ." And she'd be right back on track with her book. We can use that same strategy to help the host or hostess stay on the subject we're there to discuss.

I (Marilyn) had just the opposite thing happen on one interview. It was set for an hour and once the host introduced me, he shut up! I talked for about five minutes, anticipating him to break in with another question any time. He never did. Except for commercials, it was virtually a one-hour monologue. I learned that day that silence, unlike the Retriever, is *not* golden!

Most women need to be conscious of their voice level. Ladies tend to talk in too high a pitch. Practice lowering your voice if you're a female. Variety is important for everyone. Project a tone both low and occasionally high. Consider your vocal pacing: Say some things rapidly, state important points slowly and emphatically.

When you're actually on the air, it's also useful to think about where this show is being aired. For instance, if you're talking to a Midwest audience, they're typically going to be turned off by casual attitudes toward sex and marriage. If you're addressing people in southern California, they have a much more relaxed and open attitude toward most subjects. If it's a nationally syndicated or network show airing many places around the country, play it safe. And if you're taping the show for later airing, don't mention anything time- or date-sensitive.

If conducting a telephone interview is nerve-racking for you, there are things you can do to make yourself more comfortable. One is to have handy some slightly warm water laced with a little lemon juice. This is a trick professional speakers use; it helps lubricate your throat. Something else to do if you're very tense is to use a bit of petroleum jelly to moisten the underside of your lips. When doing a phone interview, have something available to drink. Talking for an hour can be a strain for anyone. Before beginning, take a couple of big deep breaths and exhale slowly to relax.

We mentioned a giveaway before. Now is the time to bring it into play. Toward the end of the interview, it's appropriate for you to comment, "By the way, John, I've created something I think many of our listeners would like to have." State you have a free gift you'd like to make available (naming whatever it is). Explain that to get a copy all they have to do is send a self-addressed, stamped envelope. Then give your address. Make it as simple and quick as possible. Rather than saying "P. O. Box 3789," just say, "Box 3789." Don't take up a lot of time on the address. Ideally, you want to be able to repeat it, so make it as easy as possible. Instead of giving a long, complicated name for the publisher, say "free gift" or something similar.

Joe Sabah, who coauthored and self-published *How to Get the Job You Really Want and Get Employers to Call You*, has put $357,000 in his pocket by promoting his book via radio. He has a selling secret he revealed to us: Toward the end of the show, just before a break, he instructs listeners to get a pencil and paper because he is going to give them three tips that will guarantee them success. After he gives the tips he also gives ordering information. This clever guy sets them up with a pencil and paper to take his order number!

If you're serious about using radio to sell books, call Joe at 303-722-7200. He sells a product called *How to Market Yourself on Radio Talk Shows all Across America without Leaving Your Home or Office.* This system consists of a book, cassette tape, mail labels for over 700 radio stations, plus a current database of those stations.

After the curtain falls

An important follow-up to your interview, something often neglected, is a thank you. Send a brief note to both the producer and the host. Surprisingly, this is seldom done. It's not only polite, but wise. If you have done well on a radio show, it's quite possible you'll be invited back in a few months. This has been the experience of many of our clients. And if you've used this way of staying in touch with people, they're going to be thinking more favorably toward you.

Another wise move is to have the interview taped. If you don't tape it on your end, you can always send a cassette to the radio station *ahead of time* and ask them to tape the interview. (If it's an especially important interview, send a DAT tape for the highest quality sound.) Listen carefully to that interview. Critique it. What did you do well? Where were you particularly outstanding? What do you need to improve? You can learn much from listening to your interviews. You'll be better once you've evaluated strengths and weaknesses, and taken steps to improve them.

Of course, a good demo tape may be just the "open sesame" you need to corner an invitation on a major syndicated show.

Yes, remote talk radio interviews offer an unprecedented, free way to sell books—not to mention being the "star" of the hour. We have now given you the tools to take advantage of this opportunity. Use them wisely to increase your visibility and profitability.

Web Sites, Wisdom, and Whimsey

"It's not the book, it's the hook," states famed radio coach Joel Roberts. He is so right. Fire "Captain Bob" Smith knows the truth of that statement. "It's not the book, stupid . . . it's the different ways and ideas you pitch from the book that makes the difference." Captain Bob was seeking exposure for his *How to Get Everything You Want From the Opposite Sex*, when he realized every other relationship guru was trying to get the spotlight for Valentine's Day. So he shifted his emphasis to current national events and took the tack of "President Clinton's Situation: Could it Happen to You?" His radio interview calls tripled. It was the same information but with a different spin.

His press releases change with the season or national events. Although they all have the heading "Firefighter Ignites Your Show!," the angle for summer is vacation escapes. For Christmas, it's take the mystery out of buying gifts. Same book. Same stuff. Different twist.

Want to target 150,000,000 Americans? That's how many of us listen to radio on an average day. These listeners, representing primarily homemakers and people commuting to and from work, are spread out over some 6,500 stations. If you reached only 1% of them—then sold just one-fourth of that audience—that would equal 37,500 books flying out of your warehouse! Interested? Listen up. Many of these stations depend on the same basic news releases you're sending newspapers and magazines, only rewritten for radio. In that format, they're called a "script" and are read by "talent" that works at the station. They must run just under 30 or 60 seconds (note this time and the number of words in the top right-hand corner). Use a brief headline, make the body of the release in all *caps* and use one and a half line spacing. Try for a consumer tip angle and add your toll-free number once at the bottom. Read the script aloud to be sure it flows well, sounds punchy, and is conversational. Good luck—150,000,000 Americans. Wow!

Lock into radio stations. By moseying over to http://www.ontheair. com.text/html you can link to 644 radio stations covering the total range of formats. There are listings for alternative, Christian, classical, classic rock, college, contemporary, country, dance/top 40, jazz, news/talk, netcasts, oldies, rock, sports, and urban. Whew—something for everyone! And if you're set up for it, you can also listen live so you know exactly what goes whether the station is based in New Orleans, San Francisco, Baltimore, or wherever.

It took me fifteen years to discover that I had no talent for writing, but I couldn't give up because by that time I was too famous.

Peter Benchley, *Success and Failure*

Wonder what America's talk shows are discussing—and how you might fit in? Then surf over to www.talkers.com where the industry trade magazine serving the talk radio industry, *Talkers* magazine, is online. It can help you capture the mood of the public, not to mention glean ideas for tie-ins to current events. As the magazine continues to grow (it was started in 1990 and presently costs $50 a year for 10 issues), it adds more regular features. These now include the Washington Section, Sports Talk Radio, Tech Talk, Law Office, Programmer's Point, Hot Radio Guests (Who wouldn't want to be listed here!), Interviews, News & Gossip, Opinions, Entertainment Radio, plus letters and statistics. They also list the topics, events, and people most talked about for each week. During the Week in Review for August 17 to 21 the leading topics in descending order were: sex/scandal/politics, foreign affairs/terrorism, values/the media, the legal system, sports, the economy, gender relations, arts/entertainment, gossip/relations, and science/technical.

Internet radio meets the book world. While we're speaking about radio, Web book fans with the right equipment can now find a place to stop and listen at www.BookRadio.com. This is an online radio station broadcast exclusively over the Internet and loaded with programs devoted to books, authors, and the world of publishing. They have author readings, plus reviews and interviews. Their advertising says you can "find out about news stories that *don't* get coverage by the mainstream press." Give you any ideas? You can work this site two ways: as an informational mechanism (for instance, hear Dean Koontz talk about the process of writing, how characters drive the plot, and his methodical creative pace) and as a PR vehicle (send an email pitch to Adam@BookRadio.com).

Dynamite site for major radio contacts. Whether your authors write about computers, the political condition, African-American topics, whatever—mosey over to http://www.radiospace.com/programs.html. Talk and feast on the possibilities! Here you'll find links to sites regarding radio shows of all types in the U.S. and Canada . . . and the people behind them. Some of the stuff you can learn about the personalities, such as their hobbies and interests, may give you just the competitive edge needed to become a guest. It will take some diligence, but this site can lead you to wonderful possibilities for syndicated talk shows, nationally distributed public radio shows, other nationally syndicated offerings, plus popular local personalities and programs. Have fun!

Talk show host, while plugging an author's work on her show: "Once you put down one of her books, you can't pick it up again."

A different spin from radio. Marcia Yudkin tells of achieving a different promotional effect from radio. "This year I began doing commentaries on WBUR, the NPR-affiliated station in Boston that reaches a half-million listeners. I've done five three-minute personal essays that have aired so far. The topics have absolutely nothing to do with any of my books or with my consulting. Yet there has been a noticeable effect from a business standpoint.

"The first one I did, about music education, aired at 7:55 a.m. Precisely at 9:00 a.m. I received a call from a woman asking me to write a press release for her. She had previously learned of me from a neighbor, and hearing me on the radio prompted her to call. Fellow writers are surprised and really impressed. I expect my local seminar enrollments to grow this winter because of the exposure.

"Although I have no evidence that the radio essays have helped me sell books, I know that radio is a powerful medium for building a fan club. During the fall I presented a seminar at a bookstore in Vermont. The night before my seminar, a guy had done a reading who does commentaries for Vermont Public Radio. Two hundred fans of his showed up, some buying several copies of his book."

CHAPTER 9

Opening the Throttle: Touting Titles on TV

It's 9:00 A.M. Let the battle begin.

Currently there are 16 syndicated daytime and late-night TV talk shows. Donahue started the daytime talk show derby; Oprah took it to a fine edge; then Rosie jumped on the bandwagon. Recently, Roseanne, Howie Mandel, and Donny and Marie Osmond joined the ranks. Magic Johnson did a brief stint with his "Magic Hour," then was abruptly canceled.

So what do the TV talk show wars, with celebrity talkers serving as the generals, mean to authors and publishers? They can mean plenty. Those generals need troops to conquer their adversaries (other competing shows). So, in many cases—if your book touches on the 3T's: tragedy, transgression, or titillation—you're in! Or if you can find a hook to link your message to one of the 3T's, you may also join the victors.

The bad, the ugly, and the good

This is not to say that *all* TV talk is salacious. In September 1998, Oprah debuted a two-minute spot at the end of each show to complement her Change Your Life Television agenda. Viewers hear from celebrities and authors during this Remembering Your Spirit segment about such topics as reconnecting with yourself and doing something you find restorative.

Regis and Kathy Lee also prefer less lascivious fare, discussing food, medical topics, seasonal subjects, and interesting new products. Donny and Marie seek guests who are fun and can entertain their audience in some way. Says Marie, "This show is going to be very hip and upbeat and exciting."

On a much broader scale, millionaire Home Shopping Network cofounder Lowell "Bud" Paxson just launched the seventh national television network, Pax TV. It features upbeat, family-style programming. Some have already dubbed it the "good news" network. Further good news is that they expect to use a lot of authors with expertise on consumer-related topics or who have inspiring stories to tell.

The Fox Family Channel, another new kid on the block, has 11 hours of programming for children and families. Their Basement show is aimed at teens and tweens and accepts appropriate guests. And the Lifetime Channel has brought aboard New Attitudes, a daily 60-minute news magazine show dedicated to empowering women and girls.

Of course, capturing a spot on Good Morning America, This Morning, or The Today Show is a real coup.

Evenings we have additional choices. There is 60 Minutes, 20/20, and 48 Hours. And Dateline, the top-rated magazine show on the air, has now been expanded to five nights a week. You might try your hand at enticing the producers of Larry King Live, Charlie Rose, or the Late Late Show with Tom Snyder.

A few local markets still have early morning shows. It used to be easier to cut your teeth on local shows. We were on Sun Up in San Diego (where Regis began) many times, plus AM/Philadelphia, Good Morning in Boston, and This Day Show in Houston. Most of these programs have gone the way of the Edsel. Sunday mornings still offer some programming opportunities in smaller markets.

Strategizing for maximum results

Getting the right author on the right show can get books moving off shelves faster than a tumbleweed in a twister. Many of the tips we shared with you in the previous chapter on radio interviews also apply to TV. We won't bore you by repeating them here.

Just as you do secondary radio shows on Podunk, Idaho-type stations to gain experience, your local cable channel has public access programs where you can appear. Although these shows reach smaller audiences, they give you an opportunity to get comfortable in front of a camera and may prove effective if you have a regional guide book or a novel set in the area.

Once you've located the cable TV franchise in your community, "Call and ask about the possibilities of being a guest on one of their programs," advises Jim Cox of the *Midwest Book Review*. "Public access TV producers are *always* looking for camera fodder," he continues. "And it's a natural opportunity to become familiar with the studio setting with its lights, cameras, microphones, and people running around in the background."

Another suggestion of Jim's is to get a video cam. If you don't own one, a friend, neighbor, or family member probably does. Get someone to role play with you and do an interview. Then critique it. Did you have repetitive unconscious hand movements? Forget your 800 number? "These and a host of other interview flaws and snafues will be revealed—and solved—before going on the air for real," says Jim.

What do TV producers look for? Subject-wise they like stories involving one of the four following areas: health, heart, home, or pocketbook. Even if your book isn't specifically about one of these four areas, most messages can be appropriately "tweaked" with some creative thinking. The angle you present will either win you many appearances, or leave you as lonely as Cinderella when everyone else went to the ball. It's worth taking a lot of time and effort to come up with the right pitch.

We always preach "make it *easy* for people to do what you want them to do." This is especially important in TV. Rather than just pitching yourself as the ideal guest, think about putting together a whole show built around your topic. Then the producer's job is a cinch. Maybe it will be a panel of people you recommend. After all, you know your subject far better than any producer would, so you're the ideal person to bring together the leading experts on the topic.

Timeliness can also play a huge role. Your book needn't even be new if it addresses a hot topic. Keep abreast of the news and pounce on any issues relevant to your titles.

Because TV is such a visual medium, your pitch to them needs to vary from radio. Is there anything you could demonstrate? Can you suggest photos or other helpful visual materials? Watch the show, learn their format, then customize what you propose.

Producers love to see videos of authors (naturally you'll only send outstanding ones). Even this can present a problem, however. If you come across as a morning-show type, when you're hoping to do a funny stint on Letterman or Leno, you're pegged in the wrong slot. They can also get testy if they perceive their competition got you first.

Videotape your interview. When making final arrangements, ask the producer exactly what you need to supply to make a simultaneous dub while you're on the air. Most TV stations require Beta or other high-grade video. Of course, if you have a VCR that tapes, you can program it to record you, though this won't be as high quality.

Call the station the day before for directions. Schmooze a bit with the producer. While the host interviews you, the producer typically decides how much time you get! Speaking of time, always leave yourself plenty of travel leeway. And if you must deal with traffic at a time and location with which you're unfamiliar, make a dry run ahead of time.

Lights. Camera. Action.

"What do I wear?" is a question we hear often. Look the part. If you're discussing backpacking in the Swiss Alps, you'd look ridiculous in "dressed for success" mode. A colorful tie or scarf that calls attention to your face is a good idea. Overall, avoid patterns, stripes, plaids, herringbones, and paisleys. White can be bothersome. Ladies, leave the shiny or jangly jewelry at home. Gentlemen, be sure your socks match your shoes and are long enough so bare ankles don't show if you cross your legs. Wear something you feel good in so you can forget your appearance and concentrate on being absolutely awesome.

Take along an extra copy of your book. The one(s) you mailed often get lost—or taken home by staff who find them appealing.

Once at the studio, they'll put you in the Green Room to wait. Never have we been in one actually painted green. We've been in cubbyholes that didn't even have adequate chairs and we've been ushered into luxurious lounges where lavish free refreshments were offered.

You probably won't meet the host until a couple of minutes before you go on or until you are seated on the set. Connecting with the host helps in connecting with the audience. Naturally, viewers adore her or him, so you'll be more accepted if they sense a good rapport. In the few seconds when you're introduced, come across as warm and energetic.

Before you go on the air they may want—or *you* may suggest—a still shot of the book. (If they refuse, put your copy of the book on the coffee table in front of you, facing *out* toward the camera.) You could also ask for a crawler with your toll-free number, book title, or Web URL. (Chances are they'll say no, but you have nothing to lose by asking.)

On-the-air tips:

Smile, smile, smile. Unless, of course, you're there to talk about a tragic topic.

Look at the host or hostess, *not* the camera. It's the cameraperson's job to track you.

Assume you're always on camera from the second you sit down until you rise when the interview is over. Even though you may not be talking, the camera may pan to you. If you are fidgeting, looking disinterested, or appear smug, viewers won't like you and won't be inclined to buy your book.

Be alert to your facial expression and body language. Slouching sends a negative message. It's better to almost perch on the edge.

"Energy up." Be purposefully twice as animated and enthusiastic than usual. When you watch the tape you'll be amazed that you don't seem at all artificial.

Write your toll-free phone number on the inside of your hand. (Sound like school days?) It's easy to go blank when you're under stress; this way you can simply glance down if necessary.

Don't turn the interview into a commercial. Offer viewers real value.

Know your two or three main points backward and forward and articulate them concisely.

The best investment you can make if you want to really shine on TV is to get Brian Jud's *You're on the Air: Perform Like a Pro on Television & Radio*. This is a toolbox of information like no other. The program includes a 90-minute video of interviews with producers, hosts, and executives from major national shows: Larry King Live, Good Morning America, Maury Povich, CBS This Morning, The Charlie Rose Show, etc. There is also a media coach who reveals special techniques to prepare you to be sensational on the air. Two written companion guides have tips, checklists, and advice on how to organize a promotional tour and locate the right contact person. It's all available for $99 by calling 800-331-8355.

If radio and TV play a major role in your marketing plans, it's also wise to get professional media coaching. There are men and women who specialize in helping publishers and authors pinpoint how to pitch their books—then groom the authors on what to expect, how to "wow" audiences, and translate that success into book sales. One of our favorites for radio is Joel Roberts. You can reach him at 310-286-0631.

Will they pay your expenses? Probably not. Some do; others don't. But always ask about transportation, room, and hotel with big shows. One way around this a few prominent authors choose to take is to join AFTRA. Members of the American Federation of Television and Radio Artists are paid scale: $553 when appearing on a half-hour show, $703 for an hour. These are people expert in their fields and are considered Professional Performers. The AFTRA initiation fee is $1,042.50, and dues for six months run $42.50. For more details call 212-532-0800.

What kind of results can you expect from TV? Authors who have been prominently featured on Oprah, have seen their books soar to bestseller status. Other authors who also appeared on her show found sales to be slim, so being on Oprah doesn't automatically sell books. What does sell books is capitalizing on that exposure.

As soon as you're booked on a big show, tell the world! Alert all the chain buyers so they can get the book in stock immediately. Phone, write, fax, and email major independents, wholesalers, newspapers, and magazines in your niche. Promote your appearance and your book everywhere. Momentum is a beautiful thing to behold.

C-SPAN2's BookTV debuts. For those who enjoy literate TV, and especially those seeking wider exposure for authors and titles, the C-SPAN2 network's escalation of its weekend coverage to a full 48 hours is marvelous news. (They've folded "About Books" into this coverage, but "Booknotes" remains the same.) BookTV is now on the air from 8:00 A.M. every Saturday (eastern time) until 8:00 A.M. Monday.

Program coverage includes author readings; live signings; other book world events; tours of unique bookstores and libraries; plus interviews with authors, editors, and publishers. They will also cover serious nonfiction books focusing on biography, history, politics, and social issues. A live call-in show will anchor the evening hours.

To suggest a program idea, contact producer Robin Scullin at 400 North Capital Street, NW, Suite 650, Washington DC 20001; phone 202-626-6124; fax 202-737-6226.

Suffer from stage fright? One author's husband suggested she tell herself that only one person is watching the show: a sweet little lady in Kansas City who has the TV set on in the background as she irons. Then challenge yourself to be so interesting that the lady will put aside her ironing and start watching in earnest.

Lack of listening ability of game-show host:
"Tell me a bit about yourself. What do you do?"
Contestant: Well, I'm a widow . . .
Host: Oh, great, that's great!

A bonanza for book lovers. Booklink is just what it says: links to other book sites. This is a fabulous place for locating out-of-print books, finding specialty bookstores around the world, and perusing fascinating book sites in general. Go to http://www.gold.net/users/ds36/booklink. html. Enjoy!

Free databases await you online at http://www.gebbieinc.com/. Gebbie Press, publishers of the useful *All-in-One Directory*, provide TV and weekly newspaper databases for free. Included are 3,284 email addresses for radio and TV stations. Lots of value at this site.

PART III

Muscling Your Way into Traditional Channels

Outdistancing Distribution Doldrums: How to Capture Booksellers, Wholesalers, and Distributors

In a magical world, elves, leprechauns, Easter bunnies, and tooth fairies bring delights to the deserving. In the book business, success comes to those who establish viable channels of distribution. The world will *not* beat a path to your door. (Unless, of course, you're in the bathroom.) Happily, no matter how small or unknown you might be, you *can* play in this arena.

Let us first lay some ground rules so we're all talking the same language. Many authors and small publishers are confused about how distribution works in the publishing industry. There are actually four possible levels:

Trade distribution channels

1. Bookstores. This encompasses both the big chains, such as Barnes & Noble and Borders, and independents (also referred to throughout this book as "indies"). With rare exceptions, they don't want to purchase from you directly. Dealing with a one- or two-book publisher is too much hassle and paperwork. That does not mean, however, that they won't take your book. If Barnes & Noble, for instance, wish to place an order, they will send you a list of their approved vendors. You then simply line up with one of them, which is easy once you have a stocking order from B&N.

Bookstores in your area will often buy directly from you initially at a 40% discount for five or more books. But if the book sells through, they will typically go to a wholesaler or distributor subsequently as it is easier for them to place one large order than multiple small ones.

2. Wholesalers. The largest national wholesaler is Ingram, which caters mainly to bookstores; the second largest is Baker & Taylor, which serves mostly libraries. Both have several branches and rally for a 55% discount. We'll discuss these two behemoths in more depth later. There are also many other wholesalers, both national and regional, that may place small orders with you and typically pay net 60 or 90.

3. Distributors. They are similar to wholesalers in function, but their terms are different. They take your books on consignment, want a 55% discount, and pay you approximately 90 days after the books are sold. Although the concept of consignment sounds scary, we've sold many books via these nonexclusive distributors.

4. Master—or exclusive—distributors. There are currently nine large recognized master distributors. (A list of them appears in the Appendix.) When one accepts you (no easy task), they become solely responsible for selling your books to all other distributors, wholesalers, bookstores, usually libraries, and sometimes the gift market. They have catalogs, exhibit at trade shows, and have sales reps who present your books to buyers, so you have more personal attention.

For this privilege you pay around 65% of the retail price of the book. Of course, they must give discounts of from 40 to 50% so this isn't all gravy for them. Most of them also offer toll-free numbers and accept credit cards for consumer orders. They not only sell your books, they store them, fulfill all orders, and handle invoicing. You receive a monthly report and check about 90 days after the sale.

Going with a master distributor can be good—or bad. All your eggs are in one basket. Several master distributors have gone bankrupt, taking little publishers with them who were not paid for books sold and whose inventory was confiscated by the courts. Of course, if you haven't priced your book properly, you may find yourself losing money on every book they sell.

However, many independent publishers swear by their master distributors and feel they could never have reached the sales volume they've achieved without such an arrangement. It would be like trying to lasso a locomotive with cobwebs.

If you decide to go this route, check out candidates carefully. One good way is to request a copy of their catalog, then pick three smaller publishers at random who publish similar titles. Call them and ask about their level of satisfaction. Is the distributor's staff responsive? Do they pay according to the terms of the agreement? Have the books sold well? Are there hidden costs such as storage fees or requirements for paying for advertising in catalogs or for having their books exhibited at BookExpo America?

Then ask the distributor for their bank of record and account number. Call the operations officer and inquire about bounced checks and other undesirable financial history. Not all cooperate, but some do.

Once you've found a happy marriage between someone you want and an organization that is excited about your book, talk with your distributor early about the price point, cover design, promotion plans, etc. Their feedback can be invaluable. They have knowledge of the marketplace you'll never obtain. Work far out. Master distributors need cover mockups and sales copy many months in advance for listing your books in their catalogs.

And remember that you and your master distributor are partners. Develop a relationship not only with the buyer but also with their sales reps, publicity coordinator, the people in the warehouse, and secretarial assistants. These people are extensions of your company. Communicate! Keep them informed of important reviews, major media about to break, etc. The sales reps will use your good news as ammunition to get larger buys from the chains, jobbers, and wholesalers.

Sometimes you can catch the coattails of a larger publisher that publishes in your niche.
For this book we established an exclusive distribution arrangement with Writer's Digest Books/F&W Publications, Inc., which publishes our *Complete Guide to Self-Publishing*. It's a win/win alliance as booksellers already know and love our self-publishing title, so *Jump Start Your Book Sales* will be a natural companion book. While they handle the trade, we can concentrate on generating lots of publicity, selling via direct mail to our in-house list, and plumbing nontraditional outlets.

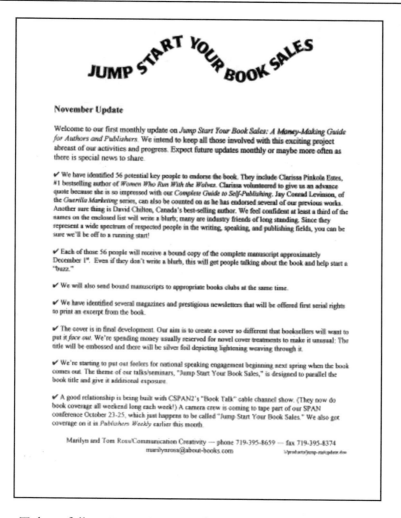

To keep folks at WDB/F&W informed and excited about this book, we began sending key players in the organization colorful one-page monthly newsgrams in October of 1998—five months before the book was to come off the press. (See the adjacent sample.) Although it seems very early, that is when the sales activity gears up. If you delay until you have books, you'll be left standing on the shore waiting for your ship to come in . . . after it has sailed.

When we give seminars, we're frequently asked, "How can I get my book into bookstores?" That's the wrong question. The real question is, "How can you get your book *out* of bookstores? You see no bookstore, wholesaler, distributor, or master distributor wants you unless you have a carefully plotted campaign for marketing the book. How are you going to sell that puppy? You need to be so passionate, so dedicated, so clever you could almost convince the Pope to switch to the Methodist Church. The tiny sliver of spine showing on shelves won't make consumers gobble it up by the thousands. It is up to you to create customer demand via publicity and promotion.

If you don't do this, the 600-pound gorilla called "Returns" will literally squash you. In this business a book isn't sold—even if it is sold and paid for—until a year has past. There is an atrocious industry standard that says any of the above entities can return your book if it doesn't sell. They will demand credit if you have several titles, or their money back if you're a self-publisher. Returns, which used to run 10 to 25%, mushroomed to around 35% in 1997, sending many publishers into financial chaos. They have leveled off some now.

Returns have caused some small presses to go out of business. Imagine this scenario: You spend $10,000 to print 5,000 books. Through aggressive merchandising, you manage to sell 2,000 to Barnes & Noble and another 2,000 to Borders. Good heavens, you have only 1,000 books left for review copies, direct mail, to fulfill radio orders, etc. Encouraged by this strong early response, you go back to press, spend another $10,000, and print 5,000 more copies. You get paid by the two chains. You're in fat city! Three months later the returns start rolling in. Ultimately you get back 3,500 of the original 4,000 sold. Of course, the chains want their money refunded. You have around 8,000 books nobody seems to want, a bill that feels like the national debt, and no way to repay it.

That is one of the main reasons we preach generating a demand for the book via nontraditional channels rather than initially focusing most of your attention on bookstores. Rest assured, when people come into the bookstores in any number asking for your book, the buyers will find *you*. Besides, the majority of Americans never go into a bookstore. They buy books at warehouse clubs, through catalogs, book clubs, on the Internet, and in specialty retail stores that cater to their individual interests.

Independents versus chain stores

The Christian Science Monitor reported in December of 1997 that independent bookstores have lost half their market share in the past five years. Hundreds closed their doors. It was like driving against traffic on a one-way street. The survivors have learned to be tougher merchandisers. They've added cafes, created more community alliances and events, wooed their customers with even greater attention. Authors such as Lisa See, Patrick McManus, Jacquelyn Mitchard, and Esther Dyson comment that independents are vital to their success.

Staff recommendations offer great promise for small presses and assertive authors. Independent booksellers are famous for hand selling books. When they read something they like, they suggest it to their customers, whose tastes they know and understand. Thus, sending complimentary reading copies can pay big dividends. It's a good idea to include a hand written note from the author or editor. If there is a local connection, be sure to mention it.

One bookseller was responsible for selling 1,500 copies of Sarah Smith's mystery, *The Vanished Child.* This honor goes to Christy Pascoe of San Francisco's A Clean Well-Lighted Place. Imagine if you could duplicate even a fraction of this success with indies in many major cities. There is no question that praise from independents for Robert Waller's *Bridges of Madison County* is what helped it develop "legs" and climb onto bestseller lists.

During the same five-year period so many indies perished, the number of superstores increased 712%. The chains are here to stay and they have changed the face of bookselling. As we go to press, Barnes & Noble leads the pack with a total of 1,011 mall and superstores. In their mall group are B. Dalton, Doubleday, and Scribner's. Their superstores include Barnes & Noble, Bookstop, and Bookstar. All of their buying is done by category and there are some 40 buyers spread across both groups.

Competition to be accepted is stiff. The overall presentation must shout "quality" from the writing to the editing, the jacket design to the interior layout. How does it stand up to other competition in the category? What are the publisher's pertinent marketing or promotion plans?

If you don't have a distributor, it's wise to contact B&N for a new title buy sheet at least 120 days before the publication date. Send along a fact sheet describing your book, a color copy of the cover, any advance reviews or testimonials, plus full publicity plans.

One bit of encouraging news is their statistics show that 47% of their sales were of books from the big conglomerate houses while 53% came from independent publishers! (A separate submission must be made for their online bookstore. See information later in this chapter.)

Another encouraging fact is that free promotion is available to selected novelists; and independent press authors have an equal chance at being selected. Four times a year Barnes & Noble chooses around 20 obscure authors for their Discover Great New Writers program. Those selected are featured in a 16-page pamphlet given to B&N shoppers. This often leads to great regional publicity. To find out the next deadline, call Kelle Ruden at 212-633-3511. Be prepared to send three galley copies, cover art, catalog copy, author bio, any advance reviews, a tip sheet, and specific publicity and touring plans. Mail to her at Discover Great New Writers Program, 122 Fifth Avenue, New York, NY 10011.

The second huge chain is the Borders group. It includes Waldenbooks, Brentanos, and the Readers Market. They have 244 Borders superstores and about 900 Waldens. Although getting the attention of headquarters seems to be difficult, one small press found the way in via her local store. The manager liked her book, called the home office and asked them to list it in the computer. So make friends with your local manager or buyer if you're having a tough time scaling the walls.

Books-A-Million is the number three chain bookstore. The Crown chain has closed many of its stores and is currently in bankruptcy proceedings. In Canada, Chapters (which also owns Coles and Smith) has 250 stores. See contact information for all four in the Appendix.

Working with the two major wholesalers

Ingram Book Company welcomes small publishers. For those who publish 10 or less titles per year and want to get into Ingram, you can find all the details about the Ingram Express program on their Web site. Go to http://www.ingrambook.com. From the main menu choose "Ingram publisher services." Click on "Ingram Express". Next choose "Click here for information on how publishers can get started with Ingram." At that point you'll have access to more information than you possibly know what to do with. Seriously, it gives all the particulars about the program, a marketing plan to fill out, a copy of their agreement, etc. There are no shortcuts; you must complete all their paperwork and agree to their terms.

If you don't have Web access, you can call their new submission line at 615-213-5350 or 800-937-8222, ext. 35369. The person currently responsible for this program is Phil Frazer, Title Expansion Manager, Publisher Relations Department, Ingram Distribution Group, One Ingram Boulevard, La Vergne, TN 37086. Reach him directly at ext. 35369, fax 615-213-5565, or email phil.frazer@ingrambook.com.

We're delighted they put together a program opening this important channel of distribution for new and small publishers who produce quality products and publicize them well.

To qualify, a book must have an ISBN, EAN Bookland barcode, the price printed on the cover, and the title on the spine. Once demand has been established, you'll be moved over to their regular status.

Baker & Taylor, though catering mainly to libraries, also crosses over into the bookstore market. Their headquarters and main facility is in Charlotte, North Carolina. They also have service centers in Reno, Nevada; Momence, Illinois; and Commerce, Georgia. To work with B&T you'll need to complete a Vendor Profile Questionnaire, give them a 55% discount, accept payment in 90 days, pay the freight, and accept returns for 100% credit. Occasionally, a publisher with books ideally suited to the library market can negotiate a shorter discount of 20 to 40%.

For full information contact Sally Neher, manager, Publishers Services, Baker & Taylor, 44 Kirby Avenue, POB 734, Somerville, NJ 08876-0734; phone 908-218-3863; fax 908-704-9315. They normally charge a fee of $125 to get you set up on their database. If you're a new publisher, we may be able to save you that expense.

In 1996 we decided to give something back to this industry that has been so good to us for over 22 years. So we launched a nonprofit professional trade association called the Small Publishers Association of North America (SPAN). We've grown to over 1,100 members, put out a meaty 24-page monthly newsletter, and offer our members many cost-saving benefits.

SPAN has an agreement with Baker & Taylor whereby they will waive the $125 fee for our members who agree to put that money toward marketing their books and provide B&T with four free stocking copies. It's a real win-win arrangement. To learn more about the association and request a free sample newsletter, visit our Web site at http://www.spannet.org, call 719-395-4790, or fax 719-395-8374.

Online booksellers offer additional opportunities

Amazon.com, the Big Kahuna of book e-commerce, cultivates the favor of small publishers. They want not only mainstream titles but also diverse and undiscovered books. The Amazon.com Advantage Program developed by Dan Camacho empowers independent publishers and authors to sell more product online. Even if your books are already listed—and they may be without you doing a thing because amazon.com scours *Books in Print* and other resources—it may make sense to participate in their new approach to Internet merchandising.

They level the playing field for little people. You can make the information about your title(s) as rich as any from Random House or Simon & Schuster. Supply everything they allow: book cover for scanning, cover sales copy, Table of Contents if it is nonfiction, excerpts, official reviews, reviews from your readers and friends (If you like this book, we hope you'll do a review for us!), publisher's statement, author's statement, etc. When a customer comes a-callin' they look for the most interesting book; they could care less who published it. So let your light shine!

With this innovative plan, small publishers will have inventory on hand with the online bookstore so orders can be filled within 24 hours—just like the major publishers—rather than the usual 4 to 6 weeks. Immediate availability translates into more sales. Statistics show that customers are more likely to purchase books they can get quickly.

Participation in the Amazon.com Advantage Program is free. Participating titles are assigned subject classifications to help give the books more visibility in amazon.com's rich subject browsing features and niche bestseller lists. (They have some 2,000 bestseller lists. Just think, while you'll probably never land on *The New York Times* or *Publishers Weekly's* bestseller lists, you could be number one on amazon.com's bestseller list of books about teddy bears or mathematical physics.)

And it's an easy way to develop a global marketplace for your titles—without *you* having to fool with all the foreign shipping hassles. Other pluses are access to aggregate daily updated sales data and quick payment. You give a hefty 55% discount off the retail price and pay the shipping. Of course, no one thing is a panacea, but this is another possible notch in your overall marketing belt.

With its 4 million books, amazon.com is not only the number one online bookstore but consistently ranks as the Web's most visited retailer. For full particulars on this new program, go to www.amazon.com/advantage. You must have email and Web access to participate. Of course, you can also sell to them at standard bookstore discounts and save 15%, but they will show your titles as not being readily available.

They also have a program called amazon.com/associates that pays referral fees to Web sites that link to it and send book-buying customers to their site. If you can't have, or don't want, orders processed on your site, this option will put a little extra jingle in your pocket.

BarnesandNoble.com offers similar options through their Affiliate Program. They also pay a small commission when you send business their way. While they don't have anything like the Advantage Program, they did put information up on several of our books, which we embellished.

They book authors for online author events "through their publishing houses or publicists." To initiate a request, your publicist should email the title, publishing date, and ISBN to Elke Villa, manager, Interactive at evilla@book.com. BarnesandNoble.com is located at 76 9th Ave., New York, NY 10011, phone 212-414-6000.

Our inquiry to Borders resulted in this email: "At this time, we do not have a specific program for independent publishers to get their titles listed at Borders.com. However, we automatically list all books listed in *Books in Print*."

Book Stacks Unlimited, though not as well known as the former sites, is another strong online bookseller with over 10,000 customers visiting daily. They were recently bought by a much larger company so watch for more action from this site. Their director of publisher relations is Jack Bashian. Reach him at jbashian@books.com or by calling 216-694-5741. He will provide you with full instructions on how to list and promote your books via their site. Check first, however, at http://www.books.com. If your titles are carried by Ingram or Baker & Taylor, they are probably already up. Of course, that doesn't mean you won't want to annotate and enhance them.

The five reasons bookstore customers buy books. 1) Word-of-mouth recommendations, 2) reviews, ads, publicity, 3) browsing the store, usually by subject or author, 4) because of window displays, dumps, end caps, or books placed face out, and 5) from staff recommendations.

Try "reverse shoplifting!" Greg Godek, author of the best-selling *1,001 Ways to Be Romantic* and several sequels, has a novel way of getting his book into bookstores. He "plants" them there—face out of course. His rationale is when customers go to purchase them at the cash register it will create havoc on the computer since it won't appear in inventory, thus bringing his book to the attention of store personnel.

Should you *under*sell your exclusive distributor? We know a publisher whose distributor placed a big reorder for her book. To fulfill that order, the publisher would have had to go back to press. When she really pinned down the distributor, however, it turned out they really only needed 10% of what they had told her. The moral is to get realistic orders not necessarily big orders.

Chains often call the shots. *The New York Times* recently reported that many large publishers are turning to the major chain stores for consultation on a variety of publishing decisions. They seek feedback on covers, titles, sales history of a given author, etc. Sometimes book contracts are actually canceled if chain buyers are lukewarm about the book. Thank goodness independent presses are capable of more individual thinking.

Bestsellerdom. "What is a bestseller?" we're often asked. There is no simple answer. Sure it's clear cut when a book lands on one of the top three bestseller lists: *The New York Times, Publishers Weekly,* or *USA Today.* But there are dozens of other "bestseller" lists. Ingram has them, so do most other wholesalers. Amazon.com has lots of them for very definitive topics. Many newspapers run ones representing their area. Bookstores often have their own. *Entrepreneur* magazine has a business bestseller list . . . and it goes on and on.

Books targeted as bestsellers have the shelf life of milk. They live the compressed existence of butterflies. For a brief period they are discussed, admired, recommended, touted, publicized. Then the window of opportunity is gone and they return to oblivion. Occasionally, books that are on the bestseller list in January end up in remainder bins in June.

Surprisingly, a book can sometimes make a major bestseller list with maybe only 35,000 copies sold if the competition that week is very light. Yet other books, whose titles will never see the type of a bestseller list, might sell a million copies. They do it through direct mail. So "bestsellers" come in many varieties and often don't ever appear on the official lists.

Make a big local splash. Virtually all bookstores have a special section for books by local authors, so capitalize on being an area writer. Always make store managers or buyers aware of the local tie-in. They constantly seek new books to keep that section fresh. Also tell them of local publicity as this often triggers them to display your book more predominantly.

Refine your mini sales call. When you phone a book buyer you have 30 to 60 seconds to make your pitch. It needs to be succinct and powerful. Tell them first who the market is for this book and how many potential buyers there are. (Yes, this is going to take some homework. Hopefully, you determined that a sizeable and reachable market existed *before* you decided to publish the title.) What is the benefit to the consumer—what problem will it solve? How is this book different from the competition? Cover these points briefly, take pride in your pithiness, and chances are you'll have the spark you need to succeed.

You know what Alfred Knopf once said about book returns: "Gone today, here tomorrow."

Penetrating airport stores. This is certainly not a market for all titles. Best-selling fiction gets most of the shelf space. But area cookbooks, local tour guides, gambling books, humor, and business titles also stand a chance. Here's how it works in most airports: The concessions, whether they be for food, books, or miscellaneous, are tightly controlled by the local airport commission. It awards the contract to the highest bidder, usually one of a few big companies that will generate the most dollars for the space allotted. (See the list in the Appendix.) In turn, they usually contract with local wholesalers, who also bid for the business. By the time everybody takes their cut, the margins are very slim.

The manager of a store typically has little say over whether a title is carried or not. Talk to them, however, to determine who really makes the buying decisions. The buyer's primary concern is margin and salability. Here is where a smaller publisher may have an advantage. You can raise the price of your book for this market by stickering the cover with a higher figure. Then everybody gets a little more profit and you are in a preferred position.

Obtaining and wooing sales reps. If you publish several title each year, an organization of commissioned sales reps, or individual reps themselves, may be interested in taking on your line. They then present it to bookstores and wholesalers. Besides the normal discounts, the sales reps typically get 10% of the list price on all bookstore sales in their territories (regardless of how they originate) and 5% of sales to wholesalers.

Sales reps in various regions can also be lifesavers when it comes to targeting the best stores for signings or the most effective media in major cities. Karen Misuraca tells of a Toronto rep faxing her a fantastic list of media, with hot prospects starred. He also explained which were the biggest and best indies and even offered to set up the events!

To learn more about using reps and how to reach them, contact the National Association of Independent Publishers Representatives (NAIPR), Ralph Woodward, Executive Secretary, Zeckendorf Towers, 111 East 14 Street, PMB 157, New York, NY 10003; phone 508-877-5328; fax 508-788-0208; email naipr@aol.com.

Once you have reps—whether through the above action, or individuals who work with your exclusive distributor—treat them like gold. Your sales can go from deuces to aces if the reps love your book. First off, educate them. Provide a sales kit for each new title. It should include a finished color cover, reviews and advance blurbs, a tip or fact sheet, table of contents (for nonfiction), an author bio including his or her hometown, an overview of who the market is, and sales bullets or a hook that summarizes the book. Forget the hype. Provide a nuts and bolts description.

But don't give up after this initial push. Keep them in the loop about what you have planned for publicity. Fax them copies of good reviews. If you stay visible, your book has a better chance of being remembered and well plugged. United we sell; divided we die.

Books-A-Million puts out its hand big time. Not only will BAM gladly take your money for in-store promotions such as "marquee posters" at the exits of all stores for $3,500 per month, they've come up with a multitude of creative options to lighten publishers' wallets. Sixty-second advertising spots in their product knowledge videos are $600; a five-minute spot on their training video is $2,500.

Want to be in the Books-A-Million Christmas catalog? Get ready to shell out $3,000. Or you can advertise on their trucks (yes, you read right) to the tune of $1,500 for one truck, $3,500 for four, and $6,200 for eight. Maybe you'd like your book or publishing image on the side of coffee cups in BAM cafes. A mere $3,000 gets you on 100,000 cups. You can sponsor lunch or a cocktail reception at their employee management seminars for a paltry $6,000. Dinner for this group? Eight thousand smackers. And the list goes on and on.

And they're not alone. At Borders it costs between $1,500 and $2,500 a month to have a book positioned in the front of the store and sold at a 30% discount. Everybody's doing it. B. Dalton, Doubleday, and

Scribners get publishers to fork over $12,000 a month to put their bestsellers in the front of the store. Barnes & Noble's section, Discover Great New Writers, allows books there if the publisher pays $1,500. Needless to say, independent publishers must find more creative ways to stand out.

Printing sell sheets for your distributor(s)? We've found these 8½- by 11-inch flyers can be an effective way to let booksellers know about your books. If you're printing a quantity anyway, tack on 500 when you go to press. Quality Books, the library distributor, is willing to include them in customer mailings to see how it works. If the results are positive, they'll move ahead cautiously. Check with Carolyn Olson at (815) 732-4450 or email her at carolyn.olson@dawson.com for details. A good source for affordable full-color flyers is Tu-Vets Corporation. Get prices at 800-894-8977 and tell Henry we said to call.

Hard work pays off in the future. Laziness pays off now.

Are you utilizing Freddie and Cecil to your advantage? No, these aren't the names of men or pets. They are Ingram programs that give you accurate book sales information on your titles.

Freddie is an automatic stock-status checker for publishers. By calling 615-287-6803 and entering your book's ISBN, you can gather information on title status, quantity available, quantity on order, sales for current year, sales for the past year, demand for the current week, even demand for the previous week.

Not only can you do this for *your* titles, but you can use it as a wonderful measurement of how your competition stacks up by entering *their* ISBNs! It's also helpful if you're considering reprinting so you can estimate Ingram's usage.

Cecil is primarily for booksellers but can yield valuable data to you as well. By calling 800-937-0995 you will find out how many books each of Ingram's distribution centers has in stock, and the number sold so far this year. And again, you can do reconnaissance on how your competition is doing. Curious about how many books amazon.com is moving? Get a general idea by tuning into the figures for Ingram's Roseburg, Oregon, distribution center, which supplies amazon.com.

One smart publisher we know checked *Cecil* to determine the inventory level at various warehouses before embarking on a radio tour. Learning his stock was depleted and probably wouldn't cover demand, he immediately faxed off a schedule of radio interviews to his master distributor, who then notified Ingram. In turn, Ingram restocked four warehouses to meet demand.

Looking for a *literary* wholesaler? The sole remaining one in the country has moved to a larger facility and doubled its warehousing space. If you do fiction or poetry, contact Small Press Distribution, Inc. at 1341 7th Street, Berkeley, CA 94710-1403; phone 510-524-1668; fax 510-524-0852.

Save your inventory from bankrupt distributors! If you have books, audios, or videos on consignment with miscellaneous distributors, or have an exclusive agreement with a master distributor, there is a special form you should file to protect your inventory in case the company goes bankrupt. This lifesaver is called a UCC1 (Uniform Commercial Code) form. It can be obtained at most stationery stores that sell legal forms, you can ask your distributor if they might have one, or check with the Secretary of State (look in the White or Yellow Pages for a phone number).

In talking with the attorney who handled Pacific Pipeline's demise, she indicated that of the 3,500 vendors involved, virtually none had filed UCC1 forms! If they had, they would have gotten their books back immediately. So you can see the power of this secret weapon for publishers. If you're unsure of how to complete the form, invest an hour with a smart business attorney for guidance. It could be the best money you've ever spent. Filling the form out correctly and keeping it current can save you thousands of dollars in lost books. There is a small filing fee involved. The list of distributors who have gone out of business—and left publishers unable to access their inventory and holding an empty bank bag—grows ever longer. Use this information to protect yourself!

What drives book sales? Most people would say distribution is crucial. We disagree. You can have excellent distribution—and end up with enormous returns. *Consumer demand* is what's crucial. If people are asking for your books, the booksellers will find a way to get them in inventory. Bookstores are bottom-line operators. If you create the demand, they'll find a way to supply. Word-of-mouth is sooooooo important. Give away complimentary copies. Do constant publicity. Create a buzz. When consumers start asking for books, they suddenly appear on the shelves.

Locating wholesalers online. The Combined Book Exhibit site has put together a list of dozens of wholesalers and distributors. Don't think this is a list of recommendations; it is simply for informational purposes. But it may help you locate some additional companies to contact about selling your books. Besides company name, address, phone, and fax, there are also links to available email addresses and URLs. Everything happens at http://www.combinedbook.com/.

The other day I felt so confused that I signed up for reincarnation life insurance.

Access over 4,500 independent bookstores through the American Booksellers Association's CIBON Bookstore Directory at http://www.bookweb. org/. Creating a "buzz"—generating word-of-mouth excitement—is a proven way to sell books, especially novels. Independents that have gotten behind books have been largely responsible for catapulting them onto bestseller lists by hand selling them. Now there is an easy way to identify and reach leading indies with reading copies and promotional materials.

The Comprehensive Independent Booksellers Online Network includes physical addresses and descriptions of their focus as well as online links. Browsing here could be a very productive marketing approach. Should you be doing a regional book or want to contact major indies in an area where you have media scheduled, you can also search by state, city, even postal code to locate stores geographically.

This is also a goldmine of 33 genre-specific categories. You can find bookstores by specialty, going directly to those that feature mystery, sci/fi, or audio, for instance. And for nonfiction, there is health, museum, new age, scientific and technical, travel, cooking, computers, you name it.

Los Angeles displaces New York as top book market. According to a ranking recently released from the ABA Research Department, the L.A./ Long Beach metropolitan area supplanted New York as the nation's biggest book market. This is good news for independent presses, a lot more of which operate out of the west coast than the east coast. More of us are now likely to be where the majority of the action is. By doing a "regional" marketing plan we can actually influence the nation's largest market segment. And costs to do media tours are far lower in California than New York. In ranking order, the top U.S. book-buying areas are: Los Angeles, New York, Chicago, Boston, Washington DC, Philadelphia, San Francisco, Seattle, San Jose, and San Diego.

CHAPTER 11

High-Voltage Ideas for Getting on the Library Speedway

Publishers and authors who neglect this channel of distribution often cheat themselves out of a lightning-bolt 20% increase in their sales! Libraries can be one of your best friends. Yet they are frequently overlooked and undervalued. The public library, rather than the Internet, continues to be a source of entertainment for millions. Libraries provide a cultural center for the community.

What is in the most demand? Library patrons love bestsellers, of course, but they also want to read first novels and midlist fiction. How-tos, health/medicine, science, history, home repair/building, biographies, reference, finance, children's books, the classics, computer/Internet, and armchair travel titles are all popular. Some volumes are naturals for libraries. *The Book of U.S. Government Jobs* has sold more than 125,000 copies. Vic Richards of Bookhaven Press reports that 25% of those sales are made up of libraries.

What's so good about libraries?

First, library sales are final; you needn't worry about returns. Second, there is often repeat business. Library books only survive so many "turns." The book must be replaced after repeated handling by patrons. According to a recent *Library Journal*-sponsored survey, nearly two-third of libraries weed and replace outdated or damaged books each year and spend about 7% of their budget on replacement copies. Stolen books must also be replaced. (This is not to suggest you should steal your books!) Libraries are key in keeping good backlist books viable, visible, and in print.

Third, and of particular interest, is that many times they buy multiple copies, more even than many bookstores. For instance, the Broward County Public Library (PL) in Ft. Lauderdale, Florida, bought 363 copies of Pat Conroy's *Beach Music* for its 33 libraries. Seattle PL took 50 copies for its 24 libraries while Memphis' Shelby County PL and Information Center gobbled up 120 copies for the 22 libraries in its system.

Fourth, people who don't normally frequent bookstores are regular library users. They often find books they want to own or give as gifts. We've been told by scores of readers that they discovered our *Complete Guide to Self-Publishing* in the library, then purchased a personal copy.

Fifth, libraries are equally interested in paperbacks as hardcovers. It used to be they only bought cloth books. But today they want to spread their budgets farther, so paperbacks are very popular. The pricier hardback books are sometimes so poorly bound that they need to be sent to the bindery after only a couple of circulations. Paperbacks don't usually wear out until after a half dozen uses.

Sixth, the well is *not* running dry. The February 15, 1998, issue of *Library Journal* told of a survey that showed more than half of the libraries (56%) stated they have more money to spend on books this year than last.

Timing does affect their decisions. Where the library is in their fiscal year will impact their likelihood of buying. If they are near the end and still have money in the budget, you're in luck. While not all run on the same fiscal schedule, normally the best time for them to order is late summer or fall.

What do they want?

It might be easier to say what they do *not* want:

■ They don't want books with fill-in-the-blanks. Why? The first patron who checks it out does the exercises and spoils it for everyone else.

■ They don't want spiral or comb binding, or saddle-stitching.

- They don't want material in three-ring binders, part of which patrons can appropriate.
- They don't want nonfiction books without indexes.
- They don't want hyperbole. Tell them the facts and stress good reviews.
- They don't want to be kept in the dark if the book has an area tie-in. A local author, local setting of the novel, etc. will create extra demand they want to be able to meet.
- They don't want schlocky-looking books. Quality is a must.

How do you influence librarians?

Librarians are very review-driven. If you capture favorable comments in *Library Journal, Booklist, Publishers Weekly, Kirkus, Choice,* or *School Library Journal,* librarians will be much more likely to purchase your books. Ninety-six percent rely mostly on reviews in these trade journals. Ofttimes they are required to justify their purchases by citing such reviews.

Their second most mentioned reason for making purchases is patron requests (90%). These carry lots of weight. Nothing creates greater demand within a library than having their customers come in and ask for your titles. Seattle tries to maintain a ratio of one copy of a title for every five requests it receives. In some libraries that ratio drops down to a lovely two or three requests. Then they'll buy a copy.

Can you impact this issue? You bet! When sending holiday cards, suggest your friends call not only bookstores but also area *libraries* to request your book. When people call or write to rave about your titles, ask them to do you a favor: Call two local libraries and two local bookstores and request the book. And when your authors are on talk shows, have them mention to the audience to ask for your book at their local library.

Besides the major review mechanisms, there are a number of lesser-known trade journals, newsletters, and regional publications librarians read. Seek them out by researching in your library (of course!). Look carefully. Some small library journals can fill in nicely behind key ones in your niche. Be sure they receive review copies for consideration; competition is much lighter here.

How else do libraries make buys? There are two main distributors that inform them about independent publishers' books. Quality Books Inc. has been in business for more than 33 years and houses about 12,000 titles from small presses. They have 20 sales reps who constantly make personal calls on librarians. They receive about 2,500 unsolicited books each month and select perhaps a fourth of them. You'll need to complete a form to work with them and, if accepted, furnish 30 copies of your book's cover or dust jacket. Contact Quality at 1003 West Pines Road, Oregon, IL 61061-9680; phone 815-732-4450; fax 815-732-4499.

Unique Books began in 1985 and functions similarly. Reach them at 5010 Kemper Avenue, St. Louis, MO 63139; phone 314-776-6695; fax 314-776-0841.

Librarians become aware of titles to order via ads in magazines, surfing the Internet, catalogs from publishers or distributors, telemarketing, and direct mail. Some small publishers create flyers to promote their books. To stand a chance in the clutter of other flyers, yours must be very professional looking and have certain ingredients. Be sure the genre is prominently announced at the top of the flyer. Include those all-important reviews! They will also want to know  about the author's credentials and something about the content (either a Table of Contents, short excerpt, or summary statement). Include a photograph of the book cover and what back matter, such as an index or glossary, it contains. And don't leave off the ISBN, LCCN, price, binding, number of pages, publication date, names of wholesalers/distributors who carry the book, and if it has CIP data.

Libraries like Cataloging-in-Publication data because it gives them ready-to-use cataloging information and saves time in getting the book onto the shelves. Unfortunately, the CIP program does not accept self-published books. You can, however, purchase *Publishers* Cataloging-in-Publication (PCIP) from Quality Books. Call the number above for details.

It isn't cost-effective to send your single flyer to libraries. Instead you might consider participating in the Publishers Marketing Association's (PMA) cooperative library mailing program. They go to public libraries; K-12 libraries; and college, junior college, and university libraries. For details call PMA at 310-372-2732. It's always hard to track the results from such mailings as rarely will librarians buy from you directly. If it works, you'll see an increase in orders from Baker & Taylor (the main purveyor of books to libraries), Brodart, Quality, Unique, and other library wholesalers. The others most active in this field include Midwest Library Service, Blackwell North America, and Yankee Book Peddler. Find contact information for them in *LMP*.

Of course, nothing stops you from putting together your own collection of publishers' flyers. Perhaps a regional association to which you belong will rent a list and do a mailing if there is enough interest. SPAN members might seek out others in the membership directory who publish in their genre and do a specialized mailing to likely libraries. For mailing list sources, see Web Sites, Wisdom, and Whimsey.

Additionally, you can call the American Library Association at 800-545-2433 and inquire about renting lists of specialized library associations. There are those that concentrate on law (3,950 names), art (1,221 names), Judaism (700), medicine (4,886), music (3,050), business and finance (2,449), education (210) . . . and the list marches on past multiple topics.

Should you want to create your own mailing list, call the administration office at large public libraries you're targeting and ask who is responsible for collection development. In most cases the choice of materials is done out of one centralized office. Staff from branches may or may not have input into the process. In some situations, selection lists are then sent out to the branches for librarians to choose titles from. But it all hinges on the central decision, so be sure you're contacting the right person.

Exhibits that reach librarians are an excellent way to penetrate the market. You probably don't want to sign up for a full booth at the American Library Association annual convention, maybe not even a table at regional events. (But if you do, ask if they offer a special Small Press discount.) There are many cooperative opportunities, however, where you can promote your titles very affordable. Both Quality Books and Unique display the books of their publishers for a small fee. Combined Book Exhibits (CBE) offers many plans for a modest representation at a wide variety of shows. Contact them at 800-462-7687. And Association Book Exhibit may also be your answer as they go to some 70 shows a year (703-519-3909).

Library shows are different from BookExpo America (BEA), which caters primarily to booksellers. Librarians are very concerned with the credibility of the author and the authenticity of the press. Publisher size carries very little weight with them, reports Ted Parkhurst of August

House Publishers. He focuses on selling to libraries, visiting with them at more than 100 exhibits. "They are looking for excellence within the subject area. A small house can begin to establish itself in a given niche with one very strong title or several consistently reliable ones," reports Parkhurst.

The main value of attending such shows is to give librarians a chance to personally examine your books and get to know you. You might offer them a "special show discount" of from 20 to 40%, but chances are they will still consolidate their buying through a wholesaler, distributor, or jobber. Some libraries are mandated to do all their buying through Baker & Taylor, for instance. Librarians do hang onto the materials they receive, however, so contact now may result in orders six months downstream.

Work with Friends of the Library

Every library has a group of dedicated volunteers called Friends of the Library (FOL). You or your authors can work with this organization in a number of ways. Jim Cox of *Midwest Book Review* (which goes primarily to librarians), suggests you contact the president, note that you would like to donate a book, and be put on the agenda to speak briefly at the next meeting. They usually meet monthly. This is also a great place for both the author and publisher (assuming they're different) to appear. Nearly every book has an interesting behind-the-scenes story.

"When you show up at the meeting, bring three things: a case of books, a stack of publicity releases, and a camera," Jim advises. Make your presentation speech, hand the book to the president, and have someone take a picture. Also mention if anyone in the room would like copies, you have extra books in the trunk of your car which are available at a discount (maybe 20% off) for FOL members. Friends groups often have their own book acquisition funding quite separate from the normal library budget. They can, and do, purchase books that library budgets wouldn't permit. Some are used as memorials or for similar occasions.

Then go home and do the following per Mr. Cox:

1. Write a letter to the editor of the town newspaper praising the FOL and their wonderful reception of you when you donated your book—and enclose a copy of the photo. This is called a do-it-yourself photo-op and hugely enhances the chances of your letter being printed—and maybe even a reporter coming out for a follow-up interview.

2. Write a letter of appreciation to the FOL president on what a wonderful time you had and if there is anything further you can do.
3. Take any positive feedback from your presentation ceremony—such as a thank-you letter from the FOL or their next newsletter with an article about you in it—and contact the regional library system, which has its own monthly or bimonthly meetings. Ask to be an agenda item for the purpose of donating your book to their regional library system's book collection.
4. Contact the next library system in your county, and then the other regional systems and libraries within your state. Repeat the process until you run out of libraries, FOLs, books, or time.

The newsletters published by FOLs hold intriguing potential. Not only do they go out to the general Friends of the Library membership, they are also usually posted in the library to be read by library patrons. Additionally, they are perused by the library staff, who are always interested in what their FOLs are up to because it often has some bearing on them and their jobs.

Go to meetings equipped with a brief article you've created on your book and yourself. Hand it to their newsletter editor (or mail it if the person isn't in attendance) as possible filler material or as the basis for them to write even more about your visit after you leave.

Speaking of articles, every state library system has a newsletter. These do not typically run reviews, however. The trick, according to Jim, is not to send in your ordinary press release, but to rewrite it in the form of a letter to the editor based on your presentation ceremony (and photo) to the local library's FOL organization. The state newsletter will be interested in what's happening to their constituent library system members. Embedded in your letter, of course, will be pertinent descriptive information on your book—including the ISBN, price, and toll-free order number.

"Think of the whole process as a ladder," Jim counsels. "The first rung is your local library. The second rung is the state regional division your local library is a part of. The third rung is the State Library Office."

FOLs also frequently sponsor authors as speakers for library events. Sometimes the library will sell inexpensive tickets; other times admission is free. Try to arrange to sell your own books or give the FOLs a discount so they can use the event as a fund-raiser. Although library users are by nature not the most enthusiastic book purchasers, it's still valuable exposure.

Get quality library and reference information at LibrarySpot. It's very complete and very fast, certainly appealing characteristics for busy authors and publishers. At www.libraryspot.com you can find general libraries online, as well as those that specialize in law, medicine, and music. There is also a Reference Desk replete with acronyms, dictionaries, encyclopedias, government info, maps, phone books, statistics, and much more. And their Special Stacks include how-to articles that put valuable Internet resources into the context of relevant research topics. Visit and we think you'll agree this site could save you a lot of time and trouble.

Sources for library mailing lists. You can rent lists from a multitude of places, depending on exactly who you want to reach:
R. R. Bowker/Cahners (800-337-7184)
American Library Association (800-545-2433)
Special Libraries Association (202-234-4700)
Library Journal for public libraries (212-463-6819)
Booklist for public libraries (312-944-6780)
School Library Journal for academic libraries (212-463-6759)

Sites for librarians yield insider info for you! Here are a couple of sites for librarians that can provide *you* with further insight for understanding and reaching this market. AcqWeb is a gathering place for librarians and other professionals interested in acquisitions and collection development. Find them at http://www.library.vanderbilt.edu/law/acqs/acqs/html. What's so exciting about this site is that it also links you to a myriad of other intriguing places. The American Library Association lives at http://www.ala.org/ (Thank goodness, a short address!) In addition to oodles of information about the ALA itself, you can access the digital counterparts of both *American Libraries* and *Booklist* here. New reviews appear every couple of weeks . . . watch for yours.

Looking to penetrate libraries? Then surf on over to http://www. sunsite.berkeley.edu/Libweb/. Here you'll find over 1,600 pages from libraries in some 60 countries. Within the United States alone they list academic libraries, public libraries, national libraries and library organizations, state libraries, regional consortia, plus special and school libraries. You can also do a keyword search here or jump to related library sites.

The librarian asked the little boy why he wanted to borrow the book, Advice to Young Mothers. "Because I'm going to start collecting moths," he replied eagerly.

Taking an electronic bite of the Big Apple. Most of us don't live within easy visiting distance of the New York Public Library. But that's no problem because an incredible collection of information awaits us at http://www.nypl.org/index.html. I (Marilyn) had a ball hopping among What's New, Resource Guides, Catalogs & Indexes, and Publications. I knew there used to be something like *Gebbie's House Organs*. But although my regional librarian went online to find out what it is now called and if it is still being published, she came up empty-handed. By entering the old name into the CATNYP search engine at the New York Public Library site, I discovered it has been assimilated into another publication and was quickly on my way to mining the information I needed.

They also have staff-compiled Resource Guides on a variety of subjects here. A publisher of children's books, for instance, should check out the recommendations and booklists under "Children" to see if they couldn't get their titles included. Ditto for Literature and Book Culture, Gay and Lesbian Studies, Ethnic Heritage, and Women's Studies. Browse to your heart's content. We defy you not to find something valuable.

CHAPTER 12

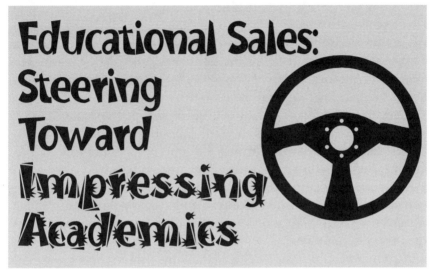

Educational Sales: Steering Toward Impressing Academics

The past few years have brought a heightened focus and renewed commitment to education. In 1999 the federal government's educational technology budget request of $721 million represents a massive leap from education technology in 1993, which was only $23 million. Title I funding continues to rise; it received $7.8 billion in funding for 1998 and 1999, an increase of 5.4% over last year.

And the list doesn't end there. Private schools are attracting more students and beefing up curriculum. Today 5.4 million students are enrolled in approximately 25,000 private elementary and secondary schools. The vast majority (61.8%) are in elementary grades. Home schooling is also flourishing. Even the corporate sector has allocated big dollars for training of employees.

This stable and growing market bodes well for small to mid-sized publishers trying to get their books adopted. It also shows great promise for authors with books that could be considered as supplemental texts. Let us explore what that might entail.

Books as supplementary texts

The diversity of curriculum and needs in education today is awesome. You may well be sitting on a book that is a perfect complement to a class being taught in K-12 (kindergarten through high school), or even for a college or university class.

Marilyn's first book, *Discover Your Roots* wound up being a supplemental text in eighth-grade history classes in both San Diego city and county schools when it first came out. They ordered by the case year after year. And our *National Directory of Newspaper Op-Ed Pages* has been used in college journalism classes.

It's all a question of finding the matches. You can become a David among the Goliaths if you aim your slingshot in the right direction. Novels can also work sometimes if the subject matter, setting, or protagonist meshes with a given educational program.

If you're new at this, one of the best free lessons available is contained in QED's Education Market Guide and Mailing List Catalog. Although Quality Education Data specializes in renting mailing lists, they also put out a very informative catalog. Change is inevitable (except from a vending machine) and they understand the ways schools are changing and how best to capitalize on this. Order your copy by calling 800-525-5811.

While renting mailing lists is certainly one way to reach this marketplace—and we'll explore it more later—there are other vehicles for penetrating education.

Advice from those who are doing

Judith Cook Tucker, publisher of World Music Press, explains that her strategy involves going to conferences and offering a workshop or demo session, or to serve on a panel. She does it with the understanding she can hand out her catalog at the sessions. Sometimes she is given a booth in exchange for her presentation. She uses it strictly as an information-dispensing device, preferring not to directly compete for sales with her dealers who are present in the exhibit hall.

Judith also watches lists of conference presenters, tracks down their phone numbers, talks to them, and sends sample books. Her hope is they will select something to use during their session. To facilitate this she permits copying of handouts. "This comes across at sessions as an endorsement by the presenter and participants rush to buy the stuff," she says.

Her third ploy is to find mail order catalogs that specialize in serving her music and social studies educators. She offers these dealers a 50% discount on 10 or more mixed nonreturnable titles. She also encourages them to stock her titles in their exhibits at conferences. In those cases the books are purchased with return privileges.

She also holds membership in professional organizations that serve the market and often writes articles that mention relevant titles. Judith further scans newsletters and journals to cull names and addresses of prospects, then sends them a catalog and personal note.

Steve Beeler, marketing director for Brookes Publishing Company, Inc., uses a combination of strategies to move their books on diversity. Direct marketing is one arrow in his quiver. He gets lists from associations, of conference attendees, from their authors—"Use all your author contacts for everything," he states. "The best list is the list *you* build." And don't make the flyers you send daunting. Steve's recommendation is that you "keep them open and airy."

He uses conferences to do market research as well as a venue to meet distributors and catalogers. "Quiz people," he advises. "Ask them what they need, like, and don't like." Steve finds potential authors at these shows as well as ideas for new projects. In one month his company went to the International Conference on Infant Studies, American Educational Research Association, National Association of School Psychologists, The Council for Exceptional Children, Head Start National Conference, Baltimore County Public Schools Early Childhood Conference, and The Child with Special Needs conference.

He is a great believer in using college and university Web sites. "They post a syllabus for every course. See what books they're using." His mailings to professors typically include a cover with the Table of Contents. Education specialty stores, such as Teacher Materials and Educational Outfitters, help him reach K-12 teachers.

He warns if you plan on doing electronic media to be aware that kids are very savvy. They want many different sensory experiences in their quest for information. And their desire for freedom to search on their own is almost insatiable. Things must be interactive; participatory elements are almost mandatory.

Dorothy Kupcha Leland, publisher of Tomato Enterprises Book Publishing, has two books: *Patty Reed's Doll: The Story of the Donner Party* and *Sallie Fox: The Story of a Pioneer Girl*. Dorothy finds out what schools need by working the bureaucracy. In California, for instance, the State Department of Education issues a Curriculum Framework. This document gives grade-by-grade explanations of what students are expected to learn. By studying it, you can quickly see where your titles might fit in. In the fourth grade students study pioneers coming west, for instance, so that's what she targets.

One of her company's books is specifically recommended in California's framework. Not only does this mean schools can buy the book with certain kinds of state funding that can only be used for books listed in the framework, it also means every teacher learns about the book, as each must read the framework document.

Other techniques Dorothy uses is pursuing reviews in *School Library Journal* and other pertinent publications. (There are some 50 magazines in the educational market. Many just publish your press releases.) She also exhibits at school-oriented trade shows and places her books in educational catalogs. She reminds us, "Schools also love to have authors speak to their students. For the right book, a school visit can mean a stipend for the author and sizeable book sales. And one successful visit usually generates additional invitations from neighboring schools."

Speaking at schools is a perfect venue for some authors and books. A children's book writer and illustrator, for instance, could regale the kids while drawing a brief sketch or having a slide show of his or her artwork and discussing the creative process. Some schools have a community resources office (or some similar name) that coordinates such functions. You, or your author, may be paid nothing, a $25 honorarium, or more. We know of one storyteller who charges a minimum of $300 a day plus travel expenses.

The key to these appearances is having some vehicle for communicating with the parents so they can buy the books. Advance notification is ideal. Then they can send in checks and the books can be personally autographed.

Working through wholesalers or distributors is important if you are serious about this market. They already have customers in place and have developed a relationship with them. Send finished books so they can see the final product and know how it fits. (For kids' books, be sure to indicate the age, grade, and interest level.) And the category must be obvious and fit into their curriculum. Check out the Dewey Decimal System for guidance here.

Random tips to help you triumph

Happily, you can market backlist titles to schools. Just be sure not to use the term or flaunt that it isn't a current book. On your sell sheet refer to it as "back in print," "classic," "category bestseller," or something similarly creative.

Want to talk with a cross-section of school librarians? Find a copy of *School Library Journal.* Each issue contains a calendar of upcoming shows.

If you have a regional title or want to start in your area and ripple out, ask the state library if they have a list of libraries. One publisher in Florida got a free mailing list for the whole state.

Another publisher recommends contacting the state departments of education themselves. Most have a staffed section devoted to assembling and sending out lists requested. You can even ask for curriculum supervisors for K-3, for instance, and get them on pressure sensitive labels either free or for a small cost. An additional plus is they are very accurate.

There are three primary sources for renting quality educational lists. Call and ask for their catalogs:

Quality Education Data (QED) 800-525-5811

College Marketing Group (CMG) 800-677-7959

Market Data Retrieval (MDR) 800-333-8802

You can request very segmented lists, such as districts by Title I funding allocation, or multicultural student percentage if, for instance, you're targeting African-Americans. You can also rent by neighborhood lifestyle, selecting only the upscale names. And you can get curriculum specialists by name covering early childhood education, fine arts/humanities, foreign languages, gifted/talented, music/physical education, etc.

Always test, test, test, before you roll out any campaign. Do a small, affordable mailing to see what works before making a major financial commitment.

Who buys? Low-priced products can generally be purchased directly by educators themselves. Sometimes teachers even buy books out of their own pockets. Professors at colleges and universities are likely to purchase on the spot with a credit card or institutional purchase order. Another group that may buy are student teachers or education students preparing units for classes. When you're trying to find funds, brainstorm where money might be had: the school library, talented-and-gifted program, PTA, etc.

■ When selling to schools one publisher offers classroom sets at a 22% discount and the schools pay shipping. Their sets include one teacher's edition, 30 student editions, and one answer key for grading purposes. Sales for those books were $500,000 in 1997 and were projected to be more than $700,000 in 1998.

■ Did you know that adding an inexpensive freebie to a book makes a big difference and is much more likely to cause a teacher to adopt it? We know of one text that came with overhead transparencies as a teaching aid.

■ For those really serious about this method of selling, QED sponsors an annual Education Marketer's Forum. You'll join industry colleagues to hear about the hottest topics and trends in education marketing. Learn the inside story on how schools operate and purchase products. You can register online at www.qeddata.com. Find loads of other useful information there as well.

Getting text adoptions in the college market

Textbook adoption is a complicated, often years-long process. It requires infinite patience. With this method of selling books, you can't throw an egg in the barnyard today and expect to eat chicken tomorrow. In fact, you may be into third generation chickens before much happens.

Professors hold the key to your penetrating the college/university market. After you've done your homework and found a match between your books and their subjects, you can try one of two approaches: 1) Send a brochure and hope they request a book, or 2) send the actual book. These review copies are called "desk copies," "examination copies," or "samples" in this industry. Gryphon House, a publisher and distributor of children's activity books, offers desk copies through its Web site at http://www.gryphonhouse.com.

If you choose the brochure route, be sure to include a complete Table of Contents and description of the book. Instructors look for thorough topical coverage. Assuming your author is well credentialed, emphasize his or her academic qualifications and any distinguished career accomplishments to impress the elitist instructors. Create some sort of reply mechanism—a Text Adoption Book Request Form—so they can easily ask for a copy of the book. If you also have ancillary value-added instructional materials, mention those as well. An instructor's manual, solutions manual, test material, etc., might make the difference on a sale.

Professors are very spoiled. Many major publishers scatter free examination copies like chicken feed. (There are those darned chickens again!) Smaller houses, while not wanting to appear stingy, can't afford to dole out hundreds of free books to instructors. There is a happy medium. Instructors who adopt your book and verify same with an order of 10 or more copies keep the desk copy as a free gift.

Otherwise they pay up or return the book. Jossey-Bass, a medium-sized business publisher sends a professor a 60-day examination copy. If the book is not adopted, the professor can either buy it for personal use or return it. (Often a 10 or 20% professional courtesy discount is extended.) Apparently this policy works, as 30 to 33% of their sales are from text book adoptions.

When planning to approach educators, be aware of the adoption cycle. Eighty percent of adoption decisions are made in the spring (February 1 to May 1) for fall courses. For the winter term, the date runs from early September to late November. These are the dates instructors must make their selections, so be sensitive to these critical times. There is less pressure at the graduate level to make decisions in advance. But if you want bigger sales, you'll target undergraduate courses with their larger number of students.

Once a text is adopted, you'll probably never hear from the professor again. Several months later a purchase order will come from the college bookstore. Although they aren't the most prompt to pay, they virtually never go out of business and some even send prepayment with the order. As in any accounts payable situation, don't let things get too far behind. A gentle call at 60 days is appropriate.

Large quantity potential sales

Reading's Fun/Books Are Fun is a company that does book fairs for school teachers (and corporations) all over the country. They buy hardcover books in huge volume—sometimes 50,000 to 75,000 units—and sell them at about 50% of the retail price. Consequently, they try to pick up product at around 20% of the cover price.

They seek general appeal nonfiction books, nothing regional or specialized. It's an impulse buy. Covers need pizzazz and color. They aim to create a balance between gift books, coffee-table books, how-to titles, children's books, educational books, and cookbooks. Currently, there is great demand for good cookbooks as they lost one of their prime suppliers.

Here's how it works: They take about 20 titles at a time and leave them at a school for 7 to 10 days. The teachers preview the inventory, then remit a check for anything they want. The books are delivered at the end of the preview time. In corporations, they use display racks for about 200 titles and only stay a day or two. The generous 50% discount allows the program to be promoted as an employee appreciation event.

Since their crystal ball doesn't reveal exactly which books will work, they do initial tests. The buy for a typical test is 500 units. If that flies, you'll be as snugly confined as a yolk in an egg—and considerably richer.

There are two ways to reach them: 1) Ask your local school secretary or librarian who the rep is and approach him or her, or 2) send a sample book and pitch letter to Book Buyer, Reading's Fun/Books Are Fun, 110 South Main Street, Fairfield, IA 52556. Their phone is 515-472-8301.

Web Sites, Wisdom, and Whimsey

Attention text and academic buffs. This site will appeal to anyone writing or publishing educational materials—including textbooks, software, videos, monographs, reference books, newsletters, and multimedia CD-ROM disks. It includes book reviews, how-to advice, and a listserv for online dialog. Many other features make this a gold mine for those dealing with textbooks. Find it at http://www.winonanet.com/taa/.

Contacting college professors. Marcella Chester, the author of two novels that deal with sexual abuse, uses the Net to find possible sales outlets. She goes to the university's home page, then to the program she wants, then to the faculty, and finally to the individual professor. For instance, at one university sociology department, she found a professor who demonstrates by current work and a list of published works a genuine interest in violence against women. Now Marcella has something tangible to grab hold of when she pitches *Cherry Love* and *Wild Cherry*.

Network at the National Association of College Stores expo. If you hanker to reach the $8.15 billion college market, it might be wise to attend or exhibit at their annual Campus Market Expo. It rotates around the country and is held in March or April. For more details call the National Association of College Stores at 440-775-7777.

Tired of feeling like your home-based publishing company is small and insignificant? Here's an idea: Put a sign up in the bathroom that reads "Employees must wash their hands before returning to work."

Want to reach elementary school librarians? Strive to get a review in *Library Talk*. It comes out five times a year and reviews books of interest to elementary school librarians. Contact editor Carolyn Hamilton, 480 East Wilson Bridge Road, #L, Worthington, OH 43085-2373; phone 614-436-7107.

Site to a million links. Well, that's a bit of an exaggeration, but you can jump to hundreds of educational site links, all thoughtfully organized to help you find what you need. For 27 years, the site's originator, Pitsco, has used visionary leadership to provide solutions to many of the challenges in education. Surf over to http://askanexpert.com/.

K-12 periodicals. If you publish books for these grades, here are two magazines you should know about: *Curriculum Administrator*, Jane Ferguson, Editor, Educational Media LLC, 992 High Ridge Road, Stamford, CT 06905; phone 203-322-1300; fax 203-329-9177. *Curriculum Review*, Mike Michaelson, Editor, Lawrence Ragan Communications, Inc., 212 West Superior Street, Chicago, IL 60610; phone 312-335-0037; fax 312-335-9583.

Literacy Ads, Not-So-Smart: How to Speak and Write Like a Colleg Graduate

from the *Norfolk Virginia-Pilot*

Tips and more tips: Excellent ideas and links for selling to libraries are available at the Internet Monitor site at http://www.internet-monitor.com, a site devoted to educational publishers.

CHAPTER 13

Amplify Your Presence with Book Clubs

Many smaller publishers ignore book clubs, feeling they are the domain of major houses. Absolutely not true! In fact, we've locked into book club sales that covered all our first-run printing costs.

Book club sales do something additional for you: They build credibility by increasing a title's promotion and distribution. Book club adoption provides added PR and sales leverage. When you can splash across your book cover, highlight in your promotional materials, and tell media producers you've been selected by a book club, it proves others in the industry value your work. Furthermore, the club itself will advertise both in general and specialized media, which gives your book added visibility at no cost to you. Bookstores, even though they see clubs as competition, are influenced by news of a club sale. Bill Hannah of Stoddard Publishing in Toronto, Ontario, comments, "It aids your sales immeasurably when you can say that you've been picked up by X, Y, and Z club."

Learning the ins and outs of book clubs

There are some 160 different book clubs. The vast majority operate on a theory called "negative option." Members have the chance to say "no" to the automatic selection, but if the club doesn't hear back from them, they get the book. People are enticed to join with the promise of free or nominally priced initial books if they agree to purchase a certain number over time.

Just as there are IBMs and Macs, there are two leaders in the book club world. Book-of-the-Month Club (BOMC) and the Literary Guild (now known as Doubleday Direct, Inc.) were founded in the mid-1920s and were immediately successful. Since most Americans lived in rural areas at that time, the book clubs kept them informed about new books and made purchasing easy. Today they're still going strong.

The large clubs buy for 15 cycles a year. BOMC, for instance, typically chooses 20 to 25 books as *main* selections each year. They also offer many *alternative* selections so if members aren't intrigued by the main selections, they have other books to choose from. Main selections at the major clubs can sell as many as 200,000 copies; the main selections of medium-sized clubs usually sell around 10,000 copies. While the numbers for alternate selections can be as low as 200, this is still a marketing ploy well worth pursuing.

Happily, it isn't necessary to have an established subsidiary rights department to crack this market. We'll show you how in this chapter.

Choosing the right book club

Virtually any book published has a potential home with at least one book club. They come in as many varieties as wildflowers. In addition to the big two, there are a multitude of mid-sized clubs.

Newbridge Communications, for instance, has 24 professional book clubs covering a variety of subject areas including nursing, computers, psychology, business, astronomy, and much more. Charles Decker is club director for the Executive Program, which encompasses business and management titles and the Architects and Designers Book Service. He explains that because the Newbridge clubs are professional rather than consumer, they welcome books with a high price point. Their members rely on them for hard-to-find titles and the best books in specific subject areas.

A Newbridge "main selection buy" runs from 2,000 to 4,000 copies, while an alternate ranges from 500 to 2,000 copies. The club likes to join the publisher's print run. (Should they decide to use your book as an introductory offer, however, they will print it themselves in high numbers, usually around 100,000.) Normally, they pay the actual unit printing cost plus a 10% royalty.

"Think of a professional book club as a direct mail arm of your company," Decker advises. "It's a targeted low-cost marketing effort that reaches a specific professional market which publishers often cannot reach themselves." These nonreturnable buys, royalties, and advances can boost a publisher's bottom line.

The McGraw-Hill Companies also serve a similar group of professionals. They have offerings for aviators, architects, chemists, chemical engineers, civil engineers, electronic engineers, mechanical engineers, and those interested in electronics. They also have the Computer Book Club (for hobbyists) and the Computer Professionals' Book Society.

When we spoke with Willis Walker, book club manager for McGraw-Hill, he told us, "I buy from a lot of small publishers—everything from 150 copies to several thousand." He looks for professional reference titles or books of interest to high-end hobbyists. Although they have no math club per se, a math book might be appropriate for all five engineering clubs, so think creatively about how your titles would fit. They discount books 20% to their customers, pay all royalties up front, and often reorder popular titles. Walker offered a word of warning: "Keep to your production schedule. You have to have it ready on that date."

Dozens of smaller, more specialized clubs address individualized interests. They run a wide gamut: the Conservative Book Club, Dance Book Club, Self-Sufficiency Book Club, Graphic Design Book Club, Prevention Book Club, even Smart Practice Inc., which buys books for medical and dental offices.

Others cater to various religious interests. There's the Jewish Book Club, Guideposts Theological Book Service, Catholic Digest Book Club, and the popular One Spirit, which targets metaphysical customers.

Over two dozen juvenile clubs exist, even one for kids as young as two years old. If you publish children's books, the potential here is enormous. More juvenile paperbacks are sold through student book clubs than through any other single market. Scholastic's book clubs are available in 80% of American elementary schools and 50% of high schools. Most school book clubs feature paperbacks from a variety of publishers.

School book clubs promote themselves to teachers through direct mail, exhibits, conferences, workshops, and salespeople. The club sends the teacher monthly annotated lists of available books, which the teacher distributes. Students take the lists home, make their selections, and pay the teacher—who distributes the books when they arrive at the classroom. School book clubs usually pay the publisher a 6% royalty on the club price of the book. The Weekly Reader Book Clubs license previously published books, so a backlist title may fare well there.

Match your editorial focus with specific clubs. They have spent a lot of money to find the enthusiasts for their subject area. Capitalize on that! Call, fax, email, or write to find out how appropriate ones work. Don't make blind submissions. Know the right editor, notify them a package is coming, and follow up on its arrival so it won't be lost in the shuffle. You can expect a response within a month. Multiple submissions are fine. To really analyze their needs, get on their mailing list. You may even want to sign up for a club to study what their bulletins look like, how they pitch titles, what types of books they're buying, etc.

Understanding the submission process

It's never too early to start thinking of book clubs. Walker with McGraw-Hill indicated sometimes publishers approach him even before they have a manuscript! They might tell him of a proposal, ask his advice on the list price and title, and if he would like to see such a book.

Most larger clubs want manuscripts six to nine months before the publication date. "We welcome manuscripts as far in advance as possible. It's never too soon to send," said Sarah Gallick, an editor for the Literary Guild. Although they buy specifically for the Military Book Club, Mystery Guild, Crossings, Health Book Club, and Audiobooks, Gallick assured us, "Our clubs cover everything of interest to general readers." She advised sending to the Submissions Editor at Doubleday Direct, Inc.

No matter which club you're approaching, at this infant stage you'll need to put together a powerful package. Dazzle them! Your cover letter should include:

- ■ Estimated publication date.
- ■ Proposed price.
- ■ Anticipated number of pages.
- ■ Whether paperback or hardcover.
- ■ Trim size.
- ■ A brief description of the book and content summary. Do your homework. Include a paragraph that clearly demonstrates your understanding of the club's membership makeup and tastes. Mention titles they have carried that are similar or complementary to yours. Talk about related titles the club has offered again and again.
- ■ It would also be wise, if you're a new or small press, to include a bit about who you are to establish your company credibility. The edi-

tor wants to be assured you can produce a quality book, on time, and sell it effectively. If you've won awards for previous titles, made regional bestseller lists, received major review attention, or are recognized as a leader in your publishing specialty, by all means say so!

■ Be sure to also include an author bio, credentials for writing the book, and mention any previous books published. Add copies of favorable key reviews of the author's past titles.

■ If illustrations are an integral part of the project, it's helpful to include the anticipated number and photocopies to convey a sense of the complete work. The more important the illustrations are to the book, the more fully they need to be presented. (Don't plan on getting them, or any of your other materials, back.)

■ Have rough cover ideas? Include them too.

■ A marketing plan and publicity plans will impress them.

■ Pre-publication endorsements, advance quotes, or testimonials are great if you have any at this stage.

By working with them early, you give clubs the option of combining their print run with yours. This has a distinct advantage for *you* since it slashes the unit cost of each book printed. Or they may want the printer to use cheaper paper and binding in their edition.

If you're already into the typesetting phase, send them a copy of the galleys. But even after a title has passed its publication date, many smaller clubs will still consider it. Here's where authors themselves can get involved. Clear it with your publisher, then go after this exciting income opportunity.

BOMC receives more than 10,000 submissions a year. From this they select about 1,000 titles. We're happy to report that their submission guidelines state, "It is both a key part of our work and a personal pleasure for the editorial staff to 'discover' worthy books from smaller publishing houses. We warmly invite university presses and small presses, both regional and national, to submit appropriate manuscripts to BOMC and its affiliated clubs." To learn all about their submission process, go to http://www.smallpress.org/MajorBMC.htm.

They have 10 clubs: Book-of-the-Month Club itself (with Canadian and International branches); Quality Paperback Book Club (QPB also has a Canadian branch); The Good Cook; Fortune International Book Club, which handles business books; History Book Club; Money

Book Club; Crafter's Choice; Country Homes and Gardens; One Spirit; and Children's Book-of-the-Month Club.

Time Warner, Inc.'s BOMC and QPB are general-interest clubs seeking books with a genuinely broad appeal within their subject areas. They cover how-to, self-help, history, biography, science, math, fiction, language, spirituality, personal finance, current affairs, reference, even pets and humor. If you have a title that is unusually expensive—such as a photography, art, or reference work—it might be considered as a "dividend" book, which is offered at a deep discount to members who have earned credits through earlier book purchases.

If they're interested in a title they'll offer you an advance against royalties for book club rights. This is based on their sales and manufacturing estimates. It may seem paltry: perhaps 8% royalties with a $750 advance. With the big clubs, don't try to lean on them for more money or your deal will blow up faster than balloons in a porcupine's nest. The money is only the tip of the iceberg. Properly utilized, the prominence and propaganda value is worth a lot more.

Quality Paperback Book Club has, over the last several years, adopted books from dozens of small presses. They consistently take risks with off-beat, unusual titles from independent presses and have made significant hits out of them. "Some of the most interesting writing today is coming from small presses," stated a spokesperson. Linda Loewenthal, of QPB and One Spirit, told *Publishers Weekly Show Daily* she always tries to include a few smaller press titles in each club catalog. "They're what keep our members surprised." QPB members enjoy the unusual, the quality book with a twist that may not find mass market popularity.

Timing may play a role in your success. Major publishers tend to bunch their big books together in September/October and March/April. That leaves dry holes in the other eight months—holes small presses may be able to plug. BOMC, for instance, sometimes finds it a challenge to acquire the right nonfiction books consistently throughout the year.

Since the emergence of chain bookstore discounting, book clubs—whose appeal has revolved around offering books at low prices by mail—dare to seek additional ways to be competitive. Doubleday, for instance, may stress elements other than price. The quality of the product will be of more importance. "A club edition could include comprehensive information about the author, it could cross-reference other works by the author, it could contain illustrations by interesting people who have some relationship with the author," commented Peter von Puttkamer, a former CEO of Doubleday clubs. "It becomes a whole different product, a book one can only find in the club."

Bottom dollar sense

Book clubs are typically sold one of three types of rights. Either they purchase the right to print their own edition, often of lesser quality so they can offer it at a substantial discount. They join your print run and pay you a royalty. Or they buy finished copies from your inventory.

Just what kind of financial rewards can you expect from such a subsidiary rights sale? That varies widely. It will be influenced by whether

your title is a main or alternate selection. Understandably, main selections hit the bullseye and command more money. They are most likely to come from major houses.

With the big clubs, the royalty usually runs 10 to 15% of *their* selling price, (which will be 15 to 20% below normal retail). And they will pay you for the PPB cost, which stands for paper, print, and binding. Others will offer an advance against royalties. Should they decide to use your book as a bonus, dividend, or new member reward, the royalty is usually halved. Thankfully, there are no returns.

Exclusivity is the name of the game when dealing with the bigger clubs. BOMC and the Literary Guild, for instance, never share a title. Should you be fortunate enough to command interest from both, there might be an auction for the rights. Auctions drive advances heavenward in a hurry.

When dealing with the smaller specialized clubs, plan on giving a 60 to 80% discount. (Of course, if you've used the proper formulas for pricing your book, this will still leave you a profit.) Most publishers split book club royalties 50/50 with their authors. Don't forget to factor this into your computations.

Negotiation skills are very important here. Try to get *them* to make a commitment first. Editors of smaller clubs usually offer much less than they will settle for. We were offered $5.70 per book for one of our client's titles. When the negotiation ended, we had parlayed the price to $8 per book.

Some require legal contracts, others just a purchase order. For your own sake, be sure all details are spelled out in a letter of agreement. The terms are often negotiable. One club we sold to wanted to pay net 90, but finally agreed to net 30 when we pushed for more prompt payment. That way, there is cash in hand to pay outstanding printing bills. With some, you can even encourage faster payment by offering a 2% discount for payment within 10 days of delivery.

Don't feel the story has ended just because you've made one sale. We sold one client's book to both the Nostalgia Book Club and the Movie/Entertainment Book Club. Neither of them required exclusivity.

A caution you're not likely to read elsewhere has to do with remaindering. If a club overprints and can't sell the books, they will want to remainder them. Try to avoid allowing that in the contract as it can play havoc with your regular trade sales. If they insist on remaindering copies a year after they begin distribution, at least be sure *you* are able to buy back the inventory at manufacturing cost. Also be careful—if they plan to use photographs, illustrations, or excerpts for advertising and promotional purposes—that *you* own the rights for this use. Some stock photography houses, for instance, require extra payment if their photos are used in such ways.

At our seminars the question often comes up, "But won't it cut into my other sales if I let a book club have my book?" Probably not. Exposure with a book club creates an *echo effect*. People learn about your title through the book club—but they may buy it at a bookstore, through your own direct mail promotions, or on the Internet. So you've little to lose and potentially big bucks to gain by exploring this lucrative market.

The one exception to this is if you publish high-ticket, tightly niched books you typically merchandise via direct mail. Then a book club targeted to your potential customer could siphon off a major portion of your sales. And it might be a long-term drain. Their terms may include the right to reprint and offer the book for as long as they want.

Making Contact

So how do you find out about all these book clubs? There are two ideal sources: *Literary Market Place* (section 25) and *Book Publishing Resource Guide*, which is an affordable reference for many marketing contacts available from 800-331-8355. Both publications list dozens of clubs and appropriate contact names. *LMP* sells for almost $200, so check online at http://www.literarymarketplace.com or your closest major library for a current copy. Always call and verify the present editor's name and spelling and request current submission guidelines before writing. Pay attention to what you're doing. Don't be like the guy who spent five minutes behind a line of cars before he realized they were parked.

Book clubs—with their enormous power to influence consumers and professionals—should be a vital part of your marketing efforts. Time invested here can not only open up other opportunities for your publishing program, it can yield a new revenue stream—plus far-reaching PR and prestige.

Research online for Book-of-the-Month Club tastes. BOMC launched their Web site in June 1997. Ever since then, resourceful publishers have been auditing it to see exactly what books they have selected. Go to www.bomc.com and click on Member Views to see the 2,400 titles club members can buy. For fun, also click on Authors & Archives. Here you'll see information about award-winning books from the past 25 years, 450-in-depth author profiles, plus dozens of exclusive interviews with authors from the last 70 years, including many contemporaries.

Sell and sell and sell! Especially with smaller clubs, you needn't necessarily be satisfied with one deal. When we were ready to go back to press for our *National Directory of Newspaper Op-Ed Pages*, we alerted Writer's Digest Books, which had previously purchased it. A day later we had a verbal purchase order for 500 more! We've sold one title three times to a book club. This really helps lower reprint costs.

From the Astute Remarks Department:
"I couldn't care less about all those fiction stories about what happened in the year 1500 or 1600. Half of them aren't even true," said pro golfer John Daly as he explained why he wasn't interested in literature as a college student.

It's never too late to submit a book. When we sold *Big Ideas for Small Service Businesses* to a major publisher, they dropped the ball completely. So after the publication date had passed, we asked for and got book club rights back, then we went to work. Newbridge's Executive Program snapped up the book—even though it was no longer new. Look at your strong backlist books; you may have an unmined treasure waiting to be discovered.

Exciting search engine makes your research easy. There's an embarrassment of riches on the Internet. But where do you find them? In Yahoo!? Alto Vista? Lycos? Or one of the other countless sources? Now you can do one-stop-shopping! Go to http://www.search.com and you can access more than 250 Web and Usenet search engines from a central Web page! Instead of searching each engine individually, Search.com's "slave driver" engine organizes engines both by category and alphabetically and it eliminates duplicates. What a tremendous time saver for you. Furthermore, you can locate people's residential phone numbers and addresses here via Switchboard. It's a big, diversified, fascinating site. And they update it constantly. One week we found seven new search tools.

PART IV

Flip the Switch with Nontraditional Retail Markets

Nonbookstore Merchandising Channels to Make Sales Sizzle

Bookstores. Certainly they're a viable way to distribute books. But let us not focus solely on them. You see, when we really concentrate on something our brain interprets that as our desire, aims at it, and excludes all other ideas. For instance, if you drive down a street looking at a pothole up ahead, you will unconsciously direct your car at that pothole and hit it. To avoid "pothole" thinking, let's explore some of the dozens of other special sales possibilities for merchandising books.

Mass market outlets—which include supermarkets; drug stores; membership warehouses like Costco's and Sam's; and discounters such as Kmart, Wal-Mart, and Target stores—take a huge piece of the retailing pie.

Yet books are sold in dozens of imaginative places: home improvement centers, pet stores, gas stations, beauty salons, record stores, bike shops, auto supply outlets, winery tasting rooms, toy stores, and nurseries. And also in gourmet stores, doctor's offices, computer stores, bait shops, office supply stores, car washes, clothing stores, bedding stores, theatrical supply houses, magic shops, luggage stores, truck stops, nail salons…the list goes on infinitum. Don't rule out national parks, museums, or government agencies. And certain books are like catnip to a feline for network marketing organizations that gobble up thousands of copies for members of their multilevel down-lines.

Penetrating special sales

The advantages of special sales outlets are multifaceted. In many cases, they buy nonreturnable. They typically pay net 60. There is less competition from other books, yet greater exposure to your target market. Rather than just a sliver of spine showing, books are often displayed attractively and advantageously. And once you're in, sales typically continue for months, or even years.

These kinds of sales accounted for more than half of all the books sold in the U.S. in 1997. They're certainly more realistic than expecting to crack bestseller lists; the odds against that are overwhelming. You have to sell 50,000 copies in the first week to even have a crack at the list.

Special sales can augment the overall success of your book. Jack Canfield and Mark Victor Hanson's *Chicken Soup* series are sold in all kinds of nonbookstore places. They are merchandised in gas stations, car washes, and bakeries. Reading Is Fun, a firm that distributes books to teachers (and is discussed in another chapter), sold more than a million copies. Another company that hires college students to go door-to-door in corporate parks moved many more copies.

Publishers reach specialty buyers in a variety of ways: through telemarketing, by direct mail campaigns, or via specialty or commissioned sales reps. They also often connect at industry-specific conventions and trade shows. Timberline Press out of Portland takes three booths at the Northwest Flower Show. Other smaller publishers merely attend such events to line up distributors, catalogers, and more informally introduce their products.

So, do you need more nerve than an abscessed tooth to make it happen? No. Just get creative! Find the matches. Look for links. Similarities. Connections. Scour each book for ideas.

Specialty retailers are always on the lookout for books that go with the products they sell. Have a title for children or about parenting? Consider toy stores like Toys R Us and F.A.O. Schwarz. The latter aims to "be the ultimate place for children's books" and includes everything from classics to hot new titles. Or work with Noodle Kidoodle, Zany Brainy, Learningsmith, or the Store of Knowledge.

Gardening titles—as long as they are practical with straightforward directions, not too expensive, and have colorful illustrations—can bloom into big sales at Smith & Hawken, for instance. They seek high-quality products for their 25 stores and mail order division. Gardening is a growing (ahem) area. Books on the subject appear in home improvement centers, botanical garden shops, seed catalogues, lawn and garden shops, even country gift shops that specialize in Americana. There are special distributors, like Terrebonne Ltd. and Creative Homeowner Press, that supply books to this marketplace.

Cookbooks can also fare well in this environment. Williams-Sonoma offers books in all of its 150 stores, plus its catalog. Crate & Barrel, the home-supply and cooking store, looks for books as accessories for its 62 stores nationwide. Spokesperson Bette Kahn explains, "The company buys primarily cookbooks and coffee-table books that deal with specific products we are promoting." For example, they sold a pizza primer to go with a new pizza set and a book on how to make ice cream for an ice cream machine.

The Nature Company has 120 stores in malls around the country and carries a wide variety of books. While science and nature-oriented titles are naturals, their stock also includes books on travel, field guides, art/photography, cooking, general interest and niche children's books, and tomes on animals, sea life, and birds.

If your titles tend to be inspirational or motivational, then Successories, Inc. is a retailer to investigate. They have nearly 100 stores in the United States plus half a dozen abroad. And they also produce a snazzy catalog with wide distribution. Company chairman/CEO/founder Mac Anderson wants to triple the number of books they carry in the Personal Motivation Library. (To reach buyers at any of the firms listed in this chapter, contact a local branch and ask for headquarters information.)

Getting your books into the National Park System can be a real coup. It can also be time-consuming and frustrating. One publisher admitted it took three years to crack this outlet. Every park system has its own buyer. Their purchasing process is complex and sometimes political.

It's a good idea to bring them on board before the book is published. Talk with appropriate park personnel during the editorial stage. By getting them involved early it creates ownership and trust, and helps the sale move along faster. Find out what holes they are trying to fill. They're real sticklers on accuracy. And the credibility of the author and photographer is important. A good place to start is the biannual trade show put on by the Conference of National Park Cooperative Association. If your book is already done, give away review copies generously. (Don't be as cheap as the guy who shares shoes with a neighbor who works nights!) Their review committee needs product to evaluate.

Author and publisher success stories

Vicki Lansky, author of many books from major publishers, has given several of her titles "second lives" when they went out of print. Then she goes after special sales. Her edition of *KoKo Bear's Big Earache* sells almost 5,000 copies a year to pediatric ear, nose, and throat specialists. And her *Vicki Lansky's Divorce Book for Parents* sold 30,000 copies in 18 months largely because of mailings to divorce lawyers, mediators, therapists, and other professionals in the divorce world.

After 12 rejections, F. Lynn Harris self-published his first novel, *Invisible Life.* One of his main sales outlets was beauty salons. He managed to move 5,000 copies, after which he was "discovered" by Anchor. His first novel and second book have sold over 300,000 copies.

Charlene Costanzo tells of deciding to place her book, *The Twelve Gifts of Birth* in OB/GYN and pediatric waiting rooms. After dropping off books at two offices in a nearby medical center, she returned home to a phone message from someone ordering three books. How's that for quick results?

Jerrold R. Jenkins of Rhodes & Easton tells of selling more than 10,000 copies of *Deer Camp Directory* in places that sell beef jerky and six packs. And *Buck Wilder's Small Fry Fishing Guide* has become one of the hottest paperbacks in Michigan. Rather than bookstores, the best place to purchase the fishing primer is at your friendly neighborhood gas station. (And that's no fish story.)

A book of short fiction titled *The Homeward Bounder and Other Stories* found its home in a marine supply company of all places. Author Floyd Beaver keeps his boat in a slip near the store and has sold over 300 copies by chatting it up and hand-selling it to store customers.

A number of years ago we worked with a client who had a book about raw foods titled *The UNcook Book.* We sold it to a variety of health professionals, who in turn resold it to their patients. It went to chiropractors, dentists, progressive MD's, wellness centers, etc.

We've heard of a poet who calls corporations offering to do a 15-minute reading at their board meeting and personally autograph books for each board member. He sells 20 to 50 books at a whack.

We asked Bobbie Christensen the strangest place she had ever sold books and were told the following: At virtually every KOA campground she stays at while putting herself on an author tour, she puts up a flyer at the front desk and marks on it, "Meet the author at site #X." She says it works very well.

First-time novelist Dirk Wyle pairs the tone of the hard-boiled mystery with the intricate scientific detail common to the medical thriller. This allows him to target *Pharmacology Is Murder* to pharmacologists and toxicologists (obvious hooks), graduate medical students (the story is set in a medical school), Mensa members (the protagonist is a Mensan), sailing enthusiasts (the protagonists also lives on a sailboat), and Miami lovers (the author lives there and the story is set in Miami). If more novelists would identify niche markets like Dirk does, they would sell tons more books!

Connie Evers, publisher of *How to Teach Nutrition to Kids*, reports that her most successful nontraditional marketing strategy has been to keep on top of child nutrition grant recipients. She researches on the Internet. The USDA posts a list each fall of the states that received grant money, including how much and who is administering it. The Maternal and Child Health people also post their list of grantees. Connie sends a nice promo package and a copy of the book to these folks. This has resulted in several orders in the hundreds and a couple of orders for over a thousand copies. "Find the recipients and help them spend their money," is her advice. Give you any ideas?

Own your niche by establishing national distribution

Suppose you have an idea for matching your book with a nontraditional retail outlet. Here's a proven formula for success. Get 8 or 10 books in the store, even using consignment if you must. Provide a point-of-purchase display so the books are by the cash register as an impulse item. Go back two weeks later and see how things went.

If the books sold out, replenish them, then use the Yellow Pages to pinpoint more similar local stores. Take the same approach. Once they also have proven themselves, ask one of the store managers who the regional wholesaler is for their industry. Contact the supplier and tell them about your successful local test; suggest they do the same thing on a regional basis.

Expect to give them a 50% discount and don't breathe a word about returns!

Once this is working, pitch them about going national. At this point be prepared to bring in your big guns and give them lots of support. Consider doing in-store events. Maybe run ads on a co-op basis. Follow up consistently with telemarketing. Discuss having the author in their booth at trade shows to autograph books and schmooze with prospects. See if there is any way you could automatically package your book with one of the other products they represent. Start a two-sided 8 ½- by 11-inch quarterly newsletter to tout successful store campaigns, provide ongoing information, and keep them jazzed. You have just developed a national distribution chain. Congratulate yourself!

Be smart. Join their industry trade association. Subscribe to appropriate trade journals. Become as savvy as they are about their industry; it could become your largest customer.

Going after gift store sales

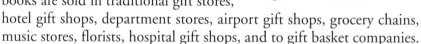

If you have the right kind of book, this can be a wonderful market. Gift books are usually smaller; have enticing, colorful covers; and involve an impulse topic that is fun, inspirational, gourmet, or kookie. These books are sold in traditional gift stores, hotel gift shops, department stores, airport gift shops, grocery chains, music stores, florists, hospital gift shops, and to gift basket companies.

When you design book covers test them in gift shops, not bookstores. And be sure to price your books to meet gift store standards. Remember when writing these books they are what they say they are: items to be purchased as gifts. Write accordingly.

What does the money side look like? Most gift shops need a 50% discount; larger chains often demand 55% but it's nonreturnable so a sale is a sale. If you work through gift reps, their commissions run around 15 to 20% so be sure to figure that in. Distributors typically require 55% and pay net 60. You can find a helpful special report on gift book marketing at http://www.bookzonepro.com/gift.html.

Wholesale gift shows can play a major role in selling to the gift industry, whether through reps in a showroom or temporary booth, or by displaying product at your own booth. The major shows run January to September. The granddaddy of them all is the National Stationery

Show in New York. Other big ones include the California Gift Show, Chicago Gift Show, GiftSource West, San Francisco International Gift Fair, and the New York International Gift Fair. To learn dates and particulars check *Tradeshow Week* at the library.

If you're targeting this area, another place to find show dates, plus glean many useful tips and leads, is in *Gift & Decorative Accessories* and *Giftware News*. You should also belong to the Gift Association of America, 608 West Broad Street, Bethlehem, PA 18018; phone 610-861-9445; fax 610-861-0948.

Museums can mean megabucks

Few authors or publishers realize that museums are the destination for over 600 million visitors each year. Most museums sport gift shops. These stores represent a multimillion-dollar industry and, happily, books play a large role in these receipts. The museums have a focus, which is to provide books that further visitors' knowledge. In addition to those who personally throng to these shops, many museums put out catalogs that reach thousands upon thousands of added potential customers.

The subject possibilities are virtually endless and apply to both adults and children. While titles on art, natural history, nature, and science might be expected, interest areas straddle a variety of other topics. Have books on theater, dance, or music? Many museums will be interested. They also are attracted to crafts, gardening, architecture, computers, history, antique collecting, animals, fish, photography, and sports, to name more categories.

Let's take a look at some actual titles that are flourishing in museums to get a better feel for the texture of what works: *Paintings of New England* romanticizes New England's alluring forests, hills, mountains, and coastline. *The Indispensable Cat* documents the feline's relationship to people in history, literature, and art. *The Look of the Century* is an encyclopedic guide that celebrates the genius in design. And for those who want a manual of pictorial thought and practical advice on new ways to see and capture the world around them, there is *Paint*.

Other titles run the gamut from *Mysterious Ruins* to *Peaceful Kingdom: Random Acts of Kindness by Animals*, from *Stinky Smelly Hold Your Nose Science* to *The Art of Construction*. Then there's *Death Valley, Bubble Monster, Getting into Art History, The Civil War Infantryman, The Atlas of Languages, Log Cabin Cooking, In Celebration of Women, The Vanishing Tribes of Burma, Book of the Medieval Knight,* and *Great White Sharks*. Anything there sound similar to something you publish?

When we interviewed Brenda Knight, the sales and marketing director for Conari Press, she noted that museums are a "very important market" for them. One of their titles, *Uppity Women of Ancient Times*, has sold over 30,000 copies. She believes museums and gift shops were responsible for 40% of those sales. Conari gives a 50% discount and sells nonreturnable. Museums are also helping them reach a strategic target market of animal lovers for their newly released *Peaceful Kingdom: Random Acts of Kindness by Animals*. It's doing well in zoos and aquatic parks. Her advice is to "educate yourself. Go to museum stores. They have an amazing depth and breadth of selections."

An area blossoming in museum stores is miniature books. This "honey-I-shrunk-the-art-book" movement transforms works that normally sell in the $30 to $50 price range into affordable $4.95 to $11.95 treasures. Although they can't quite compete with their larger cousins, this represents a small but significant category for certain publishers such as Abbeville Press, Running Press, Applewood Books, Andrews and McMeel, and Phaidon.

As you can see, culture wears a coat of many colors. This is a natural marketplace for books. But is it also fraught with the difficulties of reaching the appropriate buyers, slow pay, and returns? In a word, "No!" These folks are generally friendly, well organized, and pay promptly. They can amount to great volume over time, especially if you're fortunate enough to score with the likes of the Smithsonian.

Since they are part of nonprofits, many are limited by their educational charters to stock only books directly relating to the subject matter of the museum. So you need to find the matches. Children's museums, however, have greater latitude. Some museums even have resource centers for teachers and cater to them in their shops as well.

Another way in the door might be through special exhibitions. At the Harvard University Art Museum Shop, the manager is constantly rotating books to accommodate the museum's 22 annual exhibitions. Each one lasts from six to eight weeks. You'd be surprised how many books you can sell during that small window of opportunity if you find the right hook. Do you have a travel story or novel using the setting, a regional cookbook, or photography of places being featured in the traveling exhibition?

Penetrating this marketplace begins by joining the Museum Store Association, Inc. (MSA). It is the only professional museum retailing association and offers many advertising and promotional opportunities to communicate effectively with museum store managers, buyers, and product developers. Museums—some 1,800 of them—representing art, science, history, botanic gardens, zoos, and aquariums belong. MSA's members constantly search for new merchandise that complements their institutions' educational missions.

Exhibitor Affiliate Member dues are $175 annually and run from January through December. Marketing opportunities include access to their membership directory, a complimentary listing therein, discounted rates on display advertising in MSA publications, eligibility to purchase mailing labels, and the ability to sign up for booth space at the MSA Expo, held in conjunction with the association's annual meeting. Booths start at about $1,000. You can also seek free publicity for your titles in the Discoveries section of their quarterly museum store magazine.

Reach the Museum Store Association, Inc. at 4100 E. Mississippi Ave., Suite 800, Denver, CO 80246; phone 303-504-9223; fax 303-504-9585.

Another marketing tool comes from the American Association of Museums. They publish *The Official Museum Directory*, which includes detailed descriptions of the focus and offerings of each museum, notes if they have a store, and provides full contact information. It can be ordered by calling 800-521-8110, ext. 2 or checking a major library. The 1999 edition sells for $229.

We recently received a glorious 4-color, 92-page catalog from the Museum of Fine Arts, Boston. This holiday catalog contained great gifts under $50. And we're pleased to say six of those pages were devoted exclusively to books. Who knows how many museums send out similar catalogs and how many thousands, perhaps millions, of potential customers they reach?

Museums can indeed mean megabucks for you. Couple your materials to their collections and watch the cash flow.

Web Sites,
Wisdom, and
Whimsey

Reaching National Park Visitor Centers. The National Park Service has an extensive Web site at http://www.nps.gov. It includes a park index. By clicking on "visit your parks," you can then search by theme. To experiment, we entered "airplanes" and "marine life." Both had many links to potential sales outlets.

Museum marketing data on the Net. One particularly useful site can be found at http://www.yahoo.com/arts/museums_galleries_and_centers/indices/index.html. It will take you to many fascinating links. Visit http:/ /www.museumca.org/usa/ for an eclectic collection of WWW sites connected with museums, galleries, and archives in the United States. You can access them alphabetically, by state, or by type (art, children's history, miscellaneous, multidisciplinary, science, and technology).

Another stop on your museum Web tour should be http:// www.amn.org/central.htm. This takes you to the Art Museum Network, the official Web site for the largest art museums in North America. With some creative research, you can locate forthcoming events and recent acquisitions that may lead to additional book sales. For instance, the Houston Museum of Fine Arts recently had a special exhibition, Splendors of Ancient Egypt. A nonfiction book slanted to that topic or a novel set in ancient Egypt could have done well there. And the Art Gallery of Ontario just received a large donation of Inuit art. Here again, a book tie-in awaits. Some sites also allow you to search by artist or theme, thus making it easy to target your marketing efforts.

If you come to a fork in the road, take it!

Looking for customized individual help with this and other aspects of your project? Consider participating in our Jump Master Marketing System. See page 349 for details.

Sell books on the party plan. Move over Tupperware. Watch out Mary Kay. Here comes Dorling Kindersley Family Learning (DKFL)—and maybe you! Like all multilevel marketing, DKFL is based on enthusiasm and building a network of other distributors. For an investment of $99, distributors get an inventory of books worth $130, a business strategy guide, sales training program including video and audio tapes, and startup supplies and forms.

Distributors make between 25 and 40% on their sales and work with individuals and families in homes, schools, preschools, and daycare centers to help them build home learning centers. According to DKFL, they had 10,500 distributors in the U.S. at the end of 1997. That's one mammoth network marketing down-line!

Their products are developed primarily for the party plan and include much multimedia. Children's books take center stage, but they also include adult hobby, reference books, and such topics as cooking, fashion, and golf. A medium-sized publisher with a strong list in the right niche might do very well with this nontraditional approach. You can learn more by visiting their Web site at http://www.dkfl.com/. Their entire distributor compensation plan is presented online.

Selling directly to your niche market. Along this same line, BrightIdeas, a Concord, Massachusetts, direct sales education software company, hires mothers to sell to other mothers looking for computer programs for their kids. "The maternal bond helps establish trust, which is critical in the selling process," they report. Perhaps you could use a similar approach or develop a home party plan to merchandise your product line.

Attend fiction genre conferences. Connie Shelton tells of doing well when attending conferences geared to her specific genre. Writers, readers, reviewers, booksellers, and fans gather at these events. It's a great venue for making a name for yourself as an author, especially if you can wangle a spot as a speaker or panelist.

Networking is the order of the day. "If you've done your pre-publication homework and sent regular notices to your key contact list, people in the genre should have already heard of you before your first conference," Connie says. She tells of introducing herself to fans and booksellers and getting the reaction, "Oh, yes, I've heard of your book." At one conference she met Dulcy Brainard, then the mystery reviewer for *Publishers Weekly*. "She had missed reviewing my first book, but since that meeting has reviewed every other title we've submitted," reports Connie.

CHAPTER 15

Turn Up the Current with Catalog Sales

Catalog sales: Easy? Profitable? Ongoing? Yes and no. Well actually, no, yes, and yes. There are more than 14,000 printed catalogs in existence. Thousands more wait to tempt surfers on the Internet. Getting your books in them isn't easy. You're not going to be as lucky as the guy who accidentally installed the deer whistles on his car backwards—and everywhere he went he was chased by a herd of deer. Catalogers won't chase you. It works the other way around. Smart authors and publishers are in hot pursuit of them.

While almost any book can find a home in a catalog if you are inventive and persistent enough, certain types flourish in this marketplace more than others. General interest books, cookbooks, children's books, self-help/how-to titles, and coffee-table books lead the pack. Hardcover works especially well as catalogers want to drive up the price point. You might, however, be able to bundle several related paperbacks to make an attractive set. And the low-end general catalogs sometimes like inexpensive paperbacks as impulse items.

This is an ever-growing opportunity. More catalogs were mailed in 1997 than in any of the previous 10 years: 13,905,653 estimates the Direct Mail Association and the U.S. Postal Service. This industry experiences growth in sales of 6% per year. According to Simmons Market Research Bureau, 56.6% of all adults bought from a catalog in the last

12 months. What are these purchasers like? Overall, demographic statistics show that buyers tend to be married, female, and between 35 and 54.

Why this is such an attractive sale

First, virtually all catalogs buy nonreturnable. No more risk. No more wondering if half the books will arrive back in your warehouse or on your doorstep in six months or a year.

Second, most pay in 30 days. This unheard of practice in the publishing industry is as refreshing as a cold beer on a hot day.

Third, they buy over and over and over again. Once you've made the sale, they'll purchase your book for as long as their catalog remains in print (sometimes for as much as a year). And if your title is a good seller, they'll put it in the next catalog, and the next.

Fourth, rarely do they require exclusivity. That means you can place the same book in many different catalogs.

Fifth, they usually pay the freight. This frees up your capital for more important things.

Sixth, you get free exposure to hundreds of thousands, oftimes millions, of consumers. Not all of them will buy through the catalog; some may purchase at a bookstore, through a book club, or another channel of distribution.

Seventh, backlist is welcome. Catalogs couldn't care less if your book is two, three, or more years old—as long as the information is still fresh. So you can pursue this avenue of profit at any time and for older titles.

The range of subject matter

Catalogs come in as many varieties as Ben & Jerry's flavors. They cater to an enormously wide variety of whims. Here are just a few examples of consumer ones: There are sports catalogs like Gold Day, Bike Nashbar, and American Tennis Mart. For crafters there's Stitcher's Sourcebook, Keepsake Quilting, and Woodworkers' Store. Interested in games and novelties? How about Spy Headquarters, Magic Masters, or the Gamblers Emporium? Those seeking better health turn to The Vitamin Shoppe, Allergy Resources, and Healthy Living.

Businesspeople read office supply catalogs from Quill, Viking, and Reliable—or find inspiration in Successories. They also browse in-flight catalogs on various airplanes, and buy many computer and other high-tech products via mail order offerings and the Internet.

These business-to-business catalogs are flourishing even more than ones directed to general consumers. This is evident when looking at *Catalog Age's* fifth annual ranking of the top 100 catalog companies. Here's the line-up of the top 10: Dell Computer Corp., Gateway 2000, J.C. Penney, Digital Equipment, Micro Warehouse, Spiegel, Fingerhut, Viking Office Products, Land's End, and CDW.

Of course, not all catalogs are specialized. No doubt you're familiar with the offerings of Walter Drake, Lillian Vernon, and Hanover House. Perhaps you also receive the Wireless or Signals catalog of more upscale gift offerings. And for those who really like to shop expensively by mail, there is Bloomingdales and Neiman-Marcus, not to mention the Metropolitan Museum of Art's catalog.

How to find appropriate catalogs

You probably receive possible candidates in your mail on a weekly basis. Yes, it's what you used to consider "junk mail." Now it may be grist for your sales mill.

There are many directories that list catalogs, which are typically grouped according to subject matter. Most are quite expensive; you probably want to look at them in a public or university library before considering a purchase. Here are some to investigate: *The Directory of Mail Order Catalogs* (lists over 7,000 general catalogs), *Directory of Business to Business Catalogs* (contains 6,000 business catalogs), *Mail Order Business Directory* (lists 10,000 catalogs and mail order firms), *The Directory of Overseas Catalogs* (contains information on over 1,300 mail order catalog companies from around the world), and the *National Directory of Catalogs* (9,000 mail order catalogs).

To reach folks living in our neighboring country to the north, research in the *Catalogue of Canadian Catalogues*, which has about 1,000 entries. Then there's the *Kid's Catalog Collection* with over 500 catalogs featuring books, toys, and clothing for children. And the Direct Mail Association publishes the *Great Catalog Guide*.

Our favorite is a very affordable directory ($24.95 versus the $100+ for most of the others) called *The Catalog of Catalogs*. Although it is designed with consumers in mind, you can use it handily to track down possibilities in some 850 categories. To give you an idea of how obscure some of these topics are, here's a list of their newest categories: astrology, block printing, bulletin and chalkboards, calculators, gingerbread houses, pagers, safes, scooters, thermometers, and wines.

In a resource the size of a hefty phone book, they cover 14,000 catalogs in all. This is a superb place for market research. You can order by calling 800-331-8355. We're impressed by the detail of this reference's organization. Let's say you have a cookbook you'd like to sell via mail order. If you look under "Foods," there are no less than 22 different categories ranging from ethnic to health and natural, from meats to sugar-free and dietetic. Ditto for gardening. If your horticultural tome is about bonsai, herbs, orchids, rock gardens, vegetables, wildflowers, or a dozen other sub-subjects, you'll have a field day. (Pun intended.)

Trade shows are another hot place to find catalog matches. Most big conferences hold an accompanying trade exhibit. Look in the *Encyclopedia of Associations* to target major organizations in your field. Determine where and when their next convention is. Go armed with books and promotional materials and walk the aisles. Talk with vendors. Seek out those with related products. Many of the firms exhibiting produce catalogs you might never see otherwise. If you have a "gifty" book, gift shows are another fine place to meet potential bulk buyers.

What about the magazines published in your field? A careful read of their display and classified ads is likely to reveal catalogs aimed at your audience. Don't think just of consumer magazines. Also peruse trade journals and newsletters.

How it all works

Most catalogers will want to do a test first. This usually involves a purchase of a few dozen copies to as many as 1,000 for a huge catalog. If the book passes their test, the rollout order can mean a few hundred copies—or as many as 50,000. Subsequent orders for major catalogs may end up being your biggest revenue producer.

Timing can be important. For holiday catalogs, you must catch them very early in the year. By April their selections will likely already be made. Generally, most companies tend to purchase in two seasons: Fall negotiations are completed by the end of July for delivery the beginning of September. Spring buys are finished by December 1 for delivery February 1.

Not all follow this schedule. Some publish as frequently as quarterly, bimonthly, even monthly. The average is seven to eight times a year, so they're always looking for new product. And if you miss one window of opportunity, don't fret. Stay in touch as they may consider your books at a later date.

Most independent publishers give catalogs a 50% discount. This works fine until you start dealing with the big boys. Larger catalogers will send you a product submission packet and *their* contract with required discounts and terms. Don't be surprised if they want 80% off the retail price. If you've priced your book properly, you can give them that on orders of several thousand and still make a profit. Remember you have no expenses or financial risk: They produce and mail the catalogs. A few will charge more for the book than your stipulated retail price.

It's important, once you've negotiated a catalog sale, you be able to supply books. Sounds simple doesn't it? Not so. This stocking issue can get as sticky as fly paper. You need to have a good channel of communication with the buyer so you have adequate stock, yet aren't sitting on inventory they won't eventually want. And if your book really takes off, you must be prepared to turn a reprint within four to five weeks.

If you're really serious about making a commitment to this marketing strategy, it's wise to read the trade journal of the industry, *Catalog Age*. If it's not available in your library, you can get subscription information by calling 800-775-3777 or check them out online at http://www.mediacentral.com/CatalogAge. You can access selected stories from the current issue, check their archives, or do a keyword search. Other good publications for those interested in this area are *Target Marketing, DM News*, and *Direct Marketing*.

Know your reader

When you see a catalog targeted to this audience, treat it like gold! For indeed, it can be like finding buried treasure.

For instance, The Successories, Inc. holiday catalog is a bonanza of opportunity for business book publishers. They carry books that inspire, teach, and motivate—such titles as *Anatomy of a Leader; Motivating Today's Employees; Attitude, Your Internal Compass; 1,001 Ways to Reward Employees*—and an extensive library of books of quotations guaranteed to brighten your day.

Another catalog that concentrates strictly on business books is Schwartz's Gazette. They mix scores of business, professional, and technical books with an interview with Tom Peters, thus offering potential customers valuable editorial content. This is a strategy more and more catalogers are using to get people to actually *read* their offerings.

Of a more general nature, The Paragon's Favorites holiday catalog mixed a few books among clothing, jewelry, knick knacks, etc. The *Kids Paper Airplane Book* they carry would make a great gift, as would *Special*

Words, a collection of over 200 actual letters organized by theme to make gracious correspondence a snap. *Women Make the Best Friends* also found its way into this catalog, as did a source book titled *Unbelievably Good Deals That You Absolutely Can't Get Unless You're a Parent*, and a consumer guide on saving money dubbed *How to Figure It*. Does this give you any ideas?

Success secrets for approaching this market

Do your targeted catalogs carry books? Great. If not, you have a bigger challenge. They just don't carry books *yet*. Often you'll notice their other products are more expensive than your book. So how can you build your ticket to get it into the range of their other merchandise?

Think packaging. Can you combine it with another complementary book from a different publisher? Or maybe you can develop a "mini kit" with a couple of other nonbook items that relate to your topic. (A book on training your puppy with a pooper scooper and a dog toy, for instance.) One catalog we researched included The Feng Shui Kit. It consisted of a 112-page instruction book, a compass, mirror, and sheets of stickers.

Make it *easy* for them to want you. We recommend developing a one-page sell sheet that is reproduced on your letterhead and contains all the vital information. See the following Catalog/Retail Information Sheet. Here are some guidelines on the actual process:

- ■ Pinpoint likely catalogs using the strategies outlined above.
- ■ Call and request a copy (most have toll-free numbers and will gladly provide a free copy).
- ■ Study it. Consume it. Think about it. Relate it to your product(s).
- ■ If it looks promising, call again. This time you want the buyer's name (get the spelling too), address, direct phone number, fax, and email. Request any available submission forms or guidelines.
- ■ Complete their form if applicable; write a benefit-oriented sales letter that emphasizes why their customers need your book and citing specific examples of their current offerings that relate to it. Include your sell sheet, a book cover or photo, and important testimonials or reviews. It is also wise for *you* to write a catalog blurb in their style. Bingo—you've just made their job that much easier. Most agree it's better *not* to send the book at this stage.
- ■ Follow up two weeks later with a phone call. Find out when their decision-making committee will meet. Offer to send a sample book.

- At the designated time send the book (along with copies of all the previous PR materials).

- Follow up two weeks after the committee was to meet if you haven't heard anything. (If the answer is "no," try to find out their objection so you can overcome it at the next round of meetings.)

- Don't get discouraged. Be tenacious. When we published *Country Bound!* a few years back, we were sure it was a natural for *Mother Earth News*, which had a self-contained catalog in their magazine. But we could never get to "yes," let alone catch the decision maker. Finally, on our *fifth* call, we reached the woman, gave her our pitch— and were promptly put on hold.

She came back a couple of minutes later saying, "You know, you're right. I just pulled your book off the bookshelf and it is right for our readers." Then she gave us a purchase order for several cases. We sold to *MEN* month after month, year after year thereafter.

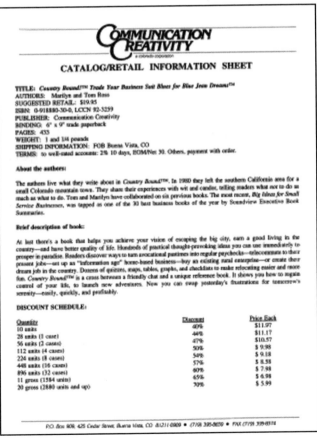

When you've had initial correspondence and they come back with a Vendor Information Sheet, they're serious. At this point you probably want to ask some questions:

1. Do you need a cover transparency?
2. What are your projections: how many copies do you expect to sell over what period of time?
3. Will my catalog blurb copy work or may I see yours?
4. When will the catalog drop (mail)?

Happily, as an independent publisher or author your chances of cracking this market are just as good as a major house. (Probably better because you care more and will be more dogged.) So if you want a close encounter of a profitable kind, get on the trail of catalogs, stalk them relentlessly, and grin all the way to the bank.

A plethora of catalog possibilities awaits you online. And it's easy to order the catalogs as you identify likely ones. You can take a general approach: Visit various search engines and plug in the word "catalog" plus the subject of your book and see what comes up. Or you can go directly to the following sites and do searches for topic-specific catalogs:

Buyers Index (http://www.buyersindex.com)

Catalog City (www.CatalogCity.com)

Catalog Mart (http://catalog.savvy.com)

Catalog Link (http://cataloglink.com)

Catalog Site, The (http://www.catalogsite.com)

Catalog of Catalogs for Teachers (http://edweb.sdsu.edu/index Teacher_Catalog.html)

Conduct a customer survey—and gain more customers! It's no secret that our best customers are our present customers. But are we serving them as well as we could? Why not devise a brief consumer survey that you send out with individual book orders to see if you're hitting the mark? Ask questions that address the following issues: order ease, shipping speed, price point, content, writing style, etc. Also inquire about upcoming related topics they would like to see. (Feedback here can shape your whole future publishing thrust.) And why not invite them to give you names and addresses of friends or relatives who might also enjoy your books? Our customers appreciate it when we care enough to stay in touch. Additionally, they—and only they—can tell us things we really need to know.

Reach 3,500 mail order catalogs in 55 categories! If you aspire to place your books in catalogs, this site is like finding a pool of cool water in the middle of the Sahara. We pulled up catalogs for travel, craft supplies, sex/erotica (all in the name of work, you understand), office supplies/equipment, plus cooking/food prep. In each category we identified catalogs that already carry books. (Of course, just because they don't include them in their line of merchandise *now* doesn't mean they won't if you're convincing.) Then we got smart and did a global search for "books." That netted 200 listings of various catalogs. Suffice it to say this is a bonanza of places to sell your products. To access them go to http://www.buyersindex.com. You can then either connect directly to a catalog's individual Web site or find general contact information.

"Never give up" is a worthy motto. We approached the Real Goods Catalog back in 1992 when *Country Bound!* first came out. They refused us flat. We tried again a couple of years later and weren't welcomed any more graciously. The book, however, was in the 1998 Holiday Catalog. It only took six years!

Why isn't phonetic spelled the way it sounds?

References galore all in one spot. For easy surfing, we suggest you bookmark http://www.refdesk.com/. Here you'll quickly access over 290 links to reference and research information, 260 search engines covering 19 categories, a virtual encyclopedia covering 45 subjects, and loads more. You can read *USA Today* and other worldwide newspapers, plus find headlines and summaries for the following topics: top stories, business, technology, world, sports, entertainment, politics, health, weather (five-day forecasts), human interest (including crime), and community (including a Latino link). Looking for a publicity news peg? What a time saver this will be as you scan for breaking news stories on any of the above subjects. Another intriguing link goes to "My Homework Helper." Though the title sounds sophomoric (and we're all seniors, of course), the material is broad in depth. You can find out about architecture, astronomy, aviation, birds, building, the census, chemistry, dentistry, diamonds, drug abuse, gravity, guitars, health, leadership, magic, Mars, nutrition, oceanography, physics, plumbing, and much more. What a great place to research!

Free **book exposure at trade shows.** Two ways to accomplish this is to work with catalog houses that sell your books and niche distributors that carry your titles. They often exhibit at major trade shows in their specialty areas. Why not call your catalog rep or distributor contact and ask what shows they will be attending? Figure out which ones are a good fit for your titles, then suggest that your product be displayed at their booth. They have to put *something* on display . . . why not make it your books? And if your author lives nearby, consider having him or her available in the booth to sign copies and schmooze.

CHAPTER 16

Enterprising Internet Strategies: Tech It to the Max

So you're ready to stake a claim on the wild, wild Web. Just as some companies rent space in physical shopping malls, your Web site is a digital retail storefront with an infinite number of shelves, total customer convenience (you're open 24 hours a day, 365 days a year), and a global reach. Mary Westheimer of BookZone, the Web's largest publisher community, says many of their publishers report one-third of their sales come from overseas. You also have a vehicle to communicate with your customers via email. Others may surf the Internet; we want to show you how to *harvest* it.

But perhaps you feel a bit like the man who remarked, "There has been an alarming increase in the number of things I know absolutely nothing about! Don't send me updates," he quipped. "I need down dates!" Yes, high-tech marketing can certainly be mystifying. In the next few pages we'll pierce the secrecy, solve that riddle, and lay out a game plan to take advantage of this powerful opportunity. Of course, in this brief chapter we can't cover all the bases. We'd strongly recommend you study the many books available on creating a Web site and fully utilizing the Internet.

Getting your Web feet wet

It's only natural, once you have a site, for you to want to create a presence—make your new marketing medium pay off in reach and revenues. With an estimated 1 million new home pages appearing on the Web every month, the challenge to stand out from this cyberspace crowd of eye candy grows ever daunting. Yet according to *Input*, the overall global Internet market is expected to soar to $200 billion by the year 2000. A study by Veronis Suhler forecasts that online spending for consumer books will be $2.1 billion by 2002. That's up from an estimated $150 million in 1997.

Statistics now tell us that 41% of U.S. households own a PC. And Web TV now gives those without computers the ability to access the Internet through their television sets!

More good news: A recent University of Michigan business school study of 11,000 customers found that *books*, along with computer equipment, are among the most popular products purchased online. So you're smart to be getting set now so you can work out any bugs and really be ready when Net use hits critical mass. Already, congestion is beginning to rear its monsterous head. A few years ago Yahoo, considered by many to be the best search engine, came out and found you. Now it takes as long as eight weeks to appear there . . . if they even agree to list your site—they don't include them all, as others do.

Many people still shun the Internet because it's too slow. They have no patience to sit and wait. But that's about to change. The problem is the bandwidth of transmission lines. As it increases, images will appear on the screen faster and the Internet will become a marketing tool unlike anything we've ever experienced! While today it seems like traveling in a covered wagon, tomorrow it will be like racing in a Ferrari. People will find it essential . . . just as they do the telephone and the fax.

The question is often asked, "Is anyone making money on the Web?" The answer is a qualified "yes." The majority of Americans still aren't online, so this naturally impacts sales. Those who are making money offer the right products or services for this audience and have developed unique marketing habits.

Please don't think of your Web site as just another brochure. To be successful online, you need to make a commitment. You must take personal responsibility to allot the time to do what it takes . . . or assign that task to someone else. It requires patience. Frequent updating. Experimentation.

Be aware that online marketing simply offers another method for reaching prospective customers. It should be part of your marketing mix. Don't abandon your traditional publicity and sales efforts. They should all be used in tandem. In that way, you create a synergy where each effort reinforces the others. One of the interesting things about the World Wide Web (WWW) is that it has a ripple effect. People may learn about your books online, then go to a bookstore or elsewhere to purchase them. If you properly "work" your site, you'll not only get direct orders, but you'll also see an increase in traffic from booksellers, wholesalers, distributors, and libraries. Media types may find you—or your authors—there as well.

Each thing feeds the other. A survey conducted by NetSmart of New York City found that 27% of Internet users have already purchased items online, while 46% ended up buying products at traditional retail outlets after finding out about them on the WWW. A whopping 81% of them used the Net to research new products and services.

Smart students of the Web realize that generating direct orders from their site is only one way to use this medium. With a guest book, you can also build a list of prospects for future titles, increase consumer awareness of your company and titles, gather information about customers' preferences to guide future product development, test consumer responses to various prices and titles, even solicit manuscripts and recruit authors.

Now let's move ahead and investigate the specifics of how to untangle the Web. If you want to spin yourself a successful home, you'll use a rifle-shot strategy rather than shot gunning. We'll be discussing how to attract more people to your site, get greater exposure for yourself, practice electronic schmoozing, become an online celebrity, use email to the maximum, and more.

Giving to get: adding value

In the restaurant business, the old adage is "location, location, location." On the Web it's "content, content, content."

There is a Universal Law that says the more you give, the more you get. Nowhere is that truer than online. Savvy marketers enrich their sites with valuable information. Then people come to visit your site because they can find helpful or entertaining data there. This is considered "value added"—meaning you give something extra.

Let's look at an example. Hal Higdon is the author of various books, including *Boston: A Century of Running*. On his Web site he posts weekly columns and other information for runners. He currently gets about 6,000 hits a week. Naturally, visitors also find information about his books and sometimes order. The reason they come in the first place, however, is not to find out about the books. They come for the helpful articles; the fact they order is a byproduct. And they keep coming back because he makes it worth their while by providing ever-changing informative content.

Your imagination is the only limit to what you might include. A cookbook publisher could have copies of recipes. And perhaps a luscious photograph of the finished dish. The publisher of a book on classic cars might include photos of some of these beauties. Trivia quizzes work well, especially for fiction. Perhaps you offer a free autographed copy to the first person with all the correct answers. Novelists could also include an essay, short story, or the first chapter of a book as a teaser. You might offer a downloadable coupon.

Excerpts from nonfiction books are a natural. Then the prospect can get an idea of the level of sophistication, the writing style, etc. (You might also attract a magazine editor interested in purchasing serial rights or electronic rights.) Weekly or monthly tips related to a book's topic are also winners. Consider developing a brief electronic newsletter to attract traffic to your site. By creating info-tools about your products, you serve as well as sell. Look for creative ways to put bytes in your bark.

NorthSouth Books, which launched its site in May 1996, gives added value to its catalog approach by including author bios, sneak previews of its upcoming titles, essays, plus information on nonbook items related to its popular Rainbow Fish series. (Of course, the Internet is ideal for publishers large enough to have a catalog. Instead of spending a small fortune on printing, shipping, postage, mailing list rentals, etc., you post your catalog online.)

Putting whole books on the Web

Some publishers are even putting their entire books online—and selling more of the hard copy versions. The National Academy Press put 1,700 of its books on the Net. The result? Some books are selling two to three times the previous level! MIT Press is experiencing similar results. "It's great advertising," says the Press's director. "For each of our electronic books, we've approximately doubled our sales."

The rationale is few are going to sit there and read a whole book online. And it costs money and time to download—which just gives you loose sheets of paper. This was proven very dramatically when the Starr Report went up on the WWW. It didn't hurt book sales one iota when the identical material was both free on the Net and sold in bookstores. On the contrary, it seemed to stimulate paperback sales, pushing the book onto best-seller lists.

Travel guidebook publishers are another group happy with Web publishing. "When we first put the entire text of our *Rough Guide USA* on the Internet, there was this big, collective gasp," recalls associate publisher Jean Marie Kelly. "The second edition has sold three times as well as the first and I'd guess up to half those sales come from having the book on the Web," she reports.

"People are discovering books on the Internet first, then looking for them in bookstores," agrees Bill Newlin of Moon Publications. It gives potential customers a taste of what a book offers.

If you want to extend your content into new markets and reach a worldwide audience of researchers, students, businesspeople, and general consumers, it may make sense to sell electronic versions of your books. Electronic Book Aisle (EBA), which avows to provide "Great books in an instant" is one possibility.

Unlike amazon.com and other online retailers, Electronic Book Aisle specializes in selling texts in completely digital format. Instead of shipping physical books, they download the book into a customer's computer via the Internet. Customers pay a flat fee (typically discounted from the full retail price) to get the entire book electronically. Interestingly, EBA works *with* many online retailers, which are encouraged to build a link from their site and are paid a 7% referral fee for purchases.

"We're open to any project that it makes sense to be selling in electronic format," reports spokesperson Bruce Newburger. Although they are dabbling in a number of fiction works, how-tos have been their bestsellers so far. EBA works on a nonexclusive distribution basis and pays an amount equal to 50% of net revenue. Of course, there is a cost involved in producing your book in an appropriate electronic format. To see what they have to offer and view their distribution agreement, go to http://www.bookaisle.com.

Another similar vendor is www.NetBooks.com. They allow authors to post their books on the Web with freely accessible excerpts. When ordered by an Internet user, the books download directly to the user's computer. This bypasses the need for printing, warehousing, and conventional shipping. They also offer talking books online to bring the ease of use and practicality of books on tape to the world of the Internet.

Search engines: how everyone can find you

A search engine, sometimes called a directory, is a Web site that helps you locate others . . . and guides them to finding you. It's like an interactive index. You type in a key word, such as "florists," and up pops a list of florists and florist-related sites. People browsing online for information about astronomy, for instance, will find your book on that topic. With search engines, "being well-connected" takes on a whole new meaning!

There are hundreds and hundreds of these. You've probably heard of several: Yahoo, Infoseek, Lycos, Alta Vista, Magellan, HotBot, and Excite, for example. They identify your site by key words.

It's a good idea to pick these key words and phrases *before* you write the text for your site. Then you can include your selections often within the content. Repetition is important. That helps encourage the search engines to list you higher.

Think carefully about the information you want to convey before you decide on these key words. In what categories do you want to be included? Remember that the purpose is to *entice* people to your site, not describe everything that's there. You want to attract your target audience, titillate these prospects, then get them to visit out of need or greed.

In addition to key words, you'll need a short paragraph—about 25 words—of description. In registration, words are precious. (To publishers and authors, words are always precious. But you know what we mean!) If the title of your site is "The Complete Guide to Self-Publishing," don't start your description with those same words. Likewise, don't duplicate words found in your URL. By the way, URL stands for Uniform Resource Locator—it's the address of your Web site (http://www.YourCompanyName.com).

To enhance your search capabilities, shorter key word strings are better. Some engines chop off the end of long descriptions. You might even submit 10-word strings at different times. Then these sets of key words would be distributed and embedded in the search routines.

Using a divide-and-conquer approach is wise. List with so many each day or each week. Saturday and Sunday mornings are often the best times for the do-it-yourself registration process.

Some search engines, called "spiders," don't rely on receiving submitted information; they go out and automatically fetch your pages for indexing. Some of them follow links from the address they are given;

others don't. Note which don't follow all subsequent pages as they are the ones to which you'll need to submit underlying pages.

But don't think once you're done, you're done. It's a good idea to check periodically and re-register as this can get you closer to the top of the list. Be sure, as you add new pages or features to your site, to alert the search engines. Submitting to each individually takes a while. Keep in mind the "paste" function to trim your time investment. Of course, you already have that succinct, benefit-oriented statement about your book if you followed our earlier advice. Plug it in over and over, especially to the directories that require you to submit information to them.

One way to keep yourself organized is to start a notebook to track your online marketing activity. Have one section devoted to search engines, another to links, another to newsgroups. (More on these two shortly.) Keep track of when you submitted, the results, and create a tickler system for when to check back.

Does all this effort pay off? "By being on the Internet, our products and services have been noticed in ways we never before imagined," reports Bill Ronay of Decatur, Georgia. "A Russian tourist agency came across our Web site. Several email contacts later, we now provide listings of several thousand events per year to them for the purpose of arranging tours for their customers." It opened up a completely new market for his publications in *The Ronay Guide* series.

When entering a URL, be sure to always include the "http://www." prefix. While some software programs don't require it, older ones do.

Links level the playing field

People love to surf and lurk, cruise and peruse, browse and behold. Links from other sites to yours allow them to instantly jump to you. Depending on how assertively you cultivate them, you may get more hits from links than from being listed on search engines.

Your aim is to find other sites with similar or complementary information, products, or services. Let's say you've written a banana cookbook. You'd want to contact the Banana Importers Trade Association, the Banana Promotion Council, sites about healthy eating, fruit, cookbooks, banana growers, etc.

So where do you find this plethora of possibilities? Now it's *your turn* to use the search engines! Enter "bananas" in any search engine and you'll be busy for hours clicking on relevant home pages, evaluating their usefulness to you, and tracking down email addresses of the owners or Web masters.

To make the actual contact, craft a brief message that compliments their site, explains who you are, what your URL is, and why a link would make sense. Sometimes your creative connections will be "reaching" with these links, so be sure to make your rationale clear to them. Most will want what is called a "reciprocal link." That means they will require a link from your site back to theirs. Links are usually free.

Advertising on the Net

Should you want to spend a little money and get truly aggressive, you can also purchase classified ads on some sites. They are cheap because you get limited exposure. The other advantage is they're quick. Within literally hours you can begin to see results. And online classifieds provide a great test mechanism. Debating between two titles? See which gets the most inquiries.

"Banner ads" are another advertising possibility. They are just what they sound like: little rectangular signs on someone else's site that announce your product or site, with a connecting link. Costs range from $20 to $350 per 1,000 hits. That means the number of times a site is visited over a certain period of time. This can be cost-effective for certain very targeted titles, for example, a golf book promoted on a site for golfers, a wheat-free cookbook announced on a site devoted to those who can't tolerate wheat, or a book on quilting advertised on a site for quilters.

Once you've found the right site or sites, you need to find the right message and present it in the right way. Go for pain or gain. Briefly state what problem the book will solve—or tell what fundamental desire the book satisfies.

When designing your banner use bright colors and animation. Always add the words "click here." If you can, place your ad at the top of the page and repeat it at the bottom. As in all advertising, track results to ensure maximum return on your investment.

Of course, amazon.com and barnesandnoble.com offer publishers and authors unprecedented opportunities for advertising their products to a global audience. In chapter 10 we delve into details about these online booksellers.

Electronic schmoozing = free publicity

The Internet is a lot like direct marketing in that it allows you to specifically target your market. Because the online world is fragmented into thousands of different groups, you can find and reach your potential customers easily. They literally sort themselves out for you! Bird lovers hang out here, *Star Trek* fans there—physicians can be found somewhere else, herbalists another place—and so on.

These gatherings of folks into Special Interests Groups (SIGs) are called by many names: newsgroups, forums, listservs, chat groups, etc. Newsgroups are on the USENET. "Forums" is usually the term used for Web-based and online service (AOL) areas. "Listserves" are mail lists that operate by email, while "chat groups" are typically online services.

You can win exposure, credibility, and customers by becoming an active participant in appropriate discussion groups. Networking online is the next best thing to being there. Better sometimes. Instead of merely working a room, you can work the whole world! It's the perfect way to make contacts in special interest groups.

Franklin White (online name of "Stelow"), is a twentysomething who shared a conversation in a chat room on America Online that paid off in spades. The live chat was the genesis of a significant six-figure book deal with Simon & Schuster. Laurie Chittenden, host of Ask the Editor, signed him up for the two-book deal. S&S published his first novel, the previously self-published *Fed Up with the Fanny*, in 1998.

A good first step when visiting a new group is to read their Frequently Asked Questions (FAQs). This general information will answer many of your queries and lay the groundwork for participating in the group.

There is an art to approaching folks online. Soft and subtle are the "open sesames" of newsgroups. Don't ask for the order; instead offer to send information to their email address. If you come on with a strong sales pitch, you'll be "flamed," which means people will send you hostile electronic messages. Judith Broadhurst enjoys excellent word-of-mouth for her newsletter and writing classes by making herself a constant presence in writers' online forums.

You've got to be customer-centered, not self-centered. One of the best ways to introduce yourself to a new group is to ask for help. When you receive positive responses, thank them . . . and be sure your email signature—which we'll discuss shortly—has a tag line about your publishing company or book.

Another approach is to dole out free samples. Offer information that will entice a response. Have a book on accounting? Maybe you'll put together 10 Year-End Tax Planning Tips. You could offer a short mailing list, a report, newsletter article, contacts, etc. Messages you post are identified by a one-line description. Make it short and catchy: Free

Tax Planning Tips Save You $$$. When you email them the promised item, be sure you insert a plug for your publication(s) at the bottom and refer them to your URL.

Wonder how many newsgroups there are? Estimates place the figure at more than 15,000! If you're a beginner in this electronic realm, check out http://web.presby.edu/~itbell/usenet/ for guidance.

How do you locate the news useful to you? Here are four possible sites to delight your soul. They cover every imaginable topic and facilitate electronic "chatting" with others of relevant interests. When you subscribe, you'll typically receive subscription verification plus information about what to do if you wish to leave the list. Don't lose the latter as it's sometimes more difficult to get off a listserv than on!

By going to http://www.lsoft.com/lists/listref.html you'll find some 14,000 lists. And at http://www.liszt.com a whopping 84,792 lists await you, along with some intriguing free offers. At http://www.neosoft.com/internet/paml/bysubj.html you will locate a conveniently alphabetized list that goes from "abuse" clear through "youth." And DejaNews has a newsgroup search engine at http://www.dejanews.com/ that should also prove helpful.

Still another approach is to email liszter@bluemarble.net. List key words in the message portion. This is going to a computer, not a human, so only list words; don't make sentences. When the list is complete (it will probably take anywhere from 20 to 40 minutes), prepare to prospect for gold! Just remember the old divide-and-conquer advice. You can only investigate a few each time. You have nuggets here for lots of digging. Yes, it's slow and laborious work. But the potential is enormous.

Liberally posting free information also works well. Susanna Hutcheson is a direct mail specialist who spreads her wisdom around the Net. She posts an article each month to a dozen forum libraries on CompuServe and to three newsgroups. The results? An average week brings 5 faxes, 5 phone calls, and up to 20 email inquiries from serious prospects.

Bulletin board systems: new version of the town crier

A close cousin of SIGs are computer bulletin board systems (BBSs). These are electronic versions of the old-fashioned corkboards where notices were posted. They come in various sizes, colors, and styles. Some are run by commercial enterprises, others by local groups, SIGs, or hobbyists. According to *Boardwatch* magazine, there are more than 65,000 public bulletin boards and perhaps as many as 150,000 private ones nationwide. BBSs have three sections: message, file, and conference capabilities. All can be used successfully for PR.

Some operate on a broad scale, others locally. To find local ones, check the library, computer stores, or computer user groups. It's a good idea to participate in major local BBSs; they often have a ripple effect that goes far beyond area boundaries. Most BBSs have different forums, or sub-categories. Although a few charge for their services, many are free.

Here's how they work: A person chooses one of the forums—"Reviews," for instance—then types in a note that future people can read. For example, a user might write, "I thought *Snow Crash* was a waste of time. I much preferred *Zodiac*, which was Stephenson's second book."

The next day another BBS user who read the notice might respond, "If you were disappointed by *Snow Crash* (I was too), maybe you should read Gibson's *Johnny Mnemonic*. Much more fun." By auditing this BBS you get honest reader feedback and plug your own products.

Hot new PR tool: cyberspace talk shows

Appearances on such shows as Oprah, Leeza, or Sally Jesse Raphael are not the only way to attract attention. You can be the center of attraction at special online events where you make live appearances for an hour or two. At America Online's Center Stage, for instance, there are four cyberspace "auditoriums," each with a capacity of 5,000 so there is a good chance of getting on if you can angle your subject to hitchhike on something in today's headlines. Coordinator Amy Arnold is encouraging: "Even if a proposal is not appropriate for Center Stage, it might fit one of the other areas." Try contacting the service or forum administrator for details on how to appear: RJScottV@aol.com.

Most appearances typically draw crowds of about 300 participants. However, transcripts of these events might reach another 300 people, many of whom are journalists or freelancers looking for story angles.

Suggestions for being effective online don't vary greatly from what you would do for typical media: 1) Provide the host with an introductory script with details on how to buy the book, 2) alert people about where it can be purchased online and give a toll-free order number, 3) provide a list of sample questions to ask you, and 4) keep your answers short and remind people they can find more details inside your book. Mention the title.

It's also a good idea to require that they include ordering information at the beginning and end of the transcript. And remember that, unlike radio, this is a visual medium. Including an interesting graphic or photo with your initial materials will increase your success ratio. It may also be available to those with the proper software in audio and video.

Getting booked here is similar to a TV show, yet you have the convenience of doing it from your home or office, as you would a radio phoner. "Sell us on your idea," advises a CompuServe spokesperson. "We have 2.8 million subscribers online, so it should have universal appeal." Even more targeted ideas, however, stand a chance with product managers in an appropriate specialty. For a proposal kit, call 614-457-8600.

Watch forums to see if a "thread" develops that fits your topic. A thread is a series of messages centered around a specific topic. When author Lisa Reid looked in on CompuServe's My Family Forum she decided this was a prime place for a guest appearance. The sysop (system operator) agreed and she did a stint on *Raising Kids with Just a Little Cash.* Lisa was prepared and had her uncle and dad standing by to pop in electronically and ask where they could get the book.

One literary agent we know of schedules his authors for electronic book tours. He posts notices on appropriate bulletin boards that an author will be available at a given time and place to answer questions about a certain topic. You can reach thousands of people in a short time with this approach.

Steve Miller, the author of *How to Get the Most Out of Trade Shows,* set up his own forum to give him higher visibility and credibility. He did a series of seminars online by loading several 1,000- to 1,500-word articles on different trade show topics into the forum library. After reading them, subscribers could ask him questions based on the information. He responded to over 200 questions on the public forum and received another 50 or so private messages via email. A spinoff was that an association asked him to upload his seminar lectures on their Internet bulletin board, then proposed they hire him to facilitate another online seminar.

Guest appearances online are an excellent way to promote books and authors. Be sure to get your share of this free publicity.

Email allows you to outsmart your rivals online

Email—used in tandem with Web site search engine registration, links, participation in SIGs, and guest appearances—forms a solid foundation for Internet success. With over 40 million users in this country alone, it's hot and getting hotter. According to a recent Forrester Research report, that figure will zoom to 135 million by the year 2001. And that's just the numbers for the United States! Email lets you lob statements and comments to online forums, not to mention influence individuals and reporters around the world.

Wally Bock, who authored *Cyberpower for Business*, uses it in a multitude of ways:

- As part of a regular contact strategy
- To set up mailing lists as a way to create virtual teams
- For surveys
- To send birthday greetings
- To forward articles that might interest a prospect
- As a follow-up device
- To deliver his newsletter
- For placing orders
- To acknowledge orders placed with him
- To get past gatekeepers who guard the telephone

John Kremer tells of attaching several review chapters of a manuscript to an email message and sending them to an editor. It arrived in seven seconds, didn't cost any postage, and made it easy for the editor to work with the material. (Are you encouraging your authors to submit this way?) By the way, John's new *1001 Ways to Market Your Book* is an ideal complement to this book. Order it at 800-331-8355.

The first and foremost way to use email as a marketing tool is to develop a "signature." This refers to a small file automatically attached to every message or newsgroup post you send. Properly thought out, it becomes a soft-sell commercial, yet is appropriate "netiquette" because it doesn't compromise traditional standards forbidding advertising.

Naturally, it will include your name, company name, phone, fax, snail-mail address, email address, and URL. It should *also* include a line with your book title or a brief statement of your publishing company thrust. This is like wearing an online name tag.

You can locate the email addresses of prime journalists. Briefly email them to identify yourself and give your area of expertise. Then when they're looking for a resource for a story, you're in their files!

Many who visit your site will not buy. But if you encourage them, they'll leave their email address to receive future information. Treat these online leads like any others. Don't settle for a brief email reply and hope they'll decide to purchase. Get their snail mail address so you can send them things through regular mail too. Or do periodic mass email mailings. Follow up again and again.

Toot your horn to promote your site

Newspaper, newsletter, and magazine editors are always looking for interesting sites to write about. Publicity about your Web site is a terrific way to generate traffic. Hold a zany online contest, become a unique information resource, or create an elaborate story within your site to pitch to these publishers. Use the traditional press release, sent via email or snail mail, to trumpet your message to those who can get the word out.

And don't overlook online magazines, called "zines." There are thousands of online publications that might be interested in your books. The subjects they cover range from alternative lifestyles to cooking, health to politics, religion to sports. We've discovered a wonderful place to locate them. Go to http://www.dominis.com/Zines. Pick a category, then for an even more definitive sorting process, enter a key word and search. You'll quickly find a list (with links) to many appropriate online magazines or newsletters.

Dan Kennedy, author of *How to Make Money with Your Ideas*, says his site has been most useful in reaching the media for publicity. Editors, columnists, and freelancers, as well as radio and TV producers, are using the Internet more and more to seek story ideas and interview subjects. Keep visible and they'll come to you!

When Tony Alessandra's site—built around his book titled *The Platinum Rule*—was mentioned in *USA Today,* there was an immediate and dramatic jump in the number of visitors. Tony was able to crack this prestigious national newspaper because his site features an interactive survey where visitors can answer questions and learn more about their own personality or that of someone else, which is the theme of his book. (Remember what we said about "value added"?)

The wrap up

You never know from day to day where the Web will take you. As we were putting the finishing touches on this chapter, a call came in from a *Wall Street Journal* reporter. She is doing a story on independent publishing and wanted an interview. When we asked how she had heard of us, she replied, "I found your SPAN site through Infoseek on the Web." So now we'll get national publicity in one of the most prestigious publication in the land, all as a result of our Web site!

Gail Golomb tells of a pharmacist from Michigan who contacted her because of her site. He not only ordered her book, but they discussed several issues regarding kidney stones from a pharmacist's point of view. When she offered to supply his pharmacy with the book, he liked the idea. Thus in one online contact, she 1) made a direct sale, 2) got a potential subscriber for her newsletter, 3) made a new professional distribution contact, and 4) cultivated a future buyer/seller for other books.

The Web has unlimited potential. None of us even has the slightest clue of what this tool will mean to us in another decade. Sure, it provides a new way of conducting worldwide e-commerce. Yes, it links you with more media than you've ever imagined. Although much of the outcome is in the hands of technology—and people's acceptance of it—you can still have a huge impact on the results. Be proactive. Get involved. Make this a magical part of your marketing mix.

Don't be intimidated into thinking you must rush out and print all new literature to include your URL. One approach is to have it printed on a quantity of see-though labels, which you then affix in strategic places until you're ready to reprint your literature, or have a rubber stamp made. Put it everywhere! On:

business cards	*advertisements*
letterhead	*invoices/statements*
envelopes	*articles about you (or your authors)*
shipping labels	*articles/columns by you (or your authors)*
flyers	*newsletters*
brochures	*inside your books*
catalogs	*on phone answering/voice mail messages*
postcards	*during radio/TV interviews*
order forms	

Visit (and get listed with) Nerd World. No, you don't have to be a computer geek to appreciate this site. It gets a whopping 2,000,000 hits each month and has 260,441 links, so we're talking about the big time here. The site features 23 leisure and knowledge categories with scads of subcategories. For instance, we pulled up "health" and found the following subtopics: beauty therapy, books—health and fitness (YES!), e-zines on health, family health, first aid, fitness, health news and information, health reports, living, marketplace—health and fitness, medicine, mental health, nutrition, self-improvement, skin care, support groups and programs, and weight loss.

Whew! This is an incredible place to research—both for editorial content and marketing opportunities. And they reference books on such subjects as history, parenting, religion, travel, biography, cooking, humor—you name it. Go to http://www.nerdworld.com/ and go for it!

Dramatic Web use. According to an American Management Association survey of 3,500 of its members, 22% used the Internet for purchasing products and services in 1997. That is projected to leap to 52% in 1999. Active Media Incorporated, which tracks Internet business, forecasts exponential growth. Web-generated revenues hit $24.4 billion in 1997. And they estimate an incredible $1.5 *trillion* in sales for 2002!

Active Media goes on to say that Web sites with two years' experience are twice as likely to be profitable as the newest arrivals: those that have been in existence for fewer than six months.

So should you have a Web site? Yes. This is a learning process. Begin to prepare now for the fortune that lies waiting to be unearthed on the Web. We've had our sites for SPAN (www.SPANnet.org) and About Books, Inc. (www.about-books.com) up for over two years and we're still tinkering and fine-tuning to get them just right. It takes time, experimentation, and testing to find the best approach. That's why we say get on the Internet *now* so you'll be ready when the multitudes strike at the turn of the century.

Internet publicity tips galore. Steve O'Keefe, who is known to many publishers for his consulting services and his excellent book, *Publicity on* *the Internet*, has launched a truly useful resource center at http://www.olympus.net/okeefe/pubnet. A visit here will have you leaping all over the Internet to other fascinating possibilities, as he includes links to more opportunities. You'll find sections on self-promotion resources, paid promotion possibilities, registration resources, chat spots, the search gang, newsgroups, media contacts and people finders, etc. This is definitely one to bookmark.

Web Marketing Forum a bonanza! Now you can easily access articles about general strategies for Internet marketing via http://www.wilsoninet.com/HyperNews/get/forum/strategy.html. Here you'll find, for instance, "Using contests and giveaways to promote business," "Going global with your business," "Creating links to celebrity home pages," and "Analyzing your Web site traffic." While some of these and other articles may be self-serving and used as vehicles to sell Web services or hosting, many offer valid information. Under the section on "Promotion," there are links, tips, and incredible strategies for increasing traffic to your site. And a click on "Trends" lets you find out in what direction the winds are blowing.

Computer cuties
Ram: a male sheep
Rom: a ram after a sex change operation

Hanker to know more about e-commerce? Then go to http://e-comm.internet.com/. Here you'll find a comprehensive resource for news about electronic commerce. This is also a gateway to hundreds of sites and resources on the WWW devoted to the evolving electronic commerce industry. You'll love their links. There is also a library with an extensive compilation of articles and reading lists. Their resources section offers details about online commerce regulations, research groups, consortium, newsgroups, industry standards, and more.

Use the grocery store to improve your Web site! (No, we haven't lost it. Honest.) In fact, we've discovered there are many common denominators between supermarkets and publishers. Why not learn how to entice customers to buy more from the research and strategies used in the fiercely competitive grocery industry? Two important factors were revealed in the most recent Point-of-Purchase Advertising Institute's "Consumer Buying Habits Study": 1) 70% of purchasing decisions are actually made in the store, most of which are unplanned, and 2) shoppers are more likely to purchase a product that is highlighted via an in-store display.

So how do we translate this information into Web book sales? Help those who come to your site by highlighting certain items like the grocery store end-of-the-aisle displays that draw shoppers' attention to products. Feature your biggest seller, however, not a "dog." Push your strengths. Notice the razors, cigarette lighters, playing cards, glue sticks, etc., to tempt one at the checkout stand? Mimic that merchandising tactic. Choose high-profit items and feature them prominently at the end of your order form (the equivalent of a checkout stand). By tempting those who are already ordering with an additional impulse item you can definitely build your sales. So "check out" what they do the next time you go to the grocery store. This kind of market research can yield big dividends.

Learn about everything from anarchy (5,768 listings) to zebras (259 listings) here. This site gives you access to the conversational forums of the Internet. Many Usenet groups are archived for a month to a year on Dejanews. You can search by keywords and find virtually anything. This will save you countless hours rummaging through Usenet news groups. In fact, rather than reading all the postings every day, you could just enter the subject you want to know about and see what comes up. Although you lose the aspect of active participation, it's a wonderful time-saving technique. Reach them at http://www.dejanews.com.

Definition of a keyboard:
a device used to enter errors into a computer.

Get a head start on your Internet marketing. BookZone offers its Internet Marketing Toolbox—which contains the Internet Marketing Checklist, Online Marketing Worksheet and Internet Marketing Log—for free at http://bookzonepro.com/mkttoolbox.html. You'll get instructions on how to use each component, too!

CHAPTER 17

Premiums and Incentives Super-Charge Your Bottom Line

Selling thousands of copies of your books to one company, organization, or association is a phenomenal money maker. These are called premium or incentive sales. Books are a growing segment of the overall premium/incentive market, increasing approximately 8% a year in the burgeoning $25 billion-a-year industry. Besides giving a gigantic boost to your bottom line, the beauty of these sales is they don't compete with your other marketing efforts. You are paid when the books are shipped, the sale itself is great PR—and these companies never heard of returns.

Further good news is you don't need the magic of David Copperfield to pull it off. Premium sales usually consist of about 60% inspiration and 40% perspiration. We'll guide you to cultivate and close these colossal sales.

Think big, really BIG. How big? Quantities range anywhere from 500 to 100,000 units. There have even been a few sales into the millions. The majority fall between 5,000 and 20,000 copies—certainly worth the effort of any self-respecting independent press.

Is this really doable? You bet! Kim Gosselin of JayJo Books, L.L.C. received a check for more than $330,000 for the sale of 110,000 of two of her titles: *Taking Asthma to School* and *Taking Asthma to Camp*. Nice going, Kim!

And just before Christmas, Diane Pfeifer of Strawberry Patch pocketed $68,100 for selling 15,000 copies of her *Gone with the Grits* book to Quaker Oats. You'll hear from both these ladies later in this chapter.

Books as premiums

Books have "high perceived value," make impressive gifts, and work in all sorts of ways. Businesses use them to create goodwill, strengthen existing ties, and foster new relationships. Manufacturers buy them as an incentive for their sales force and as dealer rewards; corporations purchase them for gifts and as training tools. Companies like books because people don't throw them away. They represent a gift with long-lasting appeal.

The largest segment is probably sold as consumer incentives: traffic builders to encourage people to come into a store or rewards for a consumer who participates in an offer. Product tie-ins often take the form of money-off coupons or rebate offers.

One of their most common uses is as a promotional piece or in-room gift for incentive travel programs. "We found them [books] to have a very high perceived value," says Kevin Krueger, director of department store sales for Regal Ware, Inc. This Wisconsin-based maker of kitchen appliances and cookware goes on to say, "Also on the plus side for us, they are a relatively cheap and easy premium to offer."

Premiums also serve as lower ranking prizes in contests or sweepstakes, as a thank you when one customer refers another, as a gift for listening to a direct selling pitch, or as a reward for spending X number of dollars.

Financial institutions have long been heavy users of premiums. They love coffee-table books, financial guides, regionals, and titles that appeal to mature consumers. These books are given for opening a new account, making a substantial deposit to an existing one, taking out a loan, or maintaining a certain balance over a specified period.

Government agencies, American embassies, and consulates around the world sometimes purchase bulk quantities of books. Additionally, there are special promotion agencies and sales incentive houses that exist solely to put together premiums with purchasers.

Books are also used in conjunction with magazine, newsletter, and newspaper subscriptions. *Working Mother* magazine shipped thousands of customized hardcover limited editions of *The Beardstown Ladies' Stitch-in-Time Guide to Growing Your Nest Egg* to increase renewals. Of course, it also increased the "nest egg" of the publisher. Mike Royko, columnist with the *Chicago Times*, wrote a book titled *Sez Who? Sez Me*. It was used as a circulation booster by his paper.

Sometimes premiums are considered to be self-liquidating. That means the company buying the books charges recipients a discounted amount that covers the investment put up by the company. Here's an example of how this works: When we spoke with the special sales director at E. P. Dutton, they were in the process of positioning *Winnie the Pooh* with Lever Brothers. In turn, the food manufacturer offers purchasers of Mrs. Butterworth syrup half price off the book when accompanied by a proof of purchase coupon. Dutton anticipates selling 80,000 copies. The consumer will ultimately foot the bill. Dutton will cash the check.

No major publisher dominates the field. In fact, many ignore it completely. It's estimated that only one in five trade houses really pursue premium sales. What a wonderful opening for small and mid-sized publishers and clever authors! To capitalize on this situation, let's examine what some of the "biggies" do.

Success examples

Better Homes and Gardens is one of the most aggressive publishers to exploit this market. They often spin out parts of their larger cookbooks into 16-, 32-, or 64-page booklets. Their red plaid cover has high recognition value and is trusted by consumers. For that reason, their premium sales typically start around 50,000 copies and sometimes run into several million. They also team with manufacturers on complete books. In one especially successful match, Frigidaire bought one of their titles to give to refrigerator purchasers. This giveaway was credited with boosting refrigerator sales by 44%!

St. Martins Press used an innovative twist to sell one of their titles. When they heard the Sylvania 19-inch TV had been voted the "best in its field," they convinced Sylvania to buy their book of lists, *The Best of Everything*, as a premium.

Emergency Medical Procedures made a bunch of money for Prentice Hall. Getty Oil asked that the cover be redesigned for them, then bought a large quantity at 60% of retail to be used in auto dealerships and by sales reps.

What's hot

If you decide to pursue this avenue, be aware premium customers swarm around certain areas as bees do around honeycombs. Here are the most popular topics: cookbooks, sports, health/fitness, how-to, reference, and children's books. Business books of many stripes have appeal: possibilities include training manuals, books on change/leadership/ethics, and sales guides.

Certain industries are more likely to participate in premiums and incentives. Food and beverage companies are heavy users, as are appliance makers. Then there's the automotive field, especially for tires, batteries, and accessories. Pharmaceuticals are another huge possibility. And, of course, banks and savings and loan institutions often present gifts to their customers. General corporate tie-ins run a wide gamut: gifts to VIP customers, stockholders, board of director members; incentives for members of the sales force; training tools for various departments.

There are no limitations. *USA for Business Travelers* was a natural for airlines, hotels, credit card companies, and travel agencies. *In Search of Excellence* zoomed to stardom partly because of imposing corporate sales. You're bound only by your own imagination. Bear in mind, of course, companies or products favorably mentioned in your book are always prime prospects. You may even want to purposely include certain ones during the writing/editing stage with this strategy in mind.

And you needn't be confined to using the whole book. You might excerpt a part, chapter, section, even certain recipes to suit a given customer.

Creating customized editions

Customizing the book is often the "open sesame" for corporate sales. A *sponsored book* will have a personalized cover. For certain it will include the company name, maybe even a logo or product photograph. Clever publishers design the book's interior so they can remove the bastard title page and/or pages of quotes and reviews in the front and substitute a Foreword by the CEO. Thus only one print signature needs to be changed.

Major publishers typically won't customize until the customer is at the 5,000-unit level. It can be done economically in lesser quantities, however, if you're going back to press anyway. For smaller quantities, another approach is to affix a round or oval gold sticker, which has been imprinted with the customer's name, in one corner of the cover.

Applying creativity

How do you dream up premium matches for your books? Roger Von Oech says in *A Whack on the Side of the Head,* "Discovery consists of looking at the same thing as everyone else and thinking something different." Let us embark on such a journey of discovery. To succeed at premium sales, we must get out of our normal marketing rut: expand concepts, open ourselves to new paths, practice creative thinking. Here are some guidelines to help you accomplish just that:

1. Look for links, similarities, and connections between your book and companies, products, slogans, even associations and nonprofit organizations.
2. Scour each book internally for ideas.
3. Ask, "What's the fit?"
4. Play the "What-if" game. Follow it with some contrary-to-normal condition or idea.
5. Probe the possible, the impossible, the ridiculous.
6. Challenge the rules. Ignore "we've always done it this way" thinking.
7. Seek the second right answer. It may be an offbeat, but often innovative, solution.
8. Don't be judgmental. Let the ideas flow.

By the way, *A Whack on the Side of the Head* had several corporate takers. IBM bought 2,000, Hewlett Packard picked up 700, and Control Data took 600 copies of this handbook to creativity. You too can climb on this lucrative bandwagon.

The mechanics of how it works

The one drawback to this merchandising strategy is that nothing happens fast. Sometimes it seems like premium and incentive deals take about as long to mature as trees do to grow. Sales take months, sometimes years, to develop. But they are worth waiting for!

Diane Pfeifer of Strawberry Patch tells of working on one deal for *four* years! It's not that it was so difficult; the Quaker Oats contact people just kept changing. They will put a coupon offer in 4 million boxes of grits offering the book. (So this may not be her last sale to them either.) Quaker got a 55% discount off the retail price of $9.95; Diane got a fabulous, and well deserved, Christmas present.

Examples of Premium Book Sales

We hope one or more of these case histories will trigger an idea for you. Some books and premium buyers make unusual bedfellows.

■ *The 17 Laws of Successful Investing* sold to Cosmair, Inc. to be used for educating retirement plan participants. Rich Rodman of Alidan Press gave only a 20% discount on the 500 books. Because large corporations have been mandated by law to provide financial planning information to their employees, this may be only the tip of a very large iceberg. Do you have a book that addresses an issue that companies have been mandated to cover?

■ Bill Gordon sold more than 1,000 copies of his *Ultimate Hollywood Tour Book* to the Auto Club of Southern California.

■ R. L. Stine's *Goosebumps Thrillogy* found their way into more than 30 million bags of Frito-Lay products. (It would break your heart to make a sale like that, wouldn't it?!) Pepsi put a coupon for a free Stine book on 35 million 12-packs and 6 million 24-packs of pop. Not to be outdone, Hershey Chocolate offered mail-in coupons for free copies of the books in 52 million newspapers! These particular books weren't offered for sale in any bookstores; it was strictly a premium marketing campaign.

(continued on next page)

Most sales fall in the range of 5,000 to 100,000 copies. Your customer may want to buy a couple of hundred units for initial testing purposes before committing to a large quantity.

Be flexible. Some premium purchasers will want to customize the cover to include their name, logo, slogan, or product photo. Talk with your printer and allow for this extra expense when putting together the deal. They may buy all, or a part, of your book. They may want to make slight modifications to the text or add something to make it more appealing to their customers.

And now to the $64,000 question: What do you charge? Whatever the traffic will bear. On amounts up to 5,000 units, 50 to 70% off the retail price is typical. In large volume, experienced buyers will expect to pay manufacturing costs plus 10%.

Be sure to get a written purchase order or agreement that spells out all details, such as who pays the freight. If there is any question about the integrity or financial status of the company with which you're dealing, insist on at least half payment before you go to press, or establish an escrow account to hold the money. In some cases, publishers get lines of credit from banks based on the company for whom they are going to publish and the purchase order presentation. Go for the balance being due on delivery, certainly no later than 30 days afterwards.

When we discuss this topic in our seminars, attendees often ask if they can sell to more than one company. The answer is a qualified "yes." Your customers have the right to demand exclusivity—either within their industry or their geographical area. You don't sell to Pepsi, for instance, then go to Coke and try to strike a deal. Did you connect with a regional savings and loan? Don't muddy the waters by contacting their competition in the area. If you peddle a book on household hints to a washing machine manufacturer, steer clear of similar manufacturers. Of course, nothing is stopping you from tying in with Arm & Hammer baking soda, etc.

Finding the golden needles in the premium haystack

As you might expect, there is a directory for this industry. Finding it is like discovering manna from heaven. Go to the reference or business section of a major library and request the *Directory of Premium, Incentive & Travel Buyers*. Your best business contacts are right there: 12,000 corporations plus 19,000 premium and incentive buyers by name, title, address, phone, and fax. Additionally, you can find prospects by city or state, company name, or type of product or service they sell.

Examples of Premium Book Sales (continued)

■ Westcliff Publishers racked up a sale of 100,000 copies of their *The Colorado Scenic Calendar* when Coors Beer decided to give it to their distributors, who then doled the calendars out to retail accounts as holiday gifts.

■ The executive director of the Software Publishers Association bought 1,000 units of Dan Janal's self-published *How to Publicize High-Tech Products and Services* to give as a premium to their new members. And the associate publisher of *MacUser* magazine took another 500 units so his ad reps could give them as presents to their clients. Now when Dan walks through computer conventions people stop him because they recognize him from his picture on the book. (Not bad publicity for a guy who also makes his living as a speaker.)

■ Dorothy Kupcha Leland managed to have Public TV in Sacramento pick up two of Tomato Enterprises' books as a premiums on a membership drive. This centered around the 150th anniversary of the Donner party. Those who contributed at the $125 level could choose a bundle of products for children consisting of *Patty Reed's Doll: The Story of the Donner Party, Sallie Fox: The Story of a Pioneer Girl,* and a small doll. Additionally, Dorothy was interviewed on PBS and the book was shown on TV throughout the program.

(continued on next page)

Examples of Premium Book Sales (continued)

■ The American Indian Movement selected *Wisdom Keepers* to express thanks to special donors. Beyond Words Publishing in Hillsboro, Oregon, had nice success with this premium promotion.

■ Dr. Tony Alessandra, a much-in-demand professional speaker, spoke free for several corporations that each purchased 600 copies of his *The Platinum Rule*. He made his $10,000 speaking fee in book profits. He also sold 200 copies to U.S. Life and customized them in an unusual way: A large sticker was placed on the inside front cover with a note from the company and Tony's autograph. Thus, a generic book was quickly and easily customized.

■ A Long Island, New York, realtor purchased bulk copies of that region's Zagat restaurant guide to give to new home buyers. Look for ways to create synergy between your regional title and area businesses.

■ Dearborn Financial Publishing, Inc. did a special customized print run of their *How to Buy Your Home . . . and Do It Right* for an east coast branch of Northwest Savings. The S&L gave the books away to people applying for mortgages. Dearborn pocketed 40% of the $14.95 price for each unit sold.

■ Judy Dugan sold her self-published book *Santa Barbara Highlights and History* to a local bank that was celebrating the opening of a new branch. The 5,000 copies went to

(continued on next page)

(If your corporate coffers are flush, you can purchase a copy for $259.95 by calling 800-223-1797.)

This secondary research, however, is but the tip of the iceberg. What about checking trade shows and exhibitions yourself to locate suitable matches? The library has reference directories that list such shows all around the country. There are also trade show/exhibition sites listed on the Web. Perhaps one will be held near by so you can do hands-on primary research. If you publish a book about Crock-Pots or woks, for instance, small appliance trade shows are a bonanza of potential incentive sales contacts. Ditto for books on computers.

Just as we have BookExpo America and regional book shows for publishing, the premium/incentive industry does likewise. The granddaddy is The Motivation Show, held in the fall at McCormick Center in Chicago. This event has been going on for 65 years and attracts some 25,000 people. Decision makers who attend seek premiums and incentives to increase sales and foster attitudes of loyalty. Many also have internal company agendas such as strengthening productivity, reducing absenteeism and employee turnover, or improving work habits and leadership skills. For more information on the show, call 630-850-7779. There are also regional shows in New York,

California, Texas, Ohio, and New England.

Go where manufacturers of related products will be. Position yourself with others interested in your market. Think about who else reaches your potential readers and how your book can serve their needs. Maybe you've identified cereal companies as a target (they're ideal for kid's books). Perhaps it's garden equipment manufacturers or the maker of a well-known beverage.

Sometimes an ad agency will be the conduit through which you connect with a sale. Eileen Johnson, formerly of Dearborn Financial Publishing, Inc., tells of being contacted by ad personnel who saw one of their books in a bookstore. The client, U.S. West Direct, was looking for a book on customer service to mail as an appreciation gift to their Yellow Page advertisers. They chose Dearborn's *Talking with Your Customers*, buying 2,000 in the fall of 1996 at a 60% discount to use as a test.

So while the first step is identifying likely industries, perhaps the larger challenge is finding out how to reach the players in these industries who might be interested in

Examples of Premium Book Sales (continued)

every customer who came in during the first week.

■ *If Life Is a Balancing Act, Why Am I So Darn Clumsy?* has found a lucrative home with Amway. Author/publisher Dick Biggs has sold over 4,000 copies to a top Crown Ambassador distributor. Do you have a title that might appeal to network marketing groups?

■ In an unusual combination, Parke Davis Pharmaceuticals buys *Tales for Travelers* from Penton Overseas to mail to doctors along with advertising for new drugs. Although these brief tales, which are conveniently folded like a map, have nothing to do with pharmaceuticals, the 30-minute stories provide quick and exciting journeys of discovery for busy doctors. Penton Overseas also merchandises quantities to AAA, cruise lines, travel consortiums, and luxury hotels, which use them as gifts for evening turn-down service.

■ Lilac Press sold 1,000 copies of their first printing of Dr. Bill Parsons' *Cholesterol Control Without Diet: The Niacin Solution* to a drug company in Oregon. Then they peddled 500 copies to a similar firm in Minnesota.

purchasing your book in bulk. Get online and hold onto your hat! The *Thomas Register of American Manufacturers* awaits you in cyberspace. This is a massive directory of virtually every company that manufactures virtually every thing in the U.S.

The beauty is you can do key word searches that pull the information immediately to your fingertips. Got a cookbook you want to sell to a food company or appliance manufacturer? Bingo. Have a camping guide? You could approach camper manufacturers (58 companies listed); trailers, travel (61); or RV parts, accessories and supplies (129). The list goes on and on.

Once you've accessed the appropriate product heading, you can either use their internal hyperlink to go directly to the manufacturer's site, or contact them via fax if they are not yet on the Web. The other good news is membership to access this information is free and takes all of about 30 seconds. Furthermore, if you can't locate the category you want, they offer a customized search feature. Tune in at http://www.thomasregister.com. Of course, if you're not on the Web, you can use the paper version of *Thomas Register of American Manufacturers* in the business or reference section of a major library.

You might also want to check *Hoover's Handbook of American Businesses*. It has one-page overviews of companies, complete with contact information, number of outlets, earnings, what they sell, and a list of key competitors—which could lead you onto many other marketing possibilities. Find them on the Internet at http://www.hoovers.com or in your main library. Their database contains some 7,800 major U.S. corporations.

While capturing information, always include the name of a primary contact person. Titles vary from company to company. You really want the VP of Promotion or the Promotion Director or Promotion Manager. But you may have to go to the VP of Sales or Marketing to locate the above person. If you're going after a food manufacturer, Diane Pfeifer advises, "Find the *brand manager* of that particular product. It cuts hours off your research."

Do your homework. Know the company you're targeting. Look them up on the Web. Get a copy of their annual report by calling their office and speaking to the public relations office or, if the company is local, check in the library. Call the librarian at their major local newspaper. An article may have run about them lately that gives you new insights.

Using Premium Reps to Peddle Your Wares

These sales reps usually have substantial corporate training in sales and marketing and were often former premium managers themselves. They are sharp individuals with incredible contacts who specialize in forging the right marriages between premiums and product offers.

If you are fortunate enough to attract a member of this ready-made sales force, expect to pay a commission of 5-10%. Of course you *don't* pay salaries, pension plans, health insurance, expense accounts, etc. as you would to a salaried employee. Nor do you wait 90-120 days for your money as we in the publishing industry are so often forced to do.

Most premium reps belong to the Incentive Manufactures Representative Association, Inc. (IMRA). You can reach this organization at 630-369-3466, 1805 North Mill Street, Suite A, Naperville, IL 60563.

Of course, membership in IRMA would put you in immediate contact with about 150 reps as you hobnob at their annual Marketing Conference. This four-day working meeting is devoted to the analysis of industry trends, problem solving, and knowledge sharing between reps and manufacturers like you.

IMRA also publishes *The IMRA Handbook*. While the hefty price of $225 will dissuade some, those really serious about pursuing this avenue will find practical, proven ideas here for organizing and managing an incentive department, interviewing reps, plus developing appropriate sales support materials. You'll discover why middlemen can be more important than end users. Along with the *Handbook* you get other goodies such as a model contract, membership list, and a set of rep member labels. This makes it easy to solicit their interest.

Strategies from the sage of premium sales

Before premiums can take you to the promised land, you need someone who knows the way. Kim Gosselin of JayJo Books is the supreme guide. "You can get rich selling books as premiums," she declares. Kim has racked up a total of over $1.5 million in premium revenue working out of her home and by herself, so she knows! This lady could sell sand to a sheik. She also does hourly consulting. Call 314-861-1331 for details.

Here are some of her secrets: Once you've identified the right contact person and done you homework, call and make a short pitch. If there is interest, send a package and proposal. This will not be your normal mailing. To catch the potential buyer's attention for one of her titles, she enclosed the book manuscript in a clear plastic backpack—complete with custom imprinted pencils carrying their company name, bookmarks, and a full-color cover.

Another time she hired a specialty ad company to do a prototype of a big clear aspirin bottle with the prospect's logo on it, then placed her book inside. Other times she makes up a fancy gift basket. (If you have a cookbook, include cookies made from one of the recipes, measuring spoons, and a nice pot holder in your basket.) Be creative. Don't just send a proposal in a manila envelope. "That first impression may be your last. Make it look the best it can be," she counsels. "Send it FedEx or UPS overnight."

Call two weeks later and try to set an appointment for a presentation. "If they give you an appointment, they're half way sold," she says. During that presentation, show your passion for the project. Passion sells! Explain to them how you're creating a win/win situation, how it's going to increase their sales. Have your discount policy ready. Her prices range from 50 - 80% off the retail price with payment net 30. "Ask for the order," she instructs. "Why don't we test market 10,000 and see how it goes?" Always have something dramatic you can leave behind.

You may run into objections:

1. "We have no money left in the budget," they tell you. Counter it with a suggestion that they write it into next year's budget.

2. "We can't afford it." Could they comarket it with another compatible company?

3. "Our lawyers will have to take a look at the book." Fine.

4. "We want our name on the cover, a message from the CEO, our brand mentioned in the recipes, commercial plugs in the book . . . yada, yada, yada." Wonderful. Give them anything they want—and are willing to pay for.

Kim is a great believer in servicing the sale before, during and after. If you constantly please the customer, they may be interested in buying more books. What size cartons do they want? Do the cartons need to be labeled specifically for them? How many on a pallet? During printing, she does a personal press check to guarantee their name and logo are perfect on the cover. She calls their warehouse to alert personnel when to expect the shipment. It's called customer service.

After the books are delivered, she sends personal thank-you notes to the marketing director, production supervisor, secretary, anyone who was part of the deal. And she remembers them at Christmas with gifts. But it doesn't stop there.

Kim sends a Customer Satisfaction Form. Are the books okay? Is there anything you'd like to change for future runs? How's the book doing? Has it increased your sales? "Go for the gold," she encourages.

She has sold one company 10,000 to 15,000 copies of one title every year for 5 years. "Repeat business is the key. Create a club or a series to keep them coming back."

No questions, there are BIG bucks to be made in premium sales. We wish you much success!

Primary trade journals of the industry can help expose your book to potential buyers and further educate yourself. The biggest is *Potentials in Marketing* (50 South Ninth Street, Minneapolis, MN 55402). They run free "new product" color photos and blurbs. Needless to say, the competition is ferocious. If they pick your book, they refer interested people to a reader's service "bingo" card, which is a postcard where premium buyers are invited to circle appropriate numbers for more information. The magazine then sends you a computer printout of the names of information requesters.

You could get hundreds of requests for more information. Statistics show about 1 in 10 will typically gel when promptly followed up. If your budget is flush, and your title an especially likely premium candidate, you may even want to run a display ad in this publication.

Other magazines that go to potential customers are *Incentive* (355 Park Avenue South, New York, NY 10010) and *Promo* (11 Riverbend Drive South, Stamford, CT 06907).

Strategies for courting area premium sales: There may be a wealth of opportunities waiting in your backyard. Here are some ideas to woo local business.

■ Get a mailing list of corporations and associations in your community from the local chamber of commerce.

■ Contact the corporate librarians at large companies in your area. They can tell you who buys what for their organization.

■ Call the administrative assistant of key decision makers for research.

■ Learn as much as you can about their business and needs so you can suggest suitable books.

■ Begin a dialogue with the key decision maker.

■ Instill in them the concept that books are the ideal choice for gifts and staff incentives.

■ Check for professional groups such as human resources associations or training and development associations in the area that might buy business books.

■ When you receive a small order, perhaps an individual manager buying books for his or her staff, use this as an entry to reach further. You might be able to sell products to the director of human resources for the entire company or to the CEO for Christmas presents.

■ Position yourself as a premium resource. Set up a program that helps area companies understand how to reward employees with books or use books to prospect for new customers. Use suggestive selling.

The early bird gets the worm, but the second mouse gets the cheese.

Ad agencies can be death to premium sales. If you approach a large corporation and they talk about getting their agency involved, say pleasantly but firmly that you only work directly with the company. Otherwise, the agency is likely to feel jealous that *they* didn't come up with the idea and nix the whole project.

Once in a while, however, PR/ad agencies can be worked to your advantage. We know of one author who scheduled herself for an "appearance" at a major San Francisco PR firm. It turned out her book was just what the account executives needed to push a product, so they bought 12,000 copies!

CHAPTER 18

LinkThink: Strategic Alliances to Ignite Your Book Sales

There are innumerable ways you can partner with other businesses or organizations, sell more product, and sweeten your margins. We call this LinkThink. You may have heard it referred to as affinity marketing, forming strategic alliances, or fusion marketing. It's sort of like braiding hair: You take a handful of unruly strands, weave them together, and create unity.

Even tiny publishers and ingenious authors can create "glitz by association." It isn't brain surgery. It takes vision. Creativity. Resourcefulness. Imagine it's Christmas Eve and you are presented with an unassembled toy and no instructions. How do you put it together? Trial and error. Fitting this to that. Trying one thing with another. That's what LinkThink is all about: Finding the matches. Who already reaches your customer base? Ponder this for awhile and you're sure to come upon an idea that seizes your soul.

Examples from other industries

Carolee Jewelry teamed up with Estee Lauder cosmetics a few years ago to create a new and exciting way to wear makeup and jewelry. An in-store promotion called Custom Color Consultations gave women complimentary make-overs. The beauty consultant determined whether the customer had "warm" or "cool" skin undertones, then the Carolee representative coordinated a pearl ensemble to go with the customer's new cosmetic shades.

General Electric refrigerators teamed up with Culligan Water. When people went to their G.E. fridge's ice maker to get a drink of water or for ice cubes, it was compliments of the Culligan man. Starbucks is on a caffeine high. They have partnered with United Airlines, which serves Starbucks coffee.

Calvin Klein Cosmetics can now be found in music stores. Yep. The new fragrance, cK, is targeted to both men and women and is available in 85 Tower Records stores. A Klein spokesperson said it's selling the fragrance in record stores because of the "synergy between music and fashion." (Seems a little to us like opening a clothing store in a nudist camp, but what do we know?)

Binney & Smith was concerned their flagship product, Crayola Crayons, was too low-tech by today's standards. So they forged an alliance with a software development company called Micrografx, which developed digital crayons and a software drawing program for kids that can be used on home computers. It was a marriage made in heaven.

"Happy Holidays from the Hyatt Downtown and Tattered Cover" read the $59 gift coupon. The Hyatt Regency in downtown Denver combined with the wonderful Tattered Cover bookstore to offer an evening's stay in the hotel and a $10 gift certificate for a book. What a nice and imaginative holiday treat.

Publishing partnerships

The latest news is that Coca-Cola's research indicates that while regular Coke drinkers only buy one or two books a year, those who consume Diet Coke purchase seven or more books per year! They also tend to be adults instead of youngsters and 60% are women. So...the company is joining with HarperCollins, Penguin Putnam, Random House, and Doubleday to put excerpts of new books in cartons of Diet Coke. A whopping 35 million packages will carry 32-page excerpts from new books. These appetizers are meant to tempt readers to devour the rest of the book.

It's a wondrous concept, we only wish the four publishers were independent presses rather than the giants. But you don't have to be the size of Coca-Cola or Random House to put together meaningful deals.

The Junior League of Houston formed a strategic alliance with the city's largest grocery store chain, Randalls, to promote the League's cookbook, *Stop and Smell the Rosemary*. The ladies gave the grocery chain a very tasteful thank you in the front of the book—and received marketing valued at $57,000 in return! It consisted of more than a half million grocery bags with a recipe and their order phone number, radio tag lines, ads in the *Houston Chronicle* and the grocer's circular (which goes to 5 million people statewide), plus in-store promotions to sell the book.

Another example of a retailer combining with a publisher is a Dillard's department store in Littleton, Colorado. They sponsored Pretty as a Picture, a five-class course on social etiquette for young ladies aged 5 to 16. It covered visual poise, personal grooming, and social etiquette. Included with the course was a copy of the book *Pretty as a Picture*, a $19.95 value.

We had an interesting experience with *Country Bound!* I (Marilyn) discovered that United National Real Estate specializes in selling rural property. Research revealed they have more than 300 affiliated offices around the country and publish two catalogs a year. These nationally circulated "wish books" are replete with tempting photographs and descriptions of rural hideaways: ranches, farms, country estates, homes in small towns, rural business opportunities, land, you name it.

I figured that if they carried our book it would help them sell more property as one of the main reasons people don't move to small towns is because they can't make a living there. Aha! The entire second part of *Country Bound!* addresses the issue of how to prosper in paradise.

I tracked down the company president, convinced him to give us 15 minutes of his time, and Tom and I headed for Kansas City, Missouri. We ended up persuading him to not only run ads in the catalog, but also include brief excerpts from the book. His share was 20% of the retail price. But the real value was that it helped solve one of his major problems.

The last time we tabulated the figures, which was almost a year ago, we had sold $14,978 worth of books to this one source. What appeared on the surface as incompatible as combining a tin cup with a silver spoon proved profitable for all. Look for the links.

Nonbook-related crossover marketing can apply to fiction as well. A Zebra romance, *Spring Bouquet*, teamed with national floral distributor Superflora. Inserted in the back of the books were coupons good for $10 off on flower orders. It all lined up as neatly as Pringle's potato chips.

Special Dates to Piggyback On

Why not capitalize on the calendar to build sales? If you're looking for PR tie-ins to special days/weeks/months, visit http://dailyglobe.com/day2day.html. This is similar to *Chase's Annual Events* and provides literally thousands of possible publicity hooks to give your books a fresh perspective. Here is a year's worth of possible money-making monthly marketing maneuvers:

January promotional ideas. After the holidays, it seems like everybody's thoughts turn to diets, fitness, and New Year's resolutions. And therein lie wonderful angles for PR. In fact, January is National Diet Month (and National Soup Month for those of you doing cookbooks). Maybe you can inject a motivational, inspirational, or health-related backlist title with fresh pizzazz by giving it a "new beginnings" twist to tie in with all those resolutions everyone makes—and needs help keeping.

PR tie-ins for *February*. Of course, with Valentine's Day, and President's Day falling this month, there is much grist for the creative publicist's mill. But you needn't stop there. It is also Vegetarian Month, American History Month, Black History Month, and Celebration of Chocolate Month (yummy!) Additionally, there is Pay Your Bills Week (yuk!), National Crime Prevention Week, and Health Education Week.

(continued on next page)

Carol Fenster, Ph.D., president of Savory Palate, Inc., uses a multitude of strategic alliances to sell her *Wheat-Free Recipes and Menus* and the other titles in her Special Diet Series Cookbooks. She does joint venture mailings with her local asthma and allergy support groups. These go to public and high school libraries. Health professionals who diagnose and treat persons with food allergies are also high on her list. Local physicians (including allergists and ear, nose, and throat specialists), nutritionists, and naturopaths are beginning to recommend the book.

She is also working with the Department of Agriculture, Cooperative Extension Service, and several other groups who are interested not only in nutrition and diet but also in promoting alternative grains, such as quinoa, amaranth, and teff. These are all used in the book. The organizations refer interested callers to her and mention the book in their publications. Carol also sends short press releases accompanied by recipes to selected newspapers in cities that have Whole Foods Markets, Wild Oats, or Alfalfa stores. The book already sells well there. Her aim in all this shameless self-promotion is to also generate awareness and build goodwill, as well as to move product.

One of her primary distributors is Nutri-Books, a division of Royal Publications, Inc. in Denver. To help build a strong relationship with the sales and purchasing staff, she prepared a luncheon using recipes from the book to demonstrate that dishes prepared with alternative ingredients can look and taste as good as their wheat-laden counterparts. Thus, the sales reps can personally "testify" that wheat- and gluten-free foods can be delicious.

The editor and publisher of a newsletter dubbed *Food Writer* (610-948-6031) decided to investigate widening her subscription base. Even though the newsletter focuses on writing and publication, it provides numerous outlets and media contacts, both online and off, for authors to market their work. Many of these outlets also market other culinary things. So Lynn Kerrigan sent samples to companies that had nothing to do with food writing. They, too, can use the information. She also reasoned that approaching public relations companies dealing with foods would increase her circulation. Such strategic alliances are igniting new profit centers in her newsletter business.

Collaborating with newsletters and associations

Newsletters may well be your entry into new profit centers as well. Bev Harris of Talion Publishing has had gargantuan success working this synergistic angle. In fact, she sold a political book to one association

---

Special Dates to Piggyback On (continued)

March roars in like a lion. The biggie for many independent presses and self-publishers is that this is Small Press Month, which lends itself to much local and regional publicity. It is also National Procrastination Week. (But if you practice that you won't get any PR!) And it's National Feminine Empowerment Month, National Craft Month, and National Talk to Your Teen About Sex Month. Glenn Miller has a birthday on March 1st, Jerry Lewis on March 15th, and Edgar Cayce on March 18th. What great fodder for books on music, humor, and psychic phenomena. World Day of Prayer occurs in March, as does St. Patrick's Day—not to mention National Organize Your Home Office Day, Garden Book Week, and American Camping Week. Have fun!

Suggestions for *April*. This month is replete with things that connote new hope: Easter, Daylight Savings Time, plus the birth of spring and all things green and growing. Can you hitch your book to that theme? In April we have Professional Secretaries Day and Take Our Daughters to Work Day, great tie-ins for business titles. There is also Pets Are Wonderful Month (we agree!), National Humor Month, and International Twit Award Month. This time of year also finds both Harmony Week and Hate Week occurring, not to mention taxes are due, which could be a perfect connection for books on how to reduce stress. (continued on next page)

Special Dates to Piggyback On (continued)

May = **money-making publicity ideas.** Promotional opportunities for this month abound. Mother's Day is a huge book-buying event. With some creative thinking, you can probably slant a news release for a book that is only peripherally related. Then contact local radio stations and newspapers, plus pitch independent booksellers to feature your book in their window or for an interior display. Armed Forces Day and Memorial Day provide fuel for related titles. And if you're a poet, how about arranging readings for May 31st, Walt Whitman's birthday? Have something on the environment? May 27th, Rachel Carson's birthday, may be just the hook you need. Pegging the topic of your book to a day, week, or month can lead to expansive national publicity—or set the stage for intriguing local exposure. Take, for instance, the publisher of the novel, *The Emerald Necklace*, who got a jewelry store to feature it during May. Why? Because emeralds are the birth stone for that month, of course!

Are you taking advantage of *June* opportunities? Got a book on fishing? Or antique cars? Or a biography of a famous man? Are you pitching it to booksellers and your distributor for Father's Day? Have something about rock and roll or the Beatles? Paul McCartney's birthday is June 18th. If you have published a work whose main character is blind, or a nonfiction book that deals with improving your sight, you

(continued on next page)

newsletter for a 50% discount and made a $120,000 profit within 16 weeks! No cost to her. No risk. No returns.

Every book has multiple niche markets. Step one on your path to payday is to identify the associations and newsletters that reach these markets and learn *everything* about them. Starting with the largest, really do your homework. Get on the Internet and research. Print every page of the association's Web site. Get a feel for their issues. Learn key player's names. Read their mission statement. Highlight pertinent points. If they don't have a Web site, phone their headquarters, tell them you're a freelance writer, and ask for their latest newsletter, membership brochure, articles about them, etc.

Now you're prepared to "structure the benefits, probe for their needs, and close a deal," says Bev. "Make sure it has some benefit for them. Phrase it so it's important to them, like some way of serving their membership." These are not your typical entrepreneurs. "Money" is a dirty word.

"Listen carefully to what they say," Bev advises. According to the fascinating special report she publishes *(How to Market Your Book to Associations and Newsletters;* call 425-228-7131 to order or visit her Web site at http://www.talion.com), it's smart to structure three different proposals for approaching them. She seldom has to go beyond number one.

How do the actual mechanics work? After you've closed the deal, the objective is to get them to review and endorse the book within the newsletter itself, then include a separate order flyer. Make sure you either take the orders or fulfill them so you'll have accounting checks and balances. Create a letter of agreement that spells out who does what and gets what.

A similar partnering arrangement can be worked with regular subscription newsletters. Many depend on revenue from "stuffers" that are mailed along with their newsletters. In this case, they include a flyer you provide and each takes part of the money generated. Newsletter publishers *are* entrepreneurial. The idea of making extra money will appeal to them.

Books as fund-raisers

Many publishers and authors are teaming up with organizations that have an affinity for a book's topic. Margaret Malsam sold 225 copies of her *Meditations for Today's Married Christians* at the National Theresian Convention of Chicago, then donated $375 to the organization. She offers prudent advice for dealing with nonprofits: "Don't say 'I will give you 50% off.' Instead say, 'I will donate $5 for every $10 book purchased.'" Margaret also makes up flyers so they can mail in orders and

Special Dates to Piggyback On (continued)

might use Helen Keller's birthday of June 27th as a news angle. Of course, June is a natural for any book that would make a graduation gift. And many brides and grooms tie the knot this month. Think about your list and how you can target specific timely events to promote individual books, plus give backlist titles a boost.

July dates on which you can capitalize. Embrace National Independent Bookstore Week. Have you set up something with your local indy? Arrange a reading, signing, or mini-seminar. *You* take the initiative to publicize it to local newspapers and radio. (Why not offer to give the radio stations 10 or 12 free books for them to give away to help promote the in-store event?) As independent publishers we have a natural liaison with independent booksellers. Do you publish mysteries? Then see if you can't piggyback on July 17th, which is Earl Stanley Gardner's birthday, for some media attention. And don't overlook using Independence Day as a hook. Your message needn't be strictly patriotic. One can declare their "independence" from spousal abuse, overeating, illiteracy—any number of things. Get creative.

Think back-to-school for *August*. If you have reference titles, college survival guides, even simple recipe books that would appeal to busy college freshmen, now is the time to roll out the publicity campaign big time. There are also a lot of birth-

(continued on next page)

Special Dates to Piggyback On
(continued)

days in August around which you could plan a PR campaign. Garrison Keillor is the 7th, Alex Haley the 11th, Ray Bradbury the 22nd, and Michael Jackson the 29th. That gives you an excuse to push humor, African-American studies, sci/fi, music, and any number of other imaginative twists.

Promotional ideas for *September* include Banned Books Week, which provides a natural media opportunity to highlight the importance of free expression. One of the more obscure holidays, National Grandparents Day, falls in September. And with both Rosh Hashanah and Yom Kippur occurring this month, the possibilities for Jewish-themed books are ripe. Notable literary lights' birthdays that might also yield a peg are Agatha Christie (15th), F. Scott Fitzgerald (24th), and William Faulkner (25th). Strip off the blinders and look ahead for special days, weeks, months, or people for a fresh publicity angle.

October promotional possibilities abound. October is National AIDS Awareness Month. If you have a book on AIDS, related diseases, or safe sex, partner with local healthcare professional organizations to set up tables at their meetings and donate part of the book sale proceeds back to them. October is Mystery Month for you fiction folks. National School Lunch Week falls this month—that's a new one, eh? Why not work creatively with local teachers to organize a school reading group

(continued on next page)

codes her post office box number with the acronym of the organization. "Suggest they sell the book at conferences, conventions, meetings, etc.," she advises.

Diane Pfeifer has been selling her *Angel Cookbook* as a fund-raiser for three years. Catholic organizations are a perfect match with recipes like Dominus Vo-Biscuits and In Excelsis Mayo. She sells a minimum of 300 at a time on a nonreturnable basis and gives them a 40% discount. People apparently talk about the book, as she reports getting a ton of reorders at full price.

This can work for old books as well. Ellen Perry Berkeley is a trade-published author with a backlist title she has been peddling to humane societies and animal welfare groups since the early 1980s! She gets a 40% discount from her publisher (also earns a royalty) and donates $3 of the $12.95 retail price for every copy sold by the fund-raising organization.

Ellen has this down to a system: She has a standard homemade flyer explaining the fund-raising opportunity for *Maverick Cats: Encounters with Feral Cats*. It reads in part: "If you can make this offer known to your membership, either by mentioning it in your newsletter or (better still) by running my flyer with its coupon as a page in your newsletter, I then do all the rest. Individual orders come to me. I send out individual books (personally inscribed, as desired, for gift purposes). Periodically I send your group a check. Your only chore, after the initial announcement in your newsletter, is depositing my checks." Makes it sound very attractive and simple, doesn't it? Some organizations have worked with her for years.

The order flyer includes several stunning reviews and promises fascinating information from scientists around the world, plus touching stories from the author's hillside in Vermont.

Sports Barn Publishing Company recently published *The Soccer Mom Handbook.* They form strategic partnerships with soccer clubs and tournaments. Here's their pitch: Buy a box (100 copies) of the $9.95 books and get them for half-price, enabling you to make about $500 reselling at the cover price. Since soccer tournaments draw between 1,000 and 5,000 kids, most accompanied by a parent, it's a wonderful target market. Average clubs have 20 to 40 teams of 15 to 18 kids each. Last we heard, they had sold to six organizations in the early stage of the campaign.

Dick Barnes of Sports Barn offers several tidbits of advice: Find groups that are used to fund-raising and aren't embarrassed by or afraid of it. You want to convince them to use your book, educate and persuade them to raise funds in the first place. "Get paid up front," he counsels. "If they say they don't have the money

Special Dates to Piggyback On (continued)

that meets during lunch to discuss specific books? Of course, there is Columbus Day and United Nations Day. And Halloween screams in on October 31st, replete with a plethora of opportunities.

November **dates for possible PR pitches.** Early November is National Authors' Day, certainly a natural to build a story around. National Children's Book Week occurs this month. Two wonderful humorists were born in November: Will Rogers on the 4th and Samuel Clemens (Mark Twain) on the 30th. Additionally, Election Day falls this month, as does Veteran's Day and Thanksgiving. These three events furnish excuses for any number of ingenious twists.

December **dates on which to hang your hat.** Whether you wear a baseball cap, fedora, tam, cowboy hat, beret, or helmet, there is an appropriate date in December on which to capitalize. The Christmas/Hanukkah/New Year's Day cycle is the biggest buying season of them all. But many literary lights and famous people also have birthdays that fall this month. One of them may also give you a PR hook. How about Walt Disney on the 5th, Willa Cather on the 7th, Nostradamus on the 14th, Ty Cobb on the 18th, Kit Carson on the 24th, or Rudyard Kipling on the 30th? You can promote everything from poetry to sports to children's books—and more—by capitalizing on this list. Go for it!

until they sell the books, suggest they use a credit card." Be sure the group has an adequate worker base and a large enough outlet it can approach. They won't sell 100 books if an event is only going to draw a couple hundred people.

A further suggestion from Dick is to provide covers for signs and other inexpensive sales aids to help the organization—and to encourage spillover purchases later. "I've prepared my standard three-color flyers along with stickers to put on them that tell where to get the book." The stickers read, "Buy your copy at registration or the main souvenir tent."

Scott Jordan of Freedom Publishing Company recounts that since their books came out, their most consistent success has been fund-raisers at elementary schools. The books are *Benny Gets a Bully-Ache* and *Benny's Coloring Book From A to Z.* Both feature Benny the Bull, the mascot of the Chicago Bulls basketball team.

Author Jane Bomberger reads the story to a packed assembly of several hundred children while Benny the Bull acts out the action from the story. The school pays the Bulls to have Benny there, gets a 30% discount on books, and sells them at full price. They make money and Freedom pockets almost $1,000 on every two cartons of 72 books. In one year they did 50 performances and have now branched out to northern Indiana, Jane's home territory. They hope to keep her and Benny busy in every school in the Chicago area and Indiana.

Think cooperation, not competition, advises Jay Conrad Levinson, author of the *Guerrilla Marketing* series of books. He explains fusion marketing as "making not only the competition but also every business around you a marketing partner. Help them in return for helping you." Maybe it's a shared mailing. Perhaps a referral program. Our friend Joe Black (*not* the one of movie fame) coined a wonderful word for turning competition into cooperation. He calls it "coopetition."

Establishing drop-ship arrangements. Although you won't make enough from drop shipments to fund a cruise to the Orient, it's a steady way to sell books. We have drop-ship deals with several individuals and companies that sell our various books. You, too, may think of others with whom you can partner to develop a similar program. Someone with a compatible title might tuck your flyers into their mailings when they fill book orders.

Here's how it works: They get an order, prepare a shipping label, and send you a check for your portion (50 or 60% of the retail price). You cash the check, fill the order, and add the new customer to your database. It's a painless win-win exchange.

Stop throwing pity parties! Have you ever noticed when you throw yourself a pity party, nobody comes? Not every brilliant idea you hatch will jell. Some people (dense idiots that they are) simply won't see the value in partnering with you. When that happens, accept "no" graciously. It's important that you don't shoot yourself in the foot…then admire your own marksmanship. Just because you had a setback is no excuse to kick back. The next person you approach may be enthralled with your proposal. Be persistent and apply LinkThink!

Did you hear about the man who was so stupid he thought magna cum laude was a cloud formation?

Hand-deliver books when possible. Because Savory Palate, Inc. is located in Denver where one of their primary distributors is based, Carol Fenster personally delivers all orders to Nutri-Books—and takes food every time she goes. The staff is more likely to hand-sell her books because they know her and know the quality of the tasty recipes.

Strategic alliances are hot in "Virtualville," according to Mary Westheimer of BookZone. Look for Web sites that serve your audience but don't sell books. Offer to build them a bookstore or link to your site. They can get a percentage of the sale without having to touch the books, and your titles get increased exposure.

CHAPTER 19

QVC and Home Shopping Network: Adding Mileage to Your Campaign

Where can you get 12 minutes (and often much more) of *free* television time and reach 66 million viewers without spending a cent for advertising? On the home shopping shows and networks, that's where!

This is also the place where tiny companies can become big businesses literally overnight. Many inventors feel this is the fastest, cheapest way to launch a product. Once successful, you can use that achievement to leverage your way into other channels of distribution.

"QVC is a great source of promotion. Maybe the viewers are not all buying, but they certainly are watching," says their former merchandising director Amy Rosen. *Bookselling This Week* quoted Rosen as confirming her employer was pursuing the book market "in a big way." For those selected, the exposure is instantaneous and immense.

And there's also an ego boost. When you—or your author—are captured by the camera, you join no less than Mary Higgins Clark, Anne Rice, Hugh Downs, Julia Clark, Barbara De Angelis, astronaut Alan Shepard, and Senator Bill Bradley. But celebrity status isn't at all necessary. Art Ginsburg, author of the *Mr. Food* series, has sold more than 1 million copies of his books on QVC. He has become part of the family.

Success story extraordinaire

Joanna Lund, who originally self-published her *Healthy Exchanges Cookbook*, has become the queen of QVC, having sold over 1.5 million copies of her various books in three years. But it was like trying to fingerpaint with Super Glue—it took six months to break in. Yet in January 1997 she was the Today's Special Value with a set of three titles: *Thirty Meals/Thirty Minutes, One Pot Favorites,* and *Party Fare.* She sold over 200,000 books in less than 70 minutes of air time!

When we interviewed her, Joanna emphasized that "not every product is suited for TV sales. It's no reflection on the book. Every book needs to find its right audience." She went on to explain that if your book would interest shoppers in Penneys, Wards, and Sears (in other words, if it is for the masses), it may be right for QVC.

Merchandising needs evolve

In days of yore, the typical viewer was seen as a curler-crowned, slipper-wearing housewife. But not anymore. Today's shoppers are sophisticated. Demographics show the customer base is led by young professional families.

While gold jewelry initially dominated the airwaves, these shows have branched out to include fashion apparel, home furnishings, music, electronics, and *books.* In fact, QVC is a bookstore that broadcasts live 24 hours a day, 7 days a week, 365 days a year. In 1995, they sold more than 2.2 million copies of about 40 titles. Book sales topped $20 million in 1996.

They decided books were so important they put out a call in *Publishers Weekly* in the spring of 1996 for appropriate projects. The response to their ad was so overwhelming, they had to automate instructions. Today they reach 66 million homes. In 1997 they enjoyed total revenues of $2.1 billion.

When you get a Vendor Relations packet from QVC you'll discover you must first complete their Product Data Sheet and attach a color picture of your book. (Don't send actual books initially.) Their programming is thematic and encompasses food, jewelry, apparel and accessories, health and beauty, and the home. Your book needs to fit within one of these segments. They promise to contact you in writing within three weeks from the time they receive your information.

Perhaps you can penetrate this bonanza on a regional basis. Twice before QVC has gone to all 50 states to choose entrepreneurs to be on a state show, such as "The Best of Colorado." A fair share of authors end up being part of this program.

Their main competition is Home Shopping Network (HSN), a huge player reaching over 69 million households. They receive about 175,000 calls a day, and have revenues exceeding those of QVC. HSN gets more than 25,000 product applications per year. To toss your hat in the ring, you'll need to complete their extensive Vendor Information Kit, plus send a photo of the book. They'll reply in about a month.

Other contenders for the eyes, hearts, and wallets of TV viewers are ValueVision, which began in 1991 and had sales of $89 million in 1996. They are anticipated to merge with National Media Corporation and relocate.

Another rival for TV viewers' paychecks is Shop at Home, Inc., which reaches over 30 million TV households and caters more to men. Thankfully, they have a simple one-page application form.

What does it take to be successful?

Does the book have mass appeal? While cookbooks have been the staple for years, today's home shopping shows are also interested in books about health, financial issues, self-help, home fix-it, inspiration, New Age topics, even romance fiction. The big thing is, "Can you demonstrate it in some way?" That's why cookbooks remain so popular. Of course, there must be something special, timely, and topical about your title that makes it stand out from the crowd. Maybe you package it with something else to create a "kit."

Is the quality outstanding? HSN's reputation is like gold to them. They must consistently provide their viewers with quality merchandise. Don't skimp here. Look for ways to offer real value and make your book topnotch. Merchandise must pass several rigorous quality inspections and the exact quantity ordered must be delivered on time.

Does the pricing work? Do you have the proper price margins? They will want to sell at slightly below the normal retail price and will probably expect a 50% discount. Be prepared to haggle but don't be too insistent. The final price will depend on the product, how many they order, the time of year, etc. If you haven't priced your book right, the numbers won't work. Regarding the desired price point, books must typically sell for more than $15 and less than $30. Less expensive titles might be bundled to reach a more substantial figure. That's what was done with the 12 children's books in the Weekly Readers Editors Choice

Collection. It broke all records for one-day sales figures by moving over $1.4 million in product.

Can you come up with a relevant demonstration for TV viewers? It's imperative you think visually. How can you demonstrate your product to make viewers want to grab their credit cards and rush to the phone? Bill McAlister, who sells the Smart Mop via this TV medium, came up with an ingenious way to show the features of his hard-to-describe product. He brought a 12- by 12-foot piece of linoleum flooring to his demonstration. Then he proceeded to dump a bucket of mustard, ketchup, relish, and eggs all over it. "It took us only a minute to mop up all that gook," recalls McAlister. "The buyers were blown away."

Do you have the capital or financing to produce large quantities? Most books sell in the neighborhood of 3,000 copies. But some do much better. For those that sell well, they will invite the author on again soon—and probably additional times—so you must be able to turn the print run quickly and on short notice. It's important to reassure them you can meet the demand.

Here's the procedure for dealing with the TV giants:

1. **Obtain a vendor relations kit.** This gives you the basic information for product submission, along with the appropriate forms. Read it thoroughly before starting to fill it out. This is the time to let your writing skills shine. (See contact information in the Appendix.)

2. **Determine the right buyer.** This is easier said than done. Some companies are very closed-mouthed with names. Try to verify the same person is still responsible for buying books.

3. **Hone your pitch.** Make a grand entrance! Be energetic. Talk in "sound bites." Joanna advises, "Be sure you know your main points. Three to a maximum of six works best. And if the host is a take-charge person, be prepared to let him. Just slip them in at appropriate points."

Experts in the field recommend sending a videotape of you pitching and demonstrating your product to edge out the competition. Terrie Macfarlane and Lisa Rubino, who self-published *Beat the Clock Cooking,* did just that and came away with a 5,000-copy sale.

They host a cooking show on a community access TV channel. By showing a demo of their other on-camera work, the 10-minute tape aptly displayed their experiences.

4. Prepare to go onsite and perform. If they are impressed, the buyer will ask for a sample—then set an appointment for you to come in, answer questions, and do a mock on-air pitch. (By the way, this trip is on your dime. They do not pay expenses.) It could, however, be one of the most important times of your life! Don't blow it by not being prepared. You are literally auditioning. Be ready to demonstrate your product's unique capabilities and describe its appealing features. Tell what problems it will solve for viewers.

Interject drama any way you can. Should you be in costume? Will props make it more interesting? What graphics can you provide? Give it flash!

One businesswoman prepared for her interview by setting up a table at local swap meets. This gave her a forum for live demonstrations and personal interaction. By the time she went on television, she had fielded all sorts of questions and was secure in her answers.

Authors are ideal to push their books because they have such passion for them. Being knowledgeable and sincere is a must. Having charisma is a definite plus. If your author is timid, think about having a spokesperson or hiring a professional demonstrator. The ability to present well is every bit as important as the product itself.

You may want to get a consultant's guidance on presentation and packaging. Because they know the intricate details of what a home shopping sales buyer requires, their experience and know-how can sometimes count even more than your product's potential.

5. Get ready for action. The period from product acceptance until show time is typically 6 to 12 weeks. This is not a deal for the faint-hearted. Books are generally obtained on a returnable basis. The good news is only 7 to 9% actually bomb because consumers already know what they are getting from the demonstration. Unsold books are returned to the publisher in about 90 days. QVC does pay freight both ways. If your product scores big, be aware you'll be expected to pump up production fast and furiously.

Dr. Tony Alessandra, professional speaker and author of *The Platinum Rule*, shared some of his insider secrets with us for priming the pump. Viewers can call in during the show to talk about the product.

So once Tony was firmly scheduled, he let everybody in his personal contact arena know to call in and give an on-air testimonial about how his book helped them! He coached his friends to keep it crisp and to call in a few minutes prior to his being on as they would be put on hold. QVC has a counter you can see. Whenever someone calls in with a good testimonial the sales shoot up, Tony reports.

His advance strategies also included working their Web site (http://www.qvc.com) to get a buzz going ahead of time. That way loyal viewers are eagerly looking forward to seeing the author. In the Books Directory, which is iQVC's bookstore, there is a section where people can write their own views and reviews. Comments like the following are helpful: "This is Marilyn Ross and on August 2nd I bought Tony Alessandra's new book, *The Platinum Rule*, and it's fabulous!" (plus some more superlatives and why the book is helping you, etc.).

Tony also stresses that you must have your two or three significant points down pat. "Be able to articulate what it does for the reader in 30 seconds or less," he counsels. "A quick story about how it helped somebody—in their relationships, to save money, etc.—works well." Suggesting they buy two is another of his tactics. "Buy one for yourself and one to give as a gift to your sister, mother, colleague"—you get the idea.

The home shopping shows and networks can indeed add magic to your marketing mix. They can even be responsible for turning you into a mogul-in-the-making.

QVC plans to go into the business of publishing themselves beginning in the late spring of 1999. They will develop custom titles specifically for their audience, particularly in the cookbook area. (They have one program dedicated to books: "Cookbook Corner.")

It isn't all bad news, however. Further plans include their repackaging titles originally published by other houses. They will customize these books or make them a special edition. For consideration here, contact Jill Cohen at QVC Publishing, 275 Main St., Suite 103, Mount Kisco, NY 10549; phone 914-242-7190; fax 914-242-7196.

Not content with last year's figures of 1.3 million adult books and 1.7 million children's books sold, they also intend to go into other venues such as selling their titles to the chains and independents. Just the competition we need. Groan.

You know it's going to be a bad day when you get a tattoo—and they spell it wrong.

Foreign possibilities. If things work out here and your book travels well, you might explore foreign opportunities. There's CHSN-Canada, QVC-UK, QVC-Germany, and TV Shop-France. Or you may want to further "channel" your efforts with other TV venues. Possibilities include infomercials and direct response commercials. Although costly, they allow you to capitalize on a product previously proven suitable for TV audiences.

Three brief hints. 1) If you have just written or published a first novel, stress that it is *first* fiction. Some reviewers and writers are more likely to give neophytes consideration, hoping to be credited with "discovering" the next Toni Morrison. (And any novelist should get a copy of Connie Shelton's *Publish Your Own Novel*. It's stuffed with smart marketing tips. Order at 800-331-8355.) 2) Do promotion in the town where you *used* to live. Home-town-boy-or-girl-gone-to-make-good-in-the-big-city turns you into a more valuable commodity. 3) Arrange to have an overrun of the covers printed. They make wonderful sales pieces and are inexpensive to do while you're already on the press.

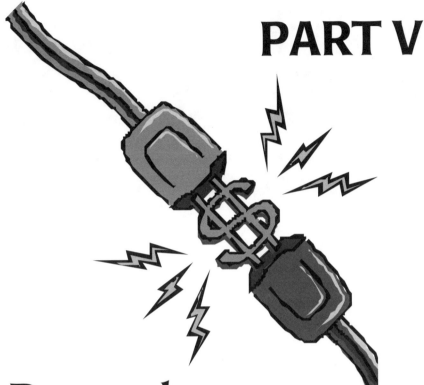

PART V

Powerhouse
Direct Marketing
Techniques

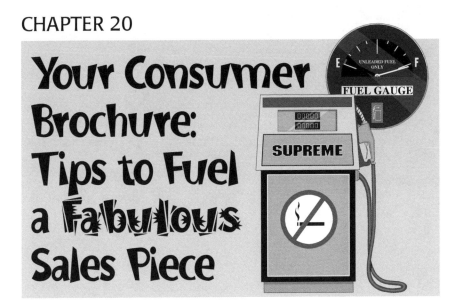

Your Consumer Brochure: Tips to Fuel a Fabulous Sales Piece

Every product or service needs promotional literature to convince potential buyers of its merits. A book is no exception. Publishing companies with several titles typically put out catalogs, which have brief blurbs about each of their books. This works well for the trade: bookstores, wholesalers, and libraries. But what about reaching consumers directly? How do they learn about the benefits of a specific book unless you've developed a brochure or flyer devoted exclusively to that title?

It becomes obvious that smart authors and small publishers require some device to promote an individual book to a single customer. Shouldn't you have a brochure that stands out from the pack—one with snap, crackle, and pop? You'll use this piece of literature in a multitude of ways: It's fast and effective when responding to daily inquiries from potential book buyers. You can hand it to prospective customers whom you meet in person. It makes an ideal direct mail piece to use when prospecting for sales. You can use it as a bounce back to routinely stuff in packages and letters you mail. And it can be placed on tables at trade shows, book fairs, and networking events.

Your brochure has an additional function: A well-crafted one also serves a peripheral PR purpose. Attach a copy of it to other paperwork when talking to your banker. Or if you consult in the book's subject area, include it with proposals.

Initial planning decisions

Don't fall into the trap of thinking once you've produced a brochure, your marketing is done. Although an important component in your overall arsenal, it is only part of the marketing mix—one of some 15 key weapons.

A good plan is to a book promoter what a scalpel is to a surgeon—not a substitute for skill, but a tool to increase success. Think about how you'll use your brochure. Will it be to promote an existing book? To announce a new one? Who is your target audience? What are their likes and dislikes? Will you provide a quantity of brochures to other authors or publishers who distribute your book? If so, leaving a place for them to customize it with their own ordering information can be a smart move. Is there an advantage to coding or folding some differently than others? Of course, it never hurts to study the competition. Take up a collection. Learn from what other book promotional pieces do well—and note things to avoid.

We're not talking about thousands of dollars here. While four-color photographs reproduced on glossy paper and cut into unusual shapes make for an impressive piece, this isn't necessary. There is a happy medium between that extreme and black ink on white paper. It is important that you project a quality image. Your brochure is your salesperson. Think of an 8½- by 11-inch or 8½- by 14-inch (legal size) piece of paper, printed on both sides and folded to fit into a normal #10 business envelope. This is an ideal size as it easily slips into a man's inside jacket pocket or a woman's handbag. Depending on the size of the paper used, folding creates six or eight surfaces, or panels. Now that we've determined the size of our brochure, it's time to consider what it will contain.

Including the right components

Just as a loaf of bread needs flour, liquid, yeast, and other ingredients, a successful brochure needs standard elements. Form follows function. Conclude what the contents should be first, then think about design. If you try it the other way around, you'll feel like you've been caught in a thunderstorm with a leaky umbrella. The design should grow logically out of the subject matter. We'll be talking more about design specifics later.

First grab the potential buyer's attention. This is usually done with a headline and an eye-catching graphic on the front panel. Its sole purpose is to lure the reader into the brochure. Next have introductory copy that addresses the specific needs or problems of your prospects, then explains how the book will meet those needs or solve their problems.

Include an author biography to establish credibility. State your qualifications to write the book; mention appropriate affiliations that contribute to your credibility. And include a photograph. People like to see the folks they are dealing with. An inexpensive source for author photos is the Glamour Shot franchises located in many shopping malls. Just be sure to tell them it is for business purposes so they don't try to put you in a feather boa. With a cookbook or travel guide, a color photograph of the book is a real plus.

Photos often need editing just like manuscripts. In this case, it takes the form of retouching or cropping. Delete extraneous background and focus on the author to achieve the best results. (As an aside, we got quite a kick out of a client who was a little late getting us his author photo. His excuse? "It took this long for two artists working full-time to retouch the age spots—and they both wound up with carpal tunnel syndrome!") Photo captions are a good place to emphasize key benefits. They are one of the best-read parts of a brochure.

And while we're talking of photographs, by all means include one of the book. Perhaps the thumbnail sketch from your graphic designer will suffice to give a reasonable portrayal of the book until you can photograph the real thing. When doing photographic work, ask the photographer to add a new perspective by changing his or her point of view. Shoot down from a ladder or up from floor level. This adds freshness to your photographic images.

Impartial third party accolades are another key element. Testimonials in the form of advance comments or endorsements give clout to your overall message. Try to get a diversity of comments. Think about your target audience and include quotes that will appeal to different niches of potential buyers.

Include a money-back guarantee. Give your prospective customers every reason to trust you. After all, you're expecting them to send you money for something they have never seen or handled. Guarantees are sales stimulators. If you're offering a quality product, returns will be a tiny fraction of sales. Anybody who sends back a good book is so dumb they'd buy a solar-powered flashlight.

Features Versus Benefits

First make a list of the features that make your book unique or better than the competition. To guide you in this process, we've done a features/benefit comparison for a custommade, wooden lawn chair.

Features:

1. Hand-crafted

2. Made of teak and brass

3. Curved back

4. Adjustable back angle

5. Natural teak finish

Now determine the benefit of each of these. Translate the lawn chair features (and those of your book) into benefits—things that meet your *customers'* needs:

Benefits:

1. Heirloom quality

2. Strong, durable, maintenance-free, naturally resistant to weather

3. Excellent back support

4. Comfortable, perfect for a nap in the afternoon sun

5. More in harmony with the natural landscape than a plastic or aluminum chair

Ask for the order. Just as a good speech has an introduction, body, and conclusion, so does a brochure. You must close the sale. Tell readers what you want them to do: Call your toll-free number or send in the order coupon. You can create a sense of urgency by encouraging them to act "today," "now," or "immediately."

Be sure to add an order coupon. It can be attached or done as a separate form. But don't overlook a reply device; tests prove coupons multiply responses. It's also a good idea to include ordering information in small print somewhere else on the brochure. That way when the coupon is detached from the main part, people can still find you. And if your brochure is designed as a self-mailer, the back outer panel must be devoted to the address section. Include your toll-free number—and your email and Web site addresses, too.

Sales sizzle: stress benefits over features

There are a few individuals on this earth who could sell sand to a sheik, but most of us have to work at being strong salespeople. You'll seduce prospects much faster with a "you" or "your" approach rather than "me," "we," "our," or "I." All of us like personalized copy that addresses our needs. When you emphasize benefits instead of features, you tell the customer what he or she will get out of the deal—you give tangible reasons to buy. And you slant the essence of your book, its special mystique, toward solving consumers' problems.

Let's look at an example of how to write benefit copy: Suppose you have a book on entertaining. Instead of listing what goes into planning a dinner party, tell prospective readers their dinner party will be a smashing success. That's the end result they want. If your title is about memory improvement, point out that these techniques will have them astounding their friends and impressing their business associates. And they'll never need to be embarrassed again because they've forgotten someone's name.

Got a book on inventory control? Don't preach about how you'll set up and monitor their inventory control system. Instead tell them inventory shortages and surpluses will be a thing of the past. Maybe your title is about physical fitness. People don't want to hear about diet and exercise. Instead romance them by explaining how they—and their friends— will see a marked improvement in their appearance and stamina. Emphasize the result people want.

To arouse a potential buyer, use punchy verbs and adjectives. Yet don't totally unleash your imagination. Terms like "miraculous," "magic," or "spectacular" sound exaggerated and unconvincing. On the other hand, words with honest pizzazz produce the greatest positive mood change. Cut through the communications chatter with clear, memorable copy that offers prospects viable solutions to nagging problems.

Kinds of brochure readers

There are three types of brochure readers. The *casual reader* spends a few seconds scanning the headline on the front panel. The *interested reader* opens your brochure and reads the headlines, subheads, and photo captions—but nothing more. The *serious reader* devours everything. Your aim is to convert casual readers to interested readers, then to serious readers. This tells us is we better concentrate some mighty creative effort on headlines and subheads. They are the carrots dangling before prospective book buyers.

Be aware of what we call "information shaping." How one presents information—what isn't said as much as what is—can prove a creative way to present your story. The media constantly molds information to suit their own purposes. Take, for instance, the two teams that played against each other. It is easy enough for the winner to say,

"We won!" But a clever loser might comment, "We came in second." Statistics are *shaped* when they are taken out of context.

One last thought about writing copy: Avoid terminology or information that "dates" your brochure. Rather than saying the book has been in print for three years, say since 1996. If you must include information that will soon change, consider putting it on a separate sheet that will fit into the regular brochure. It will be much cheaper to produce than redoing the whole brochure. And watch photographs so they don't show faddish clothes or other tipoff that will rapidly make your brochure obsolete.

So we've explored how to plan your brochure, include the right components, and add sales sizzle by stressing benefits over features. Now we move ahead to the visual aspect of this important sales piece.

Designing for "aye" appeal

Graphic design is the body language of a brochure. As you grapple with this issue, there are several questions to answer. What tone will you set? Friendly? Elegant? Humorous? Professional? Avant garde? Decide on the feeling you want to convey. Of course, this is not exclusively the domain of design. Copy must work with graphics to establish a harmonious whole.

Unlike ads, which tell your story on one flat surface, a brochure allows the reader to see only the front panel initially. Your headline must seize attention. Be succinct and benefit-oriented. Generate interest. The adjacent photo or graphic should actively support and correlate with the headline. Together they make a forceful statement to woo readers inside.

One trick for giving your brochure variety and focusing attention on key points is to use "call out" boxes. These are frequently employed in magazine articles where they extract a sentence or two from the text and run it in larger type. This gives you another shot at interested readers. If the headline doesn't catch their fancy, perhaps your call out box will.

For visual diversity there are other options besides photographs. Illustrations can be tailored to your needs and add zest to an otherwise dull brochure. If you can't afford an artist, there's always clip art. Today a wonderful array is available in software programs or sometimes even free online.

When you're planning how the various elements fit together, give special consideration to the order coupon. Put it on an end panel facing out for writing convenience. Then it's easily clipped and doesn't destroy the rest of the brochure when removed. This also gives you greater flexibility. Need a brochure for more institutional purposes—such as a mailing to libraries, bookstores, or wholesalers? Simply cut off the order coupon, add a sheet explaining your Terms and Conditions, and you have it! If you're using a self-mailer approach, plan your address panel back-to-back with the order coupon—especially if you do a lot of direct mail campaigns. That way when people return the coupon you have the coding on their address label on the back and can track which mailing list is pulling best.

Also consider what you want on the address panel if you're heavily into direct mail. Including a few words of "teaser copy" here increases the odds of tempting recipients inside. Do you need a bulk mail permit number? Should you be printing accepted postal terminology to get the piece forwarded and the new address sent to you for list cleaning? Check with the post office to make sure what you're planning satisfies all postal regulations.

Let's talk a moment about type. Typefaces have different personalities. Some are casual, some formal, some sophisticated, some just plain fun. Unless you're going for a specific effect, stick to standard typefaces. And don't mix too many different styles. One face for the text and another for headlines typically works well. A reminder when using your logo: Work from an original rather than taking one off a business card or letterhead. This sacrifices sharpness.

Did you know that words in all capitals are difficult to read, not to mention less visually pleasing? In fact, lowercase text is read 13.4% faster than copy set in all caps. So be wary of putting headlines in all caps. Large blocks of text set in italics are also tiring on the eye. You can have the right-hand margins justified (meaning all the same length) or kept ragged right. The latter gives an open feeling as there is more white space.

Cost-effective production tips

Perhaps the best advice we can give you is to proofread carefully. Then do it again. And again! Nothing is more aggravating—and costly—than getting 5,000 brochures from the printer only to discover a glaring error in a headline or a wrong digit in an address. Errors at this point are as unwelcome as ants at a picnic. In addition to diligently proofing regular text copy, carefully examine addresses, phone numbers, fax numbers, email addresses, and URLs. Watch the spelling of reviewers' names, all headlines and subheads, and any photo captions. These elements are easily overlooked and computer spell checkers can sabotage you. Double-check every detail. Get someone else to inspect things too; one person can repeatedly overlook the same error.

Two colors of ink are preferred, but even one color used creatively will do the trick if you must be very budget conscious. Please don't settle for plain old black ink. Going to a color only adds about $15 and will energize your literature. Look at Pantone Matching System (PMS) color swatches at an artist supply store, typesetter/designer, or your printer. There's no need to settle for the standard blue, red, green, etc. Black and one PMS color are also attractive and cost-effective. By the way, studies show younger people prefer bright hues, while older folks respond to soft colors.

To get more mileage out of ink, think about using screens of 10, 20, or 30%. This lays down a lighter shade of the color over which you can print text in the full strength ink color. For additional variety, consider making the front panel 100% of the color and reversing the headline in white.

While we're discussing color, there's another option: How about using a colored paper stock? Just be sure to take into consideration what will happen when you add the ink color.

Nowadays paper is a large part of the expense of any printing job. Consult with your printer to see if they stock a paper in quantity that will work for you. Glossy coated stocks will cost more but add an elegant look. They come in various weights. Beware of one too flimsy as its lack of substance will downgrade the feel of your brochure. Another tip is to inquire if they have any paper left over from another job. Sometimes you can pick up these remnants really cheap.

Get a written price quotation (not an estimate) from several printers. You may be surprised at the wide variance in charges. Think through your project first and determine what the bid should include. What quantity? Most people print at least a year's projected supply. How many folds? Are halftones needed for photographs? Any trims? Bleeds? What is their turnaround time? If they say 21 days they probably mean more than four *working weeks,* not three calendar weeks. Encourage printers to suggest cost-cutting measures. And when the job is done we recommend you get the camera-ready art back. Then there's no question about who has it if you need to make changes before going back to press next time.

A compelling brochure is a sure-fire way to cultivate consumer purchases—and help you get back to press faster with your book! Without one you're like a turtle in a horse race. These tips will enable you to get swiftly out of the starting gate and create winning sales literature to promote and sell more books.

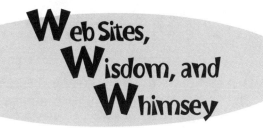

Let your sales materials catch a free ride. Do you automatically stuff promotional literature in books you ship and monthly bills you send? Why not sail your offers into consumers' or trade accounts' hands? All it costs is the paper it's printed on. These "buck slips," as they're called in direct marketing lingo, can round out your marketing mix and add a few more dollars to your coffers. You might also get the publishers of newsletters targeted to your niche to include stuffers with the next issue if you offer them 50% of the sales.

Best Typo
A daily column titled "News in a Minute" misplaced a blank space, creating a much more eye-catching headline: "New Sin a Minute."

Small details can yield big results. Have you any idea what power decimal points, commas, and zeros pack? When writing promotional materials pay attention to how you express numbers. When you want to minimize prices, write "Only $20." On the other hand, to maximize savings say "Save $20.00." And pay attention to whether you write $1,634 or $1634. The latter is perceived as less. These tiny tweaks can have a subtle, but important, impact on your results.

Want a professional to critique your promotional materials? The Rosses have created the Jump Master Marketing System, a unique customized plan that provides marketing evaluation, consultation, and guidance. This individualized coaching kicks in where *Jump Start Your Book Sales* leaves off. For more details about how you can have Marilyn as your personal mentor, see page 349.

> **"My daughter is studying to become a famous writer," grimaced her father. "I asked if she ever has trouble with punctuation." "No, I'm never late for class," was her reply.**

How to "guarantee" more business. Want to increase sales for your books or audio or video programs? Looking for a vehicle to increase your direct marketing results? Guarantees may well be your answer. Offering a guarantee relieves apprehension on the part of potential purchasers. It lets them know that if they are dissatisfied, they have recourse. Interestingly enough, if you've created a sound product, very few people will take advantage of your guarantee. There are many kinds of guarantees: all the way from seven days to a lifetime.

Statistics show that the longer the guarantee, the *less* likely you are to have returns. Consumers somehow figure there is no urgency in returning the merchandise and keep putting it off. Ultimately they forget. Even though it may sound ludicrous, a lifetime guarantee is often more effective than a seven-day guarantee. As well as guaranteeing the product itself, you may want to reassure purchasers in other ways. For instance, guaranteeing delivery within 48 hours. Or in the case of audio tapes, guarantee the replacement of a defective tape.

CHAPTER 21

Lightning-Charged Possibilities in Direct Mail

Someone once observed a successful direct marketer must have a hog's nose, a deer's legs, and an ass's back. It's a tough medium. Yet carefully conceived and executed, direct marketing to consumers can be a powerful and lucrative merchandising tool for selling books.

It masquerades under a variety of names: mail order, direct response, direct marketing, and direct mail. Some people even have the audacity to refer to it as "junk mail." Mastery of this medium depends on imagination, persistence, and following established rules. If you want to be a mogul-in-the-making, study them well.

Planning for profits

Prior to embarking on a direct mail program, spend time planning—especially your budget. Not everything warrants using direct marketing. Consider your price point. Is your book expensive enough to make this approach worthwhile? Today, you'll need a retail price of $24.95 before the numbers make sense. If your product falls far below that and you don't have a catalog of several titles, consider partnering with another author or publisher to raise the stakes and lower the investment.

Clients frequently ask us what results to expect. If you're selling a high ticket item like a Mercedes Benz, 0.5% would be acceptable. On the other hand, if you're pushing the typical book, 2% is considered a good return.

We favor a different formula, however. You need to make at least 2.2 times the money you spend for the mailing. Include the costs of copywriting and design if you hire it done, printing, list rental, postage, and mail processing if you use an outside firm.

No doubt you're wondering about the response timing on direct mail (DM). Once the mailing is out, how does the response come in and when is it finished? Third class bulk mail is typically delivered in two to three weeks. Your response will be 75% finished within four to six weeks. You'll see a few additional orders for a couple more weeks. By eight weeks most mailers consider the response final.

Seldom will a one-shot effort shake lose the desired results. You need a concerted, ongoing plan. Since the amount of third class bulk mail has escalated dramatically over the last few years, to effectively penetrate the market you must often do repeated mailings. And re-member that one form of advertising reinforces another. Launching a well-thought-out direct marketing campaign can create an ever-widen-ing ripple of sales.

Components of a successful campaign

A good direct mail package is like the couple who captures first place in a dance contest. It's lithe, limber, and all the body parts work in rhythm. It may be as lively as a rhumba or as smooth as a waltz, but it does the job: It gets response!

Your direct mail campaign needs to "work" in several areas. First, it must present the right offer. Next, the copy writing has to be strong. Finally, the mailing list needs to be good. Let's dissect these components.

Your offer is the stimulus that creates the decision to buy. Price often plays an important role. One company tried selling their product all the way from $24.95 to $79.95. Ultimately, they found it moved best at $39.95. Other aspects that affect offers have to do with whether you provide a discount, offer a money-back guarantee, include a gift (often called a premium enhancement), or suggest a deluxe alternative.

Injecting humor into your program can also be rewarding. That was the approach taken by KSK Communications Ltd. for their client, Wolverine Software Corporation. The objective was to increase sales of

Wolverine's teaching and simulation software among college engineering professors. Using a humorous caption and a whimsical cartoon of a wolverine, they developed a well-targeted self-mailer that pulled more than a 2% response.

Package contents

The traditional direct mail package consists of an outer envelope, a letter, a brochure, an order form, and a business reply envelope (BRE). More elaborate packages include additional pieces.

Outer envelope

If you hope to hit the Yellow Brick Road to DM success, you'd better pay a lot of attention to this element. If you fail here, it doesn't matter what's inside. But most publishers feel a little like Dorothy at the gates to the Emerald City.

Just how does one go about baiting the hook? How do you get from the "to oblivion" pile and into the "to open" stack? There are three schools of thought. One says, "If you've got it, flaunt it;" another goes for elegant simplicity. The third advocates being a sneaky Pete. Here's how they work.

Some envelopes shout for attention. Most of these sport a "teaser message." Clever copy can do an excellent job of provoking the inquisitiveness of recipients and pulling them in. (A word of caution here: Don't give away the punch line. If you reveal the entire sales pitch on the envelope, people have no incentive to go inside.)

Many business-to-business mailers must get through a secretary to obtain a response. That's tough. In this case you need elegant simplicity. Competent secretaries are shrewd gatekeepers. They screen for executives in nearly 87% of cases. To win their approval, be so sharp looking—so distinctive—so legitimate—so professional—they can't resist.

The object of sneaky Pete is anonymity, to camouflage any resemblance to junk mail. Rather than a return address of Brookside Publishing Company, you might use BPC or a person's name and street address in the return. With this approach you need to type or, better yet, handwrite the recipient's address rather than using computer generated labels, which would immediately give you away. These envelopes carry a postage stamp instead of being metered mail. While obviously this tactic isn't practical for large mailings, it can be fruitful in small doses. An

Direct Marketing Sales Letter Checklist

Does the headline attract attention by promising an important benefit?

Is interest built quickly by enlarging on the promise?

Have you appealed to the emotions to arouse a desire to possess?

■ Have you emphasized the unique features of your book, but stated them in *benefit* terms?

Is one central idea emphasized so strongly it avoids confusion?

Have you included believable testimonials (either here or in the brochure)?

Do you offer a guarantee?

Is your letter organized and designed to be inviting and easy to read?

Have you closed with a clear call for action?

Is a postscript included?

envelope that's anonymous has a better than 50-50 chance of getting opened out of sheer curiosity.

Sales letter

The letter is your salesperson. It accounts for 65 to 75% of the orders you get. The brochure is responsible for 15 to 25%; the order form for 5 to 25%. Fail at the letter stage and your mailing is doomed. (See the adjacent checklist.)

This is one place where more is usually better. A two-pager out-pulls a one-page format, four pages is often stronger. You're asking people to part with their money. This takes information and persuasion. It isn't done with a brief message.

The secret to success here is saying what the prospect wants to hear, *not* what you want to say. Forget features. Savvy marketers write from a benefit standpoint. Stress how your book will solve readers' problems— make them healthier, wealthier, wiser, sexier, or whatever. Start with a powerful headline. Write in easy words, short sentences, brief paragraphs. You want simple language the average person can understand. The goal is to keep them reading, not re-reading! Keep the format open and airy. Use underlining and CAPITALS for emphasis. Include a punchy, intriguing P. S. And be sure to ask for the order several times.

For minimal expense, a direct marketing campaign can be targeted to many *different* audiences by simply customizing the sales letter. You can use the same brochure but slant to the needs of different constituencies by what you say in the letter.

Brochure

While many direct mail packages sport huge, elaborate, four-color brochures, this isn't necessary for most books. An 8 ½- by 11-inch or 8 ½- by 14-inch sheet, printed on both sides, and folded into panels that fit a number 10 business envelope works well. Put your selling message on the front; it works like a headline. Incorporating advance comments, reviews, and testimonials lends clout and dilutes apprehension. Again, ask for the order. Tell the reader specifically what to do.

Pretend you're writing to one person. Envision what that individual is like. What age? Sex? Income level? Education? Interests? Hot buttons? Keep it friendly and personal in tone. Talk in specifics. Rather than saying this is "an inexpensive investment," you might tell prospects it "costs less than you spend for a daily paper." Often the brochure picks up where the letter left off, going into more detail about the benefits customers will gain. For more specifics on brochure development, review chapter 20.

It often makes sense to ensure customer satisfaction by offering a money-back guarantee. This reassures people. Many publishers are concerned about the number of returns they will get, yet there's a peculiar paradox here: The stronger and longer the guarantee, the fewer returns you'll receive.

When we write promotional literature for a full-blown direct mail campaign, we usually put the guarantee in a fancy box and add a personal signature, thus focusing attention on this important aspect in the offer. So when you are looking for another way to increase business, remember that guarantees alleviate buyer concerns. By advertising that you back your merchandise, you invite those who might be apprehensive to make a positive buying decision.

Order form

Order forms are frequently treated like Cinderella...ignored and unadorned, they stay home while the rest of the package goes to the ball. As in Cinderella's case, this can be a grave mistake. Busy people may scan your letter and, if the proposition interests them, go directly to the order form. Never stop selling. Use a benefit-laden headline on the order form—one that encompasses your offer.

Put opportunities before obligations, rewards before restrictions. Encourage people to "act now," "respond today," or "call immediately." Order forms should be cleanly engineered to make it *easy* for people to respond. Provide specific instructions and lots of contact point options and payment mechanisms. Include a toll-free phone number, fax number, and email address for credit card purchasers. Explain that you take checks or money orders and where to send them. To be sure your order form is user-friendly, fill one out yourself.

Business reply envelope (BRE)

Some mailers use a business reply envelope. Once again, the idea is to make it easy for the prospect to respond. Although most feel these postage-paid envelopes increase results, this adds considerably to your costs. If you don't supply postage, be sure to print a box with the words "place stamp here" in the upper right-hand corner of the envelope. Our sense is the BRE step can be omitted for book sales.

Other alternatives

All-in-one mailers

Full-fledged direct marketing packages are not an inexpensive way to sell products. Yet a modified version of this dynamic merchandising method can be viable for virtually every publisher. Companies with budgets as tight as banjo strings can wrap all these elements into one. This typically takes the form of a brochure designed as a self-mailer.

That's the approach taken by one small press in Portland, Oregon, that specializes in books about the graphic arts. About 70% of their orders come this way. They mail approximately 250,000 pieces a year and get close to a 4% return. They prefer to say everything in one piece. "We hire a terrific illustrator to create a grabber 'poster' image, then make the piece communicate as clearly as possible," explains a spokesperson. Their results increased noticeably when they went to two-color, then four-color.

Statement stuffers

Some firms praise statement stuffers. These are typically flyers inserted in monthly bills. Another form of direct marketing is catalogs. And you might consider developing a co-op mailing with a complementary company. By combining your in-house lists and sharing the costs, you literally divide to multiply.

Card packs

Card packs are another intriguing possibility. Stan Feingold, president of Visual Horizons in Rochester, New York, feels they are an "excellent additional marketing tool to supplement traditional ways of doing business. I can't buy mailing lists or do a solo mailing at a profit," he explains. "The only thing I can do profitably is to go prospecting in a deck. And there are a lot of companies like us. We're niche marketers."

Because your card is often in a deck with those from Fortune 500 companies, this provides positive "guilt by association" positioning. Says Feingold, "You look just as good as General Motors." Card packs are best used for books, courses, series, or kits with a price point of $49.95 or more. If you publish high-ticket products, this could be an excellent vehicle for boosting sales. Watch your mail for samples and contact the card pack publisher/owner.

Unmasking mail list culprits

To be successful in DM, it takes the right offer and a package with pizzazz. But stopping there would be like trying to sit on a three-legged stool . . . with one leg missing. Many feel the most vital ingredient is the mailing list. These databases of prospect names are the carrier pigeons of today's commerce.

Lists, and the strategies surrounding them, can be confusing. Yet knowing how this facet of direct marketing works is critical to your success. So let's unmask the mail list culprit.

There is a major misconception: You don't buy lists, you *rent* them for one-time use only. If you want to use that list again, another rental fee is due. (Don't try and cheat; lists are seeded with decoy names so the owner knows if it is being used without authority.)

Once someone has responded directly to your mailing, however, you can legitimately add their name to your own in-house database. Lists rent anywhere from $50 to $170 per thousand names. But don't just look at dollars, look at results.

When you rent several lists, there is often name duplication. This can be eliminated by requesting a "merge-purge." This is a computer program that merges lists together and purges the duplicate names. You don't want the expense of sending several pieces to the same person . . . or the unprofessional impression such a mailing leaves with the recipient. A good merge-purge program will also typically identify undeliverable names, such as those with incomplete zip codes, so you don't have to pay for sending them.

Using list brokers

Just as agents serve as a conduit to join authors and publishers, "list brokers" match those who want to do a mailing with available lists. They earn their living like a yenta—matchmaking. These men and women are specialists who make all the arrangements for one company to use the lists of another.

Your broker is a consultant in many ways. He or she is responsible for knowing about the more than 35,000 lists available, doing any research necessary for you, then recommending the best possible lists for your offer. As you get more involved, your broker may be able to negotiate prices for you, help evaluate results, and give you advice on many aspects of your direct mail plans. Used wisely, a good list broker can be a valuable member of your sales team. He or she can guide you to expand or reduce your potential universe through geography, selects, functions, and title addressing.

But don't put all your confidence in someone else. Having gotten this far in *Jump Start Your Book Sales,* your own creative juices should be surging. DM expert Dan Kennedy suggests looking for inventive matches. If you have a book on chiropractic, for instance, you should be renting the lists of buyers from BackSaver or Magnetic Therapy catalogs. Would you believe there are 32,000 buyers of a device that hunters use to mimic turkeys or deer? What a natural if you have a book on hunting advice or cooking wild meat.

And what about clubs? Dan reminds us there are "Beer Clubs, Wine Clubs, Coffee Tasters Clubs, Chocolate Clubs. Travel Clubs . . . ." Not to mention various fan clubs. You can get breakouts by state, zips, gender, etc. If you have a regional guide on the beer pubs of Colorado, for instance, this could be one of your best marketing ploys.

Jo Ann Martin, co-owner (with Vickie Hutchins) of Gooseberry Patch in Delaware, Ohio, tells of getting a list on her own through the Yellow Pages—and not receiving one single response. Now she works with a consultant. "Get someone with experience in list management and brokering," she counsels. "You need someone who knows what they're doing." Apparently her consultant does. From a starting point of distributing 7,000 catalogs in 1985 for a gross of $27,000, Gooseberry Patch sent out 4 million catalogs in 1997.

Sue and Bob Prenner traded careers as successful lawyers to launch the Ben Silver Corporation, which manufactures blazer buttons stamped with insignias in cloisonne enamel or gold. While Sue heartily recommends getting professional help, she observes, "No list broker has your inherent sense for your customer demographics. You need to use your intuition to get a good sense of where your market is." She believes a broker can direct you into less obvious areas and is especially useful in analyzing returns and seeing what works.

This expert help doesn't cost *you* anything. List brokers are typically paid a 20% commission by whoever owns the list. Because they must survive on these commissions, they're interested in working with companies that contemplate doing volume mailings now, or will be good long-range customers.

Philip Dismukes, president of Information Marketing Services, Inc., in Fairfax, Virginia, recommends, "Fit your needs with their [the broker's] capabilities and interests." Dismukes feels one of the biggest mistakes a direct marketer can make is failing to understand a key feature of every mailing list: how it was put together. "Your best names are 'responders'—people who have previously paid money in response to a direct mail solicitation," he explains (see the sidebar).

To find quick professional help, let your fingers do the walking. Brokers are cataloged in the Yellow Pages under "Mailing Lists." The largest assembly of lists is contained in *Standard Rate and Data's Direct Mail List Rates & Data (SRDS)*. This whopper volume resides in your main public library. Here you'll discover detailed information on who rents what, plus firms and individuals who serve as list brokers.

You'll be amazed at the tightly niched groups of buyers you can reach through this source. One New Age publisher reports wondering  if his book was too New Age for Christians...that is until he found the *Christian New Age Quarterly* magazine, which deals with what each group can learn from the other. He also wondered if he was too New Age to interest Republicans. Lo and behold, he found a list of New Age Republican donors!

Be careful list brokers don't oversell you. Quality is more important than quantity. You might ask which customers repeatedly rent the lists your broker recommends, then check with that firm's marketing manager to determine results.

Brokers aren't interested in talking with you, however, until you're ready to rent at least 5,000 test names. Therefore, let's look at how you can begin generating lists on your own.

Direct Marketing "Freebies"

Here are free sales aids, publications, and services that can help you generate better results from your direct marketing campaigns.

■ A valuable freebie is *How to Compile and Maintain a Mailing List.* It goes into such topics as database construction—where to find the data for your customer list—how to locate inquiry, prospect, and suspect names—ways to keep your list clean and efficient—and how to physically store and work it. Get a copy by contacting Quill Corporation at 100 S. Schelter Road, Lincolnshire, IL 60069; 800-789-1331.

■ Two dynamite specialized publications are available on a complimentary basis to serious publishers who request them on company letterhead. They are *Target Marketing*, 401 N. Broad St., Philadelphia, PA 19108 and *DM News* at 100 6th Avenue, 6th Floor, New York, NY 10013-1689. Not only do they carry how-to articles and columns but also revealing case histories of what works—and what doesn't.

■ The U.S. Postal Service puts out several things you may find useful. We were supremely impressed with their *Direct Mail Delivers Kit.* It contains a 3-ring binder of case studies and advice, a 96-page book titled *The Business Guide to Advertising with Direct Mail,* and a free hardcover guide from Random House

(continued on next page)

Prospecting for effective lists

There are many enterprising ways you can personally obtain obscure yet productive lists. Some of these ideas are plain vanilla flavor; others are like pistachio ripple.

An excellent place to secure intriguing lists is through associations. The *Encyclopedia of Associations* indexes organization names and key words in Part 3 of their three-volume set. There is an association for absolutely every interest, from the American Kite Fliers Association to the National Council of Savings Institutions, the Railway Historical Society to the Center for Environmental Research.

Often you can rent their membership lists quite inexpensively. If they don't rent it, but publish a directory, there are a couple of other alternatives: You can either buy the directory or join the organization, then compile your own list.

Directory of Directories is also a productive place to prospect. More than 6,000 reference works are logged in this volume. They run the gamut from sports to acting, medicine to gardening, ecology to feminism. Obtaining obscure directories isn't always easy. Seek unusual ones through special interlibrary loan arrangements. Don't work with anything outdated.

If you're doing a regional title, consider localized mailings. Talk with your local postmaster about SCF (Sectional Center Facility) carrier routes. These are the paths area carriers walk or drive. By coordinating an area map with the carrier routes, you can determine the number of carriers and get counts.

The post office has written instructions on how to sort your third class (bulk) mail to be cost-effective for you and efficient for them. Or you can find a mailing service in the Yellow Pages to handle all the actual details.

Cultivating your own in-house list

Your own customer mailing list can become one of your company's most valuable assets. These are people who have already bought from you. Assuming you do right by them, they will buy from you time after time. Jo Ann Martin increases her list by encouraging customers to send in referrals for their friends. "These are very valuable names," she comments. "We track all customers to know what they spend and when."

Direct Marketing "Freebies" (continued)

titled *Being Direct: Making Advertising Pay.* (Oh, to have made *that* premium sale!) Order it by calling 800-THE-USPS (800-843-8777), ext. 2085. Ask for the free kit.

■ *Memo to Mailers* is a free monthly newsletter. To subscribe, write National Customer Support Center, U.S. Postal Service, 6060 Primacy Parkway, Suite 101, Memphis, TN 38188-0001.

■ Uncle Sam also offers a complimentary service to help direct marketers correct undeliverable addresses. It's called Operation Mail. This program puts addresses in standardized form and assigns the correct 9-digit ZIP code to each. A random sample is actually forwarded to individual local post offices where the deliverability of each is scrutinized. Ultimately, you receive reports of addresses and the new standardized form, plus an explanation of those addresses that could not be matched. This can save a lot of wasted postage dollars! Talk to your local postmaster for more details.

They have surveyed their buyers as to age, sex, whether they have children or own a house, the amount of money they spend on mail order purchases, where they live, even what magazines they read! This educates Martin. Using her present customer demographics, she knows precisely what kinds of outside lists to rent.

After you've amassed 5,000 or so names, you can also go into the list rental business yourself by contacting companies listed in *SRDS*. Or you can barter your list for other ones. This plays an important role in the strategy for Ben Silver Corporation. "We exchange lists a great deal," says Sue Prenner. "About half of the time we use our own list. The other half we exchange it for another good list. This reduces our mailing costs dramatically." Because she sells unique merchandise, Prenner finds her in-house list in demand and isn't concerned about competitors.

Whether you rent your names or use them exclusively yourself, good list management is essential. Databases should be updated, cleaned, and evaluated on a regular basis.

Mailing smarter

With postage hikes announced on a regular basis, you need to be more savvy than ever. Forget mass mailings. Shrewd marketers are targeting their mailings to the most refined marketplace they can find.

In this business it's important to test, test, test. Be sure to do this before you roll out with big numbers. When generating your own lists, you could start testing with as few as 200 names, although 500 or 1,000 will give you a more realistic response. After all, 2% of 200 would only be 4 orders. When playing with the big boys, you have to rent a minimum of 5,000 names for a test.

Request an "nth" name selection for a good random cross section of the file. This avoids the problem of having every contact be from California—or New York—when buying habits for the two areas differ significantly.

Once you find a list that works, roll out big time and keep mailing to it (seasonal offers excepted) until it peters out. When you get going in DM you may be renting several lists to go out at the same time. How do you track which one is working best? You can "key code" your labels. Instruct your list broker to put "BPC," for instance, on one list to differentiate it from the other. Of course, you must make sure the customer knows to include the key on order forms (maybe they peel off the label and affix it to the order form, or write in the code.) On phone orders your telephone staff needs to be trained to ask for it. Otherwise the coding will be useless.

So how are these names supplied? The methods vary, depending on what you're doing. Pressure sensitive labels you can apply yourself. Cheshire labels require a letter shop to apply them. You may well want to outsource this job to a service bureau or letter shop, which you can find in the Yellow Pages. (It takes a lot of time to put out a 5,000-piece bulk mailing.) If you plan to merge-purge several lists, you'll need them on magnetic tape. Many letter shops also require mag tapes, so be sure to find out their requirements if you plan to outsource your mailing.

Escalating postage costs mean list cleaning is getting higher priority. Accuracy is vital; you can't afford to waste postage on dirty, undeliverable pieces of mail, which are called "nixies." Ask your broker about a list's nixie rate. Also inquire if the list owner guarantees that a certain percentage of the names are deliverable. There's no point in paying to put out mail that never reaches its destination.

Understanding the kinds of lists available

There are several kinds of lists. Some are extremely effective; others aren't worth the labels they're printed on. To help you better grasp the differences, here are your choices:

Compiled lists are derived from phone books, reference manuals, and other directories. Therefore, they are generic rather than targeted. In most cases, compiled lists don't perform very well.

Publisher R. Marilyn Schmidt of Barnegat Light Press is the exception to that rule. She told us of getting up to a 15% response to lists she compiles. This press publishes books on seafood. To get names she looks in organization directories for fishing clubs, found a directory of seafood markets, etc. Her distribution is both wholesale and retail and extends from coast to coast and into Canada.

Occupant lists include every household in a given geographic area. While not usually relevant for publishing, they could be helpful if you have a tightly niched regional book.

Response lists pull better than the first two types because they're made up of people who have already bought related products or services. These individuals have a proven propensity to purchase by mail.

Hotline lists contain names and addresses of people who have bought within the last three to six months. Because they are more current, they're also more expensive—and more productive.

Your in-house list is the best there is! These people have already bought from you. They trust you; they're far more likely to buy from you again.

If you see direct marketing playing a large role in your marketing mix, contact the Direct Marketing Association, Inc., 1120 Avenue of the Americas, New York, NY 10036, 212-768-7277; http://www.the-dma.org. These folks are the true experts in the DM field.

Armed with all this ammunition against the mail list culprit, you're sure to make better use of your mail list dollars—and reap more profits in return.

Are you on the right (any?) Web mailing lists? Liszt is a huge directory of Internet mailing list information that could make your work life a lot easier—and your play time a lot more fun. No, these are not advertising pitches. Most are chock-full of literate, mature newsletter pieces that you can have delivered free to your email address each day or week. Another facet of mailing lists is discussion groups on highly targeted subjects. The whole purpose of Liszt is to help you *find* mailing lists that might interest you, then get information about joining.

A word of caution: Be sure to research a list before you join. Otherwise here's what could happen. Let's take pitbulls, for instance. This could be a newsletter or discussion group for owners of that species of dog—or it might consist of those who crusade against pitbulls. It might be a group of stockbrokers who meet for lunch on Mondays and call themselves the "Pitbulls." It could be ex-jocks from a team dubbed the "Pitbulls." Or even groupies who love a new rock band called "The Pitbulls." See what we mean? These groups often have a strong sense of community and you don't want to barge into the wrong environment.

Also be sure not to sign up for anything that doesn't give clear directions on how to get *off* the list in case it doesn't measure up to your expectations. At http://www.liszt.com over 85,000 choices await you. They cover social issues, recreation, religion, science, computers, foreign countries—you name it. Have fun!

Want association mailing lists? MGI Lists calls itself the "Association List Company." Among others, they have lists covering healthcare, education, science, and youth at risk. Call them at 800-899-4420.

Bestseller status: boon or bane?
Of course, the higher an ape climbs in a tree,
the more of his rump shows.
And when you become a best-selling author
you gets lots of fan mail . . .
especially from men in prisons.

How much direct mail is too much direct mail? Let's say you put out a mailing and get a 3% response, which is considered very good. Should you go to that same list again? If you mail a follow-up offer within six months to those same prospects, expect to get half your original response. Armed with this statistic, you can easily compute if it will be profitable to hit that list again. By the way, prices for using the same list are often cheaper the second or third time around. Ask your mailing list broker about this or negotiate with the list owner if you rent directly.

Frustrated by returned mail when you try to reach customers in your database? Have we got a nifty solution for you! Switchboard is a directory of people, businesses, Web sites, and email addresses. The next time the post office returns mail and it looks like a dead end, go to http://www.switchboard.com and enter the person's old address. This can help you retrieve up to 90% of former good customers who slipped through the cracks.

Need lists to reach the book publishing industry? Although targeting consumers for your direct mail certainly may make sense, you might also want to do what is called business-to-business mailings. That is when you, as a business, reach out to another business. Cahners Business Lists is an easy one-stop place to find such lists, whatever your needs. Here's a sample of what you can get:

■ Selling books? Try *American Book Trade Directory* to reach book-stores and wholesalers; *American Library Directory* to contact libraries.

■ Sending news releases? Investigate *Working Press of the Nation* to reach newspapers and magazines, or use *Ulrich's International Periodicals Directory* for contacting publications worldwide.

■ Arranging author interviews? Try a list from *Working Press of the Nation*, or *Broadcasting and Cable Yearbook* to target radio and television producers.

■ Seeking other like-minded publishers? You'll find them in *Publishers Address Directory* or *Literary Market Place*.

For information on all the above lists, plus tons of specialty possibilities, call 800-337-7184 and ask for John Panza.

Want sophisticated help with direct mail? You'll find it at http://www.horah.com. If you are into serious DM, this site is worth checking out. Their postage chart will help you determine the costs of direct mailing and what discounts are available. They can also calculate the weight and thickness for you before the paper pieces are even off the printer. And there are articles and checklists on cutting costs, etc.

Looking for free money? You may be sitting on a pot of gold in your mailing list. Although renting your mailing list is strictly ancillary income, it can bring in substantial dollars and offset your own mailing costs. A handful of big catalog companies rack up an annual income in 10 figures just from list rental!

Publishers Mailing Lists (PML) is a mailing list brokerage and management company serving independent publishers. Currently they manage over 50 separate customer mailing lists representing health care; human resources management and business; holistic health and lifestyle; plus book, tape, video, and seminar buyers. If you work through them you can expect a royalty of approximately $40 per thousand names for each rental. For more details, contact PML at 508 North 2nd Street, Suite 203, Fairfield, IA 52556; phone 515-472-7188; fax 515-472-5729.

I'm writing this slow 'cause I know you can't read fast.

ZIP + 4 means extra savings for direct mailings. Coding Accuracy Support System (CASS) certification refers to the extra four digits after normal ZIP codes. If you rent mailing lists from others, look for this feature. If their lists are not prepared this way, try requesting a discount as you will be deprived of the lesser mailing fees. The post office is trying to get away from hand sorting mail. They decided that giving a business discount for the ZIP + 4 is a practical way to get businesses behind the movement.

Seeking contacts in Canada for bookstores, libraries, schools, or media? The perfect source is the Association of Canadian Publishers, 110 Eglinton Avenue W., #401, M4R 1A3 Toronto, Ontario, CANADA; phone

416-487-6116; fax 416-487-8815; or email info@canbook.org. You can also purchase the *Directory of Canadian Media* from them for $329.95.

News and resources for printing, graphic arts, direct marketing, and the publishing industry await you. We found several goodies at the North American Publishing Company site. They have an interesting Publishing Business Center and when we clicked on *Target Marketing* magazine, it led us on a merry trail to articles in the present and past issues of the magazine. One, "Market Focus: Book Club Buyers," was especially relevant. If you're into direct marketing, this is a site you should bookmark. Find it at http://www.napco.com/. And if your company qualifies, you can also get free subscriptions here for *Target Marketing* and *Publishing and Printing Executive.*

How do you tell when you're out of invisible ink?

More DM goodies live at http://www.mailingstuff.com/. Find vendor lists, printing and lettershop information, and much data relating to direct marketing here.

CHAPTER 22

Speaking and Teaching to Speed Up Profits

Speak and ye shall sell. Tapping into the presentation market, which includes seminars, workshops, lectures, classes, demonstrations, and readings, can open lucrative doors for additional book sales. In fact, Chicago author Bill Joseph earned more than $2 million during a five-year period from seminar fees. That was much more than the book itself generated. Yet his book was the key to getting students to attend the seminars.

Before Tom Peters gained fame as an author, he was earning $42,500 a year. Now he gets nearly that for a single day's speaking engagement! Peters has cut back to 125 talks a year and is booked far into the future. Although these gentlemen are the exceptions, there can be big bucks in what is known in the trade as back-of-the-room sales.

Developing back-of-the-room sales

Some entrepreneurial authors not only peddle their own books but put together kits of additional compatible materials. These are then combined, shrink-wrapped, and offered at special discounts to seminar attendees. A charismatic author/speaker could promote not only his or her own books but other titles as well. This is grand slam bookselling. This approach also works well for a publishing house with several titles in the same genre.

271

Just as oregano gives added zest to spaghetti sauce, you can give book sales new zip by exploring this avenue. Lectures or seminars work well for nonfiction; demonstrations are excellent for cookbooks, new diet regimes, and certain how-to topics. Readings are the most suitable vehicle to highlight poetry and fiction. You have a captive audience who, when properly primed, are eager to buy.

It's always easier if you can find an organization or business to sponsor your presentation. Perhaps Friends of the Library or a local bookstore that features poetry readings and novel excerpts would work. A gourmet shop is a natural for food demonstrations. Anna Aughenbaugh of Starlight Publications says, "Presenting cooking classes at health food stores, church groups, and county extension clubs has been very successful. This also provides a reason to put a news release in the paper."

When I (Marilyn) wrote *Creative Loafing*, I convinced a San Diego recreational association and a savings and loan to sponsor seminars on Creative Loafing. We sold lots of books to the folks who attended those events.

Nadia West, the author of a very specialized local history about California gold country titled *River of Red Gold*, sold more than 10,000 copies largely due to her speaking endeavors. In the beginning, she talked about her book, then moved into entertainment—expanding to costumed living history enactments, storytelling, and leading tours. She even does scholarly presentations, such as a recent convention of the Western History Association. Today she speaks two to four times a week; the sponsoring organization handles the publicity.

If your aim is book sales rather than personal glory, choose the places where you appear carefully. Although authors with a flair for the spoken word can volunteer as guest speakers at business, professional, civic, or social groups, this quickly becomes a time gobbler with minimal results. It's hard to sell a general interest book to a general interest audience. But if you have a title on collecting foreign coins, get yourself invited to address a group of numismatics and watch sales zoom.

Launching your own seminar program

Should you decide to launch your own seminar program, be prepared to work hard and spend money. Advertising and promotion are crucial. How will you attract attendees? Will you use a direct marketing campaign? Buy newspaper space advertising? Use radio spots? Develop a referral fee arrangement? Send news releases to key media?

How much must you charge to make a profit? When and where will the seminars be held? How will prospects get information and sign up? Who will handle registration and book sales? Overseeing all the details can be an arduous task. Take it from folks who have done it both ways; it's a heck of a lot easier to just walk in and do your shtick.

Besides a lot of work, self-sponsored seminars can be expensive. Suppose you plan on doing a mailing to 5,000 people. Have any idea what that will run? You'd better! To rent the list you'll probably pay around $500. Prices to print a direct marketing package vary greatly. You might get by with about $1,000; more likely you'll spend double that. (And we're assuming here you write the promotional copy yourself. Many people elect to hire a seasoned professional for this crucial step.)

Then there are the costs of a fulfillment house to physically do the mailing. This tacks a few more cents onto every piece. Bulk mail for this size list will typically be about 25¢ a piece. It doesn't take a mathematical genius to deduct that you'd better have a lot of people at a reasonable price, or a few people at a high price, to make any money.

Working through established adult educational facilities

Extended studies or adult education facilities sponsor seminars on a wide range of subjects. There are learning centers all across the United States and Canada that specialize in quenching the thirst of adults who want continued learning. Some are noncredit courses sponsored by community colleges or universities. Others are called the Learning Annex, (headquarters in San Francisco), Colorado Free University (Denver), Open U (Minneapolis), Leisure Learning Unlimited (Houston), and the Learning Connection. Look on the Web or in a local phone book to find contact information for cities where you wish to propose a class.

The Learning Annex contacted us to do courses in their four outlets. The classes typically run three hours on weekend nights and are often held at a hotel. They run $29 to $39 and instructors get 15% of the receipts. Classes are set and work on their catalogs begins three to four months in advance, so you have to plan ahead.

Some of these centers have huge mailing lists. In many cases, hundreds of thousands of people who don't attend are still exposed to the title of your book. Julian Block, noted tax attorney and author, always asks schools that offer his adult education courses to mention his *Julian*

Block's Year-Round Tax Strategies in any instructor bio. Though people may not attend his class, they become aware of the book as a resource.

At The Learning Annex, product sales are permitted and you keep 100%. Estimates are that 40 to 80% of the students will purchase something. Of course, if you have a $9.95 book, this won't amount to a lot. Better to package multiple products to create a "kit" of books, and perhaps audio and video, for those really serious about learning. Give a discount for the entire package.

Self-publishing expert Dan Poynter tells of placing a copy of his book in front of each student. Sales shot up from 10% of the room to 50% when people were able to handle and examine the book at their leisure.

Honing your presentation

Your actual presentation style has a lot of bearing on how book sales go. If you're a dynamic, animated speaker, people are much more likely to want to take home a memento of the occasion: your book. Friendliness and a smile go a long way in winning over an audience. Make people feel welcome and comfortable, and they'll be on your side.

A recent study revealed 55% of the audience responds to your body language and facial expression, while 37% react to your voice—including pacing, pitch, inflections, and overall delivery. Only 8% react to the actual content of your message! Based on these findings, it's the show that makes it go!

There are little tricks for making your presentation successful. Audiences love stories, so come up with anecdotes to illustrate your main points. They also adore humor. You don't have to be a funny person to interject levity into your presentation. Simply find a joke that fits the situation. (And don't introduce it as "a joke." If it falls flat, then you aren't embarrassed.)

If you pick a few receptive-looking people around the room and talk directly to them, your eye contact will be good and everyone will feel included. Remember, you are there to speak not give constant commercials. Referring to and showing your book a couple of times will be enough to whet audience members' desire to own a copy if you deliver otherwise.

But be sure to take along an adequate supply of books. Sounds simple, right? Yet many authors deliver a compelling speech, rouse their audience to action, then have to turn away sales because they don't have enough stock on hand to meet the demand. What a waste.

Also take along customer brochures. But *don't* leave them in a conspicuous place. You want people to make a buying decision now, not have the excuse of maybe ordering later. Sometimes a person might want to pass along information to a friend or colleague who may be interested in your title. Only then do you subtly slip them a brochure.

Another key strategy is to make it easy to buy. If you plan to use this method of merchandising, arrange to offer Visa and MasterCard. And post small display signs to announce you accept credit cards. It is wise to charge a round number like $7 or $10 or $20, rather than $7.30 or $9.88 or $19.65. That way customers aren't bothered fishing for change to pay sales tax and you aren't tied up over pennies while those who want to spend dollars wait unattended. You can afford to absorb the tax anyway as these sales are usually at full retail price.

Most professional speakers coach the person who introduces them. Many go so far as to provide a typed, double-spaced "canned" introduction. That way, there is no temptation for the introducer to say something like, "Jim really needs no introduction." Every presenter needs and deserves a well-rounded introduction to establish his or her credentials and set the stage properly. Professionals also ask the person introducing them to wrap up the presentation with, "You can get your personally autographed copy of Jim's new book by stopping to see him now at the table in the back of the room." This reminder is often the clincher.

Tips for becoming a paid presenter

It never hurts to query an organization about whether they have a budget for speakers. Most often, the answer will be "no." But sometimes they will offer you an "honorarium," which can range anywhere from $25 to several hundred dollars. Frequently, they will help with expenses. This typically includes transportation, hotel, and sometimes meals.

If you discover they do have a budget for speakers, try to find out what it is *before* you volunteer financial information. If they can afford $1,000, for instance, and you tell them your fee is $500, guess what you will be paid? You might want to have a lesser fee structure when speaking to nonprofits, as we do.

Require a deposit to hold the speaking date. We learned the hard way how important this detail can be. A few years ago we were hired to speak to a national organization. Since they were picking up the travel tab and paying us a nice fee, we decided to build book signings and PR around the speaking engagement. Two weeks before we were to give the seminar, they canceled. Our ethics dictated we do the trip as we had made other commitments. Now we require half down when booking a date. That gives our client more motivation to make the engagement work, and it gives us a pad if they do cancel. The balance of the fee is due the day we speak.

Other things we cover in a letter of agreement is how long the presentation will be, its title, and exactly what expenses the client is picking up. We also get in writing that we have the right to sell not only our own books but also other related titles the audience would find helpful. *We* provide the sales copy for their brochure, flyer, and/or newsletter.

Another issue that may come up is audio- or video-taping. More sophisticated clients like to tape you and sell copies to those who couldn't attend. We think this is fine as long as *we* get a master of the tape and also have the right to sell it. This is a cost-free way to get a professionally done audio or video to add to your own product line.

You may be able to convince your client to purchase a copy of the book for each attendee. We did this when speaking recently to an association and actually made more on book sales than we did on our fee! (And it was nice not to have the usual back-of-the room crunch after we spoke.) They liked the value-added aspect of giving attendees a gift. Suggest this idea. And if they tell you there is no money in the speaking budget for such expenses, probe to see if a different budget might have funds, such as an education budget or a participant materials budget.

Sources for more exposure and information

If you feel like you need Viagra so you can "stand and deliver," let us offer another option: Toastmasters International has more than 6,000 groups around the country where men and women gather in their communities to get comfortable speaking in front of an audience and practice honing their public speaking skills. It is a wonderful training ground. For more information write P.O. Box 9052, Mission Viejo, CA 92690; phone 949-858-8255; or fax 949-858-1207.

For more sophisticated learning, we highly recommend the National Speakers Association. (Members of NSA are listed in a directory, receive a monthly magazine of insider tips, can gain tremendous insights at the annual convention and regional workshops, and have the option of joining area chapters for networking, support, and promotion within their area.) Our fellow colleagues in NSA are a uniquely caring group of folks. For information write 1500 South Priest Drive, Tempe, AZ 85281; phone: 480-968-2552; fax: 480-968-0911.

Dottie Walters, CSP, can be a budding speaker's best friend. She and her daughter, Lilly Walters, authored *Speak and Grow Rich*, which overflows with techniques and shortcuts used by today's top professional speakers. Dottie also edits and publishers a newsmagazine called *Sharing Ideas*. For subscription information, call: 626-335-8069 or fax: 626-335-6127.

Are you an east coast poet or novelist? Then Poets & Writers, Inc. might sponsor a reading or workshop program in the state of New York. In one year, they doled out over $200,000 to authors. Presentations are given at libraries, "Y's," community centers, small presses, universities, museums, hospitals, prisons, bookstores, and religious facilities. Reach Poets and Writers, Inc. at 72 Spring Street, New York, NY 10012; phone: 212-226-3586.

Of course, not every book lends itself to merchandising in the ways we've been discussing. And certainly not every author feels comfortable in front of an audience. In many cases, though, employing back-of-the-room sales nets front-of-the-line profits.

Web Sites, Wisdom, and Whimsey

Tips for your book display table. Bring your own drape or tablecloth so your display will stand out from any others. Prop up a sample of each of your books. There are wooden, wire, and plastic stands that work great. We find that having a large display of each title works best. People seem more drawn than if there are just a few copies. (Others disagree with us on this and feel you should display only a few books to create the illusion that people better hurry up and buy.) Feature signs for the credit cards you accept.

Announce during your talk that you'll have a useful freebie hand-out on your sale table. Place it in the middle of the table at the back. People will stop by for it, see your merchandise, and perhaps impulse buy. Choreograph the end of your speech so you can readily get to your table. *Don't* let yourself get tripped up by the lectern. Also avoid getting entangled in answering complicated questions at the sales table. A grace-ful, "I'll be happy to answer that question for you if you wait a few minutes until we're finished here," usually works.

Sell more books. Naturally, when you or your authors are speaking, you will autograph and sell books. But sometimes schools, organiza-tions, and companies are finicky and won't allow this. Assuming you still want to give the speech, here are some ideas to help get the "book" word out: The most ideal solution is to sell them a book (discounted from 20 to 50% depending on quantity and how hungry you are) to give to each attendee. Since that will only work occasionally, here are some alternative strategies:

1. Provide them with flyers ahead of time to include in attendee pack-ets.
2. Have flyers available on the sign-in table and prompt the registrar to offer them.
3. Write a number on each packet, then hold a drawing during your presentation, at which time you boldly display the book and present it to the lucky winner.
4. Request a mailing list of the attendees (or see if one is automatically provided in the packet) and send a flyer to everyone.

I heard that the definition of a dynamic presentation is a good beginning and a good end...with both sides as close together as possible.

Is your networking too niched? One of the most overlooked bonanzas for meeting and greeting may be your local chamber of commerce. One publisher who tried this ended up meeting a man who serves on two regional library boards. He not only gave our publisher the buyer's name but said to use his name in the introduction. And he will look for open-ings where she can speak at future library meetings.

The chamber of commerce can also be a wealth of reference pos-sibilities: ideas for people to populate your next novel or experts to answer specific questions on such technical subjects as accounting, taxes, sales, crime, real estate, etc. The more people who know about you and what you do in your community, the better your chances of making a valuable connection. Of course, if you write or publish business books, you'll be in hog heaven.

Speaker to audience: "My function as I understand it is to talk to you. Yours is to listen. If you get finished first, just raise your hand."

Trying to locate trade shows, conferences, or exhibits that parallel your book topic? Have we got a beaut of a site for you! Go to http://www.expoguide.com/shows/shows.htm. This is both a fast and smart site. We did a general search by concept for the word "environment." It not only brought up events that are obviously environmentally oriented, it also showed ones that dealt with forestry, chemicals, paper, etc. Furthermore, they are labeled "highly relevant," "probably relevant," or "possibly relevant" so you don't waste time on marginal research. Not only can this site help you easily identify shows where they may want to exhibit, it is also an easy way to target conferences where authors might be pitched as speakers.

The trouble with the guy who talks too fast is that he often says something he hasn't thought of yet.

Remedies for laryngitis. Losing your voice just before a speech can be almost as terrifying as running into a grizzly with only a switch to defend yourself. Here are some tips to ease the situation:

1. Keep quiet. Speak off the platform only when absolutely necessary to give your vocal cords a rest. Don't whisper either; that also strains your voice.
2. Avoid coffee and soda. Caffeine dries out vocal cords.
3. Sip lukewarm water with a little lemon juice.
4. Get some Ricola cough drops. They contain healing sage instead of drying menthol.
5. Use a humidifier at night.
6. Go to a health food store and get some sesame tahini. (It looks a lot like peanut butter.) Put a spoonful on the back of your throat.

PART VI

More Methods to Fire-Up Your Sales

CHAPTER 23

Alternative Master Moves to Outrun the Herd

We have so many ideas to share with you, but several of them don't fit into one of the designated chapters. Consequently, this is a medley of money-making moves to help position you ahead of the pack. Of course, it takes hard work to be successful. But you need only work half a day. (It makes no difference which half: It can be either the first 12 hours or the last 12 hours. Smile.) Now let's look at these alternative ways to generate cash flow.

Selling foreign rights to your books

The overseas market is definitely worth exploring for many titles. Although the financial havoc the Asian flu is creating has put a serious damper on several countries, others are still big buyers. China, for instance, has emerged as a strong rights market. People are hungry for U.S. product, especially business books. You can approach these rights sales before the book is even printed—or work them on backlist titles that have done well in this country.

There are two types of foreign rights deals. Note that in both situations the copyright holder is *licensing rights*, usually for five to seven years, not selling the book.

1. The first is to license the translation of the English version of the book into a foreign language. This is done for non-English–speak-

ing countries and represents a sizable translation expense for the country acquiring the book. (It's interesting to note that when a book is translated into another language it grows from 10 to 25%.)

2. The other option is to license the right to reprint the book in the English language and sell it in a given country. Since English is the universally accepted language, this is done most often. You receive an advance against royalties on future sales. The advance may be a paltry $500, or it could run to several thousand dollars. Because each book is unique, there is no absolute standard. Large countries, such as the United Kingdom and Germany, will pay more than smaller ones. Royalties run 7.5 to 10% on the first printing and usually escalate to 10 to 15% on additional printings.

For some smaller publishers like MacMurray & Beck that aggressively pursue this, subsidiary rights sales represent a substantial portion of their income. Rights sales now account for 35% of their revenue and they hope to push that to 40%. For other publishers, it is "found" money.

How do you connect with likely buyers? Exhibiting at the huge international Frankfurt Book Fair is prudent if you're pursuing this revenue stream. You can see their catalog  by accessing their Web site at www. frankfurter-buchmesse.de. Another possibility is the London Book Fair, which has become increasingly well attended by a variety of countries—especially those from the United Kingdom, northern Europe, and emerging nations.

Or you might try a more unorthodox approach. When Bill Hannah of Canada's distinguished Stoddard Publishing wanted to sell rights, he called the embassy of the country in which he was interested. After telling them who he was and providing evidence of his credentials, they agreed to set up meetings. The publishers met him with open arms and the embassy even provided a translator!

As we explained in chapter 2, your book must "travel" well, meaning it should have appropriate content for people in other countries. To attract interest, develop a rights sheet or a cover letter detailing all of the following: title and subtitle, author, ISBN, retail price, pub date, binding, page count, and trim size. (Stating measurements in both inches and metric equivalents is easy to do and will impress them.) Include a brief, vivid description. And focus on author credentials. Foreign publishers put great weight on authors' qualifications and want books by authorities in their fields.

Also include information on other titles by the same author that have sold well in the U.S. or have had rights sales. Enclose your marketing plans and any publicity tour schedule. If you are doing an especially large print run, note that as well so they realize you're taking this book seriously. Of course, you'll include full contact information for your publishing company. Immediately upon their request, courier them a reading copy of the book.

On the foreign rights sales we've had, we hired agents to negotiate the actual deal, feeling there are too many places to make a mistake. Their take is 20%. You can find them in *International Literary Market Place* or by asking around. Or you might hire an attorney who specializes in this type of transaction.

Once you've sold rights to one or two foreign publishers, be proactive and start sending reading copies and rights sheets to others who might be interested. It's surprising how one rights sale promotes another. Strive to multiply your success.

"And the award goes to..."

Just as winning an Academy Award—not to mention a nomination—has movies zooming to box-office stardom, having your book honored with an award—or even being a finalist—has its pluses. There are those who say paying an entry fee to win an award is sheer vanity. And there are others who contend such a narrow-minded attitude is pure folly.

Winona's Web took the fiction prize in the Small Press Book Award competition recently, then went on to receive a reprint offer from Doubleday. Additionally, the author signed a two-book contract with Simon & Schuster.

When a librarian or bookseller is faced with making a choice between two comparable competing titles, the one that has won an award will best the other every time. Even obscure awards are sometimes tiebreakers in the selection process.

We feel entry fees for legitimate contests should be built into your marketing budget. Spending a few hundred PR dollars and doling out a dozen or so books is a small amount to pay if you end up being one of the lucky winners. You probably pay a lot more to generate less publicity. And as assertive publicists, we're always looking for a reason to be "news." Right? Winning an award certainly qualifies!

If you were to prevail in the Rocky Mountain Book Publishers Book Design Award Contest, for instance, your book would be displayed in their booth at key area trade shows, as well as given Web site exposure on their site at http://www.rmbpa.com.

Besides the Benjamin Franklin Awards sponsored by Publishers Marketing Association, the "Ippy" (recognizing excellence in Independent Publishing) sponsored by *Independent Publisher* and *ForeWord* magazine's awards—there are scores of others, both regional and national. A good place to look for them is in *Literary Market Place*. Section 76 lists Literary Awards, which includes selected major awards given to books, authors, and publishers by various organizations.

For writers with as-yet-unpublished manuscripts, scanning section 77, Prize Contests, may yield exciting possibilities. It covers contests in fiction, nonfiction, poetry, and various mass media. Many writers' groups also sponsor contests to offer encouragement to the unpublished.

True, winning the award benefits only one book, one author, and one publisher. But *participating* in contests has many spinoff benefits. If you enter 1 of the 19 categories in the Evangelical Christian Publishers Association's Gold Medallion Book Awards, for instance, your book goes on a list of entries that is available to all Christian retailers. When you're a finalist in the Benjamin Franklin Awards, your book is displayed for all who attend the PMA function to see and placed on their Web site.

If you capture a place as a finalist in the Colorado Book Awards, as we did for *Country Bound!*, you're invited to a complimentary $40 award ceremony luncheon at the posh Denver Petroleum Club, asked to be available to autograph copies of your book, and given a press release to notify local newspapers in your area about your being a finalist.

Judges, who are typically opinion-molders in the industry, sometimes take a personal interest in your book. Not only might they buy a copy, but they may mention it to others in their circle of influence. And some contests have the judges complete evaluation forms, which are ultimately returned to the author or publisher. This can provide invaluable impartial feedback for your future publishing projects.

Contest ideas for publishers and authors

How about putting the shoe on the other foot and sponsoring a contest of your own? Here are some suggestions to get your creative juices going:

- ■ If you're publishing books on gardening, suggest that a local chain of nurseries sponsor a contest for backyard gardeners and offer to be the judge. The winner gets one of your books and a gift certificate from the garden center. Ask the chain to stock your books. And be sure to get publicity for you and the winning gardener in the local newspaper.

- ■ Ask people to submit titles for your new book. Include the winner's name in the acknowledgments section. Announce the contest on your Web site and in the newspaper.

- ■ If you're writing a self-help book and want fodder for the content, sponsor a contest on the most unusual, inexpensive, or quick way to do whatever your book is about. People will respond even if all you promise is a mention in your book. Sweeten the offer with a small cash prize or gift certificate.

- ■ Sponsor a book review contest. Ask readers to write a short review of the new book you published. In return, give them a certificate toward the purchase of any of your other books. You end up with lots of great testimonials from your readers that you can use later in paid ads and marketing materials.

- ■ Ask the food editor at your local newspaper if he or she will sponsor a contest for readers on a topic related to one of your cookbooks. Winners get copies of the book and mention in the newspaper. You can be one of the judges. The newspaper will probably do most of the legwork.

- ■ Publishers or authors of fiction can ask the local newspaper to sponsor a "complete the short story" contest. You write the beginning and readers submit their own endings. This has been done very successfully on the Web by celebrity authors.

- ■ Call one of the disk jockeys on a popular morning drive-time radio show in your area and suggest an idea for a call-in contest that ties in with the theme of your book. Donate a batch of books as prizes. Be sure to ask them to mention where listeners who don't win can buy the books. Or ask them to announce your phone number.

17 Ways to Outdistance the Herd

1. **Price point:** Are you expensive, moderately priced, or cheap?

2. **Size:** Small may be beautiful; so might large or odd-sized.

3. **Ease of purchasing:** Do you accept credit cards?

4. **Convenience:** Can people find what they need easily?

5. **Do you have a gimmick:** What makes your book better or different from the competition?

6. **Delivery:** Do you offer overnight, second-day, regular, and book-rate options?

7. **Guarantee:** Have you a money-back policy?

8. **Packaging:** Could you use innovative, reusable, or fun packaging?

9. **Giveaways:** Do you offer small free gifts to potential customers or purchasers?

10. **Piggybacking:** Can you combine two or more books, tapes, or videos to create a kit?

11. **Samples:** Could you offer booklets, quizzes, or other excerpts to entice buyers?

12. **Seminars or demonstrations:** Should your book be showcased in this way?

13. **Contests:** Would some form of competition focus attention on you?

(continued on next page)

■ If you publish children's books, team up with a local bookstore that sells them to sponsor a contest for kids. Ask them to draw pictures of certain book characters that aren't illustrated or make a paper mask depicting a favorite character.

Creating events

Creating an "event" is another excellent way to focus attention on your book. Vicki Morgan of San Francisco's Foghorn Press did this in spades for their first title, *Forty Niners: Looking Back* by Joseph Hession. To launch it, Foghorn teamed up with the Pro Football Hall of Fame to stage a media event that would tie in with the 49ers' fortieth year. It also coincided with the book's arrival from the printers. The gala evening was held at no less than the prestigious Mark Hopkins Intercontinental Hotel on Nob Hill. It featured former and current members of the San Francisco 49ers, hosted cocktails and hors d'oeuvres, door prizes, NFL films, music, entertainment, and a copy of the book. Tickets sold for a hefty $65. Three hundred people attended.

Although Morgan wanted the party to draw fans, her main priority was to capture media attention. Thirty-one members of the media showed up, including all three major local TV stations. Radio KSJO covered the party live. The bottom line, of course, is what matters. *Forty*

Niners: Looking Back came out the beginning of December. By the end of the month, 8,000 copies had been sold! Foghorn now is recognized as a real force in the publishing community and has valuable contacts with sports writers and editors throughout the Bay Area.

We did something similar for *Creative Loafing*. We joined forces with the Aerospace Museum in San Diego and presented Creative Loafing Days in Balboa Park. Portraying the shoestring leisure activities depicted in the book, we had clowns, a frog-jumping jamboree, and po-

> **17 Ways to Out-distance the Herd (continued)**
>
> 14. **Surveys:** Can you conduct a survey to generate publicity?
>
> 15. **Audience segmentation:** Should you slant toward teens? Adults? Retirees? Men versus women? Gays rather than straights? Secular or nonsecular?
>
> 16. **Service:** Do you offer extraordinary assistance to your customers?
>
> 17. **Technological edge:** Do you have a Web site? Secure online ordering? An email address for fast, free correspondence?

etry readings. Other festivities included a jousting match by the Society of Creative Anachronism, plus demonstrations by mountain men, martial arts pros, and fencing experts. Because the museum was a nonprofit organization, we qualified for dozens of free PSA (public service announcement) radio commercials spotlighting the event and mentioning the book title. Not only did Creative Loafing Days hit all three TV networks and our publishing company receive a commendation from the mayor, we also sold out the hardcover print run.

Gleaning treasures from others

Original ideas can elude even the brightest people; no one can hit the bull's-eye every time. But there is a way you can substantially increase your success ratio. How? By mining the treasure trove that surrounds you!

Every day we're inundated with hundreds of good ideas. They masquerade in the form of direct mail packages, commercials, print ads, posters, billboards, articles, jokes, quotes, catalogs, newspaper stories, greeting cards—even as conversations. Because they wear such unlikely costumes, however, we often overlook them.

Unmasked, many are naturals for marketing; others lend sparkle to your editorial products; some furnish just the right touch to a speech. Why not begin capturing these kernels of wisdom for future use?

This is done via a "swipe file"—or more accurately, several swipe files. The term "swipe file" originated because you swipe (read "borrow") an idea from someone else. Naturally, you also give appropriate credit.

We have many such collections. Most reside in file folders. One houses interesting brochure designs, unusual folds, and remarkable headlines or copy. Another contains stunning direct mail packages. Still another comprises literature on competitive books. (How can we effectively highlight the benefits of our own titles if we don't know in what ways they are better or different from their rivals?) And computer files hold quotes, jokes, phrases, and sayings.

When it's time to develop promotional materials, put together a speech, revise a book—or start one from scratch—going through your swipe files will add verve and variety. Many a book or article has been given pizzazz by a phrase, joke, or quote collected over the years. Refrain from using things from your swipe files verbatim. The idea is not to plagiarize. Let these gems serve as an inventive resource, a trigger to inspire your own creativity.

Once you tune in to developing swipe files, everything you hear or read, every place you go, every contact you make takes on an exciting new dimension! Ideas for your files are everywhere: at the post office; in the library as you peruse newspapers, magazines, and newsletters; over the Internet; watching TV and listening to the radio; chatting with friends. The possibilities are endless. Just be sure to collar the information in written form, then place it in the appropriate archive. By using this technique to cull the best from rest, you too can excel.

A potpourri of imaginative ideas

Over the years as we prepared to write this book, I (Marilyn) collected tidbits culled ideas, examples, and stories from some 30 professional trade journals and newsletters read monthly. And from conferences, listservs, and conversations with industry colleagues. Most of this wisdom found its way into the subject-specific chapters. Here are a few intriguing savvy leftovers:

■ One new publisher who had no understanding of the book business sold direct to customers via events such as craft shows where she had no competition from other books. She made friends of event organizers, who now call to remind her to reserve a booth. She qualifies as a crafter or artist because she creates her own product. This novice paid off her publishing costs in six weeks!

■ How about conducting a survey or study to get some ink? Career Press author Lisa Kanarek *(Everything's Organized)* contacted 600 women who responded about how much time they spend each day looking for lost items. The study was given generous coverage in *Entrepreneur* magazine. According to *PRink*, the best topics for surveys are those that make for stimulating conversation: health, leisure time, hobbies and interests, sports, retirement/life cycle issues, quality of life, education, the arts, and people's feelings about entrepreneurial behavior.

■ Should you sell advertising in your book? Tom Alexander, publisher of *The Best of Growing EDGE*, decided to do so and made a nice profit before the book even hit the press. He packaged the ads as a chapter called Marketplace Sources, thus giving readers sources for the ideas they just read in the book. Although Ingram and Publishers Group West turned it down, the book sold well through smaller distributors, via direct mail, and at flower and garden shows and horticultural trade shows. All the advertisers sell it even though their competition are also listed in it. And Tom reports when it is time to reprint, most if not all advertise again, and new advertisers are easy to sell since they want to keep up with their competition.

■ Speak volumes—while keeping your mouth shut. When Marcia Yudkin, a consultant and author of *Six Steps to Free Publicity* attends a networking event, she informs people who she is without ever saying a word. Instead of wearing the usual name badge, Marcia sports a 3- by 4-inch laminated color photocopy of her latest book. Even though she isn't the official center of attention, she typically sells four books at each meeting.

Customer catalogs can multiply your profits

We've created catalogs, and we've created catalogs. And we're here to tell you what works—and what doesn't. We're talking here about *consumer* catalogs, not those that would go to the trade. If you only have one or two books in print, an extremely desirable aspect of doing a catalog is you immediately have a line of books from which your customers can choose. Suddenly, direct mail becomes a viable option. And you don't have to write (or acquire manuscripts), design and typeset, or spend money to print all those books. You simply arrange to get them from your publishing colleagues.

Sounds simple, doesn't it? And on the surface it is. But underneath you'd better be paddling like a desperate duck pursued by a hungry hound. Will you recover the costs of putting together an attractive printed piece? Can you afford to carry a small inventory of each title? What are the logistics of such an arrangement? How will you use it? Let's take those questions one at a time.

We've done 32-page catalogs and 4-page ones. Smaller is better. The cost to design and produce larger catalogs often makes it almost impossible for the small publisher to realize a profit. The one we do now is printed on a colored paper stock with two Pantone ink colors. It is attractive, yet affordable. There is room for describing 12 carefully selected titles, several photographs, and a roomy order form, and it mails for one stamp.

How do you choose and get the books? We only carry books we believe offer real value, ones that complement our titles but don't directly compete with them. And we select nothing under $10 as it isn't worth the time. We call the publisher, explain we're doing a catalog, and ask what their discount is for 5 or 10 copies nonreturnable, net 60. (It will be 40 to 50%.) Previously, we tried to get books on consignment but met with resistence. We also make sure they have adequate inventory and don't intend to let the book go out of print shortly.

Here is how it works logistically: You advertise the books via your catalog, cash your customer's check or run their credit card, place your order when you receive the first customer one, and pay the vendor within 60 days. When you get low on books, you reorder. And if you're smart, when you take orders by phone you try to cross sell them additional books. (We seldom get orders for only one book.) Include a shipping and handling charge: $3 or $4 per book, less for large multiple-book orders. Payment for Canadian orders needs to be in U.S. funds, drawn on a U.S. bank or via a credit card.

How will you use your new toy? Anywhere and everywhere. Include it as a bounce-back when filling book orders, send it when consumers inquire about your book, offer a copy free for a SASE when you do media interviews. (After all, you're a "resource center" for your subject area now.) Do targeted mailings to your database. Take it to networking events, etc. As a professional courtesy, we offer SPAN members a 20% discount on all books in our catalog.

If you would like a copy of the Rosses' catalog of books on publishing and marketing, send a SASE to Make More Money catalog, P.O. Box 909-JS, Buena Vista, CO 81211.

Four success principles

1. Ask for what you want. Sure you'll be told "no" sometimes, but that's been happening since you were a year old. If you make it clear to others when you desire something, you'll also get some "yeses." Take your courage in hand and approach a celebrity unknown to you for an advance comment. You certainly won't get that endorsement if you don't ask. When you're writing sales material ask for the order—over and over again.

During print interviews, request that the reporter include your toll-free order number. (This often works well for smaller presses as journalists want to accommodate their readers and fear your books won't be available in bookstores.) Don't feel like you need to genuflect when you go after a special sales deal with a retailer who has never sold books before. Tell them why it's to their benefit to partner with you. Ask—no *insist*—that you leave books, even if you have to start out on a consignment basis.

2. Make it easy for people to do what you want. We live in a frantically busy world. The person who makes it simple and painless for us to accommodate them will probably get their wish. Write a mock review that can be used "as is" by a busy magazine or newsletter editor. Create a list of interview questions a harried radio host can use to interview you. Put together a panel of experts (yourself included, of course) so a TV producer has a canned show ready to go. Get a toll-free phone number and email address, plus credit card merchant status, so consumers can easily order your books without connecting costs. Be as flexible as a willow tree. Bend in the wind to accommodate a bookseller or customer.

3. Apply the 80/20 rule. It all started with Italian economist Vilfredo Pareto at the turn of the last century. He observed that the wealth in Italy was controlled by 20% of the people. J. M. Juran, one of the fathers of the Total Quality Management movement, applied the Pareto Principle to inventory management in 1950. The rest is history.

This formula applies universally. You'll get 80% of your results from 20% of your efforts: 80% of your orders from 20% of your customers, 80% of your publicity from 20% of your PR contacts, 80% of your sales from 20% of your titles. Your only challenge is to identify that powerful 20%—then concentrate all your energy on them! Address the vital few versus the trivial many.

In 1980 we were helping a client with a raw foods title, *The UNcook Book*. We knew that it belonged in health food stores; if we could place it there, nothing else mattered. But the primary distributor to them, Nutri-Books, wouldn't give us the time of day. They had other books on raw foods that were going nowhere. So every time we got a good review, we sent it to the buyer. Whenever we received a large purchase order, we fired him off a copy. This went on for about six months, interspersed with general notes, postcards, etc.

Then one day we got a purchase order from them for a case of books. Hurrah! Hallelujah! Yes! (Tom says it was just to shut me up.) A couple of weeks later here comes another P.O. for two cases of books. That book went on to become their number-one seller! And, believe it or not, they still sell it today—along with several other titles from that publisher. But if we hadn't applied the 80/20 rule and focused attention on that account, it never would have happened. Think about where you *must* be, then rivet all your initiative on that endeavor.

4. Follow up. Do you want to call the tune instead of paying the fiddler? Then you'd better be prepared to monitor the progress of your projects. While diligent follow-through increases your odds for success in all aspects of publishing, it's especially crucial in promotion and sales. Many sound marketing plans flounder for lack of follow-up.

Perhaps the busiest of all recipients are the media, particularly radio and TV producers. They are inundated with literature about prospective guests. No news isn't necessarily bad news. We've had things go astray here more than anywhere else. Follow-up calls, faxes, and email often net big dividends. Be persistent. We've sent as many as *four* review copies of the book before it landed in the hands of the right person and a booking resulted.

Stay in touch with the contacts you make at major conventions, regional shows, and book fairs. Reinforce what develops for you at BookExpo America. Be sure to send announcements, catalogs, letters, complimentary books, etc., to appropriate new contacts. Properly worked, connections made at these events can impact your publishing program for years to come.

No matter what facet of marketing you explore, the squeaky wheel gets more attention. We encourage clients to be politely persistent. Stopping before you get results—or a firm "no"—is like ordering an ice cream cone, then letting it melt onto the floor. Persistence + passion = success.

Don't be like the two cows grazing by the freeway. Stainless steel milk trucks kept whizzing by sporting signs that read "Homogenized." "Pasturized." "Fortified with Vitamin C." The one cow looked at the other and said, "Sure makes you feel inadequate, doesn't it?" *You can accomplish anything you put your mind—and your energy—to!*

Called yourself lately? What do other people hear when your number is called? Remember, the phone you've listed on letterhead, in catalogs, and on order forms is a *business* telephone number. When it's answered "hello," it hardly sets the tone for a business relationship. The same is true when your adorable three-year-old gushes over the telephone. Many use answering machines—some effectively, some dismally. Let's think about this: Isn't it obvious you're "either away from your desk or on another line" when you don't answer? Rather than this well-worn phrase, why not tell callers approximately when someone will be in the office (not "at home!") and promise to return their call promptly.

For many of us, the telephone is our lifeline to the world. The image we project there can make us sound like a large, responsible, customer-oriented business organization...or like a hokey mom-and-pop operation. Call yourself. See if your publishing company passes the test.

Coupons help sell products. A recent study conducted by an Ohio State University marketing professor revealed that coupons boost response to advertising—even if unused! "Coupons send more than just a discount signal to consumers," says Robert Leone. "A coupon is a draw for somebody to read the rest of the ad." How can you extrapolate that research to books? Take a look at your promotional book brochure or flyer. Does it include a coupon? Do you have an order form in the back of your book? Use them to beef up sales.

---

296 ■ Jump Start Your Book Sales

Invoices as marketing tools? Ever give much thought to your invoices and statements (beyond hoping they will be paid quickly, that is)? Maybe you should. They can also serve as a marketing communication tool. You could announce an introductory offer for an upcoming title, run a special on a slow book, or tie into a holiday with a feature promotion. Printing directly on the invoice costs you nothing and ensures your message won't be discarded. In fact, it will probably be seen by several people as most invoices pass through a number of hands for payment approval.

I recently read a novel so dull the author's school colors must have been "clear" and "transparent."

Associations have enormous potential. They can purchase your book in bulk for resale, drop-ship individual copies from a listing in their catalog, add it to a bibliography or recommended reading list, review it, or excerpt it. Furthermore, they might hire the author to speak at their annual conference or educational workshops.

Seven out of ten people belong to an association. But where do you find out about these organizations? Well, you could head to the library and consult the three-volume *Encyclopedia of Associations*. (It's too expensive for most publishers to consider purchasing.) Another alternative is the *National Trade & Professional Associations of the United States*. It covers 7,500 associations, professional societies, and labor unions and is indexed in several helpful ways. You can also go online and do a search by entering the subject you want plus the word "association." Happy prospecting.

Looking for holiday marketing muscle? Consider the oft ignored Gift Certificate. Yes, it *can* work for publishers. One of the best approaches is to give your present customers gift certificates for their friends, loved ones, and colleagues. Offer 20 or 25% off titles—and let your present customer use one too as a way of your saying "thanks." A dentist we know of increased his business by 15% using this strategy. He printed 1,000 gift certificates, which he asked satisfied clients to give to family and friends. "The recipient gets $130 worth of free dental services, and I get to form a relationship with a potential patient," reports Larry Spidel.

Of course, mention your certificates everywhere: in your flyers, on your home page, in consumer catalogs, etc. You want to pique the interest of people scouting for gifts. Involve your authors too. Give them a quantity of gift certificates to send out with correspondence and use in other creative ways. And you needn't restrict this marketing avenue to the holidays. A make-over for Valentine's Day, Mother's Day, or Father's Day opens additional opportunities.

An interesting sidelight is that one out of every four gift certificates you sell are never redeemed! That means you pocket an extra $250 for every $1,000 you sell. This method of merchandising is also nice because you get paid up front and guarantee the next purchase is from your company rather than the competition.

Want to "feed" your media contacts or "nourish" your favorite bookseller? This yummy site lets you send a gourmet postcard to favorite people. Is an appetizer of caviar or an entree of game hen or lobster and champagne your style? Maybe you're more the peach crepes or baba with rum type. Or perhaps the standbys of popcorn, spaghetti with meatballs, or chicken soup would be your choice. And who could resist white chocolate mousse? These delicacies—plus dozens more—can be emailed to your friends, business colleagues, and enemies by simply going to http://mailameal.com. Enough of this; we're off to dinner!

Mucho marketing strategies available for the asking. We're immensely impressed with the generosity of the creators of Idea Site for Business. It features 206 marketing ideas in such categories as unusual marketing ideas, customer service, prospecting, thanking, fax marketing, signage, marketing materials, Web ideas, etc. You can sign on for their A-Marketing-Idea-A-Day-by-email™ for constant encouragement, or read articles such as "Ten easy steps to creating your first E-zine." And we've enjoyed surfing through the section called "How do you market?" Lots of enterprising entrepreneurs offer suggestions of what works for them. Furthermore, press release access to over 1,800 of the nation's top business newspapers and magazines is just a click away. Find it all at http://www.ideasiteforbusiness.com.

Prospects are everywhere! As entrepreneurs, we can't afford to turn off our prospecting clock at 5 P.M. And why should we when book buyers are e-v-e-r-y-w-h-e-r-e? We've sold books at a gas station when the attendant noticed an open case laying in the back of our car, while standing in line to ship a UPS package, and while waiting (and waiting and waiting) to renew a drivers license. Always have a copy with you!

Books as door prizes. Statistics tell us people often have to be exposed to a product between five and seven (yes, *seven!*) times before they make a buying decision. So, it behooves you to get your book out there any way you can. Consider offering it (or a collection of related titles) as a door prize for your next chamber of commerce event or other service club or trade association function or auction.

Definition of market research: the first printing.

Save money at the post office. Did you know that Priority Mail cardboard flat-rate envelopes go for $3.20 no matter how much you stuff in them? You can exceed the 2-pound limit and not pay extra. If you've been spending more, you can start saving a bundle. Many publishers are turning to Priority Mail to ship individual books as the post office pays for the shipping container and it gives the feeling of excellent customer service when the books arrive so quickly.

CHAPTER 24

Sidelines, Spinoffs, Special Reports, and Stuff: Getting a Power Boost

Want to maximize your income potential? Then let's see if you might not have some hidden money makers—ways to turn an extra profit for resources you already have on hand—or related products you can create and sell to your existing customer base.

Independent bookstores do this all the time. Not only do they sell books but also greeting cards, magazines, gift items, art, reading lights, a myriad of items that appeal to their intelligent customers. For many, these items not only separate them from their behemoth competitors but represent a sizeable share of their revenue. Shouldn't we learn from their example? Other businesses do.

Sidelines, spinoffs, and special strategies are hidden money makers

Chuck Green started a design business in Glen Allen, Virginia. To help small businesses' marketing efforts, he designed documents to allow them to succeed faster. But Chuck was only one man and his ability to grow his company was finite. So he thought about how he could expand. Chuck got the idea to simplify and redefine the documents he designed until they worked as generic templates. Then he packaged these 50 templates with a 125-page manual and presto! He had Page Greats, which sold for $49. He refined it still further and now has a product with 100 templates and a $79 price tag.

Celestial Seasonings wanted to expand their market for herb teas, so they created gift baskets. We were delighted to find one for a hard-to-buy-for tea-drinking friend last Christmas. In addition to a lovely selection of teas, the basket included a fancy cup, a couple of relevant books (YES!), and some other odds and ends.

Are you tired of selling individual books? With some creative thinking, maybe your titles will lend themselves to bundling with other items to create a gift basket or information kit. Education guide publisher Peterson's bundled nine of their books—including *College Money Handbook, Private Secondary Schools,* and *Summer Opportunities for Kids & Teenagers*—into a collection. They marketed it as a package to corporate librarians and human resource managers. The pitch? "Let Peterson's help your company employees balance work and family."

Now read on to see what other authors and publishers are doing. (Also be sure to check the sidebar, Ancillary Product Possibilities, to brainstorm and get those creative juices flowing.)

Some publishers' experiences

Steve Viglione's Lighthouse Publications not only publishes the popular *I Am Priceless!*™ line of childhood keepsake books—he also does colorful bookmarks, stickers, and posters (which double as place mats) with the same theme. They serve as a profit center in themselves, as well as helping to sell more books. The directors of education at various churches purchase the inspirational, affirming bookmarks in quantity.

When he exhibits at trade shows and festivals, he hands bookmarks to people walking by. Many are so entranced by them they purchase more on the spot or come back later to order books or bookmarks. "The bookmarks have made the difference between my writing $100 worth of orders at a show and writing $1,000," Steve reports.

He primarily markets his books to New Age and Catholic churches and schools, which purchase the sticker packages by the hundreds. "Kids love stickers," says Steve. "And because teachers know they do, they'll often buy them out of their own pockets if the school budgets are too low."

The I am *Priceless!*™ Line
from the popular *My Priceless Prayerbook* by Steve Viglione

My Priceless Prayerbook:
A Childhood Keepsake of Building Blocks
to Faith, Values and Self-Esteem.
Over 11,000 copies (first edition) of this great book for kids are in the hands of parents, children and clergy around the country and in Canada. Non-denominational. 148 pages, beautifully illustrated by Steve Viglione and Becky Parish. 5 1/2 x 8 1/2, softcover. It's a winner! Sugg. Retail $12.95

The I am *Priceless!* Stickers are another great way for children to view themselves in a positive way. Designed by the author to build confidence and reinforce a healthy self-esteem. 54 count (9 stickers on a sheet, 6 sheets in a package). Sugg. Retail $1.99

The I am *Priceless!* Bookmarks are another attractive way to help kids and adults feel priceless! Sugg. Retail $.75

The I am *Priceless!* Pre-pac (free display for book and gift stores, churches or bookstores)
Includes: 24 copies of *My Priceless Prayerbook*
            24 I am *Priceless!* Stickers
            96 I am *Priceless!* Bookmarks
Dimensions: 11" wide, 3 ft. 9" tall and 15" deep

Counter Displays also available.
Includes: 6 *My Priceless Prayerbook*
        or 50 or 100 I am *Priceless!* Bookmarks
        or 36 I am *Priceless!* Stickers

Ask about the I am *Priceless!*
T-Shirts, Posters and Gift Sets!

Order Today from:
Lighthouse Publications
Boston, MA 1-800-684-1313
617-282-5780 in the Boston area. Fax 617-288-6592

He printed 5,000 packets initially at 52¢ each plus initial setup. By retailing them for $2, there's a nice markup. Steve created a colorful catalog sheet with all the specs *except* the prices. He has separate retail and wholesale price sheets to tuck in as appropriate. This also gives him flexibility if production costs go up or down.

Jane Butel of Albuquerque is a cookbook writer, cooking school owner, and chili and spice purveyor. She saw it all coming years ago and has positioned herself as the queen of Southwest cuisine. Pecos Valley Spice Co. sells a line of chiles, herbs, and ingredients used in her school and the recipes in her books. "I'm extremely vertical," says Butel. "Basically, my tangents are all built on top of each other—and they all surround Southwestern cooking."

Dick Biggs, founder of Chattahoochee Publishers and the author of *If Life Is a Balancing Act, Why Am I so Clumsy?* and a related audio, experienced a nice spinoff when he connected with Successories, Inc. (You may recall seeing their retail stores scattered in malls around the U.S. Additionally, they send out 13 million catalogs a year.) They excerpted part of his work into a 48-page booklet titled *Burn Brightly Without Burning Out* for their Power of One series. Of course, he has a full-page bio in the booklet, which draws attention to his complete book—not to mention his speaking services.

IDG Books Worldwide's Dummies series has been extended into music CDs, calendars, and other merchandise. They just signed a deal with Pressman Toy Corporation for three board games based on *Trivia for Dummies, Crosswords for Dummies,* and *Charades for Dummies.*

Just to stay ahead of the game, Tom Clancy has formed Red Storm Entertainment and concocted a multiplayer PC game of intrigue and espionage. A single-player version of the game is even packaged with each of these books in the form of a mini-CD.

With a mission "to offer only the highest quality, proven Tools, Techniques, Knowledge and Wisdom to the farrier, veterinarian, and horse owner," Butler Publishing has put together an impressive array of products and services. In addition to books and videos, they offer consulting, graduate training, continuing education, farrier services, and tools for shoeing horses. How about that for taking your publishing business to a new level?

Susan and Bill Albert have Thyme & Season Books, not to mention a special strategy for selling books while adding to their income. They publish a quarterly 16-page newsletter/catalog and charge $12 for the four issues. It is sold through ads in the back of their books and in magazines and other newsletters.

They write a mystery series with a main character, China Bayles, who runs an herb shop. So the newsletter offers a unique mix of information about herbs, growing tips, herb lore, recipes, and occasional short fiction. Additionally, their own books are included, plus almost 100 other titles appropriate for herbalists and gardeners.

They also use the newsletter/catalog, dubbed *China's Garden*, to promote their wholesale program. They've targeted over 200 herb and garden shops. When a shop first places an order, it receives a complimentary subscription to the newsletter. The Alberts report their wholesale sales have tripled since they began sending the newsletter.

More tips for success

"To make ancillary products profitable, you've got to make sure each aspect of your business feeds the others," coaches Elaine Floyd, who has a growing business called Newsletter Resources. This woman—dubbed "the Martha Stewart of Information Products"—has published four books related to newsletters, an audiotape kit, does a quarterly newsletter (of course!), has a Web site, offers individualized consulting, and is in demand as a national speaker on the subject.

Furthermore, she took a previous book, *Quick and Easy Newsletters*, and turned it into a software system that retails for $34.99. By bundling the written information with a Windows-compatible disk, templates, newsletter fillers, inspirational quotes, cartoons, and clip art, she allows the user to create a customized newsletter in one afternoon. This package was the best-selling book for Newbridge Communications' Executive Book Club last year. Busy executives value the diskette and the perception they're buying a "system" rather than just a book.

According to Floyd, providing multiple ways to learn the same information is the key to making money in the information business. (Any nonfiction publisher is really in the "information business.")

We've certainly found the triad of writing a book, speaking on the subject, and consulting about it to be an empire-building strategy. Our *Complete Guide to Self-Publishing* has been the flagship for a flourishing business for over 20 years now. (To order a copy, call 800-331-8355.)

But that's peanuts compared to what developed when Health Communications teamed with Jack Canfield and Mark Victor Hansen. There are now more than 17 titles in the *Chicken Soup* series and they've racked up sales well over 30 million copies. After the first phenomenal hit, they dished up books for pet lovers, teenagers, children, and women— all of which are enjoying near-permanent residence on bestseller lists. The latest (as we go to press) is *Chicken Soup for the Country Soul*, which has a companion CD.

A few interesting sidelights: It took the original book almost a year to appear on bestseller lists, so don't give up! Its success was driven by the authors' commitment to unrelenting PR. And it's heartening that all this achievement is on the plate of an independent publisher.

Ideas for these guys pop up faster than prairie dogs. Mark puts out a hefty personal growth catalog and sponsors high-ticket seminars on How to Build Your Speaking and Writing Empire (call 800-433-2314).

We spoke earlier about being in the information business. We know of one author/expert who schedules monthly conference calls where he invites many people to participate at once. He charges up to $30 per person for the hour. Multiply that by 20 participants and who wouldn't work for $500 an hour? But it doesn't end there. Then he sells audio recordings of the hour for $25 each for those who couldn't make the live session! Spinoffs galore!

Back-end sales can equal big bucks

Once a person has bought a book, audio, or video from you, they are your customer. And statistics prove it's five times easier to sell to an existing customer than to a new one. You now have their trust and confidence. But what are you doing about it? Why reinvent the wheel by searching for new prospects each time? Ask yourself: What am I selling? What else are my customers looking for? Who or what can I tie in with for additional sales?

These are called back-end sales and they are absolutely the most profitable because there is no cost to develop them. Did you once sell someone a gift book? Are you recontacting them before Valentine's Day, Mother's Day, Father's Day, and the holiday season to sell them one of your other gift titles? Maybe you should develop more books that dovetail perfectly with your current titles, or connect with another publisher who does complementary books.

Since we're talking about your customers, are you capitalizing on them in another way by developing an in-house database you can rent to other companies? Once you have about 5,000 names you have something others will pay for. Although this certainly won't make you rich, renting your list several times a month can be a nice boost to your bottom line over a year.

Hidden money makers are really everywhere once you start tuning in and smartening up. Good luck in finding your bonanza!

Booklets and special reports for a lucky spin

To some the lowly booklet—that 16- or 32-page stapled product—may seem of little more value than a scrap of material, a remnant. But to the wise, it can represent a substantial revenue source, a wonderful test marketing vehicle, or both. There are independent publishers who have sold over 400,000 booklets, others who sell 10,000 copies at a whack, over and over again. And some writers are discovering it is far faster and more profitable to produce a booklet than to labor trying to get an article accepted, and paid for, by a magazine editor. Booklets are an ideal venue for putting forth your own specialized how-to knowledge.

Take the case of Velty Bautista, a Michigan man who passed the postal exam test with an almost perfect score. When people asked him how he did it, he put together a 32-page study guide, which he advertised in newspapers and magazines and by putting flyers on car windshields. When folks snapped it up for $5 a copy, he knew he was on to something. Today *The Book of U.S. Postal Exams: How to Score 95 to 100% and Get a Job* is in its fifth edition and sales are in the six figures.

The Gary Kulibert family uses booklets differently. They recently returned from a camping show where they test marketed a new booklet on *Pudgie Pies* that cost them 30 cents each to produce. "New" is the operative word here: The product hadn't existed two weeks earlier. Gary's daughter wrote it in one week, completed the design and layout on Tuesday, laser printed it on Wednesday, had it folded and stapled by a local print shop on Thursday, and sold 90 copies at $3.95 each over the weekend!

The real *coup de grâce* is that the inexpensive booklet captured people's attention, thus helping sell several of their full-fledged cookbooks, including the $11.95 *Campground Cookery.*

Another nice aspect of booklets and special reports is the content can be recycled into other formats such as news releases, Web pieces, a newsletter, calendars, advertising specialty items—all without writing another word. This also allows you to introduce information at different price points.

Or you can license the content rights to other countries or corporations. Of course, booklets can be expanded into a book. Or condensed from a book into a free or inexpensive "teaser" to entice consumers to purchase the full-blown product.

That brings us to a frequently asked question: What constitutes a "book"? That depends on whom you ask. The Library of Congress says a book contains at least 98 pages. Bowker requires 50 pages to be listed in *Books in Print,* while the post office says still a different number.

Ancillary Product Possibilities

■ Audios
■ Videos
■ CDs
■ Software
■ Bookmarks
■ Publishing online
■ Posters
■ Stickers
■ Greeting cards
■ Note cards
■ Calendars
■ Puzzles
■ Board games
■ Newsletters
■ Seminars
■ Schools
■ Catalogs
■ Booklets
■ Special reports
■ Your database
■ Ingredients for a cookbook

Success story ala mode

The guru of booklets is Paulette Ensign, who has built her one-person business into a $250,000 mini-empire selling booklets and consulting with others on how to duplicate her success. Reach her at 619-481-0890 or visit her Web site at http://www.tipsbooklets.com. She has created two 16-page tips booklets that fit into number 10 envelopes. There is *110 Ideas for Organizing Your Business Life* and *111 Ideas for Organizing Your Household.*

Ensign started out on less than a shoestring. It took her several months to pay the $300 printing bill to get the first 250 copies to use as samples. This is a crucial point, however: You need actual copies before you can start making money. She sent them to newspapers and magazines asking that they excerpt and include a bio that the whole tip booklet could be had for $3 plus a SASE. The orders began to dribble in; then suddenly there was an avalanche as a major national publication gave her ink.

Since then, her merchandising accomplishments read like a Who's Who any publisher would happily be listed in:

- A major mail-order catalog company licensed rights to print 250,000 copies.
- Another company hired her to write a customized version based on the original product.
- She received invitations to do paid speaking engagements.
- An Internet contact in Italy translated, produced, and marketed it; then paid her royalties.
- She is negotiating with 10 other countries for similar deals.
- A manufacturer's rep sent her booklet to his customers instead of an imprinted calendar.
- She was hired to record an audio program based on the booklet, then given the right to sell the audio when she speaks.
- A company bought 5,000 copies to be given away at a trade show in an industry she wanted to penetrate.
- The booklet led to a 20-minute interview on an airline's inflight audio program.
- She now has a hefty database of purchasers, so renting her mailing list can also generate revenue.

Deciding on a price point

Booklets typically are inexpensive impulse buys: They usually range in price from $1 to $3.95. Some are postpaid, meaning they include postage, while others tack on 55¢. Special reports, however, often carry hefty prices for specialized and hard-to-find information. Prices range from $5 for a 4-page report to $29.95 for a 16-pager. Those targeted to businesses can even run into hundreds of dollars. Sometimes you'll meet resistence from buyers of special reports. Unsophisticated purchasers still equate weight with value, missing the point that they are paying for specialized information not the bulk of paper.

You may decide to keep your booklet price low, especially if the purpose is to get leads for selling a book. Another reason to make it a bargain is that certain magazines ideal for publicity have a limit on how high items can sell for. *Family Circle*, for instance, has a $2 limit on offers they run. Price your goodie too high and you automatically cut yourself out of this possible publicity bonanza. Another point to consider is that people will put two dollar bills in an envelope. That's about the most cash they will mail.

When Eric Gelb self-published his booklet, *Budgeting at Your Fingertips*, he purposely set the price at $3.50, postage paid. Retail bookstores offer his guide for $2.95 per copy, making it a popular impulse item. He also sells it to credit unions and community colleges to use in their money management seminars.

Brian Jud, who publishes a series of eight pocket-size booklets on various job search topics, takes a different approach to pricing. Because he sells in large quantities, mostly to colleges and state government unemployment offices, his list price is $1.45 each. When he makes a sale of 10,000 copies, he can afford to offer a generous discount and still make money. And by having a series of products he is establishing his company as the expert resource of information in that field.

Cindy Walker, marketing manager for Bradford Publishing, tried a new approach to merchandising their products recently. She's creating several 32-page booklets. The initial test one, *Creative Parenting Plans that Work,* addresses divorce and legal separation in the state of Colorado. The first time out she sold 105 copies at $12.45 each!

Production considerations

Let's look at production issues: Most booklets have a cover printed on a colored cover-weight stock. (If you use the text paper for the whole thing, it is considered a "self-cover.") Want something more elegant that won't break the bank in small quantities? Check out Paper Direct. Their phone is 800-APAPERS. They have 80-pound presentation covers in six different colors and nine different styles. (See the list of Specialty Booklet Printers in the Appendix.)

If you intend to send a photograph with your promotional news release, your cover must photograph well in black and white. Hope to get into bookstores? That can be tough for booklets. You'll need a professional-looking colorful cover with a shiny laminate surface. You can use either electronic or traditional clip art to create something attractive and inexpensive.

Inside, a brief introduction helps set the stage. You might use bullets or a repeated piece of clip art to separate ideas. If you're aiming for an older market, remember to make the type larger. Two staples at the fold hold a booklet together. This is called saddle stitching.

Marketing like a maestro

One major key to making it big in the booklet and special report business is to pick your audience carefully. (Notice we said "audience" not topic.) You want to provide information to fill a certain niche. Who are these people? How can you reach them?

Do they read certain trade journals, consumer magazines, or newsletters that might run your press release or include reference to your booklet in a feature article or resource sidebar? Are they members of an association through which you can work? Do they attend festivals where you can meet them in person? Are there corporations or government agencies that would purchase your product in bulk to give away as a premium? Figure out who your target audience is. Write for them. Then develop a marketing plan with the same gusto you'd use if you were leading the world's most talented orchestra. Here are a few specific ideas to get you going:

■ *Bottom Line* newsletters, with their huge circulation and different spins, are a perfect target to increase *your* bottom line. (They publish *BL/Personal, BL/Business, BL/Tomorrow* [for retirees and pre-retirees], *BL/Health*, and the *Tax November 29, 1998 Hotline.*) Contact the Research Editor with a booklet, news release, and cover letter at *Bottom Line/_____*, 55 Railroad Avenue, Greenwich, CT 06836.

■ Ditto for *Freebies* magazine. Ask them for a products information form by writing to P.O. Box 5025, Carpinteria, CA 93190.

■ *Family Circle* can really put Lady Luck on your side. Contact Jonna Gallo at 375 Lexington Avenue, New York, NY 10017. Since they come out 17 times a year, they are always on the lookout for a booklet offer of value to their readership—which, by the way, exceeds 5 million people.

■ *Office Systems '98* excerpted four ideas from the booklet *100 Ways to Make Customers Happy* and ended the piece with full ordering information for the 16-page, $5 product. Contact the Info to Go editor, 252 North Main Street, Suite 200, Airy, NC 27030.

■ The library may also be a candidate for sales, though not in the normal way. Have you ever researched the vertical files? These are A to Z files in traditional filing cabinets that contain pamphlets and booklets on various topics. If your booklet is under $10 you can get listed in the *Vertical File Index*. Send a sample and full ordering information to Brenda Smith, *Vertical File Index*, H. W. Wilson Company, 950 University Avenue, Bronx, NY 10452.

As you can see, booklets, sidelines, and spinoffs serve many purposes and can be sold in a variety of ways. Look at your own publishing and career plans. How can you use one of these twists to increase your revenues for virtually no cost—or quickly allow you to test a new idea? Scraps? Never! One of these ideas may be just the material out of which your success is woven.

More *Chicken Soup* ancillary products. Jack and Mark are not ones to sit still. They see dolls, toys, games, and an assortment of products to reach more people, many of whom haven't even heard of *Chicken Soup for the Soul*. One of their planned fund-raising alliances is with Tupperware International. Their 50,000 distributors are going to provide the book as a sales incentive for folks who purchase over a certain amount of Tupperware party products.

What's another word for thesaurus?

Speeches into audio and video products. If you (or one of your authors) are speaking at a high-powered conference, there is always the possibility of getting the session professionally audio- or video-taped, then spinning that off as a new product. A further idea is to *transcribe* the tape and sell it as "the transcript from the $2,000 seminar." You get the idea.

CHAPTER 25

Moving Up to Indy: Selling Your Self-Published Book to New York

We were delighted by a piece in the Sunday, April 28, 1996, edition of *The New York Times.* It was headlined "Do-It-Yourselfers Carve Out a Piece of the Publishing Pie." What a victory for self-publishing that, from the very bastion of conventional publishing, such a piece should emerge in *The NYT.* The lengthy article sent a strong and encouraging message to self-publishers and small presses: The big houses are now looking to you for the books they will publish tomorrow.

Harry Evans, president of Random House, has instructed his sales reps to scout bookstores for these diamonds. Today it's frequent for the mainstream houses to go prospecting among self-publishers. Why? With all the downsizing they no longer have staff to wade through the "slush pile." Additionally, they can save production costs by picking up a book that has already been edited and typeset. And of course, the risk has been removed. A successful self-published book already has a track record. Small publishers are now viewed as the "farm team" for the major leagues.

Huge advances now paid

It wasn't until *The Celestine Prophecy* that *real* money was garnered for these gems. Originally published by author James Redfield, it was

12 Self-Publishing Success Strategies

Self-publishing used to be the Rodney Dangerfield of book publishing. We "didn't get no respect." Today that's all changed. With originally self-published books like *The Celestine Prophecy, The Christmas Box,* and *What Color Is Your Parachute?* hitting bestseller lists—and small press titles like *Cold Mountain* and the *Chicken Soup* series further monopolizing these coveted lists—small has become beautiful.

To be successful, however, it's mandatory you adhere to certain guidelines. By following the tips below, you'll avoid the pitfalls, enhance your chances of flourishing, and perhaps end up with a book the majors clamor for.

1. Educate yourself. Publishing is a *business.* Approach it as such. There are informative books on the subject, seminars offered, and associations where you can learn the ropes and network with the more experienced. This can be very lucrative if properly approached. Conversely, you can waste thousands of dollars by blundering along without knowledge or a plan.

2. Study the competition. Don't add more to a subject that's already glutted. Be sure the topic hasn't been overdone. Just checking a local library or bookstore is *not* adequate research. Look in *Books in Print Subject Guide* and *Forthcoming Books in Print Subject Guide.* Get online and

(continued on next page)

acquired in 1993 by Warner Books for $800,000. How wise they were. *The Celestine Prophecy* was *Publisher Weekly's* 1995 longest-running hardcover bestseller. It resided on the list for 51 weeks. Redfield soon had a workbook out to accompany his bestseller, then Warner released his *The Tenth Insight.*

Next came *Mutant Message Down Under,* written and published by Marlo Morgan. It went to HarperCollins for a cool $1.7 million. This supposedly fictional account of a woman's trek through the Australian outback has captured millions of literary hearts with its message of a life unencumbered with material things.

But Richard Paul Evans is the one who really made publishing history. He wrote a little story about a struggling young family and a wealthy widow who lost an infant daughter. Titled *The Christmas Box,* this book of family values captured the fancy of the public as well as Publishers Row.

After a two-day auction with dozens of publishers vying for the rights, Simon & Schuster captured this treasure—and Mr. Evans found himself with a $4.2 million advance! (This also includes him writing a prequel, but golly, who wouldn't be willing to do that?) While most self-published books picked up by conventional publishers don't come close to these figures, there is still serious money to be made.

Putting your best literary foot forward

Many frustrated authors find themselves in a catch-22 situation: They can't attract an agent and they can't get a publisher to look at their manuscripts. We counsel them to consider this formula: Self-publish your book. Make a quality product. Sell the heck out of it. Establish a track record. *Then* approach an agent or publisher. The result will be the difference between light and the lightning bug.

When we came up with the idea of doing a book about our experiences of moving from southern California to a small Colorado town, we queried several publishers. Two were very interested. But their terms were nonsense. We were looking for at least sirloin steak; they offered hot dogs. So we self-published *Country Bound! Trade Your Business Suit Blues for Blue Jean Dreams* in 1992.

After selling more than 10,000 copies, we wanted to devote our time to other projects. In our case, the first publisher we approached took the bait. And we're pleased about that because the reason we went to them originally is we know they do a dynamite job of developing special sales. This fact was every bit as important to us as the front money.

What did we do to woo them? We sent copies of all our reviews, press clippings from newspapers and

12 Self-Publishing Success Strategies (continued)

check at amazon.com. You'll be amazed at how many books there are on the topic. Yours must be better than what's already available. Make it shorter, longer, easier to use, more informative, funnier, richer in content, or better organized. For fiction, tie into a hot topic so you have a "hook" for publicity.

3. Write what other people want. Catering to our personal desires often makes for lackluster books nobody buys. The fact is, few care about our life history or deep-felt opinions. Personal journals and impassioned tirades are best saved for family and friends, not foist upon the general public.

4. Think "marketing" from the very beginning. The time to generate marketing ideas is *before* you publish the book (or start writing if you're the author), not after you have 5,000 copies in storage. Identify your market. How can you reach them? Start folders of ideas. What catalogs might be interested? Which associations reach your potential readers? What magazines and newsletters are relevant? Can you sell the book as a premium to companies that would give it away as a gift to entice new customers—or use it internally for training? Think about who else reaches your potential customer and how you can partner with them. Do you have contacts who have national name recognition and might write an advance endorsement?

(continued on next page)

12 Self-Publishing Success Strategies (continued)

5. Get professional editing. No, we repeat *no*, author should edit or proofread his or her own work. You'll miss the forest for the trees, overlooking things obvious to you, but unclear to your reader. And it's so easy to skip over the same typo time after time. (Please spell "foreword" correctly!)

6. Create a snappy title. The right title can make a book, just like an uninspired one can be a death curse. Short is best. While clever is nice, don't sacrifice clarity. For nonfiction, be sure to include a subtitle as it gives you extra mileage in helping readers know what the book is about.

7. Include all the vital components. Just as a cake falls flat if you don't add the right ingredients, so do books. Yours needs an ISBN, LCCN or CIP, Bookland EAN scanning symbol, subject category on the back cover, the title displayed boldly on the spine, etc. (If you don't know what some of these are, refer back to #1!)

8. Have a dynamite cover. The cover is your book's salesperson in bookstores. Get it designed by a professional who understands *cover design*...not just somebody who does nice illustrations, logos, or brochures. You have enormous competition—and a wonderful opportunity to stand out.

9. Make the interior inviting. Go to a bookstore and study the insides of books. Find one with clean, "user-friendly" pages. Use this as your model. The production values of

(continued on next page)

magazines about us, plus stories on the subject written by us. Naturally, we also sent a book and indicated the number of units sold. They could immediately see they had promotable authors and an attractive, proven product.

Negotiating a win/win contract

Once they said "yes," the real work began. Before any contracts flew back and forth we negotiated what the advance would be. They came up; we went down. The book ultimately sold for a nice five-figure advance. Where they usually pay royalties based on 10% of net, we got it up to 12.5% on the first 10,000 and thereafter. We asked how they intended to market the book and they provided a detailed Proposed Marketing Plan. This reassured us they were serious about what they would do to fuel the sales flames we had lit.

You don't have to feel like a pathetic supplicant—the equivalent of a dog exposing its belly. Major publishers need flourishing new products just as we need them.

When the contract arrived, however, we were absolutely aghast. This was the fourth book we had sold to trade publishers, so we were not novices. Some of their expectations really stung. They wanted to hold the copyright in their name. They wanted the granting of all electronic rights for a paltry 5% discount and only *for promotional purposes.* We swallowed hard and reminded ourselves that a contract is a negotiable instrument.

The real zinger was the following statement: "If royalties have not been sufficient to repay the advance within 3 years after the publication of the Work, then upon demand of Publisher, Author shall repay to Publisher the portion of the advance not yet repaid." This totally unglued us! We reminded them this was a proven book. The only reason it wouldn't have earned back its advance was if *they* neglected to properly market it.

Then they offered to extend the time to five years! We explained that only made it worse; we would want the rights back long before then if it hadn't earned back the advance. They stammered that they had never removed that clause from any contract. We made it clear there would be no contract if it remained.

After tearing the contract apart and putting it back together again in our favor, we sent it off and held our breath. They balked. Big time. "It seems like you folks want too much control. I'm not sure we should work together on this," was the reply. We called and explained that we didn't want control at all, only fair treatment and assurances that they would take control and do certain things. Here are the concessions we ended up getting:

12 Self-Publishing Success Strategies (continued)

your book must meet the competition to be acceptable in the trade. It may not make sense to purchase and learn typesetting software if you're only doing one or two books, however. In that case, consider hiring an outside vendor.

10. Use a book manufacturer for printing. Don't expect your corner print shop to have the knowledge or technical capabilities to turn out a quality book. Book manufacturers are specialists in this type of printing and can save you enormous grief and considerable money.

11. Price properly. Books that are much more costly than the competition—or even sometimes a lot cheaper—meet resistence. There are formulas for determining what the unit price should be so you have enough margin to offer appropriate discounts and still make a profit. Learn them. Break them only if common sense dictates.

12. Publicize, promote, publicize, promote. Eat, sleep, and talk your books. Nobody cares as much as you do. Ongoing, enthusiastic marketing is the real key to success. Never quit. Keep your antenna out for new review opportunities, freelancers who write articles on your topic, etc. We have books that have been in print since 1979 because we're tireless promoters. You never know when publicity will yield results. We just sold a book to a woman who clipped an article we were featured in from *The Washington Post*—in 1988! Marketing is forever.

- The copyright in our name.
- The right to mutually negotiate our payment on an individual basis for electronic rights.
- An author buy back ranging from a 50% discount to 71% depending on quantity ordered.
- The right to resell books to nontrade markets. (This is a crucial point you need so you can continue selling your book to certain markets you've developed.)
- The deletion of that dreadful advance return clause.
- A stipulation that the title would not be changed without mutual agreement.
- One-half the advance paid upon signing of the agreement; the balance upon submission of the manuscript.
- A clause giving us the right to sell off our existing inventory until their new edition comes out. (Very important; you don't want to be stuck with all the present inventory.)
- Fifty complimentary author copies instead of 10.
- A clause stipulating that any major revisions would require an additional advance to be negotiated. (Watch this; most contracts pay you nothing for future revisions.)
- Deletion of the clause requiring us to give them options on our next works. (This is really silly. If they do a good job, we would naturally approach them with a new project.)
- We added a point regarding adjudication of disputes to bring in the American Arbitration Association.
- We also added a clause to protect ourselves in the event they go bankrupt.

Did we get everything we wanted? Not by a long shot. We didn't expect to. That's why we were so picky in going back to them initially. It almost backfired on us, however. They are used to dealing with authors who are eternally grateful to be offered a contract. They surely wouldn't question half of it.

Our knowledge of the industry was an anomaly. But because there was mutual respect and a willingness to compromise we were able to cobble together an agreement that gave us each what we most needed. Now we had cash flow to devote to a new product and more time to develop it.

Selling your self-published book isn't for everyone, however. Bear Kamoroff, the author-publisher of *Small Time Operator,* would be the first to exclaim, "No way!" The big publishers weren't there when he needed them. Today they would just get in his way. He has sold over half a million copies, prefers the freedom of calling his own shots, and has built-in obsolescence in his tax guide. New editions come out every few years and he enjoys his early retirement from the drudgeries of being a CPA. So evaluate your situation carefully.

"Cashing in by selling out" may be the smartest thing you can do—especially with conventional publishers so hungry for proven self-published product. Then again, it might not be so wise.

Why giving up your baby could be just plain *stupid*

Paul Nathan, the rights columnist for *Publishers Weekly,* tells of a woman who called him one day so excited because a big, mainstream New York house wanted her book. "I asked her what percentage of her sales this title contributes. She said about 75%! I asked her if she had any other sources of income. She said no."

Here was a woman supporting her family on her book sales and she was about to hand all that over to a multinational conglomerate that was offering her a feeble advance against a below-average royalty in return. But this was a big house and she was flattered. Have you ever tried to eat flattery? Or make mortgage payments with it? Or clothe your children? Don't let your ego get in the way of a sound business decision.

We have good friends who successfully self-published their book, sold almost $300,000 worth, then turned the rights over to a major house for a $25,000 advance. The big house didn't know how to merchandise the book and it withered. Meanwhile, the cash flow our friends had grown to expect quickly dried up when the advance was spent. They were hurting. In hindsight they realized they should never have let go of the book. But hindsight has been called "optical rectosis." The story does have a happy ending, though. The rights are now back in the possession of the authors—and the book is again selling like hot cakes.

After a reasonable time, ask for certain rights back. We told you earlier about how—after the major publisher to whom we sold *Big Ideas for Small Service Businesses* dropped the ball and lost out on book club sales—we got the rights back and made a terrific sale. We also approached the publisher of *Country Bound!* to let certain rights revert back to us. We now own translation, sound recordings, and serialization rights, all of which give us more flexibility in promoting the book.

Three tricks for convincing people to do what you want them to do. Professional salespeople are masters at knowing how to turn prospects into customers. Let's take a few tips from them. 1) On the phone, learn to *listen.* After your initial introduction, let the prospect talk. He or she will reveal vital needs, concerns, and objections—which you then can counter with explanations, suggestions, and recommendations for crafting a win/win deal. 2) Script your message before you pick up the phone to call a prospect. This helps you know what you want to accomplish and gives you a sense of security. (Scripts are guidelines, however, not straightjackets.)

Also think through what message you'll leave if you get voice mail and how to get around a gatekeeper. By being well prepared you'll get far better and faster results. 3) Begin your letters by quoting the recipient. We all love to be quoted, even in a letter. And it's a compliment to the individual getting the letter that you paid such close attention to what was said. Grab their attention by repeating or paraphrasing some profound statement the person made during your conversation. Then play off it in stating your case.

Want to self-publish your book? There is a broad collection of articles and excerpts, self-publishing success stories, books on publishing and marketing, FAQs, etc., at http://www.about-books.com. About Books, Inc. is our consulting firm. We accept full-service clients and offer turn-key service for busy professionals who have adult nonfiction books they want to have edited, produced, and marketed. Stop by if this describes you.

Stay in touch over, and over, and over. It typically takes five to seven exposures before a person makes a buying decision. Determine who are the top 20% of your leads and stay visible to these prime prospects. You can do it with phone calls, faxes, emails, letters, notes, postcards, book covers, reviews, copies of large purchase orders, articles that would interest them with your business card attached. You might even get a friendly colleague to call them and offer a testimonial on your behalf. Be persistent!

George Lang, a noted restauranteur, signed with Knopf to write his autobiography. Guess what it is titled?
Nobody Knows the Truffles I've Seen

"Get a time limit on the contract," advises Bear Kamoroff, "after which you can get back the rights to your book." A big publisher will typically hustle your book for one "season" (six months) and is likely to have good sales for anywhere from six months to two years. After that, the reps lose interest. They're on to the next new bestseller and your poor book languishes in the nether world of forgotten backlist, or even goes out of print.

"In my self-publishing seminars at the University of California, I've met several authors (including one famous science fiction writer) who have met this fate," Bear continues. "They were so angry and frustrated. Some had offers from other publishers to republish their books, but couldn't get their publisher to budge."

Authors who get a time-limit clause in their contracts have the possibility of hitting the jackpot *three* times: once as a self-published book, republished by a big publisher, and self-published or resold again a few years later as a revised new edition.

Looking for an agent to represent your book? Go to the bookstore! Sounds strange, doesn't it? You're not going to find dozens of agents hanging around bookstores. What you will find are dozens of books that can lead you to them. Locate the area where books like yours are shelved, then carefully read the acknowledgments. Often the author will mention his or her agent. That agent is obviously familiar with which publishers are interested in that topic. So you have a targeted lead to a person who is likely to have the right publisher contacts.

More great resources. We found Jeff Herman's *Writer's Guide to Book Editors, Publishers, and Literary Agents, 1999-2000* to be invaluable when prospecting for publishers to pick up rights to our self-published books. Another good reference is the *Guide to Literary Agents*, edited by Donya Dickerson. Of course, the industry standard of *Writer's Market* is always invaluable.

And now we'll bring this portion of the book to a close.
It's gotten longer than a fallen woman's nightmare.
We wish you success, abundance, and great self-fulfillment.
Happy Marketing!

AFTERWORD

Three frogs were sitting on a lily pad.
One frog decided to jump.
How many frogs were left?

If you said, "three," you're right.

You see, "deciding" and "jumping" are two different things.
Deciding is a thought.
Jumping is an *action*.

What ACTION are you taking today?

ABOUT THE AUTHORS

Tom and Marilyn Ross—authors, speakers, consultants, coaches—are the champions of self-publishing. This internationally acclaimed team has helped thousands of authors sell millions of books through About Books, Inc., the company they founded in 1977 and have since sold. Now Marilyn Ross focuses her energies on helping authors, small presses, entrepreneurs and professionals through www.SelfPublishing Resources.com.

Marilyn's writing career has spanned over 30 years. Currently, she is a freelance travel journalist, writes articles on business and marketing topics, and creates promotional copy. This award winning writer's work has appeared in the *AARP Magazine (Modern Maturity)*, *Essence*, *The Writer*, *Independent Business (IB)*, *Westways*, and dozens of others.

These publishing gurus have been noted and quoted in *U.S. News & World Report*, *Publishers Weekly*, *The Los Angeles Times*, *Writer's Digest*, *Bottom Line Personal*, *John Naisbitt's Trend Letter*, *Investor's Business Daily*, *Rocky Mountain News*, *Denver Post*, *San Diego Union*, *Chicago Daily Herald*, *Phoenix Gazette*, *The New York Times*, *Newsweek*, and others.

Entrepreneur magazine dubbed Marilyn a "trend tracker." Additionally, she has appeared on scores of radio and TV shows, including NPR's "All Things Considered." CNN's website featured her in a top story, *Self-Publishing for Profit*. *Booklist* said of them, "The Rosses write with realism and extraordinary thoroughness." *The San Francisco Chronicle* commented, "The authors are energetic yet irreverent, and the attitude is refreshing." They bring this same invigorating style to *Jump Start Your Book Sales*. A reporter on NPR's "Marketplace" observed, "The bible of this self-publishing craze is *The Complete Guide to Self-Publishing* by Tom and Marilyn Ross."

Marilyn has been on the faculty of Folio's New York Face-to-Face publishing conference and has spoken at colleges and universities—plus publishing and writing associations—all over North America. Writing and publishing conference planners often call upon her as a speaker. Attendees love her entertaining presentations and the results-oriented, immediately-usable information dispensed. Consider hiring Marilyn for an upcoming conference, meeting, or fund raiser. She is a professional member of the National Speakers Association, PMA, SPAN, the Authors Guild, and the American Society of Journalists and Authors.

These busy folks not only help authors successfully write, publish, and market their own books and information products—they have written and self-published 13 books of their own. Following the "success formula" they espouse, five of their titles have been sold to major trade publishers. They have intimate knowledge of the joys and frustrations of being an author.

In 1996, Tom and Marilyn Ross launched an international non-profit trade association for self-publishers, small presses, and assertive authors. The Small Publishers Association of North America (SPAN) is now the second largest such organization in the world.

Previously Marilyn owned and operated an advertising and public relations firm. Today, as a publishing consultant and marketing expert, she accepts a limited number of ongoing coaching and hourly phone consulting clients. So, if you need help shaping a manuscript, advice on book printing issues, or assistance with a profit-making marketing campaign, contact her today!

Marilyn Ross
Self Publishing Resources
P.O. Box 909-JS, Buena Vista, CO 81211
phone: 719-395-8659
email: Marilyn@MarilynRoss.com
www.SelfPublishingResources.com

Publisher's and Author's
Bill of Rights—and Obligations

We have long thought that creating a better understanding and partnership between publishers and authors would be a huge step toward making this industry both more pleasant and more profitable for all. We have walked all sides of the fence: published four books through trade houses, self-published 10 books, and acquired two titles from authors. Not big numbers to be sure but enough to give us a taste of the honey—and the gall—involved with each.

Some of the ideas presented here are unorthodox. We trust they will be given consideration. With the confidence we can all be comrades rather than adversaries, let us forge ahead.

Publisher's *Bill of Rights—and Obligations*

1. The publisher has the right to receive the manuscript on time. When this doesn't happen, subsidiary rights are affected, catalogs become obsolete, and sales reps can't sell books scheduled for that season. All the anticipated momentum is forfeited.

2. The publisher has the right to receive a completely filled out Author Questionnaire from the author, delivered when it is due. This document is used to write catalog and book cover copy, to develop nationwide publicity and marketing plans, and for other strategic purposes. By giving it short shrift, authors handicap their publishers.

3. The publisher has the right to expect reasonable turnaround time on author review of edits, typeset pages, etc.

4. The publisher has the obligation to put real marketing muscle behind the title. Having accepted a manuscript, doing less than an excellent job of promoting it is unethical.

5. The publisher has the right to expect enthusiastic author participation and cooperation for promoting the book.

6. The publisher has the obligation to communicate regularly with the author. By keeping her or him in the loop about strategic reviews, book club sales, catalog buys, foreign rights sales, big chain store orders, etc., the author realizes the publisher is working hard on her or his behalf.

7. The publisher has the obligation to provide the author with prompt and complete statements and royalty checks (if appropriate) as per the contract.

8. The publisher has the right to exploit electronic rights and sales to the maximum—and the obligation to split that revenue fairly with the author.

9. The publisher has the obligation to promptly relinquish all rights to the book to the author when the publisher decides to let the book go out of print. All camera-ready materials, film, disks, etc., shall become the property of the author. The author shall have the right to purchase remaining stock at the best remainder price.

10. The publisher has the obligation to pay the author a fairly negotiated additional advance when major revisions on new editions are required.

Author's *Bill of Rights—and Obligations*

1. The author has the right to have enthusiastic support for his or her title from the editorial, production, publicity, and sales staff. Even if it becomes an "orphan" book (where the acquiring editor leaves), there will be earnest commitment to the title.

2. The author has the right to be provided a flow chart or some other document so he or she can identify and communicate with appropriate publisher personnel.

3. The author has the right to participate in title decisions, cover jacket selection, and sales copy. Although the publisher—who is providing the money to fund the project—justifiably retains final say, author input is welcome.

4. The author has the right to have 50 free review copies instead of the usual 10. These will be given (not sold!) to strategic opinion-molders in the author's sphere of influence to start a buzz about the book.

5. The author has the obligation to get behind his or her book 110%. No one cares as much about this book as the author. The publisher has dozens, often hundreds, of titles to promote each season; the author has only one. This means being a proactive author or hiring a freelance publicist.

6. The author has the right to purchase unlimited cases of his or her own book at a 60% discount for resale to nontrade markets. (No royalties are paid on these copies.) Many authors speak and teach, and will self-promote assertively if there is viable financial return. A strong author is the book's best salesperson. Encourage this.

7. The author has the obligation to exercise reasonable expectations. He or she will probably not appear on *Oprah,* be reviewed in *The New York Times,* or hit bestseller lists.

8. The author has the obligation not to become a pest. Attempting to get sales figures other than at statement time or demanding that a backlist book receive ambitious promotion is unrealistic.

9. The author has the right to hold the copyright in his or her name.

10. The author has the right to obtain a relinquishment of rights the publisher no longer intends to pursue, such as serial, book club, and audio.

Mastering Your Marketing Plan

Initial Steps:

Create a mission statement.
Seek early endorsements.
Develop a list of key PR contacts.
Write promotional materials.
Submit galleys.
Solicit book club adoptions.

Traditional Marketing Outlets:

Appear on radio and TV.
Pursue print reviews and publicity.
Approach bookstores.
Evaluate author signings, mini-seminars, author tours.
Work through wholesalers and distributors.
Solicit libraries.
Consider schools and colleges.

Nontraditional Marketing Moves:

Go after catalogs.
Approach nonbookstore related retail outlets.
Use LinkThink to forge creative partnerships.
Consider the TV home shopping networks.
Sell books back-of-the-room while speaking and teaching.
Develop an Internet presence.
Seek out bulk premium sales.
Approach organizations for fund-raising.
Assess direct marketing possibilities.
Look for sidelines and spinoffs.
Consider selling rights to a major publisher.

Key Review Galley Recipients

Send galleys to:

Brad Hooper, Book Editor
Booklist
American Library Association
50 East Huron Street
Chicago, IL 60611
Ph: 312-280-5722
Fax: 312-337-6787
E-mail: bhooper@ala.org
www.ala.org

Alex Moore, Managing Review Editor
Foreword
129½ East Front Street
Traverse City, MI 49684
Ph: 231-933-3699
Fax: 231-933-3899
www.forewordmagazine.com

Chuck Shelton, Managing Editor
Kirkus Reviews
VNU US Literary Group
770 Broadway, 6th Floor
New York, NY 10003
Ph: 646-654-4602
Fax: 646-654-4706
E-mail: cshelton@vnubuspubs.com
www.kirkusreviews.com
(send two galleys)

Tania Barnes, Book Review Assistant
Library Journal
360 Park Avenue South
New York, NY 10010
Ph: 646-746-1818
E-mail: tbarnes@reedbusiness.com
www.libraryjournal.com

Steve Wasserman, Book Review Editor
Los Angeles Times Book Review
Los Angeles Times
130 South Broadway
Los Angeles, CA 90012
Ph: 213-237-5000
Fax: 213-237-4712
www.latimes.com

Book Review Editor
New York Times Book Review
New York Times Company
229 West 43rd Street
New York, NY 10036
Ph: 212-556-7267
E-mail: natnews@nyt.com
www.nytimes.com/books

Sarah F. Gold, Senior Nonfiction Editor or Jeff Saleski, Forecasts Editor
Publishers Weekly
360 Park Ave South, 13th Floor
New York, NY 10010
Ph: 646-746-6554
E-mail: sgold@reedbusiness.com or jsaleski@reedbusiness.com
www.publishersweekly.com
(send two galleys)

James Grainger, Review Editor
Quill & Quire
111 Queen Street East, 3rd Floor
Toronto, ON M5C 1S2
Ph: 416-364-3333, ext. 3115
www.quillandquire.com

Trevelyn E. Jones, Editor
School Library Journal
360 Park Avenue South
New York, NY 10010
Ph: 646-746-6757
E-mail: tjones@reedbusiness.com
www.schoollibraryjournal.com

Note: Also send galleys to the main newspaper in your closest major city. Find information for it and other major newspapers in *Literary Market Place (LMP)* under Newspapers Featuring Books. This reference work is available in major libraries. Be sure to use the *current* edition.

Selected Newswire Services

The Associated Press/AP
50 Rockefeller Plaza, 5th Floor
New York, NY 10020
Phone: 212-621-1500;
fax: 212-621-1679

Bloomberg Business News
499 Park Avenue, 15th Floor
New York, NY 10022
Phone: 212-318-2000;
fax: 212-980-2480

Copley News Service
P.O. Box 190
San Diego, CA 92112
Phone: 619-293-1818;
fax: 619-293-2322

Gannett News Service
1000 Wilson Boulevard
Arlington, VA 22229
Phone: 703-276-5800;
fax: 703-558-3902

Knight-Rider Newspapers
700 National Press Building
Washington, DC 20045
Phone: 202-383-6000;
fax: 202-383-6075

Reuters America, Inc.
1333 H Street, NW, #410
Washington, DC 20005
Phone: 202-898-8300;
fax: 202-898-8383

Scripps Howard News Service
1090 Vermont Avenue, NW, 10th
Floor
Washington, DC 20005-4905
Phone: 202-408-1484

UPI/United Press International
1510 H Street
Washington, DC 20005
Phone: 202-898-8000;
fax: 202-898-8057

Op-Ed Newspaper Contacts

Atlanta Journal-Constitution
72 Marietta Street, NW
Atlanta, GA 30303
Phone: 404-526-5341;
fax 404-526-5611
Op-ed editor: Dean Wakefield, 404-582-7371
700 words or fewer; pitch by fax

Chicago Tribune
435 North Michigan Avenue
Chicago, IL 60611
Phone: 312-222-3429;
fax: 312-222-2598
Opinion page editor: Marcia Lythcott, 312-222-4198
Email: comment435@aol.com
800 or less words; pitch by fax

Christian Science Monitor
One Norway Street
Boston, MA 02115-3995
Phone: 617-450-2372;
fax: 617-450-2317
Op-ed coordinator: Clara Germani
Email: oped@csps.com
Frequency: Monday through Friday, 500 to 900 words, occasionally longer
Pay scale: $100 base rate, goes up for repeat contributors

They need exclusive 90-day worldwide copyrights. Open to any subjects except medical, liquor, or tobacco. Include a two- or three-line biographical blurb.

Houston Chronicle
P.O. Box 4260
Houston, TX 77210
Phone: 713-220-7171;
fax: 713-220-3575
Outlook editor: David Langworthy, 713-220-7209
Email: david.langworthy@chron.com
600 to 800 words; email with a fax copy back up

Los Angeles Times
Times Mirror Square
Los Angeles, CA 90053
Phone: 213-237-7939;
fax: 213-237-7968
Op-ed editor: Robert Berger, 213-237-6958
Email: op-ed@latimes.com
Approximately 650 to 700 words daily; 400 to 500 words Sunday; 800 words Saturday for *Voices*; pitch by fax or email

The Daily News (New York)
450 West 33rd Street
New York, NY 10001
Phone: 212-210-2100;
fax: 212-643-7828
Op-ed page editor: Robert Laird, 212-210-1614
600 words or fewer; pitch by fax; emphasis on New York City–oriented topics and events

The New York Times
229 West 43rd Street
New York, NY 10036
Phone: 212-556-1831;
fax: 212-556-3690
Op-ed page editor: Katherine Roberts, 212-556-3652
Approximately 650 words; pitch by mail or fax

Newsday
235 Pinelawn Road
Melville, NY 11747
Phone: 516-843-2900;
fax: 516-843-2986
Currents (Sunday) editor: (Mr.) Chris Lehmann, 516-843-2909
Viewpoints (daily) editor: Noel Rubinton, 516-843-2313
600 to 650 words daily; 1,000 to 1,200 words Sunday; pitch by fax

Philadelphia Inquirer
400 North Broad Street
P.O. Box 8263
Philadelphia, PA 19101
Phone: 215-854-4531;
fax: 215-854-5884
Commentary page associate editor: John Timpane, 215-854-4406
Approximately 750 words; pitch by mail or fax

USA Today
1000 Wilson Boulevard
Arlington, VA 22229
Phone: 703-276-3400;
fax: 703-558-3935
Glen Nishimwa, 703-276-3400, ext. 4588; fax: 703-247-3108
Frequency: Monday through Friday; 400 words; must be copyrighted

The Wall Street Journal
200 Liberty Street
New York, NY 10281
Guidelines: 212-416-3512;
fax: 212-416-2658
Editorial features editor: Max Boot, 212-416-2561
700 to 1,500 words; pitch by mail or fax; must be exclusive to the *Journal* and include two-line summary of piece

The Washington Post
1150 15th Street, NW
Washington, DC 20071
Phone: 202-334-7470; fax: 202-334-5269; guidelines: 202-334-4855
Editorial page editor: Meg Greenfield, 202-334-7470
750 to 1,000 words; pitch by mail or fax; *Outlook* looks for news-driven commentary involving a mix of reporting and opinion; call first for fax number)

Master (Exclusive) Distributors

Access Publishers Network
6893 Sullivan Road
Grawn, MI 49637
Phone: 616-276-5196;
fax: 616-276-5197
Self-help, how-to, travel, New Age,
novels, children's

Associated Publishers Group (APG Trade)
3356 Coffey Lane
Santa Rosa, CA 95403
Phone: 707-542-5400
General, metaphysical, children's

BookWorld Services, Inc.
1933 Whitfield Loop
Sarasota, FL 34243
Phone: 800-444-2524;
fax: 941-763-9396
Fiction, self-help, New Age, business,
children's

Consortium Book Sales
1045 Westgate Drive
St. Paul, MN 55114,
Phone: 612-221-9035;
fax: 612-221-0124
Fiction, feminism, drama, Hispanic,
children's

Login Publishers Consortium (LPC Group)
1438 West Randolph Street
Chicago, IL 60607
Phone: 800-626-4330, 312-432-7650;
fax: 312-432-7603
General, business, self-help, sports, fiction, politics, alternative nonfiction,
gay and lesbian

Midpoint Trade
27 West 20th Street, Suite 1102
New York, NY 10011
Phone: 212-727-0190;
fax: 212-727-0195
General, business, family, children's

National Book Network
4720 Boston Way
Lanham, MD 20706
Phone: 800-462-6420, 301-459-3366;
fax: 301-459-2118
General, alternative health, business,
sports, academics

Partners Book Distributing, Inc.
2325 Jarkco Drive
Holt, MI 48842
Phone: 517-694-3205
General, nature, travel, African-Ameri-
can, cookbooks, sports

Publishers Group West (PGW)
1700 4th Street
Berkeley, CA 94710
Phone: 800-788-3123, 510-528-1444;
fax: 510-528-3444
General

Bookstore Contacts

Chains

Barnes & Noble
Small Press Department
122 Fifth Avenue
New York, NY 10011
Phone: 212-633-3454;
fax: 212-677-1634
Web: http://www.barnesandnoble.com

Borders Group
100 Phoenix Drive
Ann Arbor, MI 48108
Phone: 734-477-4000
Web: http://www.borders.com

Books-A-Million
402 Industrial Lane
Birmingham, AL 35211-4465
Phone: 205-942-3737
Web: http:/www.booksamillion.com

Chapters (Canada)
Jim Hart, New Vendor Liaison
90 Ronson Drive
Etobicoke, Ontario M9W 1C1
Phone: 416-243-3138;
fax: 416-243-8964

Independents

There are thousands of good independently-owned retail stores, both large and small. Most belong to a trade association called the American Booksellers Association (ABA). You can pinpoint them geographically and via specialty by visiting the ABA's site at http://www.bookweb.org. Or call the ABA at 800-637-0037 for more details about renting their mailing lists of specialty stores shown below with the total numbers. If your book fits one of these topics, it's a great way to single out those places that would be most interested.

Specialty Stores

African-American Books 135
Antiques & Collectibles 95
Architecture 60
Art 260
Biography 100
Business 140
Children's, Young Adult & Adolescent 1,300
Cookbooks 310
Computers 150
Crafts 70
Theater & Drama 30
Education 150
Feminist & Women's Studies 90
Foreign Language Books 95
Gambling & Games 14
Gay & Lesbian 78

Gardening 115
Health & Nutrition 160
History 290
How To & Repair 30
Humor 30
Jadaica 45
Law Books 20
Medical 75
Metaphysical & New Age 185
Military 50
Mystery 300
Nature & Outdoors 215
Parenting 100
Philosophy 110
Photography 60
Poetry 80
Political Science & Sociology 80

Psychology 240
Reference Books 288
Religious & Christian 284
Remainders 247
Romance 100
Science Fiction 190

Spanish Language Books 50
Sports 30
Scientific & Technical Books 165
Travel 188
Westerns 45

Airport Bookstores

Benjamin Books
Chris Nielson, Associate Book Buyer
26 Kennedy Boulevard
East Brunswick, NJ 08016

Host Marriot
Melissa Christian
Sea-Tac International Airport
Room 202
Seattle, WA 98158
Phone: 206-433-5611

Paradies Shops
Debbie Moore, Buyer
Lynn Bennett, Buyer
5950 Fulton Industrial Boulevard
P.O. Box 43485
Atlanta, GA 30336
Phone: 404-344-7905

W. H. Smith
Jane Love, Book Buyer
3200 Windy Hill Road, #1500
West Atlanta, GA 30339
Phone: 770-952-0705, 404-765-9480

Selected Major Catalogs

Miles Kimball
Donna Riley
41 West 8th Avenue
Oshkosh, WI 54901
Phone: 414-231-3800;
fax: 414-231-4804

National Syndications/Pub-Choice
Brian McNeese
230 Fifth Avenue
New York, NY 10001
Phone: 212-686-8680

Publisher's Clearinghouse
Joanne Freedman
382 Channel Drive
Port Washington, NY 11050
Phone: 516-883-5432;
fax: 516-767-3650

Wireless
Michele Willey
1000 Westgate Drive
St. Paul, MN 55164-0422
Phone: 612-659-3700

Signals
Judy Ryan
1000 Westgate Drive
St. Paul, MN 55164-0422
Phone: 612-659-3700

Lillian Vernon
Michelle Burroughs
One Theall
Rye, NY 10580
Phone: 914-925-1200;
fax: 914-925-1444

Premium/Incentive Trade Associations

Contact these associations for upcoming trade show dates or membership details.

Incentive Manufactures Representatives Association (IMRA)
1805 North Mill Street, Suite A
Naperville, IL 60563
Phone: 630-369-3466;
fax: 630-369-3773
URL: http://www.imra1@aol.com

Promotional Products Association International (PPA)
3125 Skyway Circle North
Irving, TX 75038
Phone: 972-252-0404;
fax: 972:258-3004
URL: http://www.ppa.org

Promotional Marketing Association of America (PMAA)
257 Park Avenue South, Suite 1102
New York, NY 10010
Phone: 212-420-1100;
fax: 212-533-7622
URL: http://www.pmalink.org

Home Shopping Networks

QVC Network—Vendor Relations
1200 Wilson Drive
West Chester, PA 19380
Phone: 610-701-8894, 610-701-1154, 610-701-8655; fax: 610-701-1356
(They refuse to publically release the name of their book buyer.)
Request a Vendor Relations package or go online at www.QVC.com and download Vendor Information.

Home Shopping Network—Purchasing Department
1 HDSN Drive
St. Petersburg, FL 33726
Book buyer: Sarah Hawkins
Phone: 813-572-8585, ext. 4066;
fax: 813-573-3702
Call 800-436-1010 for a Vendor Information Kit.

ValueVision—International
6740 Shady Oak Road
Eden Prairie, MN 55344
Phone: 612-947-5200
Book buyer: Lori Griggs (purchasing)
Phone: 612-831-0166 (purchasing);
fax: 612-947-0188 (corporate)
They do not provide forms or kits. You must take the initiative and mail or fax data profile, cost, suggested price, brochure, pictures, catalog, etc.

Shop at Home, Inc.
PO Box 12600
Knoxville, TN 37912
Book buyer: Henry Shapiro, vice President of Merchandise
Phone: 423-688-0300;
fax: 423-687-7166
Fax them your fax number, address, and phone. They will reply via fax with a simple one-page New Vendor Inquiry Form.

Specialty Booklet Printers

Leesburg Printing Company
Mike Mason
3606 Parkway Boulevard
Leesburg, FL 34748
Phone: 800-828-3348;
fax: 352-787-2210
Email: lpcben@gate.net;
NewsletRus@aol.com
Web: http://Newsletters-Print-Mail.com

Sterling Pierce
William Burke
422 Atlantic Avenue
East Rockaway, NY 11518
Phone: 516-593-1170;
fax 516-593-1401

Triangle Printing
325 Hill Avenue
Nashville, TN 37210
Phone: 800-843-9529;
fax 800-845-4767
Printing for booklet prices accepted only by fax to the estimating department.

Kirkland Offset Printing
Jerry Kirkland
7401 Princess View Drive, Suite F
San Diego, CA 92120
Phone: 619-583-3676;
fax 619-583-3887

Waveline Direct, Inc.
Jennifer Lasserty
192 Hempt Road
Mechanicsburg, PA 17055
Phone: 800-257-8830;
fax 717-795-8836

BIBLIOGRAPHY

Many of these books can be ordered from our website at www.CommunicationCreativity.com. To order a book, call 800-331-8355.

Appelbaum, Judith. *How to Get Happily Published.* Harper Perennial.

Boekhoff, Terri A., and Joshua Bagby. *The Insiders' Guide to Book Publishing.* Rudi Publishing.

Byers, Judy. *Words on Tape.* Audio CP Publishing.

DePalma, Tami, and Kim Dushinski. *Maximum Exposure Marketing System.* MarketAbility, Inc.

Floyd, Elaine. *Marketing with Newsletters.* Writer's Digest Books.

Herman, Jeff. *Writer's Guide to Book Editors, Publishers, and Literary Agents, 1999–2000: Who They Are! What They Want! And How to Win Them Over!* Prima Publishing.

Horowitz, Shel. *Marketing Without Megabucks: How to Sell Anything on a Shoestring.* Accurate Writing and More.

Jenkins, Jerrold R., and Anne M. Stanton. *Publish to Win.* Rhodes & Easton.

Jud, Brian. *You're on the Air.* Marketing Directions, Inc.

Kiefer, Marie. *Book Publishing Resource Guide.* Ad-Lib Publications.

Kremer, John. *1001 Ways to Market Your Books.* Open Horizons.

Larsen, Michael. *How to Write a Book Proposal.* Writer's Digest Books.

Palder, Edward L. *The Catalog of Catalogs.* Woodbine House.

Ross, Marilyn. *National Directory of Newspaper Op-Ed Pages.* Communication Creativity.

Ross, Marilyn and Tom. *Big Ideas for Small Service Businesses.* Communication Creativity.

———. *The Complete Guide to Self-Publishing.* Writer's Digest Books.

————. *Country Bound! Trade Your Business Suit Blues for Blue Jean Dreams.* Upstart.

————. *How-to-Make Big Profits Publishing City & Regional Books.* Communication Creativity.

Shelton, Connie. *Publish You Own Novel.* Columbine Books.

Walters, Dottie and Lilly. *Speak and Grow Rich.* Prentice Hall Trade.

INDEX

A

About Books, Inc. 15, 318
Ad agencies 220
Adult Ed Today 274
Advance comments. *See* Endorsements
Advances 284
Advertising 39
   paid in bookstores 131
   sell in your book 291
Agents 92, 200, 285, 313, 319
Airport bookstores 130, 335
Alessandra, Tony 202, 214, 237-238
Alexander, Tom 291
Alternative master moves 283–298
   awards 285–286
   back-end sales 303–304
   booklets 304–305
   contest ideas 287–288
   creating events 288–289
   customer catalogs 291–292
   existing customers 303
   foreign rights sales 283–285
   four success principles 293–295
   imaginative ideas 290–291
   special reports 304–305, 306, 308–309
Alternative press *(See also* Newspapers) 44
Alternative sources for manuscripts 23
Amazon.com 2, 20, 28, 47, 48, 51, 126–127, 129, 132, 193, 196, 313
American Booksellers Association 9, 134, 140, 334, 351
American Federation of Television and Radio Artists 114
American Libraries 43

American Library Association 139, 142
Albert, Bill and Susan 132, 193, 196, 302, 313
Ancillary products 299–309, 305
Announcements 83
Appelbaum, Judith 58, 74
Appendixes 17, 325-337
Articles, selling 71
Ask for what you want 293
Association of Canadian Publishers 268
Associations, selling to 64, 182, 262, 266, 296
Audience participation 78
Audio products 62, 309
Aughenbaugh, Anna 272
Author bio 57, 159, 245
Authors 4, 46, 55, 129, 135
Author's Bill of Rights—and Obligations 326-327
Authors Guild 4
Author tours 49, 85-88
   escorts for 90
   formula for 86
Autographed copies 89
Autograph stickers 80
Autographing books 80, 84, 89
Awards 285–288

B

Back-end sales 303–304
Backlist 3, 16, 21, 39, 55, 67, 74, 136, 149, 170, 192, 209, 226, 283, 319, 327
Back matter 17–18
Bagby, Joshua 24
Bailey, Lorilyn 79
Baker & Taylor (B&T) 18, 49, 120, 126, 128, 139, 140
Balcomb, Mary 78
Barnes & Noble (B&N) 5, 18, 75, 80-81, 119-120, 123-125, 334

BarnesandNoble.com 128
Barnes, Dick 229
BEA. *See* BookExpo America
Beeler, Steve 147
Benefits 19, 98, 246-247
Benjamin Franklin Awards 286
Bestsellers 129, 168, 303
Bibliophiles 21
Big Ideas for Small Service Businesses 164
Biggs, Dick 301
Bill of Rights—and Obligations, author's and publisher's 325-327
Black, Joe 230
Block, Julian 273
Blurbs. *See* Endorsements
Bock, Wally 201
Boekhoff, Terri A. 24
BOMC 156, 159-160, 163
Book buyers everywhere 297
Book clubs 48, 155–165
   approach 158
   author bio 159
   Book-of-the-Month Club (BOMC) 156, 159-160, 163
   choosing clubs 156–158
   cover letter for 158–159
   Doubleday Direct, Inc. 156, 158, 160
   endorsements 159
   exclusivity 161
   financial arrangements 161–162
   juvenile clubs 157
   learning the ins and outs 155–156
   Literary Guild 156
   making contact 162–163
   McGraw-Hill Companies 157-158
   Newbridge Communications 156
   Quality Paperback Book Club 159–160

rights and royalties 161–
162
school book clubs 157
sell multiple times 163
submission process 158–
161
Book displays 277
Book fairs 89
Book Industry Study Group
8
Book Marketing & Publicity
60
Book Marketing Update 60
Book markets, top 134
*Book Publishing Resource
Guide* 162
Book signings 75–90
autographing 80, 84, 89
before your event 82–84
book tours 85–86
create an event 77
during your event 84–85
escaping the ordinary 76–
77
hidden values in 76
media, working with 81-
82
nontraditional sites 78
out of the box thinking
77
pros and cons of 75–76
readings 77, 78
successful author tours,
examples of 86–89
turn signings into
extravaganzas 79–81
virtual 89–90
Book Stacks Unlimited 128
Bookstores. *See* Distribution
channels
Book tours 85–86
costs 86
grueling 86
local news 86
schools 86
timing 87
Book-of-the-Month Club
(BOMC) 156, 159–
160, 163
BookExpo America
121, 139, 214, 294
BookFlash 74
Booklets 304–309
marketing 308
price point 306–307
printers 337

production considerations
307–308
success story 305–306
Booklink 115
Booklist 43, 46, 47, 50, 137,
142, 329
Bookmarks 300
BookRadio.com 107
Books-A-Million
125, 131, 334
Books in Print 12, 127, 128
Booksellers 119–134
Bookstore chains 129, 334
BookZone.com 10, 172,
189, 206, 231
Borders 18, 71, 77, 81, 90,
119, 123, 125, 128,
131, 334
Boston: A Century of Running
88, 191
Bottom Line newsletters 308
Bounce Back from Bankruptcy
101
Bounce-backs 292
Brainstorming 20
Broadcast fax 42
Brochure, consumer 150,
243–252, 257, 275,
278
benefits over features
246–247
components of 244–246
designing 248–249
form follows function 244
planning decisions 244
production tips for 249–
251
promotional literature
243–244
readers, kinds of 247–248
Buck slips 251
*Building Your Financial
Portfolio on $25 a
Month or Less* 87
Bundling 300
Butel, Jane 301
Buzz 27, 33, 133, 134
Byers, Judy 62

C

Calendar tie-ins 94, 106
Canada 51, 79, 108, 125,
131, 155, 159, 171,
181, 239, 265, 268–
269, 272–273, 330,
351

Canfield, Jack
66, 79, 168, 303
Card packs 258–259
Carry book 73
Catalog Age 181, 183
Catalog sales 179–188
approaching this market
184–186
attractive aspects 180
Catalog of Catalogs 181
catalog/retail information
sheet 184
discounts 183
finding appropriate ones
181–182
how it works 182–183
know your reader 183–
184
persistence 187
subject matter 180–181
Catalog/retail information
sheet 184
Cataloging-in-Publication
data 138
Catalogs 147
customer 291–292
online 186, 187
selected major 335
*Catalogue of Canadian
Catalogues* 181
Cecil 132
Celestine Prophecy, The 311
Chain reaction 56
Chamber of commerce 278
Channels of distribution. *See*
Distribution channels
Chapters 125, 334
Chicken Soup for the Soul 66,
168, 303, 309
Children's books 8, 78, 85,
86, 135, 143, 148, 150,
152, 157, 160, 168–
169, 174, 176–177,
179, 210, 229, 235,
239, 288
Choice
43, 47, 51, 137, 330
Christensen, Bobbie 82, 86–
87, 170
Christmas Box, The 312
Clips 58
College Marketing Group
(CMG) 149
Combined Book Exhibits
(CBE) 133, 139

Complete Guide to Self-Publishing, The 17, 56, 102, 121, 136, 194, 303
Conferences 146, 147, 279
Consignment 120, 171, 292–293
Consolidation 4
Consumer demand 133
Consumer spending 8
Contacts 27–28
Contest ideas 287
Cook, Judith Tucker 146
Cookbooks 14, 20, 83, 84, 130, 152, 169, 174, 179, 182, 192, 195, 196, 209, 210, 215, 218, 223, 224, 228, 234-235, 238, 245, 272, 287, 301, 305, 333
Cooperation, not competition 230
Copyright 17, 24, 283
Cotton, Letty Pogrebin 4
Country Bound! 19, 59, 185, 187, 223, 286, 313, 318
Coupons 295
Cover 8, 50, 83, 159, 239
Cox, Jim 42, 48, 65, 111, 140
Craft shows 290
Creative Loafing 14, 272, 289
C-SPAN2 65–66, 114
Customer book buying habits 128
Customizing 61, 72

D

Databases 115, 304
Dated material 248
Desk copies 150
Direct Mail 183, 243, 253–269
  All-in-one mailers 258
  brochure 257
  business reply envelope (BRE) 258
  card packs 258–325
  components of 254–255
  Direct Marketing Association, Inc. 265
  formulas 254
  in-house list, creation of 263–264, 268

list brokers 259–261
mailing lists 259, 265-268
mailing smarter 264–265
order form 257–258
outer envelope 255–256
planning for profits 253–254
prospecting for lists 262–263
returned mail 267
sales letter 256
Standard Rate and Data's Direct Mail List Rates & Data 261
statement stuffers 258
test 264
Direct Mail Association 179, 181
Direct marketing 147, 183. *See also* Direct mail
Direct Marketing Association, Inc. 265
Direct marketing sales letter checklist 256
Directory of Business to Business Catalogs 181
Directory of Directories 17
Directory of Mail Order Catalogs 181
Directory of Overseas Catalogs 181
Directory of Premium, Incentive & Travel Buyers 213
Discounts 120, 140, 183, 212, 235
Discover Your Roots 13, 146
Distribution channels 119–134
  bookstores 119, 334-335
  distributors 120-123
  independents versus chain stores 123–125, 334-335
  major wholesalers 120, 125–128
  online booksellers 126–128
  returns 123, 135
Distributors 120-123
  bankrupt 133
  master (exclusive) 46, 49, 120–123, 333
  sell sheets 132

DM News 183
Door prizes 297
Doubleday Direct, Inc. 156, 158, 160
Dowell, Karen 77
Drop-ship arrangements 231
Dyer, Wayne 63

E

Echo effect 162
E-commerce 205
Editor & Publisher 41
Editorial 11–19
  back matter 17–18
  chapters to diversify 12–13
  foreign rights 15–16
  front matter 16–17
  mentions 39
  planting zingers 13–15
  titles 19–21
  USP, determining your 11–12
Educational Sales 145–154
  adoption cycle 151
  advice from pros 146–149
  catalogs 148
  college market 150–151
  commitment to 145
  curriculum framework 148
  desk copies 150
  exhibits 148
  home schooling 145
  large quantity sales 152
  mailing lists 149
  private schools 145
  random tips 149
  Reading's Fun/Books Are Fun 152
  speaking 148
  supplementary texts 146
  text adoptions 150–151
  wholesalers/distributors 148
Edwards, Paul and Sarah 64
80/20 rule 45, 293, 294
Eisemann, Pat 91
Electronic Book Aisle (EBA) 193
Email 42, 201-202
Encyclopedia of Associations 182, 262, 296
Endorsements 27–37, 159, 245
  foreword 32–33

motivate people to agree
30–31
prepare early 27–28
promote 31
you write 30
Ensign, Paulette 305
Escorts 90
Evans, Richard Paul 312
Events, creating 288-289
Evergreen topics 24
Evers, Connie 171
Examples of premium book
sales 212-215
Excerpts 71, 192, 210
Experts 33-35, 98

F

Family Circle 308
F&Gs. *See* Galleys
Features versus benefits,
examples 246
Fenster, Carol, Ph.D. 224,
231
Fiction 8–10, 18–19, 25,
30, 48–49, 51, 56, 77,
114, 130, 133, 135,
160, 164, 170, 177,
192-193, 223, 235,
239, 272, 285, 286,
287, 302, 313, 319,
333. *See also* Novel
Floyd, Elaine 302
Flyers 31, 45, 47, 57, 68,
81, 83, 86, 88, 101,
132, 138-139, 147,
171, 227–231, 243,
258, 276, 278, 295-
296, 304, 351
Follow up 58, 65, 68, 98,
140, 184, 294
Foreign rights 15–16, 49,
239, 283–285
Foreword 23, 32–33, 210,
314
ForeWord magazine
43, 51, 286, 330
Forthcoming Books in Print
12
Fox Family Channel 110
Frankfurt Book Fair 284
Freddie 132
Freebies 150, 262, 308
Freebies magazine 308
Frequently Asked Questions
(FAQs) 197
Friends of the Library 272

Front matter 16–17
Fun 10, 84
Fund-raising 227–230, 309

G

Gadalla, Moustafa 47
Galleys 39–53, 48–52, 329
cover for 50
statistics 49
timely topic 50
where to send 50-51,
329–330
Gardner, David and Tom 89
Gatekeeper 31
Genre conferences 177
Genre-specific Web sites 8-
10
Getting Your Dream Life 82
Gifts 52, 83
basket 300
certificates 296
shows 182
store sales 172–173
Giveaways 100, 104
Glossary 17
Godek, Greg 72, 128
Golomb, Gail 203
Gosselin, Kim 207, 217
Government 25, 35, 53
Grammar 23, 25
Great Catalog Guide 181
Grocery store 205
Guarantee 245, 252
*Guide to Book Editors,
Publishers and Literary
Agents* 320

H

Hand-deliver books 231
Hannah, Bill 155, 284
Hansen, Mark Victor 66, 79,
168, 303
Harris, Bev 225
Here's what people are saying
46, 57
Higdon, Hal 88, 89, 191
Home Shopping Networks
233–239, 336
Hooks 13, 44, 68, 93, 106,
109, 131, 171, 174,
255, 313
*Hoover's Handbook of
American Businesses*
216
Horn Book Magazine, The 47
How to Get Happily Published
58, 74

*How to Get the Job You Really
Want and Get Employers
to Call You* 21
*How to Make Big Profits
Publishing City &
Regional Books* 14
*How to Make Money with
Your Ideas* 202
*How to Market Yourself on
Radio Talk Shows all
Across America* 105

I

Illustrations 248
Imaginative ideas 290–291
IMRA Handbook 217
Incentive Manufactures
Representative
Association, Inc. 217
Incentives. *See* Premiums
Independent bookstores 5,
76, 79, 119, 134, 334
Independent Publisher 17, 43,
51, 286, 329
Index 18
Information business 303
Ingram 18, 48-49, 120, 125,
128-129, 132-133, 291
Ingram Express program 125
*Insiders' Guide to Book
Publishing, The* 24
Internal press 69–71
*International Literary Market
Place* 285
Internet strategies 28, 62,
189–206
advertising 196
bulletin board systems
198–199
content 191
cyberspace talk shows
199–200
electronic schmoozing
196–198
email 201–202
give to get 191
growth 204
links 195–196
newsgroups 197-198
publicity on 15, 89-90,
196–198, 202-203,
205
search engines, registering
with 194–195
signature 201
statistics 190

Web spin offs 203–204
whole books on the Web 192–194
Invoices, as marketing tools 296
Ippy 286
iQVC 238

J

James, Larry 80
Jenkins, Jerrold R. 170
Jobber. *See* Distributors; Wholesalers
Jossey-Bass 151
Jud, Brian 113, 307
Jump Master Marketing System 176, 251, 349
Junior League of Houston, The 223

K

Kamoroff, Bear 21, 317, 319
Kennedy, Dan 202, 260
Key contacts 58
Kid's Catalog Collection 181
Kirkus Reviews 43, 47, 51, 137, 330
Kremer, John 17, 201
Kupcha, Dorothy Leland 147

L

Langton, Jane 85
Lansky, Vicki 170
Laryngitis, remedies for 279
Learning Annex 63, 86, 273, 274
Learning Connection 273
Legislature 53
Leisure Learning Unlimited 273
Letter to the editor 94, 141
Levinson, Jay Conrad 230
Library Journal 43, 46–47, 49–50, 136–137, 142, 329
Library sales 135–143, 309
  Combined Book Exhibits (CBE) 139
  distributors 137–138
  exhibits 139
  Friends of the Library, working with 140–142
  influencing librarians 47, 137–140
  Internet library sites 142

mailing lists 139, 142
  Quality Books Inc. 137, 139
  renting lists 139
  requirements 136–137
  Unique Books 138, 139
  what's good about libraries 135–136
LibrarySpot 142
Licensing rights 283
Lifetime Channel 110
LinkThink 221–231
  fund-raising 227–230
  newsletters and associations, collaborating with 225–227
  other industries examples 221
  publishing partnerships 222–225
Literary agent. *See* Agents
Literary Guild 156
Literary Market Place (LMP) 29, 43, 47, 139, 162–163, 267, 286, 330
Literary wholesaler 133
Little Book of Online Romance 79
Little media 63
Lloyd, Sharon Spence 71
London Book Fair 284
Long-term thinking 72
Los Angeles Times 330, 331
Low, Alice 78
Lund, Joanna 234

M

Mailing lists 149
Mail Order Business Directory 181
Make it easy 111, 275, 293
Malsam, Margaret 227
Market Data Retrieval (MDR) 149
Market research 147
Marketing philosophy 3–10
Marketing plan, master 328
Mass market outlets 167
Mastering Your Marketing Plan 328
Maturi, Richard J. 88
McCrumb, Sharyn 85
McGraw-Hill Companies 157–158
Media
  cards 100
  coaching 113

contacts 64
  kits 98
  little 63
  questions for 57
Midlist authors 4, 135
Midnight in the Garden of Good and Evil 66
Midwest Book Review 42, 48, 65, 111, 140
Miller, Steve 200
Mini sales call 130
Mission statement 58, 99
Mock review 42, 57
Morgan, Vicki 288
Multiple sales 79
Museum Store Association, Inc. (MSA) 174–175
Museums 173–176
Mutant Message Down Under 312

N

Nathan, Paul 317
National Association of Independent Publishers Representatives 131
National Directory of Catalogs 181
National Directory of Newspaper Op-Ed Pages 146, 163
National Park System 169
National Park Visitor Centers 175
National Press Club 35
National Speakers Association 34, 277
National Trade & Professional Associations of the United States 296
Nature Company, The 169
NetBooks.com 193
Networking 27, 291, 292
Newbridge Communications 156
News 82, 286
Newsletters 41, 52, 58, 60, 64, 69, 141
Newspapers 40, 42, 67, 72, 73, 81, 92, 187
News releases 57, 106
Newswire Services 59, 330
New York publishers 4, 47, 66, 85, 209, 311
New York Times, The 56, 91, 92, 127, 129, 311, 327, 330, 332

Niche markets 226
Nonbookstore merchandising
    channels 167–177
  gift store sales 172–173
  museums 173–175
  national distribution
    171–172
  special sales 168–170
Nontraditional channels 78,
  123. *See also*
  Nonbookstore
  merchandising
  channels
Novels 10, 25, 28, 32, 77,
  103, 110, 128, 137,
  170-171, 174, 176,
  192, 197, 226, 239,
  272, 277, 279,
  296. *See also* Fiction

O

Office Systems '98 308
Off the book pages 59
O'Keefe, Steve 204
Ollstein, Captain Bruce
  Warren 78
*1001 Ways to Market Your
  Book* 201
Online *See* Internet
Op-Ed pieces 91–94, 331
  be proactive 94
  build visibility 91–92
  description of 91
  essay, crafting 93–96
  hows and whys 92–93
  newspaper contacts 331–
    332
  results of 92
  submission requirements
    92
  timing 92
  writer's bio 92
Oprah 48, 109, 114
Order coupon 246, 248
Order form 18, 257

P

Pareto Principle (80/20 rule)
  293
PartyLine 60
Party plan 176–177
Passion
  7, 55, 92, 123, 218
Patents and trademarks 22
Pax TV 110
Perry, Ellen Berkeley 228

Persistence 65-67, 187, 319
Peters, Tom 271
Pfeifer, Diane 208, 211, 216,
  228
Phoners (for radio) 96
Phone technique 34, 65, 318
Photos 50, 57, 62, 80, 83,
  245
Pitch letter 57
Pity party 231
Planting zingers 13–15
Platinum Rule, The 202, 237
Poetry 10, 22, 133, 170,
  226, 229, 272, 277,
  286
Poets & Writers, Inc. 277
Positioning 11-12, 72, 76,
  209
Postcards 57, 59, 83, 297
Post-it Notes 74
Posters 300
Potentials in Marketing 219
Poynter, Dan 34, 274
Premium/incentive trade
  associations 336
Premiums 207–220
  books as premiums 208–
    209
  customized editions 210,
    212
  *Directory of Premium,
    Incentive & Travel
    Buyers* 213
  discounts 212
  examples of success 209,
    212-215
  exclusivity 213
  handling objections 218
  hot topics 209–210
  how it works 211–213
  Incentive Manufactures
    Representative
    Association, Inc. 217
  local business 219
  matches, finding 211
  Motivation Show, The
    214
  researching 213–216
  self-liquidating premiums
    209
  servicing the sale 218
  strategies 217–219
  trade associations for 336
  trade journals for 219
  using premium reps 216–
    217

PRink 291
Print run 49
Priority mail 298
Process of publishing 24
Professional critique 251
ProfNet 33
Promotional materials
  42, 56–58, 155, 219.
  See also Brochure
Providing a solution to
  people's problems 98
Publicity 55–74
  bad 72
  customize 61
  internal press 69–71
  key contacts 58
  midget moves, mighty
    results 58–67
  off the book pages 59
  persistence pays 65–67
  print is powerful 56
  promotional materials
    56–58
  publicity for getting
    publicity 64–65
  recycle 64-65
  regional opportunities
    67–68
  results of 65
  sell articles 71
Publicity Hound, The 60, 64
Publicity on the Internet 89,
  204
Publish Your Own Novel 239
Publisher's Bill of Rights—
  and Obligations 325-
  326
Publishers Cataloging-in-
  Publication (PCIP)
  138
Publishers, don't deliver 4
Publishers Marketing
  Association (PMA)
  138, 286
Publishers Weekly (PW) 7, 15,
  19, 43, 46-47, 50, 62-
  63, 85, 89, 129, 137,
  160, 177, 234, 317,
  329

Q

Q&A 57, 85
Quality Books Inc. 19, 34,
  132, 137, 139
Quality Education Data
  (QED) 146, 149–150

Quality Paperback Book Club (QPB) 159, 160
Quill & Quire 51, 330
Quizes 57, 192
Quotes 14, 22, 34
QVC 233–239, 336
 criteria for 235–236
 Home Shopping Network (HSN) 235
 iQVC 238
 procedure for getting on 236–238
 Shop at Home, Inc. 235
 success story 234
 ValueVision 235

R

Radio interviews 58, 73, 81, 106, 95–108
 after the curtain falls 105
 author as guest 96
 be prepared 98–100
 commentaries 108
 contacts 108
 controversy, capitalize on 102
 delivery 101
 fan demographics 96
 giveaways 100, 104
 hooks 106
 media cards 100
 newsletters hawking authors 97
 on the air 101–105
 phoners 96
 potent radio maneuvers 102–103
 practice 98
 preparation for interview 98
 prospecting for shows 97–98
 providing a solution to people's problems 98
 quiz 101
 RadioTour.com 97
 Radio-TV Interview Report 97
 results 96
 set the stage 100–101
 sound bites 99
 syndicated or network shows 97–98, 104
 tactics for handling problems 103
 tape it 105

tip sheet 101
 voice level 104
Radio-TV Interview Report 97
Reading habits 7, 9
Reading Is Fun 168
Readings 77, 78
Recycling 64
Redfield, James 311
Reference 25, 142
Remaindering 162
Research 28–29, 40, 143, 163
Resource roundup 329–337
Returns 123, 135
Reverse shoplifting 128
Reviews 39–53, 56
 capturing reviewers' attention 43–45
 criteria for getting 39–40
 follow-up 45
 here's what reviewers are saying 46
 maximizing reviews 46
 mock review 42
 process, the 42–43
 promotional package 42
 review pruning 46
 spark sales 45–46
 vital information 42
 where to garner 40–41
Reynolds, Andrea 101
Richards, Vic 135
Rights, getting back 318. *See also* Foreign rights
Ripple effect 67
Roberts, Joel 106
Rosses' rules of order: 13 tips for awesome results 6
Round-up article 57
R. R. Bowker 142, 305
Rubel, Nicole 78
Rutter, Meredith 32
Ryan, Paula 101

S

Sabah, Joe 21, 96, 104
Sales leverage 155
Sales reps 130
Schmooze 79, 112, 172, 188
School Library Journal 47, 137, 142, 148, 149
Schroeder, Patricia 20
Screen Actors Guild 29
Search engines 164, 187

Self-publish 121, 123, 136, 138, 170, 197, 213–214, 225, 234, 236, 274, 303, 307, 311-320
Self-Published book, selling 311–318
 advances paid 311–312
 best literary foot forward 313–314
 declining to turn loose 317–325
 formula for success 312–313
 negotiating contracts 314–317
Self-Publishing Manual, The 34
Self-publishing success strategies 312
Sell sheets 132, 149
Sell statement 58
Seminars 27, 32, 63, 85, 88, 122, 131, 162, 200, 213, 227, 268, 271–273, 276, 288, 303, 305, 307, 309, 312, 319. *See also* Speaking
17 ways to out-distance the herd 288
Sharing Ideas 277
Shelton, Connie 177, 239
Shop at Home, Inc. 235, 336
Sidelines 299–303
Signature, Web 201
Sites, fun 10
Small Press Center 75
Small presses, growth of 4
Small Time Operator 317
Smith, Dale 86
Smith, Fire "Captain Bob" 20, 106
Sound bites 99
SPAN 21, 60, 65, 80, 87, 126, 139, 203–204, 292, 333
Spandaccini, Vic 45
Speaking 86, 104, 141, 148, 271–281. *See also* Seminars
 back-of-the-room sales 271–272
 canned introduction 275
 conferences, shows, exhibits online 279
 getting paid 275–276

presentation preparation 274–275
sell more books 278
seminar program, your own 272–273
teaching adult educational 273–274
Special dates to piggyback on 224
Special Interests Groups (SIGs) 197
Special Libraries Association 142
Special reports 304–305, 306, 308-309
Specialty stores 334
Speeches 87
Spinoffs 299–309
Stage fright 115
Standard Rate and Data (SRDS) 40, 41, 43, 261, 263
State departments of education 149
Statistics 5, 49, 124, 248
Stewart, Joan 64
Stickers 300
Stories 84
Storyboarding 23
Strategic alliances, forming 221–231
Subject Guide to Books in Print 29
Submission guidelines 52
Successories, Inc. 169, 183, 301
Survey 186, 291
Swipe file 289
Syndicated columnists 41, 47
Syndicated or network shows 97–98, 104

T

Table of Contents 17
Talk radio shows 56, 95–105, 107, 199–200
Talkers magazine 107
Target audience 15
Target marketing 183, 269
Tarila, Sophia 41
Teaching. See Speaking
Teaser copy 249

Telemarketing 65, 172
Telephone 295
Television. See TV
Ten tips 57, 101, 197
Testimonials 34
Thank-you 48, 52, 105, 141
The Ross marketing idea generator: 26 winning strategies 68
The 7 habits of highly successful publishers 44
Thomas Register of American Manufacturers 215, 216
Time limit 319
Timeliness 41, 50, 68, 74, 111
Timing 61, 82, 94, 182
Titles 19–21, 102
Toastmasters International 276
Trends 25, 57
Tu-Vets Corporation 132
TV 73, 81, 109–115
  cable channel 110
  choices: good and bad 109–110
  green room 112
  local morning shows 110
  media coaching 113
  on-the-air tips 113
  preparation for 112
  strategizing for maximum results 110–112
  what producers seek 111
  You're on the Air: Perform Like a Pro on Television 113
12 self-publishing success strategies 312
Typefaces 249

U

UNcook Book, The 170, 294
Uniform Commercial Code (UCC1) 133
Unique Books 138, 139
Unique Selling Proposition (USP) 11-12
United National Real Estate 223
URL 194, 203

USA Today 63, 72, 91, 129, 187, 202, 332
Usenets 206
USP, determining your 11–12

V

ValueVision 235, 336
Video 58, 111, 236, 309
Viglione, Steve 300
Virtual book signing 89–90
Visual variety 84
Von Oech, Roger 211

W

Waldenbooks 87
Walker, Cindy 307
Wall Street Journal, The 4, 332
Walters, Dottie 277
Washington Post 56, 315, 330, 332
Web. See Internet
West, Nadia 272
Wholesalers 120, 125–126
  Baker & Taylor 126
  Ingram Book Company 125
  locating online 133
Window display 83
Winfrey, Oprah 48, 109, 114
Wire services 59, 330–331
Word-of-mouth 56, 133–134
Words on Tape 62
Working Press of the Nation 41, 44, 70
Writer's Guide to Book Editors, Publishers, and Literary Agents 320
Writer's Market 320

Y

Yearbook of Experts, Authorities & Spokespersons 29, 35
You're on the Air: Perform Like a Pro on Television 113
Yudkin, Marcia 108, 291

Z

Zines 52, 73

Give the Gift of
Extraordinary Book Sales
to Your Loved Ones, Friends, and Colleagues

CHECK YOUR LEADING BOOKSTORE OR ORDER HERE

❑ **YES**, I want__ copies of *Jump Start Your Book Sales* at $19.95 each, plus $4 shipping per book (Colorado residents please add $1.40 sales tax per book). Canadian orders must be accompanied by a postal money order in U.S. funds. Allow 15 days for delivery.

❑ **YES**, I need__ copies of the Ross's classic bestseller *The Complete Guide to Self-Publishing*.

My check or money order for $_____ is enclosed.

Please charge my ❑ [VISA] ❑ [MasterCard] ❑ [AMERICAN EXPRESS Cards]

Name _____

Organization _____

Address _____

City/State/Zip _____

Phone_____Email _____

Card #_____ Exp. Date _____

Signature _____

Please make your check payable and return to:

Communication Creativity
P.O. Box 909-JS
Buena Vista, CO 81211-0909

Call your credit card order to: 800-331-8355

Email: Ann@CommunicationCreativity.com

Visit our website for other helpful publishing and marketing tools: www.SelfPublishingResources.com

Give the Gift of
Extraordinary Book Sales
to Your Loved Ones, Friends, and Colleagues

CHECK YOUR LEADING BOOKSTORE OR ORDER HERE

❑ **YES**, I want__ copies of *Jump Start Your Book Sales* at $19.95 each, plus $4 shipping per book (Colorado residents please add $1.40 sales tax per book). Canadian orders must be accompanied by a postal money order in U.S. funds. Allow 15 days for delivery.

❑ **YES**, I need__ copies of the Ross's classic bestseller *The Complete Guide to Self-Publishing.*

My check or money order for $_____is enclosed.

Please charge my ❑ VISA ❑ MasterCard ❑ AMERICAN EXPRESS Cards

Name_____

Organization _____

Address _____

City/State/Zip _____

Phone_____Email _____

Card #_____ Exp. Date _____

Signature _____

Please make your check payable and return to:

Communication Creativity
P.O. Box 909-JS
Buena Vista, CO 81211-0909

Call your credit card order to: 800-331-8355

Email: Ann@CommunicationCreativity.com

Visit our website for other helpful publishing and marketing tools: www.SelfPublishingResources.com

351